The Macho Paradox
Why Some Men Hurt Women and How All Men Can Help

Jackson Katz

SOURCEBOOKS, INC.®
NAPERVILLE, ILLINOIS

Dedicated to Shelley and Judah

Published by Sourcebooks, Inc.

P.O. Box 4410, Naperville, Illinois 60567–4410

(630) 961–3900

FAX: (630) 961–2168

www.sourcebooks.com

Library of Congress Cataloging-in-Publication Data

Katz, Jackson.

  The Macho Paradox : why some men hurt women and how all men can help / Jackson Katz.

    p. cm.

  Includes index.

  1. Women—Violence against. 2. Women—Crimes against. 3. Sex crimes. I. Title: The Macho Paradox. II. Title.

  HV6250.4.W65K39 2005

  362.88'082—dc22

                    2005017683

Printed and bound in the United States of America.

VP 24 23 22 21 20 19 18

"After hundreds of years of anti-racist struggle, more than ever before non-white people are currently calling attention to the primary role white people must play in anti-racist struggle. The same is true of the struggle to eradicate sexism—men have a primary role to play...in particular, men have a tremendous contribution to make...in the area of exposing, confronting, opposing, and transforming the sexism of their male peers."
—*bell hooks*

CONTENTS

❖ ❖ ❖

PREFACE

Americans like to boast that we're "the freest country on earth," and yet half the population doesn't even feel free enough to go for a walk at night. Unlike the status of women in Afghanistan under the ghastly Taliban, women in the United States are *allowed* to go out. Fanatic men in government don't issue edicts to prevent them from exercising their basic freedom of movement. Instead, the widespread fear of men's violence does the trick.

Women in the United States have made incredible and unprecedented gains over the past thirty years in education, business, sports, politics, and other professions. The multicultural women's movement has utterly transformed the cultural landscape. But at the same time, restrictions on women's ability to move about freely are so pervasive—such a normal part of life in the post-sixties generations—that many women don't even question them. They simply order their daily lives around the threat of men's violence.

And men? A substantial number of them simply have no idea how profoundly some men's violence affects the lives of all the women we care about: our mothers, daughters, sisters, wives, and girlfriends. I had no idea, either, until the lightbulb first went on when I was a nineteen-year-old college student.

Today, a quarter century later, I've lectured about men's violence against women on hundreds of college campuses. I start my talks with a deliberately provocative statement. "The subject we're here to address," I say, "touches every single person in this room—whether you're aware of it or not. Gender violence—rape, battering, sexual abuse, sexual harassment—dramatically impacts millions of individuals and families in contemporary American society. In fact, it is one of the great, ongoing tragedies of our time."

Is this alarmist hyperbole? I don't think so. An abundance of credible statistics—some from *conservative* sources—bears it out. Study after study
shows that between one in four and one in six American women will be the
victim of a rape or attempted rape in her lifetime. An American Medical
Association report in 2001 found that 20 percent of adolescent girls have
been physically or sexually assaulted by a date. A major public opinion poll
in 2000 found that two-thirds of American men say that domestic violence
is very or fairly common in the U.S., and in a 2005 national survey conducted for *Family Circle* magazine and Lifetime Television, 92 percent of respon-
dents said that family violence is a much bigger problem than people think.

But statistics on men's violence against women, while shocking, only tell
part of the story. Another part of the story unfolds in women's daily lives. To
demonstrate this concretely, I request the students' participation in an interactive exercise.

I draw a line down the middle of a chalkboard, sketching a male symbol
on one side and a female symbol on the other. Then I ask just the men:
"What steps do you guys take, on a daily basis, to prevent yourselves from
being sexually assaulted?" At first there is a kind of awkward silence as the
men try to figure out if they've been asked a trick question. The silence gives
way to a smattering of nervous laughter. Occasionally a young guy will raise
his hand and say, "I stay out of prison." This is typically followed by another
moment of laughter, before someone finally raises his hand and soberly
states, "Nothing. I don't think about it."

Then I ask the women the same question. "What steps do you take on a
daily basis to prevent yourselves from being sexually assaulted?"

Women throughout the audience immediately start raising their hands.
As the men sit in stunned silence, the women recount safety precautions they
take as part of their daily routine. Here are some of their answers:

Hold my keys as a potential weapon. Look in the back seat of the car
before getting in. Carry a cell phone. Don't go jogging at night. Lock all the
windows when I go to sleep, even on hot summer nights. Be careful not to
drink too much. Don't put my drink down and come back to it; make sure I
see it being poured. Own a big dog. Carry Mace or pepper spray. Have an
unlisted phone number. Have a man's voice on my answering machine. Park
in well-lit areas. Don't use parking garages. Don't get on elevators with only
one man, or with a group of men. Vary my route home from work. Watch
what I wear. Don't use highway rest areas. Use a home alarm system. Don't
wear headphones when jogging. Avoid forests or wooded areas, even in the
daytime. Don't take a first-floor apartment. Go out in groups. Own a
firearm. Meet men on first dates in public places. Make sure to have a car or

cab fare. Don't make eye contact with men on the street. Make assertive eye contact with men on the street.

The exercise can go on for almost half an hour. Invariably the board fills up on the women's side. This is true, with slight variations, in urban, suburban, and rural areas. Many women say the list is like an unconscious mental checklist. Despite three decades of Take Back the Night rallies and feminists raising consciousness about the politics of women's safety, few women in audiences where I've presented think about their daily routine in terms of larger cultural issues or political questions. "It's just the way it is," they say. "It's what we have to do to feel safe." (At the end of the exercise, I always hasten to point out that most sexual assaults are perpetrated not by strangers lurking in the bushes, but by men who know their victims—often in the victim's home.) Some women do get angry when they see the radical contrast between the women's side of the chalkboard, which is always full, and the men's, which is almost always blank.

Some men react emotionally when they contemplate the full chalkboard on the women's side. They're shocked, saddened, angered. Many report its effects as life changing. Many of them had never before taken the time to think about this subject. They knew violence against women was a problem in our culture, but not this big a problem. They didn't realize how far-reaching it was. They didn't think it affected them. They were unaware of—or in denial about—the fact that it has become the *norm* in the U.S. for women and girls to remain hypervigilant—sometimes 24/7—about the possibility of being raped.

How could so many men be oblivious to such a basic aspect of life for the women and girls around them? One of the most plausible explanations is that violence against women has historically been seen as a "women's issue." We focus on the *against women* part of the phrase and not on the fact that men are the ones doing it. But the long-running American tragedy of men's violence against women is really more about men and *our* problems than it is about women. We're the ones committing the vast majority of the violence! We're the ones whom women have been conditioned to fear. In the twenty-first century, it is long past time that more men—of all races, religions, ethnicities, and nationalities—faced up to this sad situation, educated ourselves and others about the hows and whys, and then went out and did something about it.

That's why the intended audience for the chalkboard exercise about the steps women take to protect themselves is actually *men.*

That's why this book is about men.

AUTHOR'S NOTE ON THE TITLE *THE MACHO PARADOX*

Because there is no explicit discussion of the phrase "the macho paradox" in the body of this book, I would like to offer readers a brief explanation about the term from two different perspectives: 1) the contested cultural meanings of the word "macho"; and 2) the way that I have used the term to describe some of the contradictory aspects of traditional notions of masculinity, as related to men's potential for leadership in the ongoing struggle to end men's violence against women.

1) The term "macho" carries multiple meanings, with both positive and negative connotations. For some Latinos, the positive characteristics of the Spanish word "macho" have been lost in mainstream English usage, where "macho" is used almost exclusively to refer to hypermasculine aggression. Traditionally, the word "macho" carried many positive associations. To be "macho" was to be well-respected, embodying traits such as courage, valor, honor, sincerity, pride, humility, and responsibility.

Since language usage has a political context, it is unfair to discuss the definition of "macho" in contemporary U.S. society without acknowledging the colonial exploitation and cultural domination of Latin America by early European and later U.S. imperial powers that characterize an important part of the past five hundred years in the history of the Western hemisphere. Thus, when English-speaking Americans use the term "macho," they should be aware that some see the negative connotation as further evidence of the ongoing effects of the Anglo conquest of Latino cultures in the southern part of the hemisphere. While some would argue that the "true" meaning of the word macho has been lost, it is important to remember that there is no such thing as the "true" meaning of words—only ways they evolve in particular cultural-historical contexts.

In any case, the term "paradox" in the book's title was intended to address any concerns that use of the word "macho" might contribute to the perpetuation of a negative cultural stereotype of Latinos. A key definition of "paradox" is "exhibiting inexplicable or contradictory aspects."

By using the term "paradox," I mean to coin a phrase that expresses both the negative and positive definitions of the word "macho" and appropriately conveys the word's contradictory meanings and rich history.

2) Many people have rightly asked, "What is the macho paradox?" Here are suggestions which form the basis for our thinking:

a. If you are a man, it is a lot easier to be sexist and abusive toward women—or remain silent in the face of other men's abuse—than it is to speak out against sexism. It is ironic that men who speak out against men's violence against women are often called wimps, when they actually have to be more self-confident and secure than men who remain silent in order to fit in and be "one of the guys." (Thus, a "macho" man, with its original Spanish meaning, would have the courage to take responsibility for controlling sexist or violent behavior in his community.)

b. The same qualities that some people ascribe to macho or hypermasculine men (see discussion above), such as "toughness" or a willingness to use violence to get one's way, can be read as expressions of weakness and cowardice. In other words, a man who beats his wife or girlfriend proves not that he's a "real man" who is "in control" and thus worthy of others' respect, but rather that he has serious problems and needs immediate help.

—Jackson Katz

CHAPTER ONE

Violence Against Women Is a Men's Issue

Most people think violence against women is a women's issue. And why wouldn't they? Just about every woman in this society thinks about it every day. If they are not getting harassed on the street, living in an abusive relationship, recovering from a rape, or in therapy to deal with the sexual abuse they suffered as children, they are ordering their daily lives around the *threat* of men's violence.

But it is a mistake to call *men's* violence a *women's* issue. Take the subject of rape. Many people reflexively consider rape to be a women's issue. But let's take a closer look. What percentage of rape is committed by women? Is it 10 percent, 5 percent? No. *Less than 1 percent of rape is committed by women.* Let's state this another way: over 99 percent of rape is perpetrated by men. Whether the victims are female or male, men are overwhelmingly the perpetrators. But we call it a women's issue? Shouldn't that tell us something?

A major premise of this book is that the long-running American tragedy of sexual and domestic violence—including rape, battering, sexual harassment, and the sexual exploitation of women and girls—is arguably more revealing about *men* than it is about women. Men, after all, are the ones committing the vast majority of the violence. Men are the ones doing most of the battering and almost all of the raping. Men are the ones paying the prostitutes (and killing them in video games), going to strip clubs, renting sexually degrading pornography, writing and performing misogynistic music.

When men's role in gender violence is discussed—in newspaper articles, sensational TV news coverage, or everyday conversation—the focus is typically on men as perpetrators or potential perpetrators. These days, you don't have to look far to see evidence of the pain and suffering these men cause. But it is rare to find any in-depth discussion about the culture that's producing these violent men. It's almost like the perpetrators are strange aliens who landed here from another planet. It is rarer still to hear thoughtful discussions about the ways that our culture defines "manhood," and how that definition might be linked to the endless string of stories about husbands killing wives, or groups of young men raping girls (and sometimes videotaping the rape) that we hear about on a regular basis.

Why isn't there more conversation about the underlying social factors that contribute to the pandemic of violence against women? Why aren't men's attitudes and behaviors toward women the focus of more critical scrutiny and coordinated action? These days, the 24/7 news cycle brings us a steady stream of gender-violence tragedies: serial killers on the loose, men abducting young girls, domestic-violence homicides, periodic sexual abuse scandals in powerful institutions like the Catholic Church and the Air Force Academy. You can barely turn on the news these days without coming across another gruesome sex crime—whether it's a group of boys gang-raping a girl in a middle school bathroom or a young pregnant woman who turns up missing, and whose husband emerges a few days later as the primary suspect.

Isn't it about time we had a national conversation about the male causes of this violence, instead of endlessly lingering on its consequences in the lives of women? Thanks to the battered women's and rape crisis movements in the U.S., it is no longer taboo to discuss women's experiences of sexual and domestic violence. This is a significant achievement. To an unprecedented extent, American women today expect to be supported—not condemned—when they disclose what men have done to them (unless the man is popular, wealthy, or well-connected, in which case all bets are off.)

This is all for the good. Victims of violence and abuse—whether they're women or men—should be heard and respected. Their needs come first. But let's not mistake concern for victims with the political will to change the conditions that led to their victimization in the first place. On talk shows, in brutally honest memoirs, at Take Back the Night rallies, and even in celebrity interviews, our society now grants many women the platform to discuss the sexual abuse and mistreatment that have sadly been a part of women's lives here and around the world for millennia. But when was the last time you heard someone, in public or private, talk about violence against women in a way that went beyond the standard victim fixation and put a sustained spotlight on men—either as perpetrators or bystanders? It is one thing to focus on the "against women" part of the phrase; but someone's responsible for doing it, and (almost) everyone knows that it's overwhelmingly men. Why aren't people talking about this? Is it realistic to talk about preventing violence against women if no one even wants to say out loud who's responsible for it?

For the past two decades, I've been part of a growing movement of men, in North America and around the world, whose aim is to reduce violence against women by focusing on those aspects of male culture—especially male-peer culture—that provide active or tacit support for some men's abusive behavior. This movement is racially and ethnically diverse, and it brings together men from both privileged and poor communities, and everyone in between. This is challenging work on many levels, and no one should expect rapid results. For example, there is no way to gloss over some of the race, class, and sexual orientation divisions between and among us men. It is also true that it takes time to change social norms that are so deeply rooted in structures of gender and power. Even so, there is room for optimism. We've had our successes: there are arguably more men today who are actively confronting violence against women than at any time in human history.

Make no mistake. Women blazed the trail that we are riding down. Men are in the position to do this work precisely because of the great leadership of women. The battered women's and rape crisis movements and their allies in local, state, and federal government have accomplished a phenomenal amount over the past generation. Public awareness about violence against women is at an all-time high. The level of services available today for female victims and survivors of men's violence is—while not yet adequate—nonetheless historically unprecedented.

There was some good news in 2005. A Department of Justice report showed that family violence declined by about half from 1993 to 2002, similar to the overall drop in violent crime during the past decade. But encouraging as it was, the study had its limitations. For example, crime between current or former boyfriends and girlfriends was not considered "family" violence. And the study did not include sexual violence. Still, we can cheer the success of our ongoing efforts but remain clear that our society still has a very long way to go in preventing perpetration. In the United States, we continue to produce hundreds of thousands of physically and emotionally abusive—and sexually dangerous—boys and men each year. Millions more men participate in sexist behaviors on a continuum that ranges from mildly objectifying women to literally enslaving them in human trafficking syndicates. We can provide services to the female victims of these men until the cows come home. We can toughen enforcement of rape, domestic-violence, and stalking laws, and arrest and incarcerate even more men than we do currently; but this is all reactive and after the fact. It is essentially an admission of failure.

What I am proposing in this book is that we adopt a much more ambitious approach. If we are going to bring down dramatically the rates of violence against women—not just at the margins—we will need a far-reaching cultural revolution. At its heart, this revolution must be about changing the sexist social norms in male culture, from the elementary school playground to the common room in retirement communities—and every locker room, pool hall, and boardroom in between. For us to have any hope of achieving historic reductions in incidents of violence against women, at a minimum we will need to dream big and act boldy. It almost goes without saying that we will need the help of a lot more men—at all levels of power and influence—than are currently involved. Obviously we have our work cut out for us. As a measure of just how far we have to go, consider that in spite of the misogyny and sexist brutality all around us, millions of non-violent men today fail to see gender violence as their issue. "I'm a good guy," they will say. "This isn't my problem."

For years, women of every conceivable ethnic, racial, and religious background have been trying to get men around them—and men in power—to do more about violence against women. They have asked nicely and they have demanded angrily. Some women have done this on a one-to-one basis with boyfriends and husbands, fathers and sons. They have patiently explained to the men they care about how much they—and all women—have been harmed by men's violence. Others have gone public with their grievances. They have committed, in Gloria Steinem's memorable phrase, "outrageous acts and everyday rebellions." They have written songs and slam poetry. They have produced brilliant academic research. They have made connections between racism and sexism. They have organized speak-outs on college campuses, and in communities large and small. They have marched. They have advocated for legal and political reform at the state and national level. On both a micro and a macro level, women in this era have successfully broken through the historical silence about violence against women and found their voice—here in the U.S. and around the world.

Yet even with all of these achievements, women continue to face an uphill struggle in trying to make meaningful inroads into male culture. Their goal has not been simply to get men to listen to women's stories and truly hear them—although that is a critical first step. The truly vexing challenge has been getting men to actually go out and *do* something about the problem, in the form of educating and organizing *other men* in numbers great enough to prompt a real cultural shift. Some activist women—even those who have had great faith in men as allies—have been beating their heads against the wall for a long time, and are frankly burned out on the effort. I know this because I have been working with many of these women for a long time. They are my colleagues and friends.

My work is dedicated to getting more men to take on the issue of violence against women, and thus to build on what women have achieved. The area that I focus on is not law enforcement or offender treatment, but the *prevention* of sexual and domestic violence and all their related social pathologies—including violence against children. To do this, I and other men here and around the world have been trying to get our fellow men to see that this problem is not just personal for a small number of men who happen to have been touched by the issue. We try to show them that it is personal for them, too. *For all of us.* We talk about men not only as perpetrators but as victims. We try to show them that violence by men against each other—from simple assaults to gay-bashing—is linked to the same structures of gender and power that produce so much men's violence against women.

We also make it clear that these issues are not just personal, to be dealt with as private family matters. They are political as well, with repercussions that reverberate throughout our lives and communities in all sorts of meaningful and disturbing ways. For example, according to a 2003 report by the U.S. Conference of Mayors, domestic violence was a primary cause of homelessness in almost half of the twenty-five cities surveyed. And worldwide, sexual coercion and other abusive behavior by men plays an important role in the transmission of HIV/AIDS.

Nonetheless, convincing other men to make gender violence issues a priority is not an easy sell. Sometimes when men engage with other men in this area, we need to begin by reassuring them that men of character and conscience need not flee in terror when they hear the words *"sexism," "rape,"* or *"domestic violence."* However cynical it sounds, sometimes we need to convince them that they actually have a self-interest in taking on these topics; or at the very least, that men have something very valuable to learn not only about women but also about themselves.

There is no point in being naïve about why women have had such a difficult time convincing men to make violence against women a men's issue. In spite of significant social change in recent decades, men continue to grow up with, and are socialized into, a deeply misogynistic, male-dominated culture, where violence against women—from the subtle to the homicidal—is disturbingly common. It's *normal.* And precisely because the mistreatment of women is such a pervasive characteristic of our patriarchal culture, most men, to a greater or lesser extent, have played a role in its perpetuation. This gives us a strong incentive to avert our eyes.

Women, of course, have also been socialized into this misogynistic culture. Some of them resist and fight back. In fact, women's ongoing resistance to their subordinate status is one of the most momentous developments in human civilization over the past two centuries. Just the same, plenty of women show little appetite for delving deeply into the cultural roots of sexist violence. It's much less daunting simply to blame "sick" individuals for the problem. You hear women explaining away men's bad behavior as the result of individual pathology all the time: "Oh, he just had a bad childhood," or "He's an angry drunk. The booze gets to him. He's never been able to handle it."

But regardless of how difficult it can be to show some women that violence against women is a social problem that runs deeper than the abusive behavior of individual men, it is still much easier to convince women that dramatic change is in their best interest than it is to convince men. In fact, many people would argue that, since men are the dominant sex and violence serves to reinforce this dominance, that it is not in men's best interests to reduce violence against women, and that the very attempt to enlist a critical mass of men in this effort amounts to a fool's errand.

For those of us who reject this line of reasoning, the big question then is how do we reach men? We know we're not going to transform, overnight or over many decades, certain structures of male power and privilege that have developed over thousands of years. Nevertheless, how are we going to bring more men—many more men—into a conversation about sexism and violence against women? And how are we going to do this without turning them off, without berating them, without blaming them for centuries of sexist oppression? Moreover, how are we going to move beyond talk and get substantial numbers of men to partner *with* women in reducing men's violence, instead of working *against* them in some sort of fruitless and counterproductive gender struggle?

That is the $64,000 question in the growing field of gender-violence prevention in the first decade of the twenty-first century: how to get more men to stand up and be counted. Esta Soler, the executive director of the Family Violence Prevention Fund and an influential leader in the domestic-violence movement, says that activating men is "the next frontier" in the women-led movement. "In the end," she says, "we cannot change society unless we put more men at the table, amplify men's voices in the debate, enlist men to help change social norms on the issue, and convince men to teach their children that violence against women is always wrong."

Call me a starry-eyed optimist, but I have long been convinced that there are millions of men in our society who are ready to respond well to a positive message about this subject. If you go to a group of men with your finger pointed ("Stop treating women so badly!") you'll often get a defensive response. But if you approach the same group of men by appealing, in Abraham Lincoln's famous words, to "the better angels of their nature," surprising numbers of them will rise to the occasion.

For me, this is not just an article of faith. Our society has made real progress in confronting the long-standing problem of men's violence against women *just in my lifetime*. Take the 1994 Violence Against Women Act (VAWA). It is the most far-reaching piece of legislation ever on the subject. Federal funds have enabled all sorts of new initiatives, including prevention efforts that target men and boys. There have been many other encouraging developments on both the institutional and the individual levels. Not the least of these positive developments is the fact that so many young men today "get" the concept of gender equality—and are actively working against men's violence.

I understand the skepticism of women who for years have been frustrated by men's complacency about something as basic as a woman's right to live free from the threat of violence. But I am convinced that men who are active in gender-violence prevention today speak for a much larger number of men. I would not go so far as to say that a silent majority of men supports everything that gender-violence prevention activists stand for, but an awful lot of men privately cheer us on. I have long felt this way, but now there is a growing body of research—in social norms theory— that confirms it empirically.

Social norms theory begins with the premise that people often misperceive the extent to which their peers hold certain attitudes or participate in certain behaviors. In the absence of accurate knowledge, they are more likely to be influenced by what they *think* people think and do, rather than what they *actually* think and do. Some of the early work in social norms theory, in the early 1990s, had to do with how the drinking habits of college students were influenced by how much they thought their peers drank. Researchers found that when students realized that their fellow students didn't drink as much as their school's "party school" label suggested, they were less likely to binge drink in order to measure up.

Social norms theory has also been applied to men's attitudes about sexism, sex, and men's violence against women. There have been a number of studies in the past several years that demonstrate that significant numbers of men are uncomfortable with the way some of their male peers talk about and treat women. But since few men in our society have dared to talk publicly about such matters, many men think they are the only ones who feel uncomfortable.

Because they feel isolated and alone in their discomfort, they do not say anything. Their silence, in turn, simply reinforces the false perception that few men are uncomfortable with sexist attitudes and behaviors. It is a vicious cycle that keeps a lot of caring men silent.

I meet men all the time who thank me—or my fellow activists and colleagues—for publicly taking on the subject of men's violence. I frequently meet men who are receptive to the paradigm-shifting idea that men's violence against women has to be understood as a men's issue, as their issue. These men come from every demographic and geographic category. They include thousands of men who would not fit neatly into simplistic stereotypes about the kind of man who would be involved in "that touchy-feely stuff."

Still, it is an uphill fight. Truly lasting change is only going to happen as new generations of women come of age and demand equal treatment with men in every realm, and new generations of men work with them to reject the sexist attitudes and behaviors of their predecessors. This will take decades, and the outcome is hardly predetermined. But along with tens of thousands of activist women and men who continue to fight the good fight, I believe that it is possible to achieve something much closer to gender equality, and a dramatic reduction in the level of men's violence against women, both here and around the world. And there is a lot at stake. If sexism and violence against women do not subside considerably in the twenty-first century, it will not just be bad news for women. It will also say something truly ugly and tragic about the future of our species.

WOMEN'S ISSUES/MEN'S ISSUES

If you are a woman and you are reading this, you know that violence against women is one of the critical "women's issues" of our time. A major national poll released in 2003 by the New York-based Center for the Advancement of Women found that 92 percent of women named "reducing domestic violence and sexual assault" as a top priority for women's movements—outpolling all other issues.

If you are a man and you are reading this, you probably agree that violence against women is a significant problem—for women. Few men tell pollsters that "reducing domestic and sexual violence" is a priority for men. Barring a recent family tragedy, it is unlikely that men would even register these issues as ones we should be concerned with. This hardly ennobles us, but is it fair to expect otherwise? Most men—and women— see these as "women's issues."

As I have stated, calling violence against women a "women's issue" is misleading at best, and is even at some level dishonest. In fact, I think the very act of calling it a "women's issue" is itself part of the problem. Here are four reasons why:

1. *It gives men an excuse not to pay attention.*

The way we talk about a subject is the way we think about it. When people call rape, battering, and sexual harassment "women's issues"—and many people do this without a second thought—they contribute to a broad shifting of responsibility from the male perpetrators of violence to its female victims. This is likely not intentional, but words nonetheless convey subtle but powerful messages. The message to women is that it is their job to prevent—or avoid—sexual and domestic violence, and they should not expect a lot of help from men. The message to men is even more insidious: they need not tune this in. It is women's burden. As long as you do not assault women yourself, you can pretty much ignore the whole thing.

The simple phrase "women's issues" eloquently reinforces this point. Guys hear "women's issues" and not surprisingly think: *Hey, that's stuff's for girls, for women. I'm not a girl or a woman. It's not my concern.* Generations of men and boys have been conditioned to think about sexism—including gender violence—as something they need only concern themselves with when forced to do so, usually by a woman in their life.

When did you last hear a man say he was concerned about violence against women not *in spite* of the fact that he is a man but *because* of it? Implicit in the notion that violence against women is a "women's issue" is the assumption that all women should be concerned *because they're women,* because all women have an interest in preventing violence against their sex, even if they haven't been assaulted themselves. It is equally true that men should be concerned, not necessarily because they have perpetrated or prosecuted these crimes, but simply *because they are men.*

This conclusion does not flow naturally from the way the subject is currently understood. But there are numerous reasons why violence against women is a men's issue. I am going to address some of the personal ones in a subsequent chapter. Still, most of the personal and professional reasons why men are, and should be, concerned are not part of the public discourse. Few people even mention them.

A lot of men (and women) are not even conscious of *how* they think about violence against women. But it's a safe bet that some men consciously use the "women's issues" label as an excuse not to pay attention. It's not that they feel somehow unfairly excluded; more realistically they have no desire to probe any deeper. When some men hear the word "gender" in the same sentence as "violence," they automatically shut down. *Not that unpleasant subject again.* Still others respond to the term "women's issues" like they do TV commercials for feminine hygiene products. They would rather not go there. Better just to turn up the music and tune it out.

Unfortunately, few men pay any discernible price for this averting of our eyes. In part, this is because we're not expected to do much or even care much about these issues—unless something happens to a woman or girl close to us. Most guys will say, "I'm a good guy. These aren't my problems." The trouble is, for a culture with as much gender violence as ours, the bar for being considered a "good guy" is set awfully low.

In fact, a lot of women actually feel grateful when men they know emerge as strong allies. When a man—in a group of friends, in a classroom, in the media—voices an objection to sexist portrayals of women in pornography, pop music, or other forms of media, or if he speaks out in support of the victims of domestic violence or sexual assault, women will often praise his sensitivity and thank him for caring. This speaks volumes about how low women's expectations are of the average guy! In this country—perhaps in all of Western culture—in the early twenty-first century, a guy can become an instant hero merely for doing what any decent person should be doing. I know that many of my friends and colleagues who do anti-sexist "men's work," myself included, are often embarrassed by this, and by the way some women shower us with gratitude for any minimal effort we put forth.

Of course, not all women are so easily impressed; some women do have higher expectations of men. Consider the case of a woman lawyer who is an acquaintance of mine. When she was in law school, she came home one day, excited to share with her boyfriend some things she'd learned about sexual-assault prevention in a workshop on gender violence. He was completely silent and uninterested. So she called him on it. "You don't seem to care," she said.

"I'm not really into that stuff; sort of like how you aren't interested in economics," he explained matter-of-factly. She was taken aback. She wondered, if the guy she's seeing is not "interested" in what her daily life is like as a woman, how could he possibly be interested in her? She said that the moment he uttered those words she knew they were through.

2. "Women's issues" are personal for men, too.

If you are a man, I have a question for you: Is there a woman in your life that you love dearly? A mother, daughter, sister, wife, girlfriend, or close woman friend? Are there many women and girls that you care about very deeply? Okay, then isn't it true that every issue which affects the women and girls that you care about affects you—by definition? Now think about all of the men who are the fathers, brothers, sons, and lovers of women and girls who have been assaulted by men. Men whose wives were raped when they were younger, but who still feel the aftershocks. Men who have daughters who are raped in college. Men who—as little boys—experienced the trauma of watching their fathers or other men assault their mothers. Millions of men fall into one or another of these categories.

Nonetheless, it is a struggle to get men to confront each other about violence toward women because so many of us have been conditioned—in our language and otherwise—either to avoid the subject altogether or to look at it through a dichotomous and competitive lens: *Men* vs. *women. Battle between the sexes. Us* and *them.* And this is definitely one of those issues that is about *them.* Isn't that why they call it a "women's issue"? But it is more than that. There are some issues that primarily affect women as a sex class, and others where men as a sex class are more concerned. You do not need a PhD in evolutionary biology to make that observation. But it is just as true that we live in the world together. Our lives are lived *in relation* to others. Women and men have familial, platonic, and sexual relationships with each other. How can something that affects women not affect men—and vice versa?

3. Men are the primary perpetrators.

Contrary to the disinformation promulgated in recent years by the so-called "men's rights" movement, the most important statistics about violence against women do not lie. The vast majority of credible researchers in sociology, criminology, and public health confirm that men commit the most serious intimate-partner violence and the overwhelming amount of sexual violence, including the sexual abuse of children. Some women in heterosexual relationships do assault their male partners, and a small number of researchers, most notably the sociologist Murray Straus, maintain that women's violence against men is a more significant social problem than many people in the field recognize or acknowledge. But while women's violence is wrong—if used for purposes other than self-defense—it is rarely part of a systematic pattern of power and control through force or the threat of force. On a wide range of issues, from domestic violence and rape to stalking and sexual harassment, there is no symmetry between men's and women's violence against each other, no equivalence. If the tables were turned, and the primary problem were women assaulting men, would we be as likely to blame the victim as we are now? Would the general public be endlessly focused on men's experience of victimization at the hands of women? Would people constantly be asking: why do men stay with the women who beat them? Somehow I don't think so. I think most of us—especially men—would be honing in on the source of the problem—women's behavior. We would ask, rightly, "What the hell is going on with women? How are we going to get them to stop assaulting us?"

But with the situation reversed, we focus not on the perpetrator class but on the victims. There's some history behind this, and some language. Ever since women succeeded at breaking silence around the historic reality of their experience of violence at the hands of men, Western and other world cultures have framed gender violence as a "women's issue." This act of framing/naming has had a profound impact on our collective consciousness, both positive and negative. On the one hand, thinking about gender violence as a women's issue has contributed to a foregrounding of the needs of female victims and survivors. The dramatic growth over the past three decades in public understanding about how violence against women harms women—how it is a violation of their basic human rights—is one of the great achievements of modern multicultural feminism.

On the other hand, focusing on what happens *to women* has helped obscure the role played *by men*—and male culture—in the ongoing violence. After all, men are not only the primary perpetrators of gender violence. We are also the not-so-innocent bystanders. As we will discuss in this book, men hold a disproportionate amount of economic, social, and political power. This means we're more responsible for those aspects of our culture that promote and encourage violence against women. It also means we're more responsible for what we do or do not prioritize in terms of prevention— including the prevention of gender violence.

On a personal level, men who are not abusive toward women nonetheless play important roles in the lives of men who are. Men who physically and sexually abuse women are not monsters who live apart from the civilized world. They are in our families and friendship circles. They are our fathers, our sons, our brothers, and our best friends. They are our fishing partners, drinking buddies, teammates, fraternity brothers, and colleagues. We too easily let them and ourselves off the hook when we call their violence a "women's issue." Do we do it intentionally? I don't know. But whether conscious or unconscious, it's an effective strategy to avoid accountability.

4. Until more men join the fight, there is no chance that the violence will be dramatically reduced.

Men already play important roles in almost every aspect of these issues, from the personal to the professional to the political. For example, men are friends and family members of women who have been victims past or present. We're also the friends and family members of violent boys and men. In a professional context, we're rape-prevention educators and batterer-intervention counselors. We're sex crimes prosecutors. We're doctors who treat women and girls who have been assaulted. We're lawyers who represent battered women in custody battles. We're judges who hear domestic violence cases. We're therapists who treat rape-trauma survivors. We're cops who show up at the door when someone calls 911. In political terms, we're policy makers who write legislation to fund women's programs. We're activists who call attention to unmet needs. We're politicians who support changes in the law to strengthen protections for rape, battering, and stalking victims.

Until now the gynocentric nature of the "women's issues" label has distorted the role that men are already playing in these issues—both good and bad. But I wouldn't be pressing this point if it were simply about appreciating men's positive contributions. We have far more serious things to worry about than the hurt feelings of some men who might feel unacknowledged. The fact is that the current practice of calling rape, battering, and sexual harassment women's issues actually hampers prevention efforts. To cut right to it, how many more woman-as-survivor stories do we need to hear (however inspiring they might be) before we figure out that violence against women isn't caused by women, and that it won't be stopped by focusing on what women can do to change their lives?

Women, of course, have been and will continue to be the leaders of the fight against all forms of sexism. But because anti-sexism has for so long been identified with women, one of the first steps in motivating more men and boys is to talk about rape, sexual assault, battering, and sexual harassment as *our* issues. Of course it could be argued that men should *already* be concerned about women's issues because we *should* be concerned about women. But regardless of whether we should be concerned, the fact remains that very few men have historically committed time, energy, and resources to the fight against gender violence. It has not been a priority for most men. That is why we need the paradigm shift. In order to occasion a true cultural transformation, we simply must convince a sizable group of men to—in the words of the famous Apple Computer campaign—"Think Different." Only with this new thinking will they be willing to invest the personal, professional, and political time and effort necessary to get the job done.

What are the stakes? Without more active male support and involvement, there is every reason to believe that the outrageously high rates of men's violence against women that we've grown accustomed to will persist indefinitely. The only meaningful debates will be about appropriate levels of funding for victim services, along with ongoing debates about criminal justice versus community-based ways to hold offenders accountable. In other words, organized response to gender violence will continue indefinitely in clean-up-after-the-fact mode, quite possibly for decades.

True and lasting change will require—at a minimum—a critical and multicultural mass of men emerging to partner with women in confronting men's violence on both a personal and an institutional level. There are signs that this is beginning to happen. Both nationally and internationally, the number of men and men's organizations that are willing to grapple with men's roles in ending violence is growing. But this is a movement that is still in its infancy.

In my mixed-gender speeches and trainings, I try to introduce this subject matter gently, in a non-threatening way, by starting with an interactive exercise. I ask the men—just the men—to participate in a little demonstration. "By a show of hands," I ask, "how many of you have either a mother, daughter, sister, wife, girlfriend, close female friend, or another woman or girl that you care deeply about?" This usually prompts laughter and some grumbling, but eventually most guys put up their hands. (I can tell that I am in for a long night when more than a smattering of men choose to signal their unhappiness at having to attend a talk about women's issues by refusing to raise their hands.)

At a talk I once gave on a college campus, there was a middle-aged white man and woman seated in the front row, looking out of place. I assumed they were married. When I asked the men to raise their hands if they had a woman close to them, the guy didn't budge. He sat there ten feet away from me with his arms folded and the hint of a scowl on his face. His posture distracted me the entire night. I kept glancing down at them and wondering: What is going on in their relationship? How did she get him to come out and hear my talk? What will they be talking about in the car ride home?

Okay, so the guy might not have liked the slightly manipulative quality of the exercise. Regardless, its message was clear: every issue which affects the women and girls that we care about affects us. Our lives are inextricably interwoven. We live in the world together, share the same beds, and eat at the same breakfast tables. We make babies together, have *daughters* together. Everything that happens to women happens to men, too.

CHAPTER TWO

Facing Facts

"If a man is offered a fact which goes against his instincts, he will scrutinize it closely, and unless the evidence is overwhelming, he will refuse to believe it. If, on the other hand, he is offered something which affords a reason for acting in accordance to his instincts, he will accept it even on the slightest evidence."
—Bertrand Russell, *Proposed Roads to Freedom*

One of the most memorable movie lines of the 1990s is from *A Few Good Men*, when Jack Nicholson's Colonel Jessup bellows, "You can't handle the truth!" at the young prosecutor played by Tom Cruise. Its power derives from Nicholson's volcanic portrayal of the career Marine Corps officer, who is indignant at having to answer, under oath, pointed questions put to him by a much younger and less war-tested junior officer. The "truth" in this case is a metaphor for the danger and ugliness in the world. Thus the colonel's admonition is really an attack on the younger man's masculinity, because a "real man" should be able to face the truth unflinchingly. At least in theory.

In reality, "real men" can be very selective about what truths they are willing to confront. Until recently, men as a group have been largely AWOL from the fight against gender violence. In one sense, it is easy to see why. Men's violence against women is a pervasive social phenomenon with deep roots in existing personal, social, and institutional arrangements. In order for people to understand and ultimately work together to prevent it, it is first necessary for them to engage in a great deal of personal and collective introspection. This introspection can be especially threatening to men, because as perpetrators and bystanders, they are responsible for the bulk of the problem.

Introspection can also be unsettling for women. Gender violence is a painful subject they would rather not think about. Some are pessimistic about the possibility for meaningful change in men's behavior. Others don't want to draw larger conclusions from what happens to individual women because, deep down, they do not want to think it could happen to them. In addition, many women worry that a close examination of men's attitudes and behaviors toward women might shine unfavorable light on men they love and care about.

But my purpose in this book is to look at gender violence as a problem and a challenge for men. In order to do this, right up front I need to explore some of the dynamics in men's lives—and psyches—that prevent them from coming to terms with the "truth" of men's violence. There are clearly some reasons why men have not faced up to the reality of the ongoing pandemic of rape, battering, and sexual abuse.

In some cases, old-fashioned guilt keeps men from delving in too deeply. They are ashamed of their own behavior and would rather not be reminded of it. Some men avert their eyes because they are afraid of what they might learn, not only about themselves, but about men around them: their brothers and friends. Finally, many men participate—in peer cultures and as consumers—in what feminists have described as a "rape and battering culture." They laugh at sexist jokes, go out with the guys to strip clubs, and consume misogynistic pornography. So even though most men are not perpetrators, they nonetheless contribute to—and derive pleasure from—a sexist cultural climate where women are put down and sexually degraded. Thus they have little motivation to examine it critically, and a lot of incentive to look away.

I READ THE NEWS TODAY, OH BOY

Long before the 9/11 attacks prompted unusually honest national dialogue about the effects of terrorist violence on the American psyche, our culture's pandemic of men's violence against women was one of the defining characteristics of our historical era. Decades before anyone had heard of Al Qaeda, one-half of the U.S. population had learned to live in near-constant fear of the other half. Gender violence has occurred with such frequency for so long in this country that many people are no longer alarmed by how common it is. It is the status quo, an unremarkable feature of the social landscape.

What is perhaps even more disturbing is that in this culture, many people see gender violence as a problem of sick or damaged *individuals*, and not as a social phenomenon that's causes—and solutions—lie in much larger social forces. So let me be clear. There is no such thing as an isolated incident of rape, battering, sexual abuse, or sexual harassment. These are not merely individual pathologies. It is not enough for us to ask in each case: "What went wrong in his life?" "Why would he do something like that?" These problems are much too widespread for us to think about them in such narrow terms.

Men's violence against women is a major contemporary social problem that is deeply rooted in our cultural traditions. This does not in any way absolve individuals of responsibility for their actions. But just as it is unfair to punish low-level soldiers and not hold their superiors accountable for the abuse debacle at the Abu Ghraib prison in Iraq, it is disingenuous to attribute the widespread problem of gender violence to an isolated collection of social deviants and let the rest of us off the hook.

The historical dimensions of the problem of men's violence become clear when you consider their awesome scope:

- *JAMA: The Journal of the American Medical Association* published one study in 2001 which found that 20 percent of adolescent girls were physically or sexually abused by a date.
- Nearly one-third of American women report being physically or sexually abused by a husband or boyfriend at some point in their lives.
- An estimated 17.7 million women in the United States, nearly 18 percent, have been raped or have been the victim of attempted rape.
- Studies show that 15 to 38 percent of women and 5 to 16 percent of men experienced some form of sexual abuse as children.
- The average age at which a child is first abused sexually is ten years old.
- As many as 324,000 women each year experience intimate-partner violence during their pregnancy.
- Women are much more likely than men to be killed by an intimate partner. In 2000, intimate-partner homicides accounted for 33.5 percent of murders of women and less than 4 percent of murders of men.
- One national survey found that 83 percent of girls reported being sexually harassed at school.
- Between one in four and one in five college women experience completed or attempted rape during their college years.
- Ten thousand porn videos are released *each year* in the U.S. alone.
- The average age of entry into prostitution is thirteen or fourteen.
- Forty percent of girls aged fourteen to seventeen report knowing someone their age who has been hit or beaten by a boyfriend.
- There are twenty-five hundred strip clubs in the U.S.
- One study found that 70 percent of women with developmental disabilities had been sexually assaulted, and that nearly 50 percent of women with mental retardation had been sexually assaulted ten or more times.
- One study showed that 37.5 percent of American Indian and Alaska

Native women were victimized by their male partners, with 15.9 percent raped, 30.7 physically assaulted, and 10.2 percent stalked.

- Eight percent of women and 2 percent of men in the U.S. have been stalked at some time in their life; an estimated 1,006,970 women and 370,990 men are stalked annually. Eighty-seven percent of stalking perpetrators are male.
- In one study, lifetime risk for violent victimization was so high for homeless women with severe mental illness (97 percent) as to amount to normative experiences for this population.
- A study of prisons in four Midwestern states found that approximately one in five male inmates reported a pressured or forced sex incident while incarcerated. About one in ten male inmates reported that they had been raped. Sexual abuse rates for women in prison vary widely among institutions. In one facility, 27 percent of women had been sexually abused. (Women in prison are most often abused by male staff members.)
- The estimated annual health-related costs, lost productivity costs, and lost earnings due to intimate partner violence in the U.S. is $5.9 billion.
- Studies suggest that between 3.3 and 10 million children witness some form of domestic violence annually.
- Between 50–70 percent of men who abuse their female partners also abuse their children.

These numbers tell a dramatic tale, but you do not need statistical proof to see glaring evidence of the problem. Just look around. Stories about men stalking, attacking, and murdering women and children make the local, regional, and national news virtually every day; especially when they have a good news hook like a famous perpetrator or a young, attractive victim. A random scan of the headlines in the metro section of the newspaper on most days in moderately populated U.S. cities will turn up stories about husbands murdering their wives, members of the clergy arrested for sex offenses, male coaches fired for sexually abusing their young athletes, corporations sued by female employees for pervasive patterns of sexual harassment by male employees, and college athletes charged with gang rape. Sometimes the metro news pages read like a morbid catalogue of violent masculinity run amok.

Regrettably, few people see the problem in these terms. For one thing, news stories and the conversations they spark are more likely to focus on the unfortunate (female) victims than on the (male) perpetrators. It is no longer taboo in many circles in the U.S. to discuss *violence against women*. But when was the last time you heard someone in public (or private) talk about the problem of *men's violence*? Also, men's violence against women has been so pervasive for so long that when they hear about it, typical Americans just shrug their shoulders in resignation, if they can muster the psychic energy to watch or read the grim news in the first place. Not that following the news would lend them greater understanding of the problem. With few exceptions, news coverage of intimate-partner and sexual violence merely contributes to the public's misperception that these crimes occur randomly and are not part of a larger cultural pattern.

I remember watching the six o'clock news on a local network affiliate in Los Angeles a few years ago. The first story was about a minor development in the ongoing drama about then-congressman Gary Condit and Chaundra Levy, the missing Washington intern whose body was later found in a wooded area. The second story turned locally to Long Beach, where a successful realtor was missing and presumed dead; her husband had just refused a lie detector test. The next story was about an incident, also in Long Beach, where a man had abducted his ex-girlfriend at gunpoint in the middle of the day at her place of business. She later turned up safe; he was arrested.

This was just the first few minutes of one random day's newscasts. You would think it was worth mentioning that each of these three stories involved abductions and possible murders of women—perhaps by men close to them. You would think it was relevant to provide some background statistics about how many women are abducted by men each year, and how many are murdered. But the anchorwoman simply reported the stories as if they were completely unrelated.

This happens all the time. Newscasts regularly report on incidents of men's violence against women without mentioning any larger social context. One effect of the ongoing backlash against feminism is that in mainstream media, knowledgeable women and men are rarely interviewed for their insight into the broader social factors that contribute to crimes against women. It is much easier—and less risky for ratings—to offer apolitical analyses of "the criminal mind" by FBI profilers and other law enforcement types. Consider, by comparison, how the news media would cover a series of attacks by white people on people of color. Would they regard them as "unrelated" and not bother to consult experts on racism?

As if out-of-context media coverage were not bad enough, let's not forget that the vast majority of gender violence is *never reported*. Most of it happens behind closed doors and beneath the public radar screen. Murders usually make the news—although the violent deaths of poor women of color are likely to be buried on page twenty-seven. But the vast majority of battering is never reported, much less covered in the media. According to the FBI, 80 to 90 percent of rape is never reported. To be sure, dramatic events involving groups of men tend to get our attention, like the sexual assaults at the

Tailhook naval aviators convention in the early 1990s, the group sexual assaults in New York's Central Park during the Puerto Rican Day festival, the rapes at Woodstock '99, or rape scandals in college athletics and the U.S. military in recent years. For at least a brief period, these assaults can spark outrage—among men as well as women—and in some cases stimulate dialogue about men's violence.

But low-level harassment and abuse from men is much less a newsworthy event than it is a routine part of life for millions of women. After the attacks on 9/11, millions of Americans suddenly paid attention to the plight of women in Afghanistan, a situation feminists had been alarmed about for years. Men's violence is a serious problem for women all over the world. In fact, a major international study released in 2002 found that one in three women worldwide has been physically or sexually abused. But for Americans it is easier to see and speak out about problems thousands of miles away than it is to look in our own backyard.

Feeling guilty?

It is long past time that men from all walks of life owned up to their part in all of this. The status quo is simply unacceptable. And while it is crucial that women and men work together to address the problem, the primary responsibility resides with men. Men, after all, are the primary perpetrators of rape, battering, sexual abuse, and sexual harassment, at least according to those radical feminists over at the FBI. So we can dispense with the idea that it is anti-male to say what everyone already knows to be true. There is an awful lot of violence against women in our society, and men commit the vast majority of it.

Is saying that unfair to men? Better yet, is telling the truth unfair to men? For those who think it is, please know that I am not going to spend a lot of time in this book catering to some men's defensiveness around this subject. Or to women who feel obliged to rush to the defense of their sons and husbands. But let me be clear. I am also not going to guilt-trip twenty-first-century American men by blaming them for thousands of years of sexism and patriarchal oppression. Men shouldn't feel *guilty* simply for being born male. That's silly. If there is a reason to feel guilty, it should be about what they do or fail to do, not about their chance placement in one gender category.

Nonetheless, when it comes to discussions about men and sexism, the concepts of guilt and responsibility are often confused. They are not the same thing. For conscientious men, especially those who are just beginning to grapple with the enormity of the problem of men's violence against women, feelings of guilt can be paralyzing, whereas feelings of responsibility at least have the potential to be energizing. Clearly we need to figure out

new ways to energize men and not give them more reasons to feel paralyzed. After all, if more men felt guilty, how would women benefit? This
point was driven home by Victor Lewis, one of the co-founders of the pioneering Oakland Men's Project. During a presentation, he asked the
women to raise their hands if men's guilt has been helpful in keeping them
safer, getting an equal wage, or making their lives less limited in any way.
No woman raised her hand.

I believe that men who are silent in the face of other men's violence—
whether the silence is intentional or not—are complicit in the perpetration
of that violence. We're not guilty because we're men. We're responsible—
because we're men—either for speaking out or for not speaking out about
other men's violence. This is hardly a new concept. Some of the proudest
moments in the history of this country are grounded in the principle that
members of dominant groups have a critical role to play in the struggle for
equality. For example, whether motivated by secular or religious beliefs,
many white abolitionists in the nineteenth century understood that they
were complicit in the "peculiar institution" of slavery unless they worked actively to end it. A similar sensibility informed the many courageous white radical
college students and mainstream white liberals who played an important role
in the Civil Rights movement of the 1950s and 1960s. Not coincidentally, a
lot of those white people were accused by racist whites of succumbing to
"white guilt."

When I work with men, I try to address the concepts of guilt and responsibility up front because I know from long experience—and a lot of trial and
error—that if the goal is to inspire more men to engage in transformative
action, we need to do more than simply tell them to stop behaving badly.
That is sure to provoke a defensive reaction. Defensiveness, in fact, is one of
the greatest obstacles to men's involvement in meaningful discussions about
gender violence. Simply stated, a surprising number of non-violent men
cannot hear about the bad things some men do to women without feeling
blamed themselves.

In anticipation of defensive hostility, many women (and some anti-sexist
men) censor themselves in discussions with men about sensitive issues like
rape, sexual harassment, and abuse in relationships. They decide that it is not
worth such confrontations with men in their professional or personal lives.
The cost is too high in terms of ill feelings and interpersonal tensions. So a
lot goes unsaid. Moreover, because defensiveness is the enemy of critical
thinking, an awful lot of men who stand to greatly benefit from reading and
reflecting on decades of brilliant academic and popular work on gender,
power, and violence instead avoid it like the plague. So a lot goes unread.

But not all men who react defensively are irrational. Some men actually have a troubled conscience, based on past (or present) perpetrations. No point in soft-pedaling this: there are millions of men in our society who (accurately) hear calls for men to speak out about gender violence as direct criticism of their *own* behavior. Many men get defensive and hostile at the mere mention of gender violence *because they have reason to be defensive*. The only way these men would not get defensive is if no one ever brought up the subject.

People who do gender violence prevention work with college or high school students are frequently told that we need to work with even younger kids, because we need to get to them before their sexist attitudes and beliefs have fully formed. Everyone I know in the field agrees, and wishes that schools and school boards would allow this sort of education as early as possible. The urgency of this need is especially apparent when you consider that 29 percent of rape victims are assaulted before they reach the age of *eleven*.

Young minds are easier to influence with pro-social, anti-violence messages. This is true for both girls and boys. But, for boys especially, it is not simply because their minds are more impressionable at younger ages. There is a more cynical explanation. Since younger people have literally been around for a shorter time, they are correspondingly less likely to have engaged in behaviors for which they have reason to feel guilty. Older guys, who have had more opportunities to mistreat girls, or to participate in particularly sexist aspects of male culture, as a result have more incentive to defend themselves, and more motives for denial. These motives make it increasingly more difficult to reach men as they get older and accumulate experiences they might be called to account for.

Self-interested denial is clearly on display in batterer-intervention groups across the country virtually every night of the week. The U.S. batterer-intervention movement has been around for a quarter century. There is a large and ever-growing database of experiences and insights provided by counselors and therapists who have run batterers' groups and thus interacted with hundreds of thousands of abusive men. There is much for us to learn from studying batterers' mindsets, because batterers are a lot more like the "average guy" than many people think.

As the batterer-intervention counselor Lundy Bancroft observes in his deeply insightful book *Why Does He Do That? Inside the Minds of Angry and Controlling Men*, many men who batter have internalized cultural beliefs about "manhood" that legitimize—in their own minds—their controlling and abusive behaviors. These beliefs did not appear out of thin air. These men are not from some other planet. Batterers often seek to minimize and deny their abusive behavior. Men who are ordered to seek counseling for assaulting their girlfriends or wives are commonly defiant—at least initially. In the face of compelling evidence to the contrary, they often flat-out deny they have done anything wrong. They also frequently invert the truth and argue that they are the true victims. *She's the problem. She's a manipulative bitch. She should be here, not me.* None of this is surprising. Men who batter are products of a society that is in deep denial about men's violence, and when forced to face reality seeks to blame victims instead.

Victim-blaming is especially virulent in incidents of sexual violence. The level of anger directed at the alleged victim in the recent Kobe Bryant rape trial, for example, provided a shocking wake-up call to activists and advocates in the rape crisis movement. In the year after she reported that she had been raped by the basketball superstar, the young woman received numerous death threats. She constantly had to move from state to state to ensure her safety and privacy. Her motives were questioned and her character impugned in the ugliest of terms on talk-radio programs, cable TV shows, and in countless locker room and water cooler conversations across the country. By the time the criminal trial began, Bryant's lawyers had successfully steered public conversation in the direction of critiquing *her* sexual practices, thus shifting attention off of Bryant's alleged pattern of sexually aggressive conduct toward women.

What explains the virulence of victim-blaming in sexual-assault cases? Perhaps one clue can be found in an often-cited study of male college students. This study found that one in twelve men admitted to having committed acts that met the legal definition of rape. However, 88 percent of men whose actions came under the legal definition of rape were adamant that their behavior did not constitute rape. This could be a result of confusion about what constitutes rape. This confusion is real in an era when the majority of boys and men are "educated" about sex through pornography, where it is normal in "non-violent" videos to see men treating women with incredible brutality and callousness. But the fact that so many men had committed rape also speaks to the reality of how pervasive the problem is—and how many "average" guys have motivation to ignore it.

Loyalty to our brothers and friends

Whether their violence is directed against women, children, or other men, most violent men are otherwise "normal" guys. They are average and unremarkable. How many times do we have to hear people on the eleven o'clock news naively proclaim, after their neighbor has murdered his wife and kids, that he is the last person they would think capable of such a crime because he was such a nice guy and friendly neighbor? The unsettling reality is that men's violence toward women is so normal that perpetrators are generally indistinguishable from the rest of us.

You can't tell if a man is a batterer by looking at him. Rapists don't have distinguishing facial features. What's more, the majority of violent men and boys are not isolated, loner sociopaths. To be sure, deeply disturbed individuals inspire morbid fascination, and thus are more likely to be featured in repeated headlines and on late-night cable programs. Because of occasional real-life figures like Ted Bundy or Jeffrey Dahmer, or the ubiquitous cultural presence of fictional characters like Hannibal Lecter, monsters have a disproportionate impact on our cultural psyche. But even they can present a normal front to the world. As the *Time* magazine headline read after the so-called BTK serial murderer was arrested in March 2005, "Was the Killer Next Door? Dennis Rader Was a Husband, Father, Church Leader—And Is Now the Man Accused of Terrorizing Wichita." Still, deranged murderers and rapists comprise only a very small percentage of violent men. Most men who assault women are not so much disturbed as they are disturbingly *normal*. Like all of us, they are products of familial and social systems. They are our sons, brothers, friends, and coworkers. As such they are influenced not only by individual factors, but also by broader cultural attitudes and beliefs about manhood that shape their psyches and identities. And *ours*.

Most perpetrators are, in fact, "*our guys*," the phrase Bernard Lefkowitz coined to describe the popular white, middle-class New Jersey boys who gang-raped a mentally retarded girl in a 1989 case that achieved national notoriety. Those boys—like the vast majority of perpetrators of gender violence—didn't speak a foreign language or adhere to strange customs. They were homegrown products of contemporary American society. There is no getting around the fact that violent boys and men are products of our culture, and as such are influenced by cultural ideas about manhood that teach individual males what is expected of them—in and out of relationships with women. *Their* violence says something about *us*.

To put it bluntly, we are unindicted coconspirators in their crimes. That uncomfortable truth is one of the many reasons why people—both men and women—have a self-interest in denying the extent of the problem. If millions of women and girls are abused and mistreated by men, then it follows that a lot of men abuse and mistreat women. Who are these men? Most of them are not strangers. Most women who are raped are raped by men they know. Women who are battered are battered by their partners. Women who are sexually harassed are usually harassed by fellow students, teachers, coworkers, or bosses. In other words, most of us who know female victims also know the men who have abused and violated them.

Who wants to think about their friends and loved ones as rapists, wife beaters, and sexual harassers? If people have reason to be in denial about the *victimization* of women they care about, isn't it even more understandable that they would be in denial about male perpetrators they care about? At least the victims are sympathetic; something bad has happened to them. But who wants to admit that men they care about have done bad things to women? The motivation for denial is particularly acute for family members of perpetrators. *What do his actions say about us as a family?* It also brings up all sorts of conflicts for friends. *Should I be loyal to my friend, even though I know he's done something wrong? I wouldn't hit a woman, but he did, and he's my friend. Are his acts a reflection on me?* Friends are also forced to make a choice. Unless they confront an abusive friend in some way and repudiate his abusive acts, the people close to violent men can be implicated either as complicit in immoral behavior or as cowards. The more you convince men of the need for them to take action, the more you challenge them to examine their complicity.

One of the underlying causes of the rampant victim-blaming that goes on in men's discussions about violence against women is that it makes our ethical choices easier. If the (false) choice is between "She's a vindictive slut who's trying to take down one of my boys," and "My friend is a rapist," it's a no-brainer to figure out which one is the easiest to live with.

Therein lies the central paradox of trying to mobilize men by shocking them about the reality of gender violence in the lives of the women they care about. If crimes like child sexual abuse, rape, battering, and stalking were relatively uncommon, it would be much easier to take comfort in the notion that perpetrators were unusual, anomalous, just bad seeds. It is less stressful to blame the demonized "other" than it is to engage in self-examination. It would be so much easier to blame this whole nasty business on deranged psychos—easier on the victims, too. But reality intrudes. Deep in our conscience we know that violence against women is committed by men whom the victims—and we—know all too well.

Buying into sexism

For men, the myth of the anomalous, disconnected sociopath exempts us from introspection when it comes to our participation in a myriad of sexist cultural practices. Rather than question how our actions contribute to the widespread incidence of gender violence, we can instead maintain the fiction that it is simply not our problem. *We're not like those pathological perps. We wouldn't do bad things to women.* This sort of distancing comes in particularly handy when introspection might otherwise prompt us to feel guilty.

By way of example, let's speculate about how some Average Joes might react when they hear on the news about a man arrested for the abduction, rape, and murder of an eight-year-old girl. Feverish media reports of the crime might include the information that police have found an extensive collection of child porn videos and magazines in the suspect's apartment. By now, this sort of news has become a regular part of the media landscape. Most people are outraged about crimes like these and repulsed by the men who commit them. Now for the tricky part. Realistically, at least some of the men who are genuinely outraged by these crimes have purchased *Hustler* magazine, or rented *Hustler*-produced porn videos. Some might even revere *Hustler* founder Larry Flynt as a "First Amendment hero."

What is the connection? Consider this. Flynt also publishes *Barely Legal*, a porn magazine whose raison d'etre is the crude sexualization and commodification of young girls. The male consumers of *Barely Legal* would likely insist that naked eighteen-year-old models with bows in their hair, spreading their legs wide for the camera, are technically "consenting adults." But everyone knows that the intent is to create the illusion that they are much younger. For years, a popular feature in Flynt's signature publication, *Hustler*, was a cartoon that followed the exploits of a fictional sexual abuser of young girls, Chester the Molester. The cartoon was discontinued only when the cartoonist, Dwayne Tinsley, was convicted of sexually abusing his real-life daughter—who claimed that the art was a chronicle of her actual victimization.

It is not possible to draw a linear causal chain from the purchase of a magazine like *Barely Legal* to the brutal rape-murder of an eight-year-old girl by a middle-aged man. Many men would be outraged at the implication. But it is equally outrageous to suggest that *no* relationship whatsoever exists between our society's pandemic of sexual abuse of children and the widespread availability of products like *Barely Legal*, where young girls' sexualized bodies are turned into commodities that adult men can purchase for their masturbatory pleasure. You do not need to argue that legal porn *causes* illegal activity in order to assert that it contributes significantly to a culture where continuously younger girls are cast as the objects of adult men's sexual desires and pathologies.

We can take comfort in the idea of the aforementioned child rapist-murderer as a horrible aberration. A monster. *We're nothing like him.* And in fairness, purchasing and masturbating to images of "consenting adults" posing as young girls is not criminal behavior. But one need not be a criminal accomplice to share some moral responsibility, or feel—if we are honest enough with ourselves—a certain degree of moral complicity.

This is yet another place where denial plays a useful function. Men who are not rapists, batterers, or sexual abusers of young girls are nonetheless citizens and consumers in a society where a shockingly high number of our fellow men are. It is much easier for us not to think about the hundreds of ways that we—directly or indirectly—contribute to their perpetration. Better to avoid the entire messy situation than have to wrestle with such troubling moral complexities.

Breaking through the denial

Men who educate other men about violence against women tend to believe that if only more guys knew what we know, a lot of them would wake up—like we did—and do something about it. After all, isn't it true that at one point, we, too, were oblivious? Something had an effect on *our* consciousness. For many of us who were educated about these issues on college campuses in the 1970s, 1980s, and 1990s, *something* snapped us out of complacency and forced us to realize that men's violence—or the threat of it—was not some abstract social problem, but rather a routine part of life for our female peers.

Maybe it started with the disclosure by a girlfriend of abuse in a past relationship. Maybe it was catalyzed by reading assigned for a college sociology or psychology class. Maybe it was hearing with shock for the first time the often-quoted statistic that "one in four women will be the victim of rape or attempted rape in her lifetime." For some men it may have been standing in the chilly evening air at a Take Back the Night rally, watching fellow female students bravely walk up to a microphone and one after the other tell stories of having been sexually abused by an uncle or raped by an ex-boyfriend. Some of us were so shocked and angered when we realized that for women in our generation these experiences were commonplace that we developed a passion to change the consciousness and behavior of other men in the hopes of affecting a wholesale shift in their attitudes and behaviors.

Our impulse was to jolt other people, to metaphorically shake them: "Can't you see? It's all around us. This isn't one of those tragedies that happens to other people. It's right here in our own families! Look at our women friends. So many of them have been mistreated by men, in some cases since they were little girls. Talk to counselors at the local women's center and hear some of the stories they hear from women *every day*. Then do the math. You'll see. It isn't hyperbole to say that this stuff hits close to home for every one of us; it's probability theory."

When I started giving speeches at colleges and high schools, I would frequently begin by quoting a sampling of gender-violence statistics, in the hope of stirring the kind of outrage in others that I felt myself. *Did you know that there is physical abuse in about one in four marriages? Did you know that over 29 percent of rape victims are raped before the age of eleven?* I would lay down some particularly egregious stats when I was straining to impress a group of seemingly indifferent men. *Do you realize that in the U.S. three women on average are murdered every day by their husbands, boyfriends, or exes?*

In tough crowds, I would do my best to reference government and law enforcement statistics—the more traditionally "masculine" the source, the better. It was a defensive tactic. When people don't want to face facts, the first thing they do is discredit the source of those facts. Why give men—many of whom have a self-interest in discrediting unflattering assertions—the ammunition to do so? So instead of using statistics from women's organizations, I began to use those from conservative establishment sources. This provided a built-in defense against the charge that the problem has been deliberately exaggerated by "man-haters and male-bashers." Admittedly, this cautious strategy has a significant downside. Mainstream statistics often dramatically understate the problem, mostly because crimes like incest, rape, and battering are so underreported to law enforcement.

I would sometimes begin a presentation by reading dozens of newspaper headlines about gruesome incidents of murder and rape that I'd clipped from local papers. *Man kills wife, self. Girl, fifteen, bludgeoned to death. Woman raped in city park. College athletes charged with rape.* I was trying to reinforce the message through sheer repetition.

Variations on the "shock therapy" approach to gender violence prevention have been a part of most rape-education strategies on college campuses for the past several decades. The idea is that by feeding students a litany of horrifying statistics, at the very least you'll communicate to them an urgency about the seriousness of the problem. But until recently, women were the students on whom most awareness-raising efforts were focused. The presumption was that scary statistics would help women see that "it can happen to me."

For women and men involved in the battered women's or rape crisis movements, especially those who deal daily with victims, convincing people—especially men—of the urgency of the situation may appear to belabor the obvious. Doesn't everyone already realize how big a problem this is? Don't they know there are survivors *in their own families?*

Well, not necessarily. A lot of people cannot face the ugly reality—or don't want to. It is important to remember that coming to terms with the extent of the problem can be disorienting, and profoundly disruptive. As a man, once you are aware of the degree to which women suffer from gender violence and all forms of sexism, you can't simply go about your business and pretend everything is fine. You have to do something about it, or else risk losing your self-respect. This is where denial comes in. Denial is a tried and true method of coping with disruptive, traumatic, or discomforting information; it is much less painful than facing the truth. Not to mention that many Americans are so desensitized by repeated exposure to violence of all kinds—in their own lives, on the news, and in the popular culture—that denial isn't even necessary.

A substantial portion of the population—including many young Americans who consider themselves world weary and media savvy— remains unconscious and unaware of systematic causes of interpersonal violence. Another young mother murdered as her little children scream in the next room? What a shame. Another college student raped in her dorm room? It's not safe anywhere anymore. Another prominent athlete arrested for beating his wife? What's wrong with these guys, anyway?

Feminists have maintained for years that all of these phenomena are linked, that in fact they are inevitable byproducts of women's subordinate social position. They are not just a collection of unrelated acts. This is one aspect of the famously insightful slogan that the "personal is political." It is also one of the many reasons why feminist ideas about gender and power threaten so many people. They represent real philosophical challenges to dominant modes of thinking, not to mention real political challenges to hierarchical and male-dominated power structures.

Call it feminist or not. If there is any hope of dramatically reducing the high levels of men's violence to which we have become accustomed, we are going to have to find a way to look beyond individual perpetrators and their problems to the culture that produces them. This societal introspection is a daunting task, more daunting even than the war on terrorism. It is a lot easier to focus on external enemies, however elusive, than it is to look inward.

CHAPTER THREE

Taking it Personally

"My father was a violent man. His physical and verbal abuse terrorized my mother and all five of his kids. I was in my fifties before I truly realized how much this experience has impacted my personality and relationships. But the cycle can be broken."
— New York Yankees manager Joe Torre

FATHERS, BROTHERS, SONS, AND LOVERS

Many years ago I was in a theater watching a movie with a girlfriend when she abruptly got up out of her seat and, without saying a word, ran out the door. I didn't know what to do. Follow her out into the lobby? Keep watching the movie and wait for her to come back? I was not sure how to react because I did not know why she had left. Was it something she had eaten? Was it something I had done? I shifted anxiously in my seat. Was she angry with me?

Later, when we discussed what had happened, I was both relieved to find out I was not responsible and amazed at my own lack of awareness. Her response had been triggered by a scene of violence. She was a rape survivor, and something about that scene brought back intense fear and pain; she had to flee. I knew about the rape, which had happened when she was a teenager. At that point we had not discussed the details of her assault, or the trauma symptoms she still experienced. I spent some time agonizing over how I could have anticipated and prevented the entire incident. But she picked out the movie; didn't she know it would have violent scenes? Eventually, as I moved through some initial—and reflexive—defensiveness, I realized there probably wasn't anything I could have done. This was not about me, after all; it was about her.

But I was not a disinterested third party; I was her boyfriend. I cared about her. How could we even hope to get closer if I had no clue about what she had been through? If she retreated rather than reached out when feeling overwhelmed, how could I possibly help? There were practical concerns. How could I know when to touch her? How could I feel confident that *I* would not inadvertently trigger another traumatic flashback?

This incident was not the first time that violence against women became personal for me—and it was hardly the last. I would have a hard time counting all the women I know who are survivors of some kind of men's violence, abuse, or mistreatment; there are way too many. And it is not just me: *every single man I know* has at least one or two women in his life who have been emotionally, physically, or sexually abused by men. Some of us have many more.

Naturally, some men think this is overstated. "Come on," they say, "it can't be as bad as all that." It is an understandable reaction. After all, it can be pretty unsettling—especially for guys who care deeply about women—to admit to themselves that violence against women is not just happening to other people but to women we know and care about. It can be pretty unsettling for women, too. There are many women who will downplay the entire subject—and their own risk of victimization—with an exasperated sneer and a dismissive remark about feminists wallowing in "victimhood."

My perspective on the problem is inevitably skewed by the nature of my work. I regularly travel around the country to attend and present at domestic and sexual violence conferences, meet and talk with students on college and high school campuses, and work with men and women on U.S. military bases. I hear profoundly disturbing testimonies of violence and victimization from women constantly. Most men who work with these issues have similar experiences. But it is not just the admittedly skewed sample of women I come across in battered women's programs or college women's centers. Men who get involved with women's issues tend to hear stories from women—and men—in the strangest of places, stories that the average guy simply does not hear. I like to think it is because we radiate compassion and empathy, but I realize that sometimes it is just because we provide the promise of a supportive ear.

Consider this curious sequence of events that happened a few years ago. I was in a bank in Boston on a sunny, cold winter morning, completing a transaction with a teller with whom I had done business for a couple of years. She was a dark-haired Italian American woman in her forties, with a thick Boston accent and a smoker's raspy laugh. We had always exchanged polite chatter but never a really substantive conversation. I was anxious about time; I told her I had to get to the airport. She asked me where I was going. When I told her Montana, she probed me about why I would be going all the way out there. "To give a speech tonight," I said.

"About what?" she inquired.

"Violence against women," I hesitatingly answered.

She leaned forward with theatrical flair, and across the teller's window confided in me with a smirk of mock secretiveness. "Let me tell you about violence against women," she said calmly. "I had a boyfriend who beat me so bad he left me in a coma. He's dead now, but I'd kill him if he weren't."

Later that day, I was in the Salt Lake City airport, trying to figure out how I would get to Montana after my flight—the last flight of the day—had been cancelled. At the airline customer service desk I told the empathetic agent— a thirty-something white woman—that if I could not figure out a way to get to Missoula, I would have to go back to Boston, because I was scheduled to give a speech that night. Getting to Montana a day late would be pointless. "What's your speech about?" she inquired. She lit up when I told her. "I could give your speech," she exclaimed. "A former airline employee has been stalking me for months," she said. "The case was just in the paper, since I filed a suit against him. Did you hear about it? I don't know what's going to happen."

As I headed back through the terminal, I wondered something that I ponder to this day: How many of the women walking by me have similar stories to tell? Were these two women a statistical aberration? Are these types of experiences so common in the lives of women in our era that they are closer to the norm than the exception? Are stories like these just beneath the surface everywhere?

There is no more effective way to demonstrate men's self-interest in gender violence prevention than to make the subject personal. Men are affected in many ways: as the friends of women who are living with abusive relationships; as the coworkers of women whose home lives are marked by episodes of tension and ugliness; as the concerned family members of girls and women who live with harassment at school or on the job; as the sons of women who were sexually abused as girls; as the sons of battered women; as the current husbands of formerly battered women; as the sexual partners of rape survivors; as the grieving fathers of murdered daughters. One of the most famous slogans of the women's liberation movement of the 1970s was "the personal is political." This is as true today as it was then. It is also as true for men as it is for women. The trick is to show men how their personal experiences with gender violence—as victims, loved ones of victims, and in some cases as perpetrators—are not simply shaped by individual circumstances or bad luck, but reflect much broader and systematic social forces.

Many women who have experienced violence keep it to themselves—or at most they confide in a few close girlfriends. Often the men in their lives have no idea. I am sure I have women friends who haven't shared this sort of information with me. But I do hear more than my share of sad stories. For women who have been mistreated by men, confiding in a man who is committed to working against men's violence can feel safer than taking the risk that a boyfriend or close friend will not know how to react or what to say. In fact, many men who get involved in gender violence prevention go through a phase where some of their female friends start to open up to them about their experiences of abuse or violence. I have a friend who had a close platonic friendship with a woman. When he got a job with an education program that had a rape prevention component, he began to share with her his newfound awareness about rape. She confided in him that she had been raped, not years before but during the time they had known each other. He was initially stunned, and a little hurt, that she had not told him at the time, but he understood why. Over time he came to realize that many women around him— including members of his extended family—had been through similar trauma.

Women's reticence in sharing these personal experiences with men is perfectly understandable. However enlightened some of us imagine ourselves, there is still a stigma attached to violent victimization, especially sexual victimization. As a result, women often fear that even "well-meaning" men will blame them for "letting" something happen, for putting themselves in a compromising position, for falling for the wrong guy, etc. Better to never raise the subject and avoid the potential disappointment.

The result is that countless men do not realize how men's violence affects the women around them. They comfort themselves with the often naïve assumption that "this isn't a problem in my family." They hear the incredible statistics that have been circulating in our culture over the past three decades but they do not think it touches *their* lives. It does touch their lives, whether or not they are consciously aware of it. In 2002, during a training I led in Los Angeles for violence prevention educators, we did an exercise where we went around the room and people talked about their experiences with violence and how those experiences shaped their attraction to issues of human rights and social justice. A gregarious man in his late fifties, who had been a teacher and social justice educator for thirty years, demurred when it came time for him to speak. He said he could not think of any relevant experiences with violence; he just liked working with young people.

During lunch, this same man took me aside and told me that he had been ruminating on the exercise all morning. He had had a revelation. Of course this subject was personal for him. What was he thinking? His mother had been a battered woman. Granted, this was before the term "battered woman" had entered the lexicon. He had grown up in New York in the 1950s, in a family where his father had emotionally and physically abused his mother. He was startled that it had never before occurred to him that this profound experience had influenced his life choices and his professional path, especially his desire to help others.

People's trauma histories can also present significant obstacles in their search for relational connection. This phenomenon was addressed memorably in the hit film *Good Will Hunting* (1997). The lead character, Will, played by Matt Damon, had been badly abused as a boy. When he started to get closer to his girlfriend Skylar, played by Minnie Driver, his vulnerability came closer to the surface, he became aggressive, and he withdrew. A similar thing sometimes happens to young women in college who begin relationships just around the time they first seek therapy for incest or sexual abuse experiences in childhood or adolescence. Therapists in college counseling centers deal with these problems on a daily basis. Many young men—and women—struggle to develop intimate relationships with women who are going through that process. Sometimes a partner can provide invaluable love and support during a difficult period, but it can be an emotionally trying time for everyone. The relationship partner has his or her own needs, and if a woman needs to focus on herself, she may or may not be fully present and available for them. Often male partners of female rape or abuse survivors feel frustrated and inadequate because, try as they might, they can not "solve" their partner's problem.

Certainly men's own behavior can be the cause of interpersonal conflicts with women. Men with the best of intentions sometimes say things and act out in sexist and abusive ways, either because they do not know any better, or because they are conditioned to mindlessly parrot what they have learned from peers or popular culture. Some men are conscious of the contradictions between what they *say* about how much they respect women and the things they have *done* as "one of the guys." Some men feel bad because in quiet, introspective moments, they have to admit to themselves that they have participated in sexist or sexually exploitative practices. Maybe they paid a prostitute for sex, or they enjoy listening to music with sexist messages. Maybe they have not said anything in situations where male friends have made degrading comments about women. Maybe they know deep down that in spite of their self-image as a "good guy," they help to perpetuate women's subordinate status. Some men, of course, feel not only bad but guilty, because they know—even if no one around them does—that at some point in their lives, they, too, have mistreated women. They know in their bones more than they could learn from any workshop or book that the problem is not just *other guys*.

Some men do not need to experience an assault against a female loved one in order to grasp the urgency of the problem. They understand that men's exploitation of women is a fundamental human rights issue that is tied to countless other social and political problems in the U.S. and around the world. But substantive reductions in gender violence require the involvement of a much broader cross section of men. Transformative social change will come about only if a critical mass of men realize that it is in their self-interest to reduce the level of men's violence against women. Self-interest is a far more powerful motivational tool than is concern for social justice. Consider how opposition to the U.S. war in Vietnam in the 1960s increased dramatically—especially among white middle-class college students—when the government instituted the draft. When your own life is on the line, or the life of someone close to you, it has a way of getting your attention.

There is a further benefit to making the issue of gender violence personal. When men can *feel* the issue in their hearts as opposed to *intellectualizing* it in their heads, they are much more likely to gain the self-confidence necessary to confront their fellow men. It often takes special courage and strength for men to risk confrontations with friends and colleagues about the mistreatment of women, to rise above possible ridicule and disbelief, and to withstand whispering campaigns about their "manhood" if they refuse to conform to sexist and abusive norms.

But the question remains: is it defensible—is it even possible—to mobilize men to work against gender violence by arguing that it's in their self-interest to do so? It is obvious that this work is in women's interest. But whether it is in men's interest is less clear—and more controversial. For example, some feminists in the 1970s advanced the argument that *all* men benefit from *some* men's violence against women because that violence—and the threat of it—is a key tool in men's continued subordination of women, from which all men benefit.

Today we know that the picture is significantly more complicated. Most importantly, men as a category are not homogenous. There are important differences between and among them. Not all men have the same interest in maintaining the current status quo. Take gay men, for example. There are aspects of male privilege that gay men enjoy. But they are also subject to some of the same discrimination and violence that women experience. In fact, violence against women and gay-bashing have a lot in common, not the least of which is that in both cases, heterosexual men—*often with something to prove*—are the primary perpetrators.

Men of color derive some of the same benefits from male privilege as dominant white males. But in other respects they do not have as much invested in maintaining the status quo as many white men do. How does it "benefit" men of color, for example, if women of color—African Americans, Latinas, and others—suffer disproportionately high rates of domestic violence and sexual assault, especially in poor communities? Poverty and racism surely contribute to the incidence of domestic and sexual violence by men of color against their girlfriends, wives, and daughters. But this violence then helps perpetuate poverty and racism in a continuous feedback loop. An early 1990s political slogan aimed at men of color put it like this: "You can't fight the power if you're dissing the sisters."

Violence against women of color (largely perpetrated by men of color) actually subverts the fight against racism and ethnic discrimination by draining the energies of so many women. How can they fight for peace and justice in their communities if there is no peace and justice in their own homes? There are also the deleterious effects of domestic and sexual violence on children. Domestic-violence researchers have documented the relationship between violence at home and school drop-out rates, gang participation, street crime, and teen pregnancy—all of which are persistent problems in communities of color.

Although it is true that men who dominate and abuse women often "benefit" from their abuse in the sense that they get what they want from it, it is also true that it is in men's self-interest to reduce the violence suffered by our mothers, daughters, wives, and girlfriends. Over the past generation, millions of boys—of all socioeconomic, racial, and ethnic groups—have trembled in fear and powerlessness as they've watched men beat their mothers. Most of these boys eventually grow up. If they can negotiate the rocky waters of male adolescence, today's victimized boys will one day be men, many of whom will develop emotional and substance abuse problems linked to their traumatic childhoods. How many men today are in therapy—or AA meetings—to deal with the effects of growing up in violent families?

Of course, there is no comparison between the pain of men who care about female victims of men's violence and the suffering of the girls and women themselves. Regardless, countless boys and men *have* suffered as a result of violence done to their female loved ones. Think about all of the boys whose mothers have been murdered. Approximately twelve hundred women each year in the U.S. are murdered by husbands, boyfriends, or exes. That is more than thirty-six thousand women in the past three decades. They have left behind tens of thousands of children.

Consider, too, all of the fathers whose daughters are raped. Parents know that seeing children suffer is probably the most difficult experience they can imagine. Is it possible to quantify the pain of parents whose daughters (or sons) have been raped? I have talked to many fathers (and mothers) who have gone through this. A father's pain can be compounded by his sense of guilt that he failed in his manly duty to protect his family, however unrealistic a burden that is. Of course mothers experience their own guilt as well. I once had a male colleague whose only daughter was raped. A few months later, in the middle of a public presentation, his grief and anger at the rapist poured forth in a way that left people sitting in stunned silence. Another friend once called to seek my advice and support when his oldest daughter was sexually assaulted in her first *week* of college. For these men, violence against women is as personal as it gets.

If you factor in all the husbands and boyfriends of women with sexual abuse histories, or who suffer post-traumatic stress disorder symptoms from past abusive relationships, or the male partners of women who are sexually harassed in the workplace, the collective numbers of all these boys and men is in the *millions*. You do not need to convince a majority of men to prioritize gender-violence prevention in order to effect significant social change. If only a small percentage of the men with a *direct personal stake* made their personal experiences political, the reverberations would be culturally transformative.

Men's concern for the girls and women in their lives

Most men care deeply about the girls and women in their lives. Millions of these girls and women live with abuse in the present; many more live with the effects of past abuse. But virtually all women live daily with the *threat* of men's violence. Women's consciousness about the possibility of assault—by a man they do not know—is so pervasive, in fact, that most women automatically take a series of precautions every day. These precautions, which were enumerated in the prologue to this book, include not walking or going out alone at night; holding their keys as a potential weapon; locking all windows and doors in the home and car; not making eye contact with strange men; not listing their full names in the phone book; not putting their drink down at a party or bar. The list goes on.

What can the average man do about this? Many say that if they are not themselves violent, it is not really their problem. But if they care deeply about women, and this is a major concern to women, then shouldn't they do something? Are they in fact obligated to act—especially if their actions can help?

By way of analogy, imagine that you were a white, middle-class South African during the apartheid era. In spite of pervasive residential and social segregation, you managed to make some black friends and acquaintances. You did not vote for the ruling party or support its apartheid policies. You did not directly exploit black labor in your home or workplace. You did not consider yourself racist.

Nonetheless, did you have a moral obligation to work against apartheid? If you did not actively behave in a racist manner, but as a privileged white person simply went about your life in the midst of this system, weren't you manifestly part of the problem? Isn't it fair to hold you accountable—morally if not legally—for failing to act more decisively to bring about racial equality? Were you being a responsible friend to black people if you chose not to get involved?

Likewise, is a man a responsible father/son/partner/friend to women if he chooses not to get involved in speaking out about men's violence? Can a man who does not personally abuse women persuasively maintain that rape, battering, sexual abuse, and sexual harassment are "not his problem"?

How about men who have been disrespectful toward women in the past, even emotionally, physically, or sexually abusive? Perhaps it was in their teens or early twenties. Or maybe in a first marriage. What if they are better men now, having since matured, or been in therapy, or had an epiphany of one kind or another? Do their earlier transgressions confer on them any added responsibility to the women in their lives—and women in general?

One of the many reasons why some men do not feel comfortable holding other men accountable for sexist behaviors is their feeling that—considering their personal histories—they are in no position to lecture other men about how to treat women. It is a valid concern. There are a lot of compromised men out there. This was one of the striking aspects of the 1992 Senate Judiciary Committee hearings into Anita Hill's sexual-harassment allegations against Clarence Thomas. Many of the Democrats on the committee were noticeably silent or gentle with Thomas, who was alleged to have had a history of sexist and boorish behavior, but was being considered for placement on the highest court in the land. At the time, numerous commentators speculated that several Democratic senators were passive precisely because to go after Thomas would mean risking their exposure as self-righteous hypocrites. Feminists argued that if there were more (any!) women on the committee, these sorts of conflicts would be avoided—and men like Clarence Thomas would have little chance of confirmation.

Men's concern about the boys in their lives

In 2000, the Family Violence Prevention Fund commissioned a study to determine what sorts of messages would be most likely to attract men to anti-domestic-violence efforts. The study found that men were much more comfortable talking with children about the problem than they were with any of the other approaches—including confronting peers or participating in a collective action.

When adult men take a stand against violence against women, they not only model positive behavior for the next generation, they help children today—including boys. Practically speaking, men who care about boys—and feel both a personal and a political responsibility for their physical well-being and emotional health—need to think about gender-violence prevention as a primary need of theirs. In the domestic-violence and sexual-assault fields over the past decade, there has been an increased emphasis on the effects of these crimes on children. National and statewide conferences are frequently devoted to the subject of "children who witness," not to mention dozens of books and countless articles. It is worth noting that the category of "children" includes both girls and boys. Hundreds of thousands of boys are routinely terrorized in their own homes as they stand by, helplessly watching as a father or stepfather abuses their mother.

This is not taking place in some abstract universe. Thousands of five-, six, and seven-year-old boys in the United States *tonight* will cower in the closet and scream as their mother is beaten—and this is not just a problem in poor or low-income communities.

One repercussion for boys who grow up in abusive homes is the damage this does to their relationships with their fathers. This is one of the many complexities of father-son relationships in our violent culture, and one of the hidden costs of men's violence. Many adult men have conflicted feelings about their fathers due to the way their mothers were treated. They might love them but harbor intense anger toward them. In some cases, these feelings can last for decades after the actual abuse has stopped. I have known men who can never forgive their fathers, and have no wish to ever speak with them again.

There was a case in Massachusetts in the mid-1990s where a man, Daniel Holland, shot his wife eight times as their son Patrick, then eight years old, slept in the next room. Daniel Holland was arrested and eventually sentenced to life in prison without the possibility of parole. Several years later, in a case that generated national news coverage, the boy initiated a "parental divorce" in order to force his incarcerated father out of his life completely. Patrick

Holland, by then fourteen years old, filed suit to terminate his father's parental rights. After the father agreed to a settlement, the boy said, "It's like a big weight's been lifted from my shoulders, knowing that I don't have to worry about him being in my life."

Consider as well the experience of boys whose mothers are sexual-assault survivors. There are no conclusive national statistics on this subject, but when you figure that female rape survivors number in the millions, you have to assume that millions of boys and men in our society have mothers who have been raped. Suffering a rape need not be a defining life experience for a woman, or in any way prevent her from being a good mother, but its ramifications can linger in the lives of her sons (and daughters).

For example, the percentage of rape survivors who develop alcohol problems is much greater than it is in the general population. There is also evidence to suggest that rape survivors are more prone to develop addictions to antidepressants, methamphetamine, or other drugs, in part as a way to medicate the effects of their trauma. Their addiction, in turn, can then lead to all manner of destructive and self-destructive behaviors, which inevitably affect the kids. Sons (and daughters) are thus often the secondary victims of the original assault by a man against their mother.

Juvenile detention centers across the country are filled with boys whose mothers are survivors—or current victims—of men's violence. How many of these boys are in the system for acting out their family traumas in antisocial ways? The poignancy of this was brought home for me when I was working as a counselor in a staff-secure detention facility in the Boston area for boys aged nine to seventeen. Staff-secure means there are alarms on the doors but no locks. One night, one of the kids in my section, a sixteen-year-old African American who lived in Boston, was on the phone in the common area, talking with his mother. It was a half-hour after lights out. I was standing quietly near the doorway, making sure the five other kids in my dorm had settled down and stopped talking to each other across the room. I was keeping one eye on Darryl (not his real name), trying not to eavesdrop too noticeably on one of the few semi-private conversations he was allowed to have. Quite abruptly he slammed the phone down and ran by me to his cubby, where he plopped down onto his uncomfortable twin-sized bed and buried his head in the pillow. I could hear his muffled sobbing. I subsequently learned that right in the middle of the phone conversation, Darryl's mother's boyfriend started to scream and beat her while her son was on the line. This sixteen-year-old—who just a few hours before had been acting the part of the nothin'-fazes-me, street-savvy tough guy—was locked up and utterly powerless to protect his own mother.

Advocates and researchers in the battered women's movement have increasingly drawn attention to this sort of trauma. Their focus has been not just on whether girls in abusive situations are more likely to grow up and become abused, or boys to become abusers. Their goal is to understand how "delinquent" and self-destructive behavior—by girls and boys—is related to the traumatic experience of growing up in a home with an abused mother. How does the violence done to a mother affect her children? How do they cope? What are some of the gender differences in the ways that children of battered women handle the abuse?

At the time, I wondered what it must have felt like to be in Darryl's position. How would I feel if I were powerless to stop a man from assaulting my mother? Would I be able to focus on anything else—the daily routine of a juvenile facility, going to class, doing chores, playing cards? I knew Darryl was feeling guilty—if not outright responsible—for his mother's suffering. He had no one to blame but himself for doing the things he had done to get arrested; but when he ran away from the facility a week later, foolishly, impulsively, who was surprised? I never learned what happened to him.

Some men who are hesitant to talk about violence against women are eager to talk about the victimization of boys and men. "Guys are victims, too," they will say, as if anyone ever implied otherwise. Yes, they are. For one thing, they are most certainly the secondary victims of other men's crimes against the women in their families. But some men (or women) who say "men are victims, too" really mean that men are frequent victims of women's violence.

Female-on-male violence is a serious issue, especially mother-to-son child abuse. But the frequency and severity of violence by adult women against adult men is often wildly overstated by "men's rights" activists. Women do assault men, and unless it is in self-defense it is indefensible. But the incidence and severity of this violence pales in comparison to male-on-female violence. It is important to emphasize that in the vast majority of cases where boys and men are the victims of violent crime, they are the victims of other *men's* violence. For example, the rape of men in prison is a shamefully common event in this country. But prisoner rape is largely a phenomenon of men raping other men (as male authorities avert their eyes). To reduce men's violence, then, is to reduce it against *other men* as well as against women.

His stories

When I first began giving speeches on college campuses about men's violence against women, the first person to raise a hand during the Q&A period—almost always a woman—would comment on how unusual it was to hear a man talk about this subject with such passion. "I'm not sure if this is too personal," she would say, "but how did you get into this?"

A friend once advised me that I shouldn't respond to predictable questions about my personal motivation, because the answers are irrelevant. "This isn't about you," she argued, "or any of the other men who speak out against gender violence. It's about the millions of female victims and survivors. It's about their lives. *Women's* lives. It's not about men. It shouldn't matter what drives a small number of you to speak out. You're just doing what decent men should be doing." While there is truth in this, there is another truth as well: not enough men *are* doing it.

In every decade since the beginning of the feminist-led anti-rape and anti-battering movements in the 1970s, there has been a steady stream of young men who have been politicized in college or graduate school who have subsequently volunteered in campus or community-based women's centers, gone to work in batterer-intervention programs, or have done other gender violence related work in social service agencies and educational institutions. But it is not enough. Untold millions of other men, guys who love and care about women and are upset by harm done to them, are not yet ready or willing to think critically about violence against women as a men's issue, or to actively do something about it. Why not? Why are so few men willing to talk straight about this subject? Why are relatively few of us willing to engage in critical dialogue—with women as well as with other men—about cultural constructs of masculinity and their relationship to the violence some men do to women?

I have had countless conversations over the years with women and men in the field—in community settings and on college campuses—who struggle daily for men to be visible allies in their gender violence prevention work, to participate in public events, serve on committees, attend meetings and other programs. Some domestic and sexual violence programs have significant male support in their communities; others have a history of tense relations with men in law enforcement, the courts, and the school system.

On college campuses in every part of the country, women's center directors and sexual-assault educators tell me repeatedly that they only have a handful of vocal male allies in the administration or the faculty. They constantly seek suggestions about how to get more. The questions are always the same: How can we get more men with power to prioritize these issues? How can we broaden our base of male supporters? How can we get more young men involved? How can we connect with the Average Joes, the young men on college campuses who "sit in the back row with their caps pulled down," as the college professor and educational filmmaker Sut Jhally refers to them—young men who would not dream of intentionally signing up for a course on gender, volunteering at their campus women's center, or engaging feminism as something more complicated than a PC attack on their manhood? How do we get these guys to think "outside the box" and to understand these issues as their own?

I have learned that the surest way to grab men's attention is to get personal. To make this about the women they know and love. It is one thing for guys to agree in principle that violence against women is a serious problem, but quite another to talk about their mothers, daughters, or wives. In order to dramatically expand the number of men who make these issues a priority, there is no better motivating force than the power of men's intimate connection to women.

I have heard countless testimonies from men about the pain gender violence caused in their lives, from the time they were boys right up to the present. Consider a handful:

- At a gender-violence prevention training on a United States Marine Corps base in Hawaii, a forty-something first sergeant with still-taut muscles bulging out of his shirt and a ruddy, freckled complexion stands up to speak. He quietly recounts the time his father pulled a gun on him when he tried to defend his mother from a drunken beating. His eyes moisten as he speaks. I wonder if this is the first time in his life that he has ever talked publicly about this.
- The top cadet at a U.S. military service academy approaches me backstage after a speech I have just delivered to the entire corps of cadets. He shakes my hand and thanks me. He apologizes for the immature behavior of some of his fellow cadets, who had done some heckling and ill-timed laughing during my speech. He assures me that there will be consequences for the rude behavior. Then he leans over, and his voice cracks as he tells me that his fiancée was raped as a teenager, and that they sat up together and cried many nights.
- A middle-aged white man who is a powerful law enforcement official in a big city government in the Pacific Northwest states plainly, in a workshop with many of his colleagues, that he has long been motivated by his abusive, alcoholic father's negative example. "From the time I was a kid," he says, "I vowed never to be like him."
- A college classmate approaches me at a reunion in Massachusetts, after a few beers, and takes me aside. He tells me that his wife sometimes wakes up in the middle of the night, flailing about and punching the pillow. She has nightmare flashbacks to the night many years ago when she was raped. He asks me, "What am I supposed to do?"
- In a workshop with ten National Football League rookies, three of the men disclose that they grew up in homes where their mother was bat-

tered. The men—all former college football stars on the cusp of achieving their professional football dreams—struggle to maintain composure as their fellow rookie sobs openly, recounting his traumatic childhood when he was forced to watch helplessly as his mother was beaten.

• A wiry, fifty-ish white man in a black leather jacket, with a limp that suggests a nasty motorcycle accident and a weathered face that hints at years of hard drinking and drugging, approaches me after a speech in eastern Washington. He tells me softly that his mother, a domestic-violence victim, committed suicide when he was fourteen. "Keep speaking out," he says, as he firmly shakes my hand and pulls me close.

It is no secret that many women in the domestic and sexual violence fields are survivors of men's violence. These women often talk publicly about their personal experiences, both to counteract the popular caricature of battering and rape victims as weak women who wallow in victimhood, and to model for other women (and men) a way to integrate personal experience with professional commitment. You can find these women on the national stage and in every community. They run shelters, youth outreach initiatives, and even batterer-intervention programs. They work as advocates, educators, and therapists.

Many men who are drawn to the gender violence prevention field have their own relevant personal and family histories. The journey for some begins when they are called on to provide emotional support for a girlfriend or wife experiencing the symptoms of trauma from a past relationship. Others are politicized when a girl or woman close to them is sexually assaulted. Regardless of where their consciousness was before this experience, supportive men who love and care about their female partners often come to see the world through their eyes, an often unsettling experience. The novelist and poet Marge Piercy offers some insight as to why in her deeply moving "Rape Poem":

There is no difference between being raped
and going head first through a windshield
except that afterward you are afraid
not of cars
but half the human race.

What does it mean to belong to the half of the human race that so many women fear? How do you figure out the best way to be a supportive partner? Can you still be one of the guys, or do you have to renounce your membership in the brotherhood of male culture? Do you betray your girlfriend or wife if you contribute, even passively, to sexist practices? One married man, who made a point of telling me that he loved his wife very much, said that he nonetheless laughed at the misogynistic routines of the late comedian Sam Kinison. He felt guilty, but he still laughed.

Until recently, these private struggles in men's lives were not even acknowledged as important, much less discussed in public. So men would keep it to themselves. This is changing, as more men write and talk honestly about their lives in newsletters, e-zines, memoirs, men's groups, music lyrics, poetry, and spoken-word performances. One groundbreaking book that discusses men's experiences of sexual violence against women close to them is *Working with Available Light*. The author, Jamie Kalven, is a human rights activist who works on the issues of gang violence and police corruption in Chicago. He writes eloquently and in painful detail about his family's emotional struggles—including his own—after his wife was sexually assaulted one day while out running.

Some men who work to end men's violence are themselves survivors of childhood trauma. Like women, many have been the victims of men's violence—physical, emotional, sexual. They take the subject personally. Several pioneers of anti-sexist men's work are rape survivors themselves. Victor Rivers, the Cuban-born actor and domestic-violence activist, frequently tells audiences the story of how he grew up as a terrorized, angry boy with a brutal madman and batterer for a father. In his memoir, *A Private Family Matter* (2005), he recounts his struggles to escape his father's legacy and find love and intimacy. Gavin DeBecker, security consultant to the stars and bestselling author of *The Gift of Fear*, says he learned valuable lessons about reacting to violence when he lived through numerous beatings of his mother by men. Casey Gwinn, a former San Diego city attorney and a Republican who is one of the most innovative and influential domestic-violence prosecutors in the country, shares his personal story in part to dispel the common myth that gender violence only happens to certain types of people. When Casey, a white Christian from a well-respected family, started to prosecute domestic-violence cases, his father sat him down and in an emotional conversation disclosed to him that his father (Casey's grandfather) had been abusive to his mother (Casey's grandmother). Sergeant Mark Wynn, a former Nashville police officer who is a national leader in the effort to educate law enforcement personnel and policy makers about domestic violence, testified at a congressional hearing in the early nineties that he grew up with an alcoholic stepfather who was so abusive that when they were young boys, he and his brother tried unsuccessfully to poison him.

Perhaps the most famous man to speak publicly about domestic violence in his family, and to use his stature to prevent it in others, is the manager of the New York Yankees, Joe Torre. Torre, whose father for many years beat his now-deceased mother, started a foundation in her memory to raise money for battered women's programs.

These male leaders—and many others—have been courageously honest about a subject long shrouded in secrecy and shame. Until the modern women's movement catalyzed unprecedented changes in *men's* lives, male culture actively discouraged such disclosures. In Western culture men have been taught for generations to "suck it up" and "act like a man" in the face of adversity or emotional difficulty. They are warned early in life never to show vulnerability to other men for fear that they will be judged weak. But as more men from all walks of life find the courage to break their silence about traumatic experiences, this stigma is gradually fading.

I have led hundreds of candid discussions about men's violence against women with groups of men not stereotypically chatty about such matters. I have watched thousands of football, basketball, and hockey players, and United States Marines, walk into rooms with arms folded and heads down, as if to say, "*Why do we have to be here?*" I know that a lot of these men come in defensive and hostile, but leave having grown from the experience.

When men talk with other men about their experiences as the fathers, brothers, sons, and lovers of women who have been mistreated by men, they see that their doubts and insecurities, as well as their sadness, are shared by many of their fellow men. They see that some of the struggles they face in relationships with women are issues that many other men face—and that they can learn from each other. There is clearly a need for more support groups for male partners of women (and men) who were raped and sexually abused. The simple act of bringing men together to have this sort of conversation can be—like women's consciousness-raising groups in the 1970s—the crucial first step in getting them to see the bigger picture.

But it is only the first step. If we are going to dramatically reduce men's violence against women, we have to understand that individual acts of men's violence are never "isolated incidents," but rather part of a larger social and political context that it is *in our power to change.*

One of the great challenges of anti-sexist men's work is that many people grasp this principle more clearly when violence is racist or homophobic, rather than when it is simply sexist. When a group of white men in Jasper, Texas, murdered an African American man, James Byrd, in 1998 and dragged him along the street for two miles from the back of their pickup truck, there was an outcry across the country from people of color *and* whites. The case became a symbol of the enduring brutality and severity of racism—and it saddened and enraged millions of *whites*, many of whom joined with people of color to redouble their efforts against racism.

When two young white men in Laramie, Wyoming, murdered a twenty-one-year-old gay man, Matthew Shepard, in 1998 by badly beating him and then tying him to a post and leaving him to die, he instantly became a symbol of the ugliness of homophobia, and the awful consequences of anti-gay bigotry and behavior. His murder saddened and enraged millions of *heterosexuals*, many of whom joined with gays, lesbians, bisexuals, and transgendered people to redouble their efforts against homophobia.

Meanwhile, it seems that every couple of weeks we hear about another case where a man abducts a girl off the streets and sexually assaults her. On average, three men each day murder their wives, girlfriends, or exes. Every few weeks, police somewhere find the mutilated body of a new victim of a serial killer. Judging from the media coverage these events receive, about the only thing they symbolize is the many disturbed people out there. People listening to the radio in their cars or watching the news in their living rooms shake their heads and lament the tragedies for the victims. They talk about what monsters the perpetrators are. But relatively few people connect individual crimes to a broader social pattern of men's violence against women. And when was the last time you heard someone say—in the wake of yet another wife-murder or sex crime—that men need to redouble their efforts to fight sexism?

The chivalry trap

A number of years ago I was in Boston with my then-girlfriend on our way to an awards dinner for a local batterer intervention program. As we walked down the sidewalk on the way to the event, I pulled her close to me and said playfully, "You'd better stay right by my side tonight. There are going to be a lot of men in the room with a history of violence against women."

I thought I was being clever, but she was not the least bit amused. "That's a really manipulative and controlling thing to say," she said dryly. "It's not funny." I had not consciously intended to make her feel vulnerable by pumping up my own credentials as her bodyguard. It was a joke. But I had nonetheless reminded her that in a world where there are a lot of violent men, she would always need protection—and not coincidentally from good guys like me.

I might have thought the comment was funny, but it came loaded with personal and historical baggage. It is an old tactic: "good guys" positioning themselves as the protectors of women from the "bad guys" who would otherwise prey on them. (It was also a thoughtless cheap shot at the men who successfully completed the program—men I respect.)

For men who are committed to working against gender violence, the question about when and if it is okay to "protect" women from other men is the source of ongoing introspection. Taken at face value, it should not be controversial. If a man—because he is stronger, knows better how to use a weapon, or is more accustomed to physical confrontation—is in a position to protect a woman from a violent man, then shouldn't he? In principle, it is not just about protecting a woman *as a woman*. It is about the moral imperative of protecting a vulnerable *person* from harm.

But there is more to it. In theory, men should be confronting other men about their sexist attitudes and behaviors toward women. For years, feminists have urged men of conscience to do just that. The reasoning is straightforward. If you are a member of a dominant group, you have a responsibility to challenge other members of your group who are acting in oppressive ways. If you do not, then your silence is tantamount to complicity in their abusive behavior. This is true about white people who challenge the racism of other whites, or heterosexuals who challenge other heterosexuals about homophobia. But it gets more complicated with men and sexism, because there is a fine line between encouraging men to challenge each other's sexism, and encouraging deeply paternalistic chivalry.

One pitfall in the effort to make the mistreatment of women a personal issue for men is the risk that it will tap into some men's traditional chivalry without challenging their underlying sexism. It is one thing to talk about the problem of men's violence against women in personal terms, couching it in words that acknowledge a man's concern for his mother, daughter, wife, or lover. The women and girls who are victimized are not nameless, faceless statistics; they are loved ones. But when the focus remains exclusively on the personal, it may only encourage family loyalty, without truly challenging men to confront the larger problem of sexual inequality and male dominance.

Another danger we have to guard against is the possibility that we might unwittingly perpetuate the idea that the solution to the problem is actually more men's violence—but done righteously by the "good guys."

I once had a spirited discussion about this subject with a man who worked with batterers. I was taking the provocative position that I wished more men today would emulate previous generations of men who beat up men who abused female loved ones, rather than take a detached or passive stance. I did not wish they would *act* on this counterproductive impulse. I yearned for their passion to be channeled from violence to other forms of effective intervention. He would have none of it. "It's that type of thinking we need to change," he said. "The idea that violence can solve anything is itself the crux of the problem."

Yet another pitfall in this thinking is that women's right to control their own destiny gets lost in the debate about how men should behave. As victim advocates point out, one of the most painful effects of being battered or sexually assaulted is the experience of a loss of control over one's body. One of the most devastating things a perpetrator does is take this control for himself. So if a man steps in to defend or avenge the victim and he has not checked in with her about what *she* needs, no matter how well-intentioned he might be, he is also depriving her of the right to take back control of her own life.

This is the dark side of chivalry. Under the guise of "protecting" or "defending" women, it prioritizes men's needs. Besides, if women are always dependent on men to protect them, they will never achieve genuine equality with men, which puts us right back where we started.

After several decades of modern feminism, chivalry still exerts a powerful tug on many men's—and women's—psyches. For men, it has been called superhero syndrome, or misguided paternalism. In spite of increasingly egalitarian aspects of male-female relations over the past generation, it is not hard to find twenty-first-century men who nonetheless have an unconscious yearning to be the knight in shining armor, ready to rescue the damsel in distress. They might express it in genteel language about being raised "never to hit a woman," or in crude revenge fantasies like "I'll kick his butt," if another man does harm to a woman he cares about. This dynamic is true for me, as well as a lot of my colleagues and fellow anti-sexist men. We might be motivated primarily by our outrage at violence and inequality, but that does not preclude us from having rescue fantasies—some of them violent—and a visceral desire to protect women and children from other men's violence and terrorism.

It is easy to find men with an impulse toward chivalry, but it is just as easy to find women who—while professing to believe in equality between the sexes—nonetheless want men to take care of them. In her bestselling 1981 book *The Cinderella Complex*, Colette Dowling argued that, in spite of the women's liberation movement, many women had an unconscious desire to be taken care of by others, based primarily on a fear of being independent. More recently, bell hooks writes that many women, including black women, long for "the stuff of romantic fantasy" that gender equality was supposed to do away with.

Andrea Dworkin characteristically went even deeper. In her fascinating book *Right-Wing Women* (1983), she explored why many women are drawn to socially conservative movements that consign women to second-class status. She maintained that these women find comfort in the implicit promise that if they give themselves over to patriarchal authority, then find and submit to a husband, he will protect them from other men's violence. The major downside to this "bargain," of course, is that women—conservative, religious, or otherwise—are much more likely to be assaulted *by their own husbands* than they are by some stranger lurking in the bushes.

On the other hand, plenty of women, especially in the post-sixties generations, recoil from the very suggestion that they need men to protect them. Many of these women were raised by parents who taught them to be self-reliant, assertive, and intolerant of sexism or abuse from any man. In addition, they were raised in the brave new world created by Title IX, when girls and women's athletic opportunities skyrocketed, and more women than ever developed their physical strength and athletic confidence. In the era of girl power and self-defense classes, it is inevitable that some women will insist that they do not need even "well-meaning" men to protect them.

What lurks just beneath the surface of the debate about chivalry is the question of men's ownership of women and the historical reality that for centuries, men have controlled women through force. This force has come in many guises—both at the institutional level, by the church or the state, and at the individual level, by physical violence or sexual coercion. So the question is ever-present: what if a man's impulse to intervene for women derives not from caring and altruism, or a sense of fairness and equality, but from a deeply held belief that women are, in a certain sense, men's possessions? What if he is coming from a place where an attack on "our women" is functionally equivalent to an attack on him, or his honor?

Consider the following hypothetical scenarios:

• A group of men in their early twenties are in an apartment, drinking beer and playing poker. At some point, the conversation gets around to a crude discussion about women's bodies, and all of the guys laugh and joke about what sorts of breasts and asses they find sexy on a woman. Then one of the guys says something explicit about the body of another one's girlfriend. All of a sudden, the offended guy slams his cards down, and the laughter stops. "Hey, watch yourself. You're talking about *my* girl," he says sharply.

• A crowd of people mingles in the parking lot of a club at closing time. A heterosexual couple stands talking with a group of people, when another man comes up behind the woman, grabs her behind, and smiles mischievously as he starts to walk away. The woman screams, and her boyfriend leaps at the man. They end up wrestling and fighting on the pavement until the police arrive.

• A high school student reluctantly tells her older brother—who is home on break from college—that the black eye she is trying to conceal with makeup was given to her by her boyfriend in a fit of jealous rage. The brother pounds his fist on the table and vows to "beat the shit out of the #@ %*# coward."

These stories—and hundreds like them—illustrate some of the problems with chivalry as a guiding philosophy. When men are driven by a desire to protect women, they are less likely to check in with the women to see if they want or need help. Ironically, concern for the woman's needs is not these men's priority. Doing what they think they are supposed to do takes precedence, regardless of what she wants.

What if the men's concern for the women is genuine? Does it matter whether or not they intended to be dismissive of the women's needs? Does it even matter *why* men react to assaults against women they care about, as long as they actually react and do something? If they are truly interested in helping women, do we give men the benefit of the doubt? Or is this subject so loaded that we have to remain skeptical of every man's intentions, even men who profess to be concerned about women's equality?

Once in the early 1990s I was giving a speech about violence against women at a new student orientation session on a small college campus in New England. During the question and answer period at the end of my talk, a young man—just a couple of months out of high school—raised his hand and said, "I can't see how anyone could rape a woman, or harm her in any way. A woman is a delicate flower who needs love and attention, not violence."

A number of women gasped; a few others laughed out loud. I took a deep breath. I was not sure what to say, because although the young man had made an outrageously anachronistic and sexist statement, he had said it innocently and seemed totally unaware of how offensive it sounded to many of his fellow first-year students. I remember blurting out something like "I'm glad you don't approve of violence, but I think you might want to reconsider what you said about women being delicate. I know a lot of women who are really strong and are decidedly not delicate flowers."

Later, a professor at the college who had been sitting in the audience told me that my response to the young man had been totally inadequate. "You should have slammed him," she said. "You shouldn't let him get away so easily with that statement."

There have been a number of media stories in recent years about the disturbing phenomenon of "honor killings" in certain Arab cultures and South Asian tribal societies. The rationale behind these murders—which persist but are not mainstream practice in Arab or South Asian countries—is that the entire family is tainted when a woman has sex outside traditional marriage, even if she is forcibly raped. She must be killed in order to restore the family's honor. Incredibly, brothers often willingly take the lives of their own sisters in these circumstances.

My take on the personal politics of gender violence is clearly culturally specific, because in cultures that practice or tolerate "honor killings," being a close relative or friend of a girl or woman who has been the victim of another man's violence presents a very different set of imperatives than it does in our culture. Honor killings are repugnant to Western sensibilities and beyond the pale in contemporary U.S. society. Even so, the underlying sexist belief system is not as alien as many Americans would like to believe. Western civilization has come a long way since the days when, under English common law, a man for all intents and purposes owned his wife. Some etymologists believe that the phrase "rule of thumb" has its origins in English common law, where a man could legally beat his wife with a stick—provided it was not as wide as his thumb. It was not until 1993 that marital rape was considered a crime in all fifty states, after years of lobbying by women's organizations. The Uniform Code of Military Justice, which sets down the law for U.S. military members, also criminalized marital rape that year.

But while many old sexist laws have been reformed or removed from the books over the past thirty years, and egalitarian relationships between women and men are the contemporary heterosexual ideal, the ideology of men's ownership of women hasn't died so easily. Batterer-intervention counselors in every county in the United States, every day and night of the week, hear men say things like "She's *my* wife, and she'll do what I tell her." And to this day, sadly, many young women confuse their boyfriends' jealousy and possessive behavior with true concern for *them*, rather than with the *boys'* obsessive need for relational power and control.

CHAPTER FOUR

Listening to Women

"Listen to Women for a Change."
—Feminist slogan

"It all started with women learning to listen to each other. The battered women's and rape crisis movements drew strength from our understanding that what happened to individual women was not isolated. At first we just wanted to help . . . later we began to hear about women's experiences, and see commonalities and patterns not only in the abuses they suffered but in the responses to them by the police, the courts, the clergy. We then began to use what we'd learned to confront men both at a personal and an institutional level."
—Debby Tucker, cofounder of the National Center on Domestic and Sexual Violence, volunteer in the first rape crisis center in Texas, and director of the first battered women's shelter in Texas

I memorized the words to "The House of the Rising Sun" before I was out of elementary school. Like some of the enduring classic tunes, that song possessed an indescribable, mystical power. I was a sexually naïve young boy, but shivers went down my spine each time I heard the signature guitar lick that opened the famous cover by the Animals. I knew what was coming: a cautionary tale of temptation, sin, and the hint of illicit sex in the dark purples and deep burgundies of a New Orleans bordello.

The most famous couplet in the song struck an especially personal note with millions of boys of my generation:

And it's been the ruin of many a poor boy
And God, I know I'm one

How many of us imagined ourselves to be that poor boy? How many of us sang along with Eric Burdon as we daydreamed about what it would be like to spend our lives in "sin and misery" surrounded by girls in black garter belts? It was not until many years later that I learned the back story behind the British group's number one hit. In order to make the lyrics acceptable for radio play in the 1960s, the Animals had changed the main character of the song from a prostitute to a gambler. But no one was fooled. We knew it was about a house of prostitution. What we did not know is that "The House of the Rising Sun" was a traditional blues-folk song from the 1920s and 1930s whose original lyrics were written in the voice of a *female* prostitute. But the classic rock version—with a male narrator—positioned the listener to identify with that poor boy. It was *his* experiences—and *his* reality—that were the stuff of fantasy for many of us sex-starved pubescents.

Then I heard Tracy Chapman's version, recorded in 1990. By that time I had sung along to "The House of the Rising Sun" thousands of times. But her words stopped me cold:

It's been the ruin of many poor girls and oh God, I'm one.

The song's meaning changed for me forever. Now, every time I hear the Animals version on the radio I think about the girls and women who are used up and kicked to the curb by the callous and indifferent men (and women) who run the "sex industry." One old version of the song has a line that says, "Tell your baby sister not to do what I have done." This had not even occurred to me until I heard Tracy Chapman's version. Up to that point, I was too busy envying the corrupted life of the "poor boy" to empathize with the girls and women who live, work, and sometimes die in the seedy and dangerous world of prostitution and sex trafficking.

It can hardly be a coincidence that my guide in this mini consciousness-raising experience was a socially conscious female artist. This often happens when women have the opportunity to describe their reality—and when men are in a position to listen and hear what they have to say. I know I have learned a great deal about gender violence and other forms of sexism from some of the women in my life. Some of this knowledge is unsettling, because it has forced me to reassess my thoughts about certain customs and rituals in male culture, as well as certain types of people. For example, a number of years ago I was in a car on the highway with a close woman friend and we passed a shiny, gleaming semi-trailer. I said something about what an impressive machine it was, how I loved trucks, and how I was fascinated by some of the varieties of trucker masculinity. She had a different take on the subject. Ever since she started driving, she said, she had been objectified, harassed, and intimidated by male truckers. They regularly leered down at her, trying to catch a glimpse of her breasts. Some had mouthed sexually aggressive comments. One man pushed a handful of twenty-dollar bills up against his window. One time a trucker actually started to masturbate in his cab as he rode alongside her car. As a result of these experiences, she has a pretty negative visceral impression of male truckers—even though she knows it is unfair to the majority of them who do not do those sorts of things. When she told me about her experience with truckers, I quickly realized why so many women I know loved the scene in the 1991 film *Thelma and Louise* where the women blew up a fuel tanker. The explosion represented a cathartic release for so many women who could identify with the female characters' sense of anger and outrage—emotions I had never before experienced in relation to trucks or truckers.

Men can learn a lot about women's experience of men's violence by simply listening to the women in their lives, and asking them questions about their perceptions. In addition, the modern women's movement catalyzed a dramatic increase in the volume of women's voices in the public sphere. Today, many women expect to speak—and be heard—in a way that previous generations of women could not even imagine. Women who have come of age since the 1970s have historically unprecedented public voices as community leaders, politicians, business leaders, members of the clergy, college professors, journalists, television producers, songwriters, playwrights, artists, novelists, and poets. (Of course white, middle-class women are much more likely to have a public voice than are women of color or poor women.) And yet public conversation continues to be dominated by privileged white men.

To cite one example: recently a spirited debate arose in newspapers across the country about the fact that women comprise less than 20 percent of opinion columnists in print journalism. Parity between the sexes might be a stated ideal, but it remains an elusive goal. An even more insidious way that women's experiences are marginalized and their voices silenced is the still-common sexist practice of using the word "man" or "mankind" to refer to "humanity," like when a headline writer invokes "man's quest for meaning," or the president of the United States talks about the benefits of peace "for all mankind." In the late 1970s the sociologist Gaye Tuchman popularized the term "symbolic annihilation" to convey the effect this sort of linguistic exclusion has on women and their ability to be recognized as full persons whose reality, scholarship, and opinions are every bit as valid as men's. As Richard Tarnas, author of the 1991 bestselling intellectual history *The Passion of the*

Western Mind: Understanding the Ideas That Have Shaped Our World View,
writes, "Like many others, I do not consider it justifiable for a writer today to
use the word 'man' or 'mankind' when straightforwardly referring to the
human species or the generic human individual...I do not believe that such
usage can be successfully defended." His explanation is that no motive—
such as style or brevity—is sufficient "to justify the implied exclusion of the
female half of the human species."

Of course sexism is also alive and well in popular culture, especially when
it comes to the question of who gets to narrate the stories we tell about ourselves. Women studio executives have made advances in recent years, but
most Hollywood films and television shows are written, produced, and
directed by (white) men. *Rolling Stone* magazine's list of the five hundred
greatest rock-and-roll songs of all time included fewer than ten that were
written by female songwriters, and *Source* magazine's list of the one hundred
best rap albums includes but a handful of women artists. Outside of the
world of entertainment, men far outnumber women in positions of economic and political influence. There is still a glass ceiling for women in the
business world and many of the professions. At the end of 2005 there were
only seven female CEOs of *Fortune* 500 companies. And of course millions
of women (and men) continue to be stifled by the deprivations of poverty
and racism. Even among relatively privileged whites, as Carol Gilligan
famously observed, girls in patriarchal culture feel significant pressure to
censor expressions of their authentic selves in order to fit in and avoid social
stigma for not being "good girls." There are generations of men who have
grown up with the modern women's movement, have learned a lot from
women, and sincerely respect women as their equals. But make no mistake:
the beating heart of the backlash against feminism that continues to this day
is the desire of some men to put the genie back in the bottle; to tell strong,
smart, vocal women to sit down and shut up—and stop complaining.

The battered women's and rape crisis movements were created by women
who had the audacity to stand up and speak out about the ongoing crisis of
men's violence. Many of the slogans that came out of those movements
reflected this theme: *End the silence, no more violence. Break the silence. Silent
no longer.* In the 1960s, 1970s, and 1980s, feminist authors wrote books about
rape and domestic violence, and feminist collectives published pamphlets
and leaflets—the precursors to today's websites and email list-serves.
Activists organized speak-outs to give a public voice to rape survivors. They
tried—with varying degrees of success—to get mainstream media to cover

violence against women as a social problem with deep cultural roots, not simply as an endless succession of salacious crime stories.

By the 1990s, all of these efforts had begun to shift the terms of the discussion toward women's experience, women's reality. But change has not come easily. The courageous women who built the movements to end men's violence—and they come from the full spectrum of racial and ethnic backgrounds—have pushed us all to look at the world through the eyes of women, especially women who have been raped, stalked, battered, and abused by men. They have achieved a great deal in the past thirty years. But their efforts have come at a huge personal cost to many of them. Women who work with battered women, rape survivors, and sexual-harassment victims—as well as women who have been at the forefront of reform efforts in the courts, law enforcement, higher education, and K–12 school systems—have routinely been ignored or marginalized by men in positions of influence and authority. I hear stories from women all the time about men in power—or in their personal lives—who just "do not get it." For many of these women, the growing presence of men in gender violence prevention evokes mixed feelings. They are happy to see more men shoulder the burden of responsibility for changing men's and boys' attitudes and behaviors, but they are also frustrated that some men can be heard in ways that women cannot.

In 1990, when I first started to give speeches on college campuses about men's violence against women, I knew that some students came out to hear me because I was a man. Likewise, when I decided to write a book about violence against women as a men's issue, I assumed that many people would be particularly interested in my perspective on this subject because I am a man. I am fully aware that this is unfair to women whose voices have been stymied or ignored. I am also cognizant of the fact that many of the ideas presented in this book originated with women, and many of my own ideas rest on a foundation that was built by women. This is true for all the men in the U.S. and around the world who are part of a growing movement of men opposed to men's violence against women. We would not be doing this were it not for the leadership of women in our own lives and in the larger culture. As a small token of the debt we owe them, I want to share some testimonies from women about their efforts to speak to men and to advocate for themselves or other women, and what happened when they did. (Note: some names have been changed and descriptive details slightly altered to protect the privacy of individuals.)

SURVIVORS AND ACTIVISTS

It is no secret that many women who work in the battered women's and rape crisis movements are themselves survivors of men's violence. It has been this way since the beginning of these movements in the 1970s, as many of the founding mothers in the field were formerly battered women or rape survivors. The experiences of survivors have always played a critical role in the movements to end men's violence; after all, they are the ones whose lives have been most directly affected. Their testimonies provide conclusive documentary evidence of the extent of the problem, and put a human face on what otherwise could be seen as dry and abstract statistics. From women who disclose to their loved ones that they were sexually abused as children to college students who talk in front of public gatherings at Take Back the Night rallies about their experiences of being raped to domestic violence survivors who testify in legislative hearings when new legislation is before the Congress, the courageous voices of women who dare to speak out loud about their own pain and trauma have provided the moral foundation of this work for decades.

One of the most powerful public education/political art campaigns ever conceived is the Clothesline Project, created in 1990 by a group of women in Cape Cod, Massachusetts. Its design is deceptively simple: a clothesline with T-shirts hung in building lobbies in college campuses, community centers, museum lobbies, and other venues. On each T-shirt is a hand-written message from a survivor of incest, rape, domestic violence, sexual harassment, homophobic violence, or stalking, or from a friend of a homicide victim. Most of the messages are written by women, some by men. The idea is to give voice to survivors in a public forum. T-shirts say things like "For years I drank to numb the pain, guilt, and shame. No one asked me. I didn't tell. Today I know a child can never be responsible for rape or incest." "Tears, blood, and scars. But I'm here. I'm winning." "What part of no didn't you understand?" "Erase my memory so I can feel free again." "You battered my body but my spirit survived," etc. People walk down the row of shirts in respectful silence and read each one. The power of this display is that while each survivor is anonymous, their T-shirt makes an eloquent and emotional statement about their refusal to be shamed into silence. For men who walk down the line and read the shirts, the experience can be deeply moving and sobering. When the clothesline is displayed on a college campus, men who have the courage to attend are exposed to the intensity of their female peers' feelings in a way that many have never encountered directly. The personal testimony contained in the shirts conveys an intensity of grief and perseverance that can touch them in a way that no recitation of statistics could ever match.

Of course it is true that survivors are not always embraced with open arms. Their stories are often ignored or disbelieved, and they are often bullied and shamed into silence. Many women who have been assaulted by men do not talk about their experiences, either to family and friends or to colleagues and coworkers. In fact, many women who work on the issues of domestic and sexual violence do not publicly discuss their own experiences. They might wish to retain their privacy, or perhaps they are concerned that people will not take them as seriously if they suspect they are motivated by personal trauma.

Recently I was talking on the phone with a woman I had come to know through our work together over the past couple of years. She runs a campus women's center at a large southwestern university. She shared with me her frustration that a number of women students on her campus had been raped or sexually assaulted by male students, and in each case the administrators with whom she was interacting seemed either indifferent to the alleged victims or openly sided with the accused men. I asked her if she could recall any instances of men listening to her and being supportive.

"The most powerful example of this was not from my professional life but from my personal experience as a college student. When I was nineteen, I was raped by a guy who lived in my dorm. He was a popular guy, a senior and a fraternity member. The next day, I confronted him about what he had done. He told me that no one would believe me because he had so much more status on campus. Soon thereafter a group of the rapist's friends began to make nasty comments to me in hallways, the cafeteria, and just walking across campus. I also began to receive menacing phone calls, and unsigned notes under my door with dark and cryptic messages. I never identified the people responsible for these messages, but assumed they were the same men. I wondered if they were doing all of this to intimidate me into not reporting that the popular guy raped me. As all of this was happening, I told a supportive male friend. He enlisted some of his friends, and over the next several months, they publicly defended me, and whenever possible, confronted the guys who were making abusive comments, which eventually stopped. To this day I draw strength from that experience, and the knowledge that there are men who will believe and support women. Sadly, this is not always true of the college women rape victims whom I advocate for, many of whom feel isolated and unsupported, especially by their male peers."

I asked my colleague if she mentioned this experience in her public talks on campus. She told me that I was only the fourth or fifth person with whom she had shared this story since college, more than a decade ago. I thanked her for sharing it with me.

Survivors of sexual violence today—women and men—are more likely than in decades past to find supportive friends and professionals who believe them and advocate for them. But the idea that men's violence is either women's fault, or their responsibility to deal with, is deeply ingrained in both women and men's psyches. In fact, one of the chief obstacles standing in the way of redefining sexual and domestic violence as men's issues is the lingering power of this sort of victim-blaming mentality. One woman who is a prominent gender violence prevention activist in the Midwest said that when she was in college in the early 1970s, she accepted an invitation from her date to spend the night after she had found her dorm locked for the night. (College students may not relate, but at the time in many traditional colleges the women's dorms were locked at curfew hour, and if you were late you had to go through the judgmental dorm mother to reenter. Men's dorms were open all the time.)

"The man ended up raping me several times, with the threat of a gun. He allowed me to leave in the morning. I truly thought I would be shot in the back. Because at the time I was a practicing Catholic, I went to a priest later that day and he told me that while it was a bad thing that happened, 'What did I expect, a young woman spending the night with a man?' I decided not to go to the police because I was so ashamed of what I had done and did not want to hear another speech about how dumb I was."

Women who are members of racial and ethnic minorities face special pressures about when and where it is acceptable for them to raise their voices and assert their own needs. According to Lori Robinson, who wrote *I Will Survive: The African American Guide to Healing from Sexual Assault and Abuse*, black women have historically been trained to always put others' needs first, to be skeptical about utilizing professional services, and to deny their own need for support. African American women who have been abused might also choose to remain silent because although they want the violence to stop, they do not want their boyfriend or husband to go to jail. If he is black, they know that he is much more likely than a white man to do time for a gender violence crime. They might also feel pressure from members of their family and community to keep the abuse private and not air "the dirty laundry" in communities of color, because it will validate the racist stereotypes held by the white majority about African American men. In other words, black women's silence is expected as a form of loyalty to their racial or ethnic group, whose needs take priority over their own needs for healing. Robinson's book grew out of her own experience of being raped in 1995 when she was on staff at the now-defunct *Emerge* magazine, which billed itself as "America's Black Newsmagazine." She explains that an article she wrote in *Emerge* about her assault and the alleged assault of an African American college student generated an outpouring of letters from readers affected by sexual violence, which convinced her of the need to write a book.

Jewish women belong to another ethnic minority that has its own special tensions around the issues of domestic and sexual violence. Historically there was a powerful sense of denial about gender violence in the Jewish community. The conceit was that "nice Jewish boys" were not like the crude and aggressive Gentiles, and hence did not have those kinds of problems. This conveyed to Jewish women who were being abused by their Jewish husbands and boyfriends that they must be at fault, or that they should remain silent for the sake of family stability. Like women from other ethnic minorities, Jewish women also felt pressure to remain silent because if they disclosed the abuse it would somehow bring shame on them and their children—or the entire Jewish community. But over the past decade or so, in defiance of those pressures, Jewish women from all denominations, including Orthodox, have organized at the local and national level to call attention to the problem of men's violence against women in the Jewish community—which occurs at approximately the same rate as in the larger society. In doing so these women have provided much-needed moral leadership on an issue of importance to the entire community, and issued an implicit challenge to Jewish men—including male rabbis—to speak out and thus not be complicit in their silence.

If women in long-established racial and ethnic communities feel pressure to be silent about gender violence issues, new immigrant women can face even more pressure, along with some added considerations. Many of them are reluctant to report abuse, or even tell anyone about it, because they do not trust the authorities. They might have fresh memories of police corruption in their countries of origin. In some cases, the man who is abusing or harassing her might skillfully use the woman's uncertainty about her immigration status—or threats to call the Immigration and Naturalization Service—as a means to keep her quiet. Frequently these women speak a language other than English, which can make it more difficult for them to communicate their problems or access services—whose availability they might not even be aware of to begin with.

Men who work in gender-violence prevention—especially those men who are recognized and well-rewarded for our work—have an obligation to acknowledge women's leadership in this area whenever we get the chance. Some of the biggest fears women have about men's entry into this movement are that they will replicate traditional patterns of egocentric male behavior, women's leadership will be supplanted by men's, and women's voices will be drowned out. These fears mirrors one of the most frequent complaints that women have about men: that they do not listen to them. Men often cut women off in conversation, or treat women's contributions to a conversation with less weight than a man's. Many women describe group conversations where they say something, and several minutes later a man says the same thing and does not give her credit. The source of this kind of marginalization of women's opinions is not mysterious: it is a logical outcome of a sexist social system that assigns unfair weight to men's opinions and minimizes women's. One charismatic woman I know in the gender-violence prevention world recounted a conflict she had with a man she was seeing.

"He had been play-fighting with my four-year-old nephew, and I argued that he should not do that, because it would lead to problems with his peers on the playground, in the classroom, etc. This is a subject about which I know a great deal, as I work in the gender-violence area and have a lot of experience dealing with the connections between various forms of violence, and the effects of this violence on children. He had no such experience or training, but he did not accept the validity of my opinion. He argued that play-fighting with a four-year-old was necessary to toughen the boy up, and implied that it was intrinsically connected to masculinity. But what really got me upset was his attitude. I felt that he did not think I knew what I was talking about because I am a woman, and therefore he did not have to take into account my opinion. Most of the times I have gotten into heated exchanges with men—in my personal or professional life—it has had less to do with unbridgeable ideological differences than with the fact that men would not listen to me or consider my opinion worthwhile."

Sometimes the opinions of women in the sexual and domestic-violence fields are not solicited or welcomed because people have a vested interest in ignoring their perspective. In other words, it is not simply that these women's opinions are minimized as a result of sexism. They are silenced because people with power do not like the conclusions they reach, especially if they are critical of how an individual or institution handles the sensitive issue of gender violence.

One woman I know runs the women's center at a small private college in the East. In order to maintain her anonymity, I am going to paraphrase her comments. According to her, violence against women is systematically ignored and hushed up by the dean of students, who is in charge of the judicial process, policies for the student handbook, and just about every other factor that influences the kind of response that women on campus face after they have been sexually or physically assaulted. She is the person on campus with the most expertise on gender violence, but is completely excluded from meetings on sexual assault and barred from providing training to the judicial board and other staff and students. She reports that in private meetings, the dean regularly yells at her, refers to rape as "regretted sex," and forbids her from talking about the concept of rape culture, which he denies exists. On her campus in 2005, a student was seriously assaulted by her ex-boyfriend in a textbook domestic violence case. Although the women's center director provided the dean with research on the risk of escalation in cases like this and had expressed concern for the victim's ongoing safety on campus, he chose not to protect the victim. The perpetrator was back on campus the Monday following his attempt to kill his ex-girlfriend. The dean actually made the ignorant assertion that this was not a dating-violence situation, since he had asked the victim if the perpetrator had hit her before and she said no.

Women who work in this field often have to contend with a lack of respect for what they do from members of their own families. Gender violence is still a taboo subject for many people, and the women who defy the taboo and face the issues in their professional or personal lives frequently pay a price for their boldness. Many women I know have had the experience at family gatherings, dinner parties, and other social events where someone has asked them what they do for work, and their answer was greeted with awkward silence and a change of subject. One woman I know who lives in the South and works in a prominent domestic-violence advocacy organization tells this story:

"I have six brothers and three sisters, and with the exception of one brother, they tend not to ask me about my work, or domestic violence in general. This is in a culture where domestic-violence homicide cases like the Scott Peterson and Robert Blake trials are on TV every night of the week. At a family reunion, my brother told me that he has many female coworkers who are in abusive relationships, and that they are completely capable of leaving. They have a job, they can support themselves, etc., but they will not leave the abuser. He asked me why. I started to explain some of the reasons that someone might not leave and he cut me off. 'Oh, don't give me any crap about some kind of syndrome,' he said. My other siblings asked if they could please discuss something else; that was the end of the discussion."

One woman who is well-known and respected nationally in the sexual-assault field has had an ongoing struggle with her in-laws around subjects related to her work. She tells the following story:

"Several years ago, during a visit to our home, my mother-in-law asked me about my work. At the time I was working at a statewide domestic-violence and sexual-assault coalition. My mother-in-law asked if there were differences between working on these issues in the Midwest, where we had recently located, compared to the East Coast, where we had previously been for many years. I responded that I noticed a more pronounced reluctance to address sexual violence overall, and that law enforcement officers seemed to have less training and to be much more biased against victims. Very few victims report their rapes in rural areas due to the social structures of small towns. Consequently, law enforcement officers have extremely limited experience investigating these crimes, which causes its own set of problems. My mother-in-law asked me what I meant by 'biased' against rape victims. I shared with her the details of an incident of outright victim-blaming, where the police refused to facilitate and pay for a hospital exam to collect forensic evidence because the responding officer simply did not believe the victim's story, because it did not match up with the mythical 'real rape,' which should have included visible injuries and a sober, well-respected victim. My father-in-law interrupted the conversation and said, 'So you don't think rape victims are responsible at all?' And I said, 'No.' He said, 'Oh, come on! You don't think that when a woman is dressed provocatively she isn't asking for it?' or something to that effect—I was so angry that I cannot remember his exact words. My mother-in-law told him that he was wrong and ridiculous."

What happened next was even more hopeful, and speaks to the fact that many women in the gender violence field have supportive men in their lives. Her husband came out of the kitchen and informed his father that one more comment like that would result in a stay in a hotel for the rest of the visit.

Understandably, all parties subsequently sought to avoid similar conversations. But the unspoken tensions in these sorts of family relationships have a way of resurfacing. She recounts a conversation she had with her father-in-law many years after the above incident.

"He said to me 'Have you actually ever really helped someone? Do you know if you've made a difference?' I was annoyed but not surprised at the arrogance of the question. What did he expect me to say? 'No, I've spent nearly fourteen years wasting my time and taxpayers' money on something that has been completely futile?' I can't help but wonder if I were a doctor or teacher with many years of experience, would they feel so free to argue with me about the causes of cancer, trends in literacy, etc.? They grill my husband for detailed information about what he does in his job, but I have never heard them question his facts or challenge basic assumptions in the mainstream of his field."

Women—especially young women—frequently hear unsolicited comments of a sexual nature from boys and men on the streets, in parks, at sports events, and in other public spaces. While a small percentage of women might actually enjoy the attention, many others feel objectified, intimidated, or angry. But they often do not say anything, because they find it less stressful to just keep their head down and keep walking, or because they do not want to give the man the satisfaction that his comment caused any sort of rise in them. I frequently hear men say that it had never even occurred to them that women feel assaulted by this sort of unsolicited commentary, in part because they read women's silence as approval. A close friend of mine shared a story with me of an incident that happened to her one day several years ago when she was on an Amtrak train. She was in the cafe car working on her computer—the project happened to be on gender equity for a major non-governmental organization. After an hour or so, she stood up to go the snack bar, and a man sitting with two other male friends began to make extremely embarrassing comments about her breasts.

"The entire train car full of people heard what he said. I was horrified and humiliated and felt assaulted. I responded by making what I consider immature and insulting comments back to the man, who I found out was drunk. One of his friends saw how upset I was, and apologized out loud for his friend. I did not know if I should move to another train car or not. I wanted to escape the embarrassment, but instead decided to hold my ground. I sat back down at my table and pretended to do my work, all the time wishing I had had the gumption to pour a hot cup of coffee in the offender's lap.

"A while later, the man who apologized for his friend came over to discuss what had happened. He told me that he thought I had overreacted to what he considered a compliment. He said he hoped his three daughters would not behave as I did if a man made comments about their bodies. I looked him right in the eye and said he had better pray that his daughters react as I did, or he may have to worry that they will be sexually assaulted or humiliated as I was. 'Humiliated?' he asked. 'Why was that humiliating? I thought my friend was admiring you.'"

This is a common perception among men. A lot of them think women like to hear unsolicited feedback about their bodies—when it is positive. Some men are genuinely taken aback that many women take this not as a compliment but as dehumanizing and invasive. My friend told him that his friend was not admiring her and his attention was not flattering in any way. His comments, she said, were disrespectful of her as a person, as a human being. "I think he really heard me," she said. "I suggested that he ask his wife what she thought about the situation, and in ten years, ask his daughters."

THE POWER TO BE HEARD

Ultimately, decisions about who gets listened to come back to questions of social power: the more you have, the more your voice is heard. That is why around the world, as women make progress in achieving economic and political power, they are increasingly in a position to push for the reform of laws, institutional practices, and customs that perpetuate gender violence. One of the first—and most important—steps in the reform process is to provide opportunities for women and girls to tell their stories, to make visible and public their experiences of violence, harassment, and abuse. For example, when an institution such as a college or the military decides to implement systemic gender violence prevention strategies—due to the initiative of responsible leaders or as a result of public pressure—they need to devise mechanisms to hear from women about how they have been treated within that institution. From 2000 to 2003 I served on the Department of Defense Task Force on Domestic Violence by appointment of the Secretary of Defense. As part of our fact-finding mission, the joint military and civilian task force traveled all over the world and met with personnel at U.S. military installations. Task force members met with commanders, enlisted leaders, military police, chaplains, and civilian social workers. But due to strong advocacy from both civilian and military members of the task force, we also met with civilian military wives who were survivors of domestic violence. Their testimony often cut right through some of the bureaucracy-speak and diplomatic niceties and told us exactly what had happened to them and how people in power had handled their cases. These women's voices made an invaluable contribution to the task force's process of designing recommendations for transforming Department of Defense policies on domestic violence.

Each time I hear a woman (or a man) talk in public about her or his experience of domestic or sexual violence (both the violence itself and then the often-ineffectual response of the authorities) my belief is strengthened that all male leaders—in educational institutions, religious organizations, sports management, the military—should be required to listen to survivors' stories as a basic part of their training. This secular form of "bearing witness" should be seen not as something that "good guys" do to learn more about women's lives, but as a fundamental responsibility of leadership.

CHAPTER FIVE

Male-Bashing?

"I am coming up against serious defensiveness, aggression, and on some occasions, personal attacks when I speak, and this is only high school! And not surprisingly . . . the strong negative reactions to even the mere mention of dating-violence education come from young white men. It's been frustrating . . . that the ones who are the most defensive, or closed off, are the ones who need to be the most open."
—Danielle Graham, victim advocate and anti-violence educator

"None love the messenger who brings bad tidings."
—Sophocles, *Antigone*, 442 BCE

Women who dare to break the customary feminine silence about gender violence are often reminded that there is a price to pay for their boldness. They certainly run the risk of evoking men's hostility and anger, because to challenge men's right to control women is to threaten men who see such control as their birthright. Sadly, women who take a strong stand against sexual harassment, rape, and domestic violence can even be perceived as a threat by some of their fellow women. Women have been trained to take care of men's feelings for so long, to stroke their egos and to curry favor with them by not holding them accountable for their sexism, that it is understandable that some women will denounce those women who expect more. This is especially true of women who do not want to risk losing status with men by appearing to side with those angry women. As a result, most women who have worked in the gender violence field have experienced some degree of social stigma.

When I give speeches on college campuses or do trainings for domestic and sexual violence professionals, I ask participants to name some of the words that are commonly used to describe women who publicly protest men's violence toward women. This exercise often evokes spontaneous laughter from some women that only partially conceals their underlying frustration and anger at the way they have routinely been shown a lack of respect. I can barely write fast enough as the women—and men—shout out the condemning words:

Bitch
Angry
Ball-buster
Man-hater
Dyke
Lesbian
Feminazi
Liar
Irrational
Aggressive
Militant
Male-basher

Then I ask women to raise their hands if they have been called one or more of those names. Not all of them raise their hands—but many of them do. Some are clearly upset about the way they have been unfairly demeaned and caricatured. Others consider the criticism so inaccurate and ridiculous that they refuse to take it seriously. In any case, the list contains enough cultural stereotypes to fill a graduate seminar syllabus. One of its key themes is the false assumption that women who dare to step outside the strictures of traditional femininity and defy male power must be lesbians. In a culture where lesbians and gays continue to confront stigma and discrimination, this can effectively silence many women—heterosexual and lesbian. But for now, I want to discuss two of the other words: "feminazi" and "male-basher."

FEMINAZI

The word "feminazi" combines two words: feminist and Nazi. Let's look at each one separately. Who are feminists? In this society and most others, they were the first people to publicly name violence against women as a social problem. They founded the battered women's movement and the rape crisis movement. They identified sexual harassment in the workplace and the schools. They were the first people to expose the sexual abuse of children. Feminists from all racial and ethnic backgrounds have been among the leaders in every social movement dedicated to expanding the freedom, dignity, and human rights of all people—women and men, adults and children. They are some of the most passionate and effective anti-violence leaders of our time—and of all time.

Who were the Nazis? They were the embodiment of masculine cruelty and violence. They were mass murderers, responsible for one of the most despicable campaigns of organized genocide and state violence in human history. One could argue that as a national movement they represent the low point—to date—in the history of our species. The Nazis are usually described as a political party driven by racial hatred, but they were also a hypermasculinist movement of white men who were obsessed with maintaining men's control over women, parents' control over children, and heterosexuals' control over gays. In this regard the gender and sexual politics of the German National Socialists are remarkably similar to those of other far-right wing social movements, including those in the contemporary U.S.

To link feminists with Nazis requires a breathtaking leap of intellectual bad faith. Not surprisingly, the person most responsible for popularizing that leap is the right-wing talk radio icon Rush Limbaugh. When he is criticized for his regular use of the term, he claims that not all feminists are feminazis. "Feminazis are those feminists who are happy about the large number of abortions we have in this country," he wrote in his bestselling 1992 book, *The Way Things Ought To Be*. Of course no such feminists exist. Limbaugh simply made up that idea to justify his use of a patently offensive epithet. But "feminazi" is undeniably a clever term of propaganda—and Limbaugh is nothing if not a master propagandist. The word focuses aggressive hostility on feminists, who by that characterization are portrayed as the despised and violent enemy. "Feminazi" has a powerful silencing effect, because what self-respecting contemporary American woman would want to be compared to the Nazis? Why say or do anything even remotely likely to inspire that association? Nazism is so deeply stigmatized in Western consciousness that any connection with it is bound to have negative repercussions. So the violence of the term "feminazi" does its job: it bullies into complicit silence women who might otherwise challenge men's violence.

MALE-BASHER

The dictionary definition of the verb "bash" is "to hit" or "to strike." Therefore, since "bash" is a violent term, a "male-basher" is a violent person. Let's follow this twisted logic. Women who voice outrage about the fact that so many men bash women are themselves the true bashers? Women who speak out *against* men's violence are the ones who are actually perpetrating violence? But the Orwellian quality of the term "male-basher" runs even deeper. It not only implies that women who speak out about violence are the violent ones; it also transforms men from the ones doing the violence into its victims. Unlike in the real world, where the vast majority of gender violence is perpetrated by men, in the strange world created by the term "male-basher," men—not women—are the ones being bashed.

This whole process would be laughable were it not for the fact that this is deadly serious business. Words like "feminazi" and "male-basher" have real effects in the world. Many women simply do not want to feel the nasty sting of being called these names or risk other negative repercussions in their lives and relationships with men that might result if they were to protest men's violence too loudly. So they choose not to get involved. They might talk to their women friends about harassment or abusive incidents they have experienced at the hands of men. They might tell an anonymous pollster that they consider rape to be an important issue. They might even take a college course on intimate violence, or read a book about the subject. In just the past few years, women readers have made bestsellers out of numerous books about women's victimization, from *Lucky*, novelist Alice Sebold's memoir of her rape as a first-year college student, to *I Am the Central Park Jogger* to Amber Frey's memoir of the Scott Peterson murder case. But when it comes to confronting men with the truth about women's experience of men's violence—or holding men accountable for doing something about it—many women are still unwilling to go there.

This is one place where anti-sexist men's voices can change the cultural conversation, because they can say things about men's violence that most women cannot, or will not, say. Even more to the point, some men will listen to other men's opinions about this subject more readily than they will listen to women's. Men are socialized to discount women's insights—especially when they might contain criticism. However, another reason why men may listen to each other on the subject of gender violence is that they cannot "kill the messenger" as easily. For example, they cannot credibly write off a fellow man with the accusation that he is anti-male. When a *man* says that men have to take responsibility for men's violence, it would sound pretty silly to call him a male-basher. In order to make that charge stick, you would have to argue that he is a self-hating man who has somehow bought a mythical feminist hard-line about men as evil rapists and controlling bullies. There is no doubt that some people actually believe that men who challenge other men's sexism are "pussy-whipped," or so eager to please women—especially feminists—that they would betray their fellow men in an effort to be "politically correct." Or perhaps they were never "real men" in the first place. But these sorts of caricatures are increasingly difficult to sustain as growing numbers of men step forward as allies of women and begin to find a public voice on these issues. Is Joe Torre, the manager of the New York Yankees and founder of a program for battered women, a self-hating man? Is the former NFL quarterback and anti-rape educator Don McPherson a feminazi? Is Victor Rivers, the former football player, actor, and national spokesperson for the National Network to End Domestic Violence, a male-basher? Are business leaders like Gateway Computer founder Ted Waitt and Homegoods president Jerome Rossi wimpy guys who fund gender-violence prevention initiatives under the spell of domineering and manipulative women? One consequence of men's increasing participation in gender-violence prevention efforts is the diminished power of terms like "feminazi" and "male-basher" to silence women.

Alleged victims and "accusers"

If the term "male-basher" silences women who speak out against men's violence, a similar process applies to the increasingly popular convention in media where alleged rape victims are referred to as "accusers." This usage accelerated during the Kobe Bryant rape case, when media commentators routinely referred to the nineteen-year-old alleged victim as "Kobe's accuser." This usage subtly but powerfully undermined the credibility of the alleged victim, furthering the mistaken impression that it was a "he said-she said" case. Language matters. Imagine if every time people said Bryant's name, they referred to him as "the accused," or "the accused rapist" Kobe Bryant. Whether it was intentional or not, the widespread practice of calling the basketball superstar's alleged victim his "accuser" no doubt contributed to a shift in people's perspective on what happened in that Eagle, Colorado, hotel room in the summer of 2003. Instead of focusing on the merits or deficiencies of the prosecution's case against Kobe Bryant, the use of the term "accuser" subtly but profoundly turned people's attention to the actions of the young woman.

As in so many rape cases—tried either in criminal court or in the 24/7 media—the effect was to put the woman's behavior on trial, not the man's. What were her sexual practices? Did she have emotional problems? What motive did she have to falsely accuse a famous man she had previously held in high regard? This fixation on her totally overshadowed questions about the actual defendant in this case: What were Kobe Bryant's sexual practices? Did the public disclosure that at least one other woman—and perhaps several more—alleged that he had groped her provide evidence of a pattern in his behavior toward women? Did *he* have emotional problems? What could have been his motives for forcing a woman to submit to him sexually just minutes after she walked into his hotel room?

The case was ultimately settled out of court early in 2005, with a gag rule on all parties. We may never hear the alleged victim's story in detail, and Bryant will never be forced under oath to describe his version of that night's events or answer other questions about his sexual practices. But the now routine practice of calling the Colorado college student Kobe's "accuser" gave Bryant a huge advantage in the lead-up to trial. The alleged victim was turned into the one doing something to Bryant—she was *accusing* him. This is the same sort of linguistic reversal that turns women in the rape crisis and battered women's movements into male-bashers—with similar effects. In fact, in the Kobe Bryant case, it almost appeared—to the casual observer— that he was not really the one who was on trial for committing an act of violent sexual aggression. Instead, *he* became the victim of *her* accusation. Predictably, this encouraged widespread anger at her and sympathy for him. The fabulously wealthy athletic champion with high-powered lawyers was transformed into the underdog. As the Lakers made their way to the 2004 NBA finals, there were countless public comments from his teammates and fans about how courageously he performed on the court while enduring an unimaginable level of personal stress. At the same time, Bryant's alleged victim received death threats and total disruption of her life ensued. Beyond her family and friends, and rape victim advocates who worked with her, how many people in the media praised her for how well she endured an unimaginable level of personal stress?

Obviously there are some women—and men—who occasionally or regularly denigrate and insult men. I would not defend this sort of prejudice or stereotyping, but I think the problem of "male-bashing" in the movements against domestic and sexual violence is wildly overstated. I have been doing this work for twenty-five years, and I have met only a handful of women whom I would consider "male-bashers." And even those women—if pressed—will acknowledge that it is not men per se with whom they have a problem, but rather with a social system that limits and does violence to the full humanity of boys and men at the same time that it oppresses and does violence to girls and women. However, I have a problem with the term "male-basher" for another reason: it serves to obscure the harmful effects of men's violence against women *on boys and men*. Girls and women are the primary victims of men's violence against them, but they are not the only victims.

Boys and men are the perpetrators of most violence. But in almost every category they are also its primary victims. So when feminists and others in the battered women's and rape crisis movements argue that we need to figure out ways to prevent men's violence, they mean men's violence against other men as well as women. In fact, cutting-edge violence prevention work

across the U.S. and the world involves attempts to transform cultural definitions of masculinity that equate manhood with power, control, and dominance. To call this work "male-bashing" is to betray an ignorance, or utter
lack of empathy with the realities of violence in the lives of boys and men—
including sexual violence at the hands of other men.

"I am not a rapist."

The term "male-basher" implies that innocent men are harmed when
women make sweeping statements about men's sexist attitudes and behaviors. Many women, in fact, are quick to rush in and defend men against the
"man-hating" feminists. In a special "Men Can Stop Rape" edition of the
feminist news journal *Off Our Backs*, the editors write that there seems to be
a kind of "statistical dyslexia" when feminists start talking about men's violence. "The statement 'most violent crimes are committed by men' is often
misheard as 'most men are violent,'" they write. "Thus . . . feminists find
themselves in conversations like this:

'Most of the violence around the world is committed by men.'
'You can't say that. My friend Jim isn't violent!'
'Nevertheless, the Bureau of Justice Statistics says that over 85 percent of
violent crimes in the U.S. are committed by men.'
'Are you saying women are never violent? Because I read about this one
woman who . . . '
'I guess her crime would be one of the 15 percent . . . '
'Some of us don't think men are that bad, you know.'"

Anyone who has ever conducted a gender violence prevention training or
given a talk about the subject to college or high school students knows that
this sort of defensive distortion from some boys and men is quite predictable.
In the late 1990s I was conducting a one-day training for thirty educators in
the Detroit area. About a half-hour into the training, a man in his late twenties
who was seated toward the back of the room interrupted me mid-sentence by
vigorously waving his hand. He was clearly upset about something. "Earlier
you said that 99 percent of men are rapists," he said, exasperated. "I cannot
sit here and listen to you any longer until you clarify what you meant. I am
not a rapist. My friends are not rapists. How can you make such an outrageous claim? And how can I take anything you say seriously until you explain
yourself?" Trying not to sound defensive myself, I explained to him that what
I had actually said was that 99 percent of rape is perpetrated by men—which
is a far cry from saying that 99 percent of men are rapists. He nodded his
head, seeming to accept my explanation.

For the past generation, women who have tried to organize public forums in academic or community settings on the topic of men's violence against women have been forced to respond to the same set of predictable questions. Will men feel welcome in this discussion, or is this going to be just another "male-bashing" session? What can we do to assure them that they will not be treated unfairly? How can we get men to participate unless we give them this assurance? Some young men display a curious need to deny their own criminality the moment someone raises the subject of men's violence against women. Gender-violence educators hear this in the classroom all the time. Guys will say, "I'm not a rapist," or "I don't beat women," when no one has accused them personally of violent acts.

Over the past few decades, there have been numerous controversies on college campuses related to instances of rape and attempted rape. Many of these incidents involved the college administration's handling of such cases. Administrators face some sticky legal and ethical conundrums: Should rape prosecutions be handled in-house, through the campus judiciary system? Are they strictly criminal matters? Do defendants who are students have the right to stay enrolled during the months, or years, while the case proceeds to trial? How do you balance the rights of the alleged victim with the rights of the accused—especially when they are both students? In some instances, alleged rapes on college campuses serve to highlight questions of shared guilt or responsibility on the part of male students. One famous case of this type happened at Brown University in 1990, when women students—upset at the university's handling of sexual-assault cases—wrote the names of alleged rapists on the walls in women's bathrooms. They claimed it was necessary to warn women about undetected rapists in their midst. Civil libertarians and others were troubled by the lack of due process for the men, whose reputations could be slandered by an anonymous author of bathroom graffiti.

One poignant incident at another New England university highlighted even more specifically some of the issues I have taken up in this chapter. In the fall of 1999 at the University of Massachusetts-Amherst, two reported rapes of women in the same vicinity on consecutive Tuesdays, caused a paroxysm of fear and anger among the students, faculty, and staff—especially women. But unlike most college rapes, which are "date rapes" and are rarely reported, these seemingly random rapes gripped the public consciousness. Not only did they feature the politically non-controversial type of rape—the male stranger springing out from the bushes and attacking women passersby—these rapes were alleged to have taken place not at night in a remote parking lot, but in the *middle of the day* in a grassy area near a pond in the *middle of campus*.

Published descriptions of the alleged assailants heightened tensions, because based solely on superficial physical characteristics, hundreds of male students instantly qualified as potential suspects. One of them wore a black ski mask. The other was described as "blond, six feet tall, and muscular." The campus reaction was swift and frantic. Women's groups organized rallies. A few parents withdrew their daughters. The administration scrambled to reassure everyone with enhanced security measures, including the distribution of thousands of "shriek" whistles. Naturally, the rapes and the community response to them became a hot topic of conversation both on campus and off. The *New York Times* ran a story. National TV news crews descended on the school, asking questions. Was it the work of a serial rapist? Was he a student? A local resident? How could women students concentrate on their studies when it wasn't even safe to walk across campus in broad daylight? Were the authorities doing all they could to prevent further attacks?

Because UMass has a strong women's center, an established women's studies program, and is located in a region known for feminist activism, the assaults catalyzed a community discussion about men's violence against women that at times moved beyond immediate concerns about public safety. Fear can have the effect of focusing the mind, and in this case there is no doubt that many women students for the first time were forced to think about rape as a *political* act affecting an entire community, and not just an expression of individual male pathology or female victimization.

But women weren't the only ones whose lives and psyches were changed. The experience politicized many men, too. For a period of several weeks, the alleged rapes and the fear they induced on campus were the topic of countless conversations. Everyday social interactions between the sexes were newly invested with nervous tension, as women were even less likely than usual to make eye contact or otherwise acknowledge the presence of men they didn't know. One positive outcome of this unfortunate situation was that male students got a chance to see, first-hand, how women's daily lives are controlled by the threat of men's violence. And through speeches at rallies, newspaper op-eds, letters to the editor, and other impassioned statements in support of their female peers, hundreds of men denounced the rapist(s). Many of them publicly identified themselves—for the first time—as allies of women in the fight against sexist violence.

Nonetheless, as days went by and no suspects were arrested, some men began to resent the fact that their maleness alone placed them under a cloud of suspicion. Of course men of color, especially African American men, are perpetually under that same cloud; but this was different, because the alleged perpetrators had been described as white. So white guys got a taste of what black men have to live with day-to-day: women crossing the street as they approach, locking their car doors when they stop at a red light, not getting on elevators when they see a single guy already aboard.

"I'm not a rapist!"—the emblematic slogan of male defensiveness in reaction to feminist anti-rape activism since the 1970s—became in this case a rallying cry. The dominant public posture of men was one of condemnation of the perpetrator(s) and solidarity with their female peers. But according to numerous observers, growing numbers of white men at UMass felt impatient and angry that even in casual interactions with women on campus they were being unjustly stigmatized. One of the few male students who dared to publicly express this anger was a first-year student who, prudently, insisted on maintaining his anonymity. He succinctly expressed his frustration—and articulated a widely held sentiment—in an interview with the student newspaper, the *Daily Collegian*. "I don't like the fact that when I'm walking behind a girl [sic], she will get scared and give me a dirty look or a bad look," he said. "I scare girls now. I know it's not their fault, but I just feel that I should be walking around on campus with a bright orange shirt that says 'I'm not a rapist!' . . . I don't like to be looked at like this, just because I'm a guy."

It would be easy to dismiss this young man's complaint, and others like it, as evidence of whiney self-absorption or unearned (white) male privilege. With the campus on red alert status because one or more men had allegedly raped at least two *women*, it must have been tempting to ridicule or ignore men who were framing *themselves* as the victims. It must have been even harder as the absurdity of some males' self-absorption reached dizzying new heights. In a certifiably Orwellian inversion of reality, *Men's Health* magazine ran a feature in September 2000 where they named UMass one of the ten most "anti-male schools in America," in part due to feminist response to the attacks on women. Women could not even walk to class in the afternoon without escorts, and yet the school was unfriendly to *males*? It is certainly unfair that because some men rape women, all men can be looked at as potential rapists. But who should men be mad at? Women for not trusting them? How about being angry at men who rape women, who give the rest of the male sex a bad name?

This reality first struck me in college when I did a lot of hitchhiking. It was not the sixties when there was a "counterculture" to provide a sense of imagined community—and real rides—for white middle-class kids with long hair and bell bottoms. I was in college at the beginning of the Reagan era, and by then there were few college students out there on the side of the road, waiting for some generous soul to defy conventional paranoia and pull over to pick them up. Sometimes I would stand there with my thumb out and watch literally thousands of cars go by. That can be very frustrating when you need a ride home and it's getting dark. But I understood why people would not stop. How could they be sure I was not a sociopathic murderer, recently paroled, waiting to lure a naïve motorist into some fiendish plot with a gruesome ending? The threat of violence was ever-present in those split-second assessments made by people passing. Especially the women. I would watch women drive by and look straight ahead, studiously avoiding even a furtive glance my way. I felt frustrated and powerless. How could I let them know that I was safe, that there was no chance in the world that I would harm them? In fact, I used to console myself that they would be *safer* if they gave me a ride. For example, I could defend them from other men if their car happened to break down in some isolated spot.

I tried not to take it personally that women almost never stopped. How could I blame them? They did not know anything about me, except what I looked like and how I was dressed. It would have been wrong to get angry at *them* for fearing me. Instead, I would stand on the side of the road and curse rapists for depriving me of half of my possible rides. Of course most men never stopped, either. But almost always one man would decide that doing a stranger a favor—and having someone to talk to on a lonely drive—was worth the risk. For women, it was just too dangerous. I was a bit stunned once when a woman actually did pull over to give me a ride, on the side of a rural highway running through a forest in western Massachusetts. I remember thinking: if I ask her where she got the nerve to pick up a male hitchhiker, she might start worrying about me. I did not bring it up.

Why some women defend men

Over the years I have heard more than a handful of men recount stories of their attempts to intervene in incidents where a man was assaulting a woman, only to be turned on and attacked by the *woman*. The men usually explain—sometimes in impassioned voices—that this greatly surprised them; they expected the woman to be grateful. On reflection their initial surprise typically turns into bewilderment, frustration, and sometimes anger. *She defended that punk who was abusing her, and attacked me? That's crazy. Couldn't she see that I was there to help her?* Sometimes the men grumpily insist that they will never again intervene when they see a man abusing a woman. Better to mind their own business. Why take the risk? It is tempting to dismiss these guys as frustrated would-be superheroes, but their reaction speaks to how a lot of men feel about women in emotionally or physically abusive relationships. *They don't want our help. They are attracted to losers. They're masochists.* It is easy to see how men might feel that way. Not having ever been a woman in an abusive relationship, many men simply do not comprehend the practical—much less the emotional—complexities of a victim's situation. And it is not just men who are in the dark. The same is often true for other women. Many of them are baffled by the seeming irrationality of abused women's behavior.

But while a woman fighting off a man who is trying to help her might appear to be displaying crazy or at best counterintuitive behavior, it often turns out that she is quite rational. As I have learned over the years from domestic-violence victim advocates, battered women are often making the best choices for themselves in undeniably difficult circumstances. A woman who is being slapped around by her boyfriend or husband might turn on a man who is trying to intervene for a number of reasons, not necessarily motivated by a desire to protect the abuser. Perhaps the woman has already succeeded in minimizing the impact of her partner's blows, and she knows that now—once the interloper inevitably leaves—she alone will have to face his full wrath. He might later take out on her his anger and shame at having been confronted by another man. *It's your fault. You shouldn't have screamed and called attention to us! This is between you and me; it's our personal business. Why are you trying to get me in trouble?*

It may be that she does genuinely care for him, and in that moment when a stranger steps in, her loyalty to him trumps her concern for her own immediate well-being. However distraught she might be about his abuse, her first impulse when he comes under attack from an outside party may be to protect him. Ethnic or racial factors could well play a role. For example, if the abusive man is a man of color, and the intervening man is white, the white man might be perceived as an agent of state authority or a lackey of the white power structure, which has historically been much quicker to punish abusive men of color than it has white men. Regardless of his race, the woman may be afraid that this incident will result in her husband/boyfriend's arrest, and he might be the primary source of income for her and her children. When they hear these explanations, most guys get it—regardless of how they might have felt at the outset.

In the fall of 2004 I was resting inconspicuously in a chair in the sparsely populated lobby of a large hall on a major university campus in the Midwest about an hour before I was scheduled to give a guest lecture on "American manhood and violence against women." A white woman in her late twenties or early thirties, dressed in black Lycra and a heavy sweatshirt, came through the main doors of the building, wheeled a bicycle through the main doors and into the lobby, and walked over to a friend or colleague she recognized. I overheard her ask him if he knew why a crowd was gathering, and what he was doing there. He replied that he was there to do audio tech support for a talk by a man about violence against women. She stood up straight. "I hope he is going to talk about the ways that women abuse men," she said. "I'm a Camille Paglia feminist. Women can be just as violent as men, you know, only they don't do it in a physical way."

In recent years women who claim that "violence against women" is not as big a problem as some feminists maintain have garnered a massive amount of uncritical coverage in the media. Some of these women—most notably the conservative scholar Christina Hoff Sommers and the academic provocateur Camille Paglia—have since the early 1990s been putting forth the view that the problem of violence against women has been radically overstated by ideological feminists with an anti-male agenda. There is no crisis, they say, just a steady onslaught of distorted statistics and scare tactics intended to recruit young women to the feminist cause, and justify budgets for women's programs. As Hoff Sommers stated in her 1994 book *Who Stole Feminism?*, "To view rape as a crime of gender bias . . . is perversely to miss its true nature . . . gender feminist ideologues bemuse and alarm the public . . . they have made no case for the claim that violence against women is symptomatic of a deeply misogynist culture."

It should come as no surprise that some people stubbornly refuse to acknowledge that violence against women is a pervasive social problem in this country, and around the world. Free debate and divergent views are important. But it is notable how much neutral or favorable media coverage these women have gotten, considering the controversial nature of their claims and the fact that the vast majority of researchers and activists in the field—women and men—strongly dispute them. For example, the work of Hoff Sommers, Paglia, and Katie Roiphe, whose 1993 book *The Morning After: Sex, Fear, and Feminism* argued that the problem of date rape on college campuses was overstated, has been featured everywhere from the *New York Times Magazine* to the Rush Limbaugh radio program. A number of other conservative women, including Ann Coulter and Laura Schlesinger, have attacked feminists for anti-male bias and for exaggerating claims about men's violence against women. Although their particular perspectives differ slightly from one another, all of these women appear to represent a conservative answer to "male-bashing" women. In fact, they would seem to be standing up *for* men. This, of course, wins them a lot of male allies, especially men who are sick and tired of hearing about how bad men are, and conservatives—women and men—who are eager to find any way to discredit the feminist analysis of men's violence as rooted in the structures of patriarchal culture.

Conservative or libertarian women who criticize women in the battered women's and rape crisis movements are valuable assets to critics of those movements because they are willing to say things in print and in public that most men would be widely attacked for saying, such as when Camille Paglia writes that a lot of battered women stay in abusive relationships because "the sex is hot." If a man had written that, he would undoubtedly be decried as a sexist and an apologist for batterers and rapists. But because Paglia is a woman, she is merely "controversial," and as we all know, controversy sells— in bookstores and campus lecture halls. It will be interesting to see how these anti-feminist women and others—including organizations such as Concerned Women for America, which opposes the Violence Against Women Act because it is supposedly "anti-family"—respond to the growing numbers of men who write and speak in support of feminists' basic arguments about men's violence against women. Much of these conservative women's criticism is aimed at feminist women, and their supposedly divisive indictment of sexism and men's violence. Christina Hoff Sommers's book, *Who Stole Feminism?* is subtitled *How Women Have Betrayed Women*. It would not be surprising if they claim that these anti-sexist men are neutered wimps who feminists have bullied into betraying their fellow men. They would almost have to take that view in order to defend their reckless assertion that feminists have overstated or even manufactured a crisis of violence against women in order to bash men. There seems to be little room in these conservative women's arguments for men who—using their free will—have come to many of the same conclusions as feminist women about "rape culture" and the connection between gender inequality and gender violence. After all, Phyllis Schlafly, one of the female icons of the far right, praised Hoff Sommers's 2000 screed against feminists entitled *The War on Boys* by saying that "We just have to recognize that the feminist movement is an attack on everything that is masculine."

Boys will be boys?

People often defend young men's abusive or violent behavior by reciting that tired line, "boys will be boys." They usually mean this as a defense of the boys. *Don't be so hard on them.* What do you expect? But the argument that "boys will be boys" actually carries the profoundly anti-male implication that we should expect bad behavior from boys and men. The assumption is that they are somehow not capable of acting appropriately, or treating girls and women with respect. Especially when their hormones kick in, because we all know how guys get when "the little head does the thinking for the big head." This entire line of thinking does a profound disservice not only to the victims and potential victims of boys' abuses, but to boys and men themselves. I am often asked if I believe there is a genetic or biological component to men's abusive behaviors. In past decades conservatives and others who did not want to validate the feminist argument that men's violence against women has deep structural roots in gender inequality would invoke various sociobiological explanations for criminal behaviors. Today some of the more popular anti-feminist academic theories can be found in the writings of evolutionary psychologists, such as the 2001 book by Randy Thornhill and Craig T. Palmer called *A Natural History of Rape: Biological Bases of Sexual Coercion*, which argued that rape was part of a procreative strategy for males. I do not think it is intellectually honest or prudent to blithely discount *any* genetic or biological factors that might contribute to men's abusive behaviors toward women. But I am convinced that if it were ever possible to prove a hierarchy of causes, genetic or biological factors—other than size differentials between men and women—would not even come close to being the most significant. Moreover, I have too much respect for boys and men to believe they are beasts whose predatory or abusive nature is hard-wired. Let us not forget that this is the argument white racists have made for centuries about men of color—an argument that was used to justify not only slavery but brutally racist methods of social control long after the end of legal slavery. "Boys will be boys" also has a self-fulfilling quality, because boys possess not only the potential to rise to people's expectations, but also the potential to sink to them. Thus the more that abusive behavior is rationalized as normal and expected, the more likely it is to occur.

One of the great insights of the battered women's movement is that most abuse in heterosexual relationships is due not to a man's inherent biological makeup, but to his learned need for power and control. The typical scenario is not that he loses control and then strikes her, but rather that he uses force, or the threat of force, to establish or maintain control in the relationship. In other words, the problem is not his anger, it is his attitude. He believes that he should be in control, and if he needs to slap her around a bit to bring her back in line, then so be it. Not surprisingly, men who batter women tend to subscribe to hyper-traditional patriarchal gender ideologies.

People who are unfamiliar with this perspective often do not automatically comprehend it. They assume that a person is likely to get violent when he (or she) has blown a fuse, or run out of measured and reasonable alternatives to getting his point across, especially when alcohol is involved. Men will often describe their abusive behavior this way: "I was so pissed off," they'll say. "She wasn't listening. I got frustrated, and after everything else that had happened that day, I just lost it." This can seem like a reasonable explanation—although never an excuse—for a violent incident. That is, it can seem reasonable to someone who has no experience working with men who batter, and who does not know the right sorts of questions to ask. I once heard a batterer-intervention counselor explain that you can not take at face value a man's statement that he "lost control" and struck his wife. You have to probe deeper. The exchange might go something like this:

"Were you in or near the kitchen at the time when you hit and kicked her?"
"Yes."
"Do you have knives in your kitchen?"
"Yes."
"Did you stab your wife?"
"Of course not!"
"Okay, did you hit her in the face?"
"No."
"Were there kids around at the time?"
"No, I wouldn't do anything like that in front of the kids."

As this typical interview demonstrates, many men will initially say they acted violently because they could not control their raging emotions, but under questioning will admit that even in their heightened state of anger, they were able to make a series of rational decisions. For example, some men will hit a woman in the face, but others will not because she might get a bruise or a black eye. If she has to go to work tomorrow, someone might find out what is going on. Better to hit her in places where the bruises are not visible. Can we say that a man who literally picks his spots on a woman's body is truly out of control? Some men will hit a woman in front of the kids, but others will not. They will only do it when the two of them are alone. If they were truly out of control, could they make those distinctions?

A recent event in the sports world provides a powerful illustration of this dynamic, although it was not specifically about domestic-violence. Late in the 2004 baseball season, during a close pennant race, the big money free-agent pitcher Kevin Brown of the New York Yankees had a bad outing on the mound. Steaming, he walked off the field and went into the clubhouse where he punched a wall and broke his hand. This upset many people, not surprisingly, because it left his team short-handed at a crucial point in the season. After the game, Brown offered no excuses. "I reacted to frustration . . . I let it boil over and I did something stupid. I owe my teammates an apology for letting my emotions take over like that," he said. A few days later Brown apologized to his teammates, Yankees management, and the fans. At a press conference, however, Brown was asked to explain why he broke his left hand, since he was a right-handed pitcher. "Years of experience," he said. Even though he was upset, Brown, a thirty-nine-year-old professional, had the presence of mind to avoid taking a risk with his pitching hand. In other words, his emotions did not really "take over." Right up through the moment when he punched the wall, he was thinking rationally and consequentially.

It is important to make the distinction between men's supposed loss of control and their use of violence for the purpose of control, because this goes right to a root cause of their violence against women. If the problem is that men simply cannot control their tempers, then the solution is to start building anger management skills into school curricula, starting in kindergarten. But if the problem is men's learned need to exercise power and control over women, then the solution is much more difficult. It requires that all of us take a look in the mirror and ask: Why do so many men in our society feel the need to control and dominate women? At what age do boys begin to learn that having power over women is part of being a man? What steps can we take in order to change that, both on an individual and an institutional level?

CHAPTER SIX

Stuck in (Gender) Neutral

"The young Jonesboro suspect's stated motive that he wanted to kill girls who had broken up with him is reported without comment. Is it so thoroughly taken for granted that males are perpetrators of violence and females their appropriate victims that we need not discuss the matter further?"
—Dr. Kersti Yllo, on the murder of four girls and one woman in the infamous
    Arkansas school shooting in 1998

NAMING THE PROBLEM

We cannot achieve dramatic reductions in men's violence against women until we can at least *name* the problem correctly. At present, few people view this violence the way I've described it in these pages: as a *men's* problem or a *men's* issue. One consequence of this failure is that there is little discussion in media—or anywhere else—about why so many American men and boys rape, batter, sexually abuse, and sexually harass women and girls. Mainstream commentary about gender violence—and other forms of interpersonal violence— is remarkably degendered. It is almost as if journalists, educators, and even activists make a conscious effort not to bring up the fact that men and boys commit the vast majority of interpersonal and sexual violence. So we hear regular reports about the "people" who commit these crimes, and we wring our hands about yet another tragic incident of "kids killing kids."

It is easy to see why mainstream language about gender violence is typically gender neutral. If we talked about it as a *men's* problem, if we asked, "Why do *men* commit these awful crimes?" the language itself would force a critical spotlight on men, and this would make a lot of people—men and women—uncomfortable. It would reinvigorate a long-dormant conversation that began in the 1970s, and point us toward a series of probing and unsettling questions: Why do so many men assault women? What is the process by which millions of loving little boys grow up and turn into controlling, violent men? Why do so many grown men sexually abuse little girls—and boys? Why do so many men sexually assault and harass women and girls? Why have relatively few men spoken out about men's violence against women?

It has been in vogue in recent years to seek explanations for human behavior not in social structures but in biology or evolutionary psychology. But how do those theories account for the wide variation in different cultures in rates of rape, domestic violence, and other controlling and abusive behaviors? Ours is by far the most violent among the wealthy industrial countries. Why? Is there some genetic deficiency in American men? Or if the problem is not on the "nature" but rather on the "nurture" side of the equation, what are we doing wrong? How can we help shape the socialization of boys to counteract whatever forces in our culture help to produce so many abusive men? For now, the absence of clear, direct language about men's perpetration practically guarantees that outside of a small group of academics, we do not ask—much less answer—these critical questions.

The ultimate responsibility for the perpetration of violence lies not with the victims but with the perpetrators. Stated another way: domestic and sexual violence are serious problems not because so many women *experience* them but because so many men *perpetrate* or tolerate them. This is a subtle yet deep distinction that has enormous implications for how we confront these issues. The goal is to establish this distinction as common sense. But in a culture where people are conditioned to blame *women*—indeed all subordinated groups—for their own predicament, it does not come naturally to focus on the harms caused by *men*.

In fact, it is an uphill fight to establish in popular consciousness the idea that violence against women is a men's issue, because to shift responsibility for abusive and criminal behavior away from the victims/women (a group with less social power) requires that we shift it toward perpetrators/men (a group with more). I have no illusions about the difficulty of this undertaking.

The shift needs to begin with language. Language structures thought, which means that for us to change our thinking about gender violence, we have to change the language we use to think about it. And in order for us to make room for new language, we have to critically reexamine the *old* language; the words, phrases, and usages that serve to maintain and perpetuate the status quo.

In this chapter I am going to highlight some of the ways that current language about gender violence hides men's responsibility and keeps many people stuck in the old paradigm: the passive and gender-neutral language that dominates the national conversation about rape, domestic violence, sexual harassment, and related problems.

But first, because language that describes social reality is ever-changing and subject to cultural and political pressures, I want to offer a Cliff Notes version of the recent history of mainstream dialogue about gender violence to provide some perspective on how it arrived at its current state of gender neutrality.

HOW DID WE GET STUCK IN (GENDER) NEUTRAL?

When the so-called "second wave" of the modern women's movement rocked the social landscape in the 1970s, one of the many cultural norms it challenged was the silent acceptance of widespread violence against women. A series of new slogans entered the cultural lexicon. "Rape is a crime of power, not of sex." "No means no." "No one deserves to be beaten." "Never another battered woman." Across the country, tens of thousands of newly aware, politicized women from across the socioeconomic, racial, and ethnic spectrum pressured local, state, and federal governments for funding to set up rape crisis centers and battered women's shelters. The first rape crisis center opened its doors in 1972; the first battered women's shelter was founded in 1976. In the late 1970s, the pioneering legal theorist Catherine MacKinnon introduced the new concept of "sexual harassment" law, and gave a name to—and legal remedies for—the mistreatment that working women had experienced for centuries. On college campuses, young feminists, taking their cue from the civil rights and student anti-war movements, insisted that administrators provide services for rape and sexual-assault victims, institute academic women's studies programs, create "safe space" women's centers, and otherwise accommodate the special needs of women students.

The brave women who successfully pushed for these reforms were guided in their thinking by two ideas: 1. That gender—along with class and race—is one of the primary axes around which human societies are organized; and 2. That gender inequality is one of the fundamental human inequalities. They were invigorated by these ideas and their implications for understanding—and improving—the lives of women and children. They were feminists.

A raft of groundbreaking books like *Against Our Will* by Susan Brownmiller and *The Politics of Rape* by Diana Russell, as well as countless leaflets, pamphlets, and newspaper and magazine articles, helped make the intellectual argument that violence against women, while *personal* in that it was experienced by individual women, and perpetrated (in a majority of cases) by individual men, was in fact a *political* crime arising out of women's subordinate social position. The original grassroots activists and national leaders of the battered women's and rape crisis movements were clear that they were advocating not simply for individual women in trouble, but for transforming the sexist system that gave rise to the violence in the first place.

These women-led, multicultural movements withstood political attacks and bureaucratic inertia to become more established into the 1980s and 1990s. But the establishment exacted a price. With increased budgets from state legislatures and other public sources came increased demands for the professionalization of services along the lines of the mainstream social services model. This meant that the women who worked in the previously grass roots, politically oriented "movement"—many of whom were survivors of men's violence and had been activists in the civil rights and anti-war movements—were now replaced by committed young professionals with social work credentials, but without "movement" experience.

Predictably, throughout the 1980s and 1990s, this had the effect of blunting the explicitly feminist politics of the 1970s anti-rape and anti-battering movements. This depoliticization was part of a larger backlash against the women's movement that prompted much distorted media coverage of feminism in those decades. To the casual observer, a feminist was not an advocate for social justice and non-violence who demanded respect and equal treatment for everyone—especially women. She was a hysterical, angry, ugly man-hater with hairy arms and legs and no sense of humor. Susan Faludi's bestselling book *Backlash: The Undeclared War against American Women* (1991) chronicled some of the absurdities of this sort of propaganda (although Faludi devoted scant space to a discussion of violence against women).

There were specific reasons why the battered women's and rape crisis movements increasingly downplayed their explicit focus on gender inequality—and men's behavior—as the root cause of violence against women. As these movements began to make progress toward breaking through centuries of silence and denial in the Western democracies about domestic and sexual violence, more and more women came forward to report crimes against them. Program directors had to lobby state and local governments for ever-greater levels of funding to meet the increased demand for victim services. In the late 1970s through the 1980s, there were very few women in political office at the state or national level. In other words, women's advocates had to convince men in power to give them money. And some of the men were real knuckle-draggers.

The early battered women's movement faced a number of formidable obstacles, not the least of which was that just as political support and funding for battered women's programs was on the increase across the country, in 1980 Ronald Reagan was elected president. Reagan had long been a leading right-wing opponent of the women's liberation movement, and his election was sure to deal an enormous blow to federal support for shelters and other victim services. Sure enough, Reagan's first budget included plans to dramatically cut federal funds for battered women's shelters.

The first responsibility of people who work with battered women, and rape and incest survivors, is to meet the needs of the women and their children. With shelters filled to overflowing and hotlines ringing off the hook, many battered women's advocates stopped publicly using 1970s language about violence against women as a tool of patriarchal oppression and other similar phrases. They did not want to risk being labeled "anti-male," lest the men in power turn off the still-meager flow of funds for direct services. They had to learn to act, and to compromise. They had to learn to smile when district attorneys made patronizing comments addressed to "you ladies," and to endure ignorant judges who lectured battered women from the bench. Most of all, if they wanted to secure the services that women and girls desperately needed, they learned to avoid telling the truth to men in power.

To this day, much of the literature produced and distributed by battered women's and rape crisis programs is written in language that avoids saying that men's behavior is the heart of the problem. In fact, you can read through dozens of pamphlets and handouts from these groups and not see the word "man" or "men" even mentioned. For example, you might see statements like this (emphasis added):

• The primary risk factor for violence is *gender*.
• Abuse is used by *one person* to gain power and control over another.
• Domestic violence is a learned behavior, a choice, and the responsibility of the *person* who uses it.
• Sexual violence can occur at any time and be perpetrated by *anybody*.
• You are more likely to be sexually assaulted by someone you *know*— a *friend, date, classmate, neighbor, relative*—than by a *stranger* in a dark alley.

One of the silliest slogans to emerge in recent years is "Domestic violence is not just a women's problem. It's everyone's problem." Why not come right out and say that it is not just a women's problem, but a *men's* and women's problem? To say it is "everyone's" problem is yet another way to avoid implicating men.

As women's programs grew cautious about how they played the gender politics of the issues, public discourse about "violence against women" became increasingly degendered. In newspaper articles and television newscasts, men who physically abused their wives or girlfriends went from being called "abusive" husbands or boyfriends to being called "domestic-violence perpetrators," or "offenders" in need of "treatment." The old term "wife-beater," which used to suggest a shameful man, gave way to gender-neutral terms like "abusive spouse." When the word "rape" even made it into public discourse, it was almost always introduced in the passive voice, as in "x number of women were raped last year at state university." To the casual observer, it appeared as if men were not even involved.

For some lesbian feminists and their allies, the gender neutrality was intentional. Their reason for using less gender-specific language was to acknowledge that not all women are heterosexual, to explicitly include lesbians, and to recognize abuse in lesbian relationships. If the language always referred to abusers as men, wouldn't that render invisible women who were battered by their female partners? But in this case, under the guise of inclusivity and gender neutrality, individual men and male-dominated institutions evaded accountability. There is abuse in lesbian relationships, and a very small percentage of sexual violence against women is perpetrated by women; but *men's* violence against women—in or outside of heterosexual relationships—is by far the more pervasive problem.

"Offender accountability" emerged in the late 1970s to early 1980s as a critical piece of what came to be known as the "coordinated community response" model for domestic violence and sexual assault. The notion that men should be held legally liable for their abusive behavior—behavior understood to be criminal, and not relegated to the private realm of individual or couples counseling—represented a major conceptual breakthrough. The implication of this shift was clear. The women who had been doing the bulk of victim advocacy work in these fields were tired of having to pick up the pieces in women's lives after men had wreaked havoc, often with impunity. It was time that men—perpetrators and bystanders alike—were forced to shoulder more individual and collective responsibility.

The idea of accountability went beyond that of individual perpetrators. If violence against women was a social problem, there had to be institutional accountability. This included accountability in the law enforcement system and the judiciary for the prosecution, sentencing, and punishment of offenders. But it also encompassed the prevention role played by political, educational, business, and religious leaders—the majority of whom are men.

Unfortunately, it is very difficult for women to push gender politics in this way while at the same time maintaining cordial relations with powerful men. Theoretically, in order to hold men accountable, women need to confront men in positions of institutional authority with uncomfortable truths. But in order to maintain those cordial relations, they often cannot afford public honesty. They cannot call men out on their personal sexism without fear of reprisals. They cannot say that masculine entitlement, not "a few bad apples," lies at the heart of our crisis of domestic violence. They cannot say—except in feminist journals and list serves that are read by an already-politicized constituency—that the U.S. incidence of rape is so high because we live in a "rape culture" that is supported by millions of men, the majority of whom would be offended at any suggestion that they are aiding and abetting rapists.

Which brings us to the current impasse, where gender-neutral language dominates public and private conversation about a problem whose roots are gender-specific. But this may be changing. Oddly enough, one effect of men's growing involvement in this work is that men are often much less reluctant than women to say openly that men's attitudes and behaviors are part of the problem. As more men speak out, we will hopefully hear less watered-down, gender-neutral commentary, and more straightforward discussion, including discussion around such touchy subjects as the relationship between men's use of pornography and the ongoing pandemic of sexual violence.

Men are in a position to utter both controversial opinions and uncomfortable facts because they are less vulnerable than women to the withering accusation that they are "male-bashers." In fact, men who work to end men's violence often possess great empathy for the experiences and struggles of other men—even when those men have hurt women and children. As so many women know, you do not have to hate men in order to hold them accountable for violence—linguistically or otherwise.

LANGUAGE MATTERS

What follows is a brief discussion of five significant events from the past few years that illustrate how gender-neutral language effectively obscures men's responsibility for gender violence: the Jonesboro, Arkansas school shooting in 1998; Woodstock 1999; the group sexual assault at the Puerto Rican Day festival in New York's Central Park in 2000; the Child Abduction Summer of 2002; and the U.S. military rape scandal of 2003–2004.

The Jonesboro Massacre: "Kids killing kids"

The first school shooting that attracted the attention of a horrified nation occurred on March 24, 1998, in Jonesboro, Arkansas. Two boys opened fire on a schoolyard full of girls, killing four and one female teacher. In the wake of what came to be called the Jonesboro massacre, violence experts in media and academia sought to explain what others called "inexplicable." For example, in a front-page *Boston Globe* story three days after the tragedy, David

Kennedy from Harvard University was quoted as saying that these were "peculiar, horrible acts that can't easily be explained."

Perhaps not. But there *is* a framework of explanation that goes much further than most of those routinely offered. It does not involve some incomprehensible, mysterious force. It is so straightforward that some might (incorrectly) dismiss it as unworthy of mention.

Even after a string of school shootings by (mostly white) boys over the past decade, few Americans seem willing to face the fact that interpersonal violence—whether the victims are female or male—is a deeply gendered phenomenon. Obviously both sexes are victimized. But one sex is the perpetrator in the overwhelming majority of cases. So while the mainstream media provided us with tortured explanations for the Jonesboro tragedy that ranged from supernatural "evil" to the presence of guns in the southern tradition, arguably the most important story was overlooked.

The Jonesboro massacre was in fact a gender crime. The shooters were *boys*, the victims *girls*. With the exception of a handful of op-ed pieces and a smattering of quotes from feminist academics in mainstream publications, most of the coverage of Jonesboro omitted in-depth discussion of one of the crucial facts of the tragedy. The older of the two boys reportedly acknowledged that the killings were an act of revenge he had dreamed up after having been rejected by a girl. This is the prototypical reason why adult men murder their wives. If a woman is going to be murdered by her male partner, the time she is most vulnerable is *after* she leaves him. Why wasn't all of this widely discussed on television and in print in the days and weeks after the horrific shooting?

The gender crime aspect of the Jonesboro tragedy *was* discussed in feminist publications and on the Internet, but was largely absent from mainstream media conversation. If it had been part of the discussion, average Americans might have been forced to acknowledge what people in the battered women's movement have known for years—that our high rates of domestic and sexual violence are caused not by something in the water (or the gene pool), but by some of the contradictory and dysfunctional ways our culture defines "manhood." For decades, battered women's advocates and people who work with men who batter have warned us about the alarming number of boys who continue to use controlling and abusive behaviors in their relations with girls and women. Jonesboro was not so much a radical deviation from the norm—although the shooters were very young—as it was melodramatic evidence of the depth of the problem. It was not something about being *kids* in today's society that caused a couple of young teenagers to put on camouflage outfits, go into the woods with loaded .22 rifles, pull a fire alarm, and then open fire on a crowd of helpless girls (and a few boys) who came running out into the playground. This was an act of premeditated mass murder. *Kids* didn't do it. *Boys* did.

We will get nowhere if we continue to ignore the way masculine socialization helps to produce abusive boys, or boys who grow into abusive men. And we are not going to further our understanding of this process by using gender-neutral language to talk about the crisis of "youth" violence. We all know deep down that the problem is not "kids killing kids." How many people, when they heard about a schoolyard shooting that involved eleven- and thirteen-year-old shooters, thought that a couple of young girls must have "lost it"? Girls and women are obviously capable of violence; quotable experts are constantly trotted out to remind us of this. A small but growing percentage of adolescent violence is perpetrated by girls. But the default category for adolescent (and most other) violence is male. Serious violence committed by girls is still rare enough that a local incident can become a major story in the national media. The brutal hazing incident that was captured on videotape in Glenview, Illinois, in 2003 is a good example. The tape showed high school senior girls kicking, beating, and forcing younger girls on the powder puff football team to eat raw fish, pet food, feces, and dirt. Not surprisingly, that story ignited millions of conversations private and public: "What's up with girls?" "Did you see how violent those girls were?" The story had legs for several weeks.

Conversely, when boys act out violently, their gender is rarely deemed worthy of comment. Few people ask "What's up with *boys*?" They say things like, "Kids today have so many problems and pressures that we didn't have when we were young." In fact, we are no longer particularly shocked by violence done by boys which—if done by girls—would create an endless amount of hand-wringing and outraged calls for action.

The Jonesboro tragedy—which preceded Columbine by a year—might have been a national wake-up call. It did help set the stage for the popularity of several "boy books" of the late 1990s, most notably *Real Boys* by William Pollack, *Raising Cain* by Dan Kindlon and Michael Thompson, and *Reaching Up for Manhood: Transforming the Lives of Boys in America* by Geoffrey Canada.

But it did nothing for the movement to end violence against women. It did not catalyze a national conversation about what it means for boys to grow up in a culture which teaches that violence against women is *manly*. Post-Jonesboro, few people asked what it does to vulnerable young boys' psyches when they grow up and learn—at home or in their peer culture, and reinforced in the media—that it is okay for a "real man" to use force when in distress, or when he has scores to settle? How does it affect them to be told repeatedly by their male family members and friends—or by movie characters, comedians, or rap/rock lyricists—that when a girl has defied, disrespected, or rejected them, it is understandable if they have the urge to inflict physical pain on them? Unless we are satisfied with the deeply cynical, reductive explanation that human males are somehow biologically predisposed to assault human females, these are not questions we can put off until the next tragedy.

Woodstock '99

Woodstock '99 was a rock/rap festival in upstate New York that turned violent, doing serious damage to the peace and love legacy of the original. Not surprisingly, it was a hugely hyped event, just what you would expect for the thirtieth anniversary of the legendary music festival. But it went badly. The audience was overwhelmingly white, with a lot of college students, mostly from the northeast. Some of the biggest names in white rock/rap performed, including Limp Bizkit and Korn. The musical reviews were unexceptional. But what captured everyone's attention was the fury of the crowd, which erupted in violence, it was said, in response to the incredibly uncomfortable, unsanitary, disgusting conditions of the grounds, the poor access to overpriced water, filthy bathrooms, etc. If the music was a disappointment, the concert planning and logistics were a debacle. According to numerous published reports and dramatic video footage, the three days ended in a frenzy of vengeful violence early Monday morning, when "concertgoers" overturned automobiles, destroyed ATMs, and looted and burned concession trailers.

The outburst would have been disturbing enough if it had been confined to vandalism or wanton destruction of private property. But in the wake of the troubled weekend, reports surfaced of sexual violence on the concert fairgrounds. Eventually, it was clear that Woodstock '99 had been the site of numerous rapes and sexual assaults, including one reported incident during the Limp Bizkit set where a young woman who was crowd-surfing was pulled down by a group of men and gang-raped.

The rape angle did get some media play. Sample headline from Salon.com: "Three Days of Peace, Love, and Rape." Someone coined it Rapestock. *Rolling Stone* published a lengthy dispatch that detailed much of the criminal violence, including numerous anonymous sexual assaults on young women who had found themselves trapped and hemmed in by angry, aggressive men, some of whom were drunk and high and bingeing on physical displays of anger and power.

The problem was the degendered way the rapes were discussed. The passive voice was everywhere: "at least four rapes occurred," " . . . this girl was being raped."

And the perpetrators were almost never identified as men. They were "people," "offenders," or "bands of concert goers." But mostly they were members of a "crowd." The dominant frame on the story quickly became how a "crowd" of people—after being subjected to a weekend of trying and uncomfortable conditions—lost its cool. Experts on crowd and mob psychology were widely quoted explaining the concept of deindividuation, or how *people* in large, anonymous groups can lose a sense of their personal boundaries and get swept up in a collective sea of raging humanity.

But it wasn't a crowd of *people* at Woodstock '99 that lost its cool. It was a crowd of *men*. The video footage of some of the looting told the story visually: it was plainly evident that dozens of men were the instigators of the rioting and destruction. Remarkably, it was rare to see explicit mention of this in print or on TV. If you read print stories about the mayhem, you would have thought that both sexes were equally involved. Moreover, coverage and commentary about the violence tended to center on the logistics failures of the event, as if the sexual assaults and vandalism were solely the result of poor planning, and had nothing to do with gender politics. And because this was Woodstock, after all, the event prompted many cultural critics to wax philosophic and melancholy about a "generation searching for its identity."

For a moment, let us take the critics at their word; Woodstock '99 was a metaphor for a generation's quest for identity. But if it is truly something about a "generation" that holds clues to the debacle, why didn't women burn and destroy private property? Why didn't women commit sexual assault? Weren't the women at Woodstock members of the same generation as the men?

To understand how misleading it is to talk about the Woodstock rapes using passive language, all you have to do is imagine the same conversation had women been the perpetrators. That would be the whole story. Girls riot! Women out of control at rock concert! Women commit dozens of sexual assaults! Those headlines would have captured everyone's attention. People desperate for insight about the gendered factors that caused the outburst would ask: "Why women? Why would they act out in this brutal way? What does their behavior say about contemporary (white) femininity? What went wrong in the socialization of girls?" But when men are the perps, either as individuals or as a group, we rarely ask these questions. Especially when it is white men. In fact, we manage to figure out ways to sidestep the questions entirely.

Here are just a few of the rarely-asked questions in the aftermath of Woodstock: How could so many men have raped and sexually assaulted their female peers at a rock concert? Why would any man—assuming he has never before raped anyone—commit such a violent act at a concert? Or anywhere else for that matter? Is there a relationship between the hypermasculine aggression of the music and the types of men who are attracted to it? Would this have happened at a folk festival, given the exact same uncomfortable circumstances? Are men with a propensity toward violence overrepresented in certain parts of (white) youth culture? What masculine characteristics are exaggerated in a crowd setting? What role does peer pressure play in catalyzing some men's aggressive behavior in crowds? What role do alcohol and other drugs play in disinhibiting some men's violent behavior? How does the pervasive influence of porn culture contribute to the depersonalization and dehumanization of women required for men to rape them? What about the *Girls Gone Wild*-style breast flashing now common in public gatherings of young men and women? Do some men interpret this exhibitionism as an invitation? Is it possible for women to be flirtatious *and safe* in these sorts of settings?

Few of these questions were even asked, much less thoroughly discussed in any public way in the ensuing weeks and months. As a result, Woodstock '99 became yet another in a steady stream of potentially teachable moments that came and went without advancing one iota our understanding of the causes or solutions to gender violence.

The Puerto Rican Day Central Park Rampage, 2000

An event with similar characteristics took place one year later in New York's Central Park. On June 11, 2000, a crowd of men in New York's Central Park sexually assaulted more than fifty women on a hot and humid day during festivities for Puerto Rican Day. The news spread at the speed of light, as words and pictures went out on the Internet and the cable news networks. The incident stunned and horrified New Yorkers, and others across the country and the world.

It began with a group of men flirtatiously spraying women with water on a steamy Sunday afternoon, but quickly degenerated into a violent frenzy where dozens of men—mostly in their twenties—aggressively and gleefully grabbed and groped women's breasts and genitals, and tore off their clothes. After-the-fact accounts of the incident would no doubt have provoked a public outcry—especially from women's groups. But the "Central Park Rampage" became a much bigger Zeitgeist moment because several men in the crowd had video cameras, which they used to record the unfolding melee. The videotapes—taken from different angles by amateur videographers—aired repeatedly on cable and broadcast news for weeks. The story had all the elements of a ratings winner: visuals of women's partially clad and sexualized bodies, a crowd of excited young men of color, scenes of violence and humiliation. It looked something like a rumble on the WWE, only real.

In the wake of this mass sexual assault, media personalities and politicians rushed to find an explanation, once again focusing their attention on "crowd" or "mob" psychology and the lack of a timely police response. Some politicians decried the assaults as a hate crime against women. But just like Woodstock '99, the national media frame was largely deceiving. Outraged commentators decried the "young thugs" who did this, not the young *men*.

Race and ethnicity were clearly factors in the media coverage. At Woodstock most of the rapists and assaulters were white, and as a result, race hardly ever came up as an issue in the discussion ex post facto. But in Central Park most of the men were African American and Latino. This no doubt caused some politicians and members of the media to denounce them as "lowlifes" and "thugs"—terms not heard about the alleged (white) perpetrators at Woodstock. This did not become the main story, but it was undoubtedly an unspoken subtext—driven by racist stereotypes—in the national media. Men of all races and ethnicities assault women. But typically race and ethnicity are mentioned—in hushed tones or shouted from the rooftops—only when it involves men of color.

Once again, not discussed explicitly was the fact that it wasn't a "crowd," but a crowd of *men*, that attacked all of these women. We later learned that the guilty men were not a collection of career criminals, but mostly "normal" men with no prior records. In fact, perhaps the most alarming aspect of the Central Park assaults was the very *normality* of the group of men. That should have been a big part of the story: how "normal" men could be disinhibited enough to sexually assault women in an incredibly callous and aggressive fashion—and laugh as they did it. This ugly incident should have prompted a long overdue national conversation about the way our culture teaches boys and men—across class, race, and ethnic distinctions—to think about and act toward women. It rightly shocked and angered a lot of people, and caused women, particularly in New York, to be even more vigilant about their personal safety. But for people who pay attention to the broader cultural environment in which we socialize young men, the most shocking thing is how often such outrageous incidents occur with so little public response.

Can anyone seriously maintain this group assault to be an anomalous event? For the past several decades, we have raised boys in a society that in many ways glorifies sexually aggressive masculinity, and considers as normal the degradation and objectification of women. Whether it is misogynistic music and video, the sexual bullying of entertainment icons such as Eminem or Howard Stern, the omnipresence of pornography and female stripping in mainstream culture, or the crude displays of male dominance and female

submissiveness that characterize the wildly popular phenomenon of professional wrestling, the images and messages routinely directed at young males
make the actions of the Central Park men perfectly logical and consistent
with broader societal attitudes.

To demonstrate how deeply imbued our society is with those attitudes, how
"normal" were the Central Park perpetrators, consider the following thought
exercise. Imagine the public response if the June 11 assault consisted of a group
of white people who targeted and attacked people of color. In that case, media
discussion would inevitably focus on racism as the proximate cause of the
attacks. Rather than "mob mentality" or sociobiological explanations for antisocial behavior, discussion would focus, quite rightly, on the persistent problem of racism and the need to teach our (white) children to respect and
embrace racial and ethnic diversity. Although that dialogue might result in few
immediate solutions, at least the problem would clearly be identified.

Consider if the gender roles in the Central Park attack were reversed—
that a group of women had attacked men. In such a scenario, media discussion would focus obsessively on what could have been going on with women
that caused them to act out in this way. But when a group of men target and
attack women, the "experts" typically opine on crowd psychology, leaving
discussion of male socialization—and the societal sexism that fuels sex
crimes—to feminist list serves, magazines, or women's studies classes.

The Child Abduction Summer of 2002

The summer of 2002 included a seemingly endless stream of sex crimes
that dominated the infotainment world. To summarize, using the standard
language: seven-year-old Danielle van Dam was abducted out of her home
in San Diego in the evening, sexually assaulted, and murdered. (Her murderer was later sentenced to death.) Little girls were kidnapped in Utah and
Philadelphia, and their parents pleaded for their safe return in what became
an oddly voyeuristic nightly television ritual. The badly decomposed body of
college student and Washington intern Chaundra Levy was found by joggers
in a wooded area. A five-year-old girl named Samantha Runnion was
snatched from in front of her home in Orange County, California, kicking
and screaming, and then later found dead, her nude little body showing evidence of sexual violation. Accompanied by their boyfriends, two teenage girls
in a rural area east of Los Angeles were forcefully abducted out of their cars
and then sexually assaulted before authorities, acting on citizen tips, were
able to confront and kill the suspect. In Massachusetts, a woman on her way
to Cape Cod was brutally murdered when she stopped to use a restroom in
the early morning hours at a highway Burger King. In Oregon, the remains

of two teenage girls were found buried in the backyard of a suspect. Four women were the victims of domestic homicide in the course of a few weeks at Ft. Bragg, North Carolina. Kennedy relative Michael Skakel was convicted in the murder of his neighbor, Martha Moxley, when they were both teenagers in the 1970s.

The summer of 2002 also gave us a number of disturbing stories from the world of men's professional sports: Superstar basketball player Allen Iverson faced charges of criminal misconduct (eventually dismissed) stemming from a "domestic dispute" where he allegedly threw his naked wife out of their house. The race-car superstar Al Unser Jr. was arrested for assaulting his girl-friend, as were the baseball pitcher Scott Erickson, and the pro-basketball star Glenn Robinson.

As many of these descriptions exemplify, the sex of the victims was usual-ly stated clearly ("girl abducted"), while the sex of the alleged perpetrators was downplayed ("authorities questioned the suspect"). As we have seen, this is the norm in news coverage about gender violence. It is so normal that most people do not even realize what is obscured. In reality, the one common char-acteristic of the perpetrators in the string of nationally publicized cases that experts assured us was "not indicative of a larger trend" was that they were all MEN. Nearly every case involved murderous, sexually violent men who aggressed against adolescent and prepubescent girls, and famous, successful men who physically and emotionally abused their wives and girlfriends.

Admittedly, the cases took place in a cluster, and had newsworthy ele-ments that produced far more national coverage than usually afforded inci-dents of gender and sexual violence, *millions* of which occur around the country annually to little public notice. Still, few leading commentators saw fit to explore the implications of the gendered nature of this wave of violent crime. Instead, mainstream media debate about "the summer of child abductions" focused largely on parents' understandable concerns for the safety of their children, moral quandaries about the nature of evil, or after-the-fact issues like the breakdown of the criminal justice system. Mainstream debate about domestic violence by athletes and entertainers focused—as it often does—largely on the relationship between substance abuse and abu-sive behavior, or whether or not famous men, or black or brown men, are singled out because of their prominence or their race.

Why does the focus remain on these interesting but arguably secondary factors, and largely avoid the central and revealing fact that the vast majori-ty of perpetrators are male, the vast majority of victims female? Consider the racial analogy. If all of the assaults that summer—or any other summer— had been perpetrated by white people, and all the victims had been people of color, would so much airtime and ink have been devoted to discussions about individuals' family experiences and psychological problems? Or would we as a culture—quite rightly—have been talking about racism?

Why, in the face of a rash of sexual and gender crimes perpetrated by men against women and girls, did influential opinion-makers tend to ignore or overlook the role played in these crimes by sexism and male dominance? Why didn't the so-called experts start out nearly every conversation about these crimes by asking: "what is going on with American men?"

There are several possible explanations:

Everybody knows men and boys are the primary perps. Why belabor the obvious? Not only do we have to face up to the fact that our culture produces abusive, misogynistic boys and men at pandemic rates, we have to *do* something about it. The key to this is the common-sense notion that in order to deal with a problem, first you have to name it. If violence is not understood as the overwhelmingly male phenomenon that it is, then subsequent discussions about its causes are destined to ignore one of the key elements.

It would be an exercise in "male-bashing." In the earlier chapter on male-bashing, I discussed how this term is used to silence feminist critiques of men's violence. As such, "male-bashing" is a classic Orwellian phrase, like "freedom is slavery" or "war is peace." To bash someone is to assault them. It follows that "male-bashers" are violent people. But wait. Aren't "male-bashers" women—and men—who have the temerity to speak out *against* men's violence? How did they get stuck with a violent label? This would seem to be less of an accurate description of who they are and more of a conscious or unconscious attempt to intimidate them into complicit silence.

Boys and men are victims, too. Most boys and men who are victims of violence are victims of *other men's* violence. Consider the sexual abuse scandal in the Catholic Church; both boys and girls are the victims of this abuse. But virtually *all* of the perpetrators are male. When was the last time you heard about nuns sexually attacking children? There is of course mother-son child abuse, and as the Mary Kay Letourneau case in Washington State reminds us, some older women sexually abuse boys. In fact, recent media stories about sexual abuse perpetrated by women against boys suggest that this crime might be more common than many people think. This type of abuse is criminal and inexcusable. Still, let us not lose sight of the much larger problem: Whether the victims are female or male, the perpetrators of violence are overwhelmingly male. The FBI—which can hardly be accused of anti-male bias—estimates that boys and men commit between 80 to 90 percent of violent crime in the U.S. each year.

Women do horrible things, too. Women are capable of horrific violence.

But when women perpetrate violence, their gender—unlike men's—is almost always highlighted and discussed. Virtually every day across this country we hear about another man who murdered his wife and kids in a gruesome fashion. But these stories come and go in the daily news cycle. When women murder their children they are likely to become household names.

For example, consider how many Americans followed the sad and tragic cases of Susan Smith, a South Carolina woman who murdered her two sons, and Andrea Yates, a woman in Texas who murdered her five children. Those stories were so hot that people talked about them with complete strangers in supermarket checkout lines. Men murder their children (along with their wives) in far greater numbers. Does anyone outside the local community remember their names?

Consider as well the controversy that ensued with the release of the female buddy movie *Thelma and Louise* in 1991. Social critics across the country—under headlines like "Toxic feminism?"—wondered whether this portended a disturbing new cinematic trend. Would we soon see a new generation of films where women were the violent protagonists? Worse still, would they be revenge-seeking women who had the chutzpah to kill men who tried to assault them? Is it possible that this might legitimize this behavior in the real world? All it took to spark this debate was *one* film where women had usurped the male prerogative for violence, even as the cineplexes continued to fill up with non-controversial movies, many of which featured unimaginably violent men.

Feminist perspectives have been demonized and marginalized in main-stream media. Some writers and academics have argued for years that a number of our cultural practices set up girls to be victims and boys to be perpetrators. But in part because feminist insights like this make a lot of people—men *and* women—uneasy, feminists are largely ignored in the mainstream conversation about (men's) violence. It is presumably a lot safer—and better for ratings—for the networks and newspapers to feature one FBI profiler after another who dispassionately describes the characteristics of deranged criminals than it is to provide a platform for actual experts on gender violence.

The exclusion from mainstream debate of those courageous enough to tell the truth about our culture's disturbing propensity to produce sexually violent boys and men hurts us all. How can we prevent violence if we do not properly understand its causes? In the absence of a more sophisticated national conversation about the deformed masculinity that lies at the heart of these ongoing tragedies, the culture that gave rise to these crimes will continue to put women and children at risk, and those of us who care about them in a state of constant fear.

The U.S. military rape scandal of 2003–2004

Many people were stunned and outraged when the *Denver Post* ran a story in January of 2004 about dozens of U.S. servicewomen who had reported to a civilian group that they had been raped by fellow troops in Iraq and Kuwait. Countless editorials were published that condemned the rapes and called for justice for the victims, who served their country in a war zone but who had more to worry about from "friendly fire" than from the official enemy.

Many of the media accounts of the military rape scandal, while condemning the rapes, nonetheless helped perpetuate the myth that rapes in the military were a women's problem. In a long and passionate editorial in *USA Today*, headlined "Rape in the military: Female troops deserve much better," there was only one passing reference to the fact that *all* of the perpetrators were men. Every other reference was to "fellow troops," "superiors," or "attackers in their own ranks." In other editorials, op-ed commentaries, and news stories, readers learned about a female officer who had been assaulted by a "subordinate." Because she was married, she faced charges for fraternization and adultery, while her "alleged assailant" had not been charged.

The language in these articles fit the general pattern of reportage about gender violence. We were constantly reminded of the gender of the victims: " . . . *women* felt they had been doubly victimized," "recent allegations fit a pattern of *female* troops who have been sexually assaulted." At the same time, descriptions of the perpetrators were conspicuously gender-neutral.

How are we going to ensure that female service members are protected from sexual assault if no one is clear about who assaults them? It is not pleasant, but these women's assailants are not disembodied abstractions. They are fellow *male* service members. They are *men* who wear the uniform of the United States armed forces. At a minimum, don't women who put their lives on the line to serve in the military deserve this kind of honest language?

PASSIVE VOICE

Have you ever heard a politician under fire at a press conference utter the phrase "mistakes were made?" In our cynical age, everyone knows this phrase is about passing the buck. If the buck truly stopped with them, a forthright leader would say, "I made a mistake," or "We made a mistake." Instead, by shifting into the passive voice, they shift the focus off of themselves. This is a tried-and-true method employed by guilty people to manipulate language in an effort to dodge accountability.

Use of the passive voice is also one of the chief linguistic culprits responsible for deflecting attention away from men's role in violence against women.

If you pay close attention, you will see that much of the national conversation about gender violence—on the Web, in newspaper and magazine articles, on TV, and in everyday speech—is dominated by passive sentences.

News stories dutifully report—sometimes in sensational fashion—the bad things that happen to women. You see it all the time in headlines: "Aspiring Model Murdered," "Girl Abducted," "Student Raped"; in statistics: "Every day, three women are murdered as a result of domestic violence," or "More than half of rape victims are raped by the age of eighteen"; or in dramatic assertions: "Millions of girls and women suffer sexual harassment in school and in the workplace." The trouble is that you rarely hear men's roles clearly stated in these crimes. This omission is not necessarily conscious. It is true that batterers often intentionally use the passive voice to deflect blame: "She went and got herself beat up." "There was a little fight in my house last night." But many people without an obvious motive to obfuscate and evade the truth use the passive voice as well.

For example, take the infamous Janet Jackson-Justin Timberlake performance during the halftime show of Super Bowl XXXVIII, on February 1, 2004. The last moment of their duet—when Timberlake popped off part of Jackson's corset, exposing her breast—became one of the most talked about incidents in pop culture history. To this day it is not clear if what happened was a "wardrobe malfunction," as Jackson described it, or a planned publicity stunt. But one thing is clear: much of the chatter about the episode concerned Janet Jackson's "exposed breast," as if it simply exposed itself. Many commentators, and people around the water cooler the next day at work, referred to the incident as the Janet Jackson incident, omitting any reference to Timberlake. It is true that he is not as big a star as Jackson, but the dance move that caused the exposure was not merely an artistic rendition of sexual expression. As described by D. C. Rybak of the *Minneapolis Star* in one of thousands of media accounts, right after Timberlake sang the lyrics "I'm gonna have you naked by the end of this song," he reached across Jackson's gladiator-type bustier and pulled off the fabric covering her right breast. In other words, the "dance" move combined with the lyric created a kind of pantomimed sexual assault carried out by Timberlake on Jackson's body as the culmination of the narrative arc of the song.

This aspect of the incident was totally overshadowed by the firestorm of controversy about the visual image of her exposed breast. In much of the media discussion, the debate centered on the question of whether this was a new low in the shameless exploitation of sexual titilation on television, as if the true problem was "obscenity" in prime time. There was little public discussion of whether it was even appropriate to eroticize a sexual assault in a culture where, according to the National Victim Center, approximately seventy-eight women aged eighteen and over are forcibly raped every hour.

The passive voice effectively shifts responsibility for violence—and the responsibility for preventing it—from male perpetrators to female victims. Consider how this works in everyday speech. The following questions all feature passive language:

- How many women were raped at this college last year?
- How many girls at this high school have been in abusive relationships?
- Approximately how many teenage girls in the United States get pregnant every year?

In each case, use of the passive voice shifts our attention off of men and boys and onto women and girls. This reinforces the idea that gender violence is a women's issue, because the focus of the conversation is what is happening *to* girls and women, not who is doing it, or why. We can rewrite these sentences in active language:

- How many men raped women at this college last year?
- How many boys at this high school have abused their girlfriends?
- Approximately how many men and boys in the U.S. impregnated teenage girls last year?

The active voice changes the meaning. If the sort of language in the second list were more common, we would certainly be more likely to hold men accountable for men's violence. The language would push us in that direction.

Admittedly, the two sets of sentences are not 100 percent parallel. For example, there is not typically a one-to-one ratio of rapists to rape victims. Experts remind us that the typical rapist rapes multiple victims, so the number of men who rape women is a lot less than the number of women who are raped. But how often does one even hear the question, *How many men have raped women?*

In the second sentence, there is also not a one-to-one ratio, in part because girls in the school might have been abused by other girls, or boys/men who were not students. In the third sentence, one parallel question to *how many girls got pregnant?* is *how many boys impregnated girls?* But most girls who "get pregnant" are impregnated by men over the age of eighteen. It is much more common for fourteen-year-old girls to be impregnated by twenty-one-year-old men than to be impregnated by their male age-peers. Men's irresponsible and often coercive sexual behavior is one of the root causes of teen pregnancy. But how often are adult men included in discussions about teen pregnancy?

The novelist Andrew Vachss makes a related point about use of the term "child prostitute." Writing in *Parade* magazine in June 2005, Vachss points out that the term implies that little children are "seductive" and "volunteer" to have sex with adults in exchange for cash. It helps to place judgmental focus on the character of the child, not on the people (overwhelmingly men) who manipulate and use them. "When we use terms such as 'lose one's virginity' in referring to adult sex acts with children instead of calling it 'rape,'" he writes, "or when we say that teachers 'have affairs' with their pupils instead of saying that the teachers sexually exploit them, the only beneficiaries are the predators who target children."

In a paper entitled "Patriarchal False Descriptions of Language" presented at the National Women's Studies Conference in 1980, the linguist Julia Penelope brilliantly dissects how the passive voice harms women. She warns women to be aware of the language they use to talk about violence, because current language convention is antithetical to offender accountability and does not serve women's interests. Penelope illustrates her point with the following sequence of sentences:

1. John beat Mary.
2. Mary was beaten by John.
3. Mary was beaten.
4. Mary was battered.
5. Mary is a battered woman.

The first sentence is a good, active English sentence. The second sentence rewrites the first, but this time in the passive voice. This does not simply change the structure of the sentence; it changes the meaning. People who take remedial writing classes often turn in first drafts that are filled with passive sentences. They hedge their bets, qualify themselves, and dance around key points. A good writing instructor will typically tell them: "Say what you mean. Take responsibility for your ideas. Be direct." But the use of the passive voice is more than just bad writing; it has a political effect. In this case it changes the subject of the sentence from John to Mary. Not coincidentally, John is at the end of the second sentence, which means he is close to dropping off the map of our consciousness. By the third sentence, John is gone, and it's all about Mary. In the final sentence, Mary's very identity—*Mary is a battered woman*—has been created by the now-absent John.

People frequently ask why battered women stay with the men who beat them. They are right to ask the question, although it is likely that some people's curiosity *about* battered women is actually frustration *with* them, because if you have never been a battered woman you rarely have a clue about the complexities of their families and relationships. Still, it is instructive that few think to ask similar questions about batterers. *Why do they beat women? Why do so many American men seek to control through force the women they claim to love?* How might the use of active language point us toward answers to these questions?

Many advocates in the field, along with academics who study domestic violence, argue that the incessant focus on the behavior of battered women is de facto proof of the prevalence of victim-blaming. Women who are the victims of violence are frequently held responsible for what was done *to* them. This is a type of revictimization that not only discourages women from seeking help or getting out of abusive relationships; it also makes it more difficult to hold abusive men accountable for *their* behavior.

Victim-blaming is popular for many reasons. In this case the passive voice—intentionally or not—deflects attention off men at the same time that it helps keep the focus on women. This, in turn, reinforces the idea that "violence against women" is exclusively a women's issue, which gets us back to the original problem: men's central role is either overlooked or rendered invisible.

The phrase "violence against women" itself contributes to this dynamic. It is so common and influential that relatively few people ever pause to contemplate what is wrong with it. But "violence against women" is a passive phrase. It contains no active agent. It is like saying, "shit happens." No one *makes* it happen, at least no one we can identify from the available evidence. It is just something that unfortunately occurs. If you insert the active agent— men—a new phrase emerges: *Men's violence against women.* It doesn't roll off the tongue as easily, but it is far more accurate and honest.

CHAPTER SEVEN

Bystanders

"'Funny thing,' [Curley's wife] said. 'If I catch any one man, and he's alone, I get along fine with him. But just let two of the guys get together an' you won't talk. Jus' nothing but mad.' She dropped her fingers and put her hands on her hips. 'You're all scared of each other, that's what. Ever'one of you's scared the rest is goin' to get something on you.'"
—John Steinbeck, *Of Mice And Men*

Most gender-violence prevention efforts over the past several decades have been based on a crude binary model: women and girls are victims or potential victims, and men and boys are perpetrators or potential perpetrators. Not surprisingly, most prevention efforts have focused on women and girls, and how they can avoid physical and sexual assault by boyfriends, husbands, acquaintances, or strangers. This female-centered approach typically includes both the dissemination of literature with headlines like "Warning signs of abusive relationships," and advice to women and girls about personal safety measures (e.g., do not accept drinks at a party or club if you do not see them poured).

But these popular strategies are not really about prevention. They are about "risk reduction" for women. Their stock in trade is to teach individual girls and women how to avoid victimization. They communicate a simple and powerful message: there are many abusive and dangerous men out there, and you need to have your guard up at all times. Until recently, however, few gender-violence prevention initiatives made it a priority to actually target men and boys, or attempted to change social norms in male culture. The high rate of male perpetration was simply taken for granted as an unpleasant fact of life.

When men were targeted for prevention efforts, in educational or community settings, they were often seen as potential perpetrators. The message to them: you need to recognize the triggers for your own bad behaviors so you can interrupt the process before you have the urge to strike your girlfriend/wife. Or, you need to develop better interpersonal communication skills, like good listening, so you do not force yourself on women sexually. Or, if you occasionally or regularly drink alcohol and then behave in a manner you cannot defend when sober, you need to get immediate help for your drinking problem.

The first problem with this approach is that it treats gender violence as an *individual* issue that is caused by a man's personality flaws. It presumes that gender violence is a type of dysfunctional behavior that can be cured with therapy or punished by jail time, rather than a specific manifestation of a deeply rooted system of male dominance. As we have seen, people constantly misrepresent gender violence as the behavior of a few bad apples.

Secondly, it is ineffective to target men as potential perpetrators because most men do not identify themselves this way. In fact, many men who have been *convicted* of gender-violence crimes still believe they are somehow different from the sorts of men who do terrible things to women. Batterer-intervention counselors report that the men with whom they work often describe their own behavior as harmless, while criticizing other men's actions as more serious and worthy of condemnation. "I am not like *those* guys," they say, as they search for definitions of "abuse" that do not include any of the acts they have been convicted of perpetrating.

There are many different types of rapists, but studies have shown that some men who rape women are so narcissistic that it never occurs to them that they have committed a crime. This delusion helps explain the countless documented incidents where a man has raped a woman and then actually asked her for her phone number so they can arrange another "date." If men who have committed horrific acts cannot see their own behavior for what it is and continue to resist introspection—in other words, if *actual* batterers and rapists tune out messages aimed at batterers and rapists—why should other men pay attention?

When I give a presentation to a roomful of men—in the sports culture, the Marine Corps, or anywhere—I do not adopt an accusatory tone. I do not say, "You guys better listen up, because I know some of you are doing bad things to women." This would not be fair, and it would not be effective. Men are bound to become defensive and hostile. They will ask themselves: *Who the hell is this person? Why is he talking to me? What does he know about me? This isn't my problem. He should be talking to the lowlifes who actually need to hear this message.*

Instead of pointing my finger at them, I challenge them. "Come on, guys," I say. "The women and girls that we care about have to live with an awful lot of sexist abuse and violence. Many guys in this room have women close to them who have been sexually abused as girls, or raped in high school or college. I know I do. There are guys in this room whose *mothers* are domestic-violence or sexual-assault survivors. If that's not bad enough, the simple threat of men's violence—the mere possibility that it could happen—orders women's daily lives. Have you ever talked with your women friends and girl-friends about the sorts of precautions they have to take when it gets dark? Can you imagine how you would feel if your freedom was restricted like that? This isn't right."

Many men nod in agreement. Occasionally they even applaud in support; but they have no idea what to do next. Because most men see gender violence as an individual problem, they figure all that is required of them is to keep a check on their own behavior. It never occurs to a lot of thoughtful and responsible men that they have a much greater role to play. This is a fertile starting point for a discussion about the concept of men as bystanders.

The term "bystander" is often associated with passivity, a description of someone who stands by while bad things happen. The 1988 Hollywood film *The Accused* reinforced this idea and took it one step further. It featured Jodie Foster in the role of a young woman who was gang-raped by a group of men on a pool table in a bar as a second group of men cheered. The movie was loosely based on an infamous real-life incident in 1983 at Big Dan's bar in New Bedford, Massachusetts. The major difference between the film and the actual gang rape is that in the former, the bystanders were convicted of a crime, while in the actual incident none of the bystanders were even charged.

Another common definition of the term "bystander" suggests an innocent witness to a crime. One of the most famous pop-culture references to bystanders was in the final episode of *Seinfeld* in 1998, where the four main characters were put on trial for the crime of being cynical and self-absorbed louts who laughed at a victim as she was car-jacked by a gang of thugs. Their attorney, a Johnnie Cochran look-alike, defended them on the basis that no one had ever heard of a "guilty bystander." In social justice education, the term "bystander" can be used to identify people who are part of an oppressive system, but are neither victims nor perpetrators. In the wake of the Holocaust much has been written and theorized about the role played by "good Germans" in allowing the genocide to occur. Research into the social psychology of bystander behavior accelerated in the wake of the 1964 case of Kitty Genovese, a young woman who was stabbed to death by a man in the public courtyard of a Queens, New York, apartment complex. The case drew widespread attention and catalyzed much interest in the academic field of social psychology because dozens of neighbors peered out from behind their window shades at the sound of the woman's screams, but no one intervened or even called the police—for forty-five minutes—as she lay dying. In a more recent infamous case in 1997, a nineteen-year-old Berkeley engineering student, David Cash, stood outside the bathroom of a Las Vegas Casino as his friend sexually assaulted and murdered a seven-year-old girl. When asked why he did not intervene, even though he knew something terrible was happening, Cash asserted that it was none of his business. Cash's disavowal of any responsibility—moral or legal—sparked a series of protests at Berkeley and an unsuccessful effort to have him expelled.

In the field of gender-violence prevention, the idea of working with bystanders has gathered considerable momentum over the past decade. In this educational context, a bystander refers to someone who is not directly involved as a perpetrator or victim of an act of sexual harassment or violence, but is indirectly involved as a friend or family member. A bystander can also be a member of a group, team, workplace, or any other social unit. The aim in focusing on bystanders is to empower them to speak up—and not to be silent and complicit—in the face of abusive behavior. This can be a daunting challenge, because there are many deep-seated cultural factors that discourage people from getting involved in the affairs of others. For many decades in the U.S. there has been widespread residential mobility and a resultant breakdown in the bonds of community. In many cities and suburbs, neighbors do not even know each other's names, and are presumably less likely to intervene in each other's lives. Also, in our litigious society many potential Good Samaritans hesitate to get involved because they are afraid of being held liable for their actions.

However, in addition to these broader cultural factors, many men and women have been socialized to be passive bystanders specifically when it comes to sexual abuse and violence. This conditioning is reflected in commonly heard statements like: "A situation between a man and a woman is none of my business," or "What goes on within a marriage is a private matter." A historical antecedent of this belief is the English common law doctrine that an assault outside the family is a public matter, but conflicts between family members should remain confined to the domestic sphere. In other words, a man's home is his castle, and no one tells the king how to treat his subjects. One of the long-term projects of feminist jurisprudence and social activism is to erode this private-public dichotomy, because the domestic sphere has been one of the key sites of women's subordination. Women's rights advocates have made dramatic progress in this area over the past quarter-century. For example, marital rape used to be considered an oxymoron, but today it can be prosecuted as a crime in all fifty states. Nonetheless, to a disturbing extent, men are still permitted to mistreat women in the privacy of their homes and relationships and suffer only limited consequences.

Feminists have long argued that we live in a "rape culture" and a "battering culture." In other words, individual acts of gender violence emanate from an unequal and sexist cultural context, within which heterosexual men are conditioned to objectify and dominate women in the sexual sphere, and exert power and control over them in intimate relationships. If we accept this, then primary prevention efforts need to move beyond short-term safety precautions for women (e.g., women being advised not to put their drinks down at parties, to park in well-lit areas, to recognize the warning signs of abusive relational behaviors, etc.).

Instead, educators need to address the attitudes in male culture that encourage or legitimize some men's abusive behavior. One way to address these attitudes is to examine and work toward changing group dynamics in male-peer culture, where rape and battering supportive attitudes are nurtured and reinforced. If more men spoke up before, during, or after incidents of verbal, physical, or sexual abuse by their peers, they would help to create a climate where the abuse of women—emotional, physical, sexual—would be stigmatized and seen as incompatible with male group norms. That is, a man who engaged in such behavior would lose status among his male peers and forfeit the approval of older males.

Ultimately, this would cause a shift in male culture such that some men's sexist abuse of women and girls would be regarded—by other men—not only as distasteful but as utterly unacceptable. In this new climate, individuals would be strongly discouraged from acting out in abusive ways because of the anticipated negative consequences: loss of respect, friends, and status, and greater likelihood of facing both legal and non-legal sanctions. In fact, if men's violence against women truly carried a significant stigma in male culture, it is possible that most incidents of sexist abuse would never happen. This is because contrary to popular myth, the vast majority of boys and men who assault, harass, and bully girls and women are not sociopaths. They are average guys. Many of them see the sexist treatment of women as normal. They behave toward women the way they think men are supposed to. If the example and the expectations of the men around them changed, they would be likely to adjust their behavior accordingly.

In a climate where men do not tolerate other men's mistreatment of women, female (and male) victims would also undoubtedly gain more support. This would set in motion a powerful chain of events. When victims feel supported, they are more likely to come forward. As a result there would be a significant increase in the number of rape, domestic-violence, and sexual-harassment reports. With an uptick in reports, authorities would face increased pressure to hold perpetrators accountable: they would be more likely to discipline employees, suspend students from school, remove student athletes from teams, and prosecute alleged abusers in criminal court. While an increase in accountability is a positive development, it is important to acknowledge that the criminal justice system historically has not been fair to all men who are charged with or convicted of assaulting women (or men). Men of color are more likely than white men to be held accountable for their crimes, especially if their victims are white. For example, in the early decades of the twentieth century, thousands of African American men were lynched by vigilante mobs of white men, predominantly in the South, based on trumped up charges that they had raped white women. This racist legacy cannot be overlooked or wished away. But the solution to this disparity is not to ease the pressure on perpetrators; it is to seek fair treatment in the application of justice. If fewer men who assault women got away with it— including wealthy white men—the anticipation of negative consequences would reinforce the need to prevent it from happening in the first place.

ONE OF THE GUYS

Boys and men of every class, race, ethnicity, and nationality face enormous pressure to be "one of the guys." This pressure begins early in life and continues across the life span. Every man who has boyhood memories of desperately waiting to be picked when the group chooses sides for playground games knows how important it is to be accepted by one's peers, but peer pressure does not end with childhood and adolescence. The anxious feelings associated with the desire to fit in or be accepted might diminish with age and maturity, but they also might not. Many middle-aged men are more comfortable talking about the pressures on young guys to fit in than they are acknowledging the conformist pressures in their own lives. I see this frequently in my work with male officers in the U.S. military. They readily agree that young male troops are highly impressionable and need guidance about how to conduct themselves as men. The officers, however, are less apt to see themselves as subject to similar influences from men of their own age and rank. Of course the specific aspects of peer group expectations vary by age. A twenty-year-old man might feel pressure from his buddies to drink copious amounts of alcohol and shout obscenities at women out of car windows. A forty-year-old's friends might instead tease him about "who wears the pants" in his marriage if he makes less money or has less professional success than his wife; and their disapproval—even if it is presented in a light-hearted manner—might feed his resentment of her. This would not in any way *cause* him to abuse her. But the goading of friends can encourage a man to believe that he needs to exercise more control over his wife in order to maintain or regain his standing in the male group. At some point this could contribute to his decision to use physical force.

These are just some of the ways that peer groups impose rigid standards for masculine behavior, including expectations for when violence is an acceptable response to a real or perceived threat. These expectations carry significant weight. As the sociologist Michael Kimmel notes in his indispensable cultural history *Manhood in America*, men care a great deal about what other men think of them. In fact, he says, "In large part, it's other men who are important to American men; [they] define their masculinity, not as much in relation to women, but in relation to each other. Masculinity is largely a homosocial enactment."

Part of the developmental challenge men face—especially adolescent boys and young men who are trying to establish successful adult identities—is to figure out how to "act like a man" and thus earn other men's respect and approval. This is not genetically hard-wired. Some boys learn their most powerful lessons about "manhood" from their fathers—for good or ill. Some boys do not have fathers, or their fathers are so emotionally or physically distant that their influence is diminished. But regardless of whether a father is present, boys and men constantly look to each other for cues about where in the male hierarchy they fit in: how they should dress, carry themselves, and interact with others, what they should say (and not say) in various social situations, and how "real men" treat women. Guys learn many of these codes of male behavior at a young age in groups, cliques, and other associative structures.

There are many different styles of masculinity that boys and men across the ethno-cultural spectrum adopt, ranging from the self-conscious and paramilitary conformity of the Boy Scouts to the ostensibly rebel masculinity of gang bangers. The peer culture dynamic on athletic teams—from youth sports through "over-fifty" leagues—is particularly influential in shaping notions of what constitutes a "real man." For some college men, fraternities play an analogously powerful role. Regular or even daily interaction in male social groups—from motorcycle gangs to golf foursomes—provides a rich source of information to group members about what their fellow men value, and what they consider wimpy and unworthy of respect. Boys and men also absorb volumes of information from popular culture. For the past generation, pornography has been by far the most important source of sex miseducation for millions of American boys and men. Over the last decade, the rise of "lad" magazines like *Maxim, Stuff,* and *FHM,* which feature scantily clad starlets on the cover, can actually be understood as instructional manuals for a certain type of upwardly mobile white, middle, and upper-class manhood.

Another critical but less-acknowledged source of information about male group norms and how "real men" act comes from fictional portrayals, especially television and movies. Over the past few decades, cultural theorists such as Raymond Williams have argued that while it is people who produce the images that bombard us daily on TV, on billboards, in videogames, and in film, it is equally true to say that this virtual landscape of images in some sense produces us. This means we are not just consumers of these images. We do not simply make our way through the thousands of images we see daily and pick and choose what we like and don't like. These images have a profound effect on who we are, on our tastes, attitudes, and the kinds of choices we make. Millions of young men (and women) take cues from television programs and movies about what is masculine and feminine and how "cool" members of their generation are supposed to act. As cultural studies scholar Douglas Kellner puts it in his book *Media Culture,* the media provide "symbolic environments" in which people live that strongly influence their thought, behavior, and style. "When a media sensation appears," he says, "it becomes part of that environment, and in turn becomes a new resource for pleasures, identities, and contestation." Consider, for example, the wildly popular *American Pie* movie series. A large percentage of white Americans in their twenties have seen one or all of the three movies. One of the signature characteristics of these movies is the glamorization of a certain type of male-centered partying culture, where men drink large quantities of alcohol to overcome their social inhibitions and to fit in, and girls are little more than caricatured objects of heterosexual male desire. The beer-soaked partying culture in *American Pie,* with its celebration of male "hijinks" and blatant objectification of women, is precisely the social backdrop to the pandemic of acquaintance rape, especially on college campuses. Does this mean that movies like *American Pie* can be said to *cause* rape? Of course not. But if there is such a thing as a rape culture, they are surely part of it. This is not a self-righteous statement. When I saw *American Pie*—in my late thirties in a theater filled with teens and twenty-somethings—I immediately recognized the party scenes, because when I was in high school and college I was immersed in similar ones. And I know for certain that millions of white men in my generation self-consciously patterned our speech, mannerisms, and sexual expectations after groups of men in movies like *Animal House* and *Saturday Night Fever*.

One explanation for the enduring popularity of gangster films like The *Godfather*, *Goodfellas*, and the HBO series *The Sopranos* is that they provide an up-close glimpse—from a safe distance—into the tensions in male culture, between loyalty to the group and the reality of cutthroat competition between its members. It is not just the violence that attracts millions of viewers, or the great storytelling and acting; these movies and programs also provide an opportunity to peer behind the curtain, to gain insight about how "real men" are supposed to act when there are no women around. Part of the appeal of these pop cultural mainstays is how the writers unmask the anxiety at the heart of male performance, including the realistic fear of violence that can simmer just beneath the surface. Journalist Nathan McCall explains in his essay collection *What's Going On* that he and some of his African American male cohorts in the 1960s and 1970s learned a lot about "manhood" from watching gangster films which featured ruthless Italian men who regularly assaulted each other and treated women as little more than property. Gangsta rap in the late twentieth and early twenty-first century borrowed a lot from these cinematic portrayals. Ironically, many young suburban white men today are powerfully influenced by black urban gangsta rappers, who in turn learned about how "real men" are supposed to act from white actors in movies that were written and directed by white men.

As always there is a fine line between the best of realist fiction and actual events. Several documentary accounts of "groupthink" in the Kennedy and Johnson administrations, for example, include anecdotes of highly accomplished male presidential advisers who remained silent in White House discussions about Vietnam policy rather than risk appearing "wimpy" by advocating less militaristic options. Carol Cohn, in a fascinating article about language and group dynamics among defense intellectuals entitled "Wars, Wimps, and Women: Talking Gender and Thinking War," maintains that narrow group norms of masculine language and behavior materially influenced the group process—and ultimately, perhaps, public policy—on issues of potentially dire consequence, such as nuclear war. Numerous insider accounts of the George W. Bush administration's push for "preventive" war in Iraq have described a clique of hypermasculine hawks—led by vice president Dick Cheney and secretary of defense Donald Rumsfeld—who effectively silenced dissenting voices inside the White House and bullied opposition voices in the media.

The dynamics of particular peer cultures can determine the reactions of individual bystanders to events around them. Because I do a lot of work with male athletes, people often ask me if there is something about sports—especially contact sports—that fosters aggression toward women. Do these guys have a hard time compartmentalizing the aggression they learn on the fields and courts, and carry it over into their personal relationships? They ask the same thing about men in the military. People wonder how you can be taught to kill the enemy and not have that affect the way you interact with people in your family.

There have been some interesting psychological and anthropological studies of male subcultures that seek answers to these sorts of questions. One fascinating study by James McBride, *War, Battering, and Other Sports*, attempts to explore the psychic terrain that links male aggression in the sports arena and the realm of the personal. This study and others lend credibility to the popular belief that certain aspects of the training for sports or the military fuel men's aggression toward women. But in addition to the violent characteristics of the various activities in which men are engaged (e.g., contact sports, military), it is important to examine how specific social dynamics in men's peer groups support and even encourage controlling or sexually aggressive behaviors. For example, an all-white men's college hockey team in New England and a Latino street gang in Los Angeles have starkly different day-to-day experiences, and they occupy very different social positions. But key elements of their respective group dynamics can nonetheless be strikingly similar, especially the way the masculine status hierarchy rewards violence, the way individual members self-consciously jockey for social position, and the way anxieties about their friends' perceptions shape the way they treat and talk about women.

The vast majority of men are profoundly influenced by both the example and the expectations of the people around them. In fact, the rugged individualist man, the solitary soul who answers to no one but himself, is a myth and a prototype; he is not a real person. The influence of peers is felt both in immediate environments and in quiet moments of reflection, and it is of course both positive and negative. Peer pressure is often characterized in negative terms, but peer influence can also be positive. In fact, some cutting-edge, gender violence prevention initiatives with boys and men, in the U.S. and other parts of the world, focus on creating and rewarding young men who respect girls and who refuse to participate in sexist rituals. This is part of the rationale behind "strength" clubs in high schools and colleges developed by the D.C.-based group Men Can Stop Rape. At the University of Maine in 2005, a group called Male Athletes Against Violence produced a series of posters that feature uniformed football players and slogans like "Join the huddle. Work together to end violence." It is unfair to always accentuate the negatives in male-peer culture without recognizing the bonding and brother-hood that takes place that is not harmful to women. Many men support and look out for each other—rather than simply *cover up* for each other. Some men feel obliged to intervene when they see a friend mistreat his girlfriend or wife, even when they know the conversation is bound to get awkward.

On the other hand, sometimes men feel as if they have to participate in sexist and even violent practices in order to be accepted into the brother-hood. These practices run the spectrum from laughing at sexist jokes to par-ticipating in gang rapes. Thus some men acquiesce even when their heart is not in it, like when a high school student remains silent in the back seat of his friend's car as his buddies shout out sexual comments to girls walking down the street, or a thirty-something professional reluctantly goes out to Hooters after work with a group of his coworkers. Many men simply learn to keep their discomfort to themselves. As the sociologist Sharon Bird argues in a 1996 article in the journal *Gender and Society*, emotional detachment, competitiveness, and the sexual objectification of women are often the crite-ria by which men judge each other. When men do not "measure up" in those terms—and many do not—they often keep their objections to themselves so as not to threaten their standing in the group.

There is a clear and disturbing illustration of this phenomenon in Nathan McCall's gutsy memoir, *Makes Me Wanna Holler* (1994), where he tells an unusually self-implicating and chilling story of his participation in a gang rape when he was a teenager in the 1960s.

"Vanessa was thirteen years old and very naïve. She thought she had gone to [an older male friend's house] just to talk with somebody she had a crush on. A bunch of the fellas hid in closets and under beds. When she stepped inside and sat down, they sprang from their hiding places and blocked the door so that she couldn't leave. When I got there, two or three dudes were in the back room, trying to persuade her to give it up . . . Some had never even had sex before, yet they were trying to act like they knew what to do. I front-ed, too. I acted like I was eager to get on Vanessa, because that's how everyone else was acting . . . She seemed in a daze, like she couldn't believe what was happening to her. . . . She looked so sad that I started to feel sorry for her.

Something in me wanted to reach out and do what I knew was right . . . But it was too late. This was our first train together as a group. All the fellas were there and everybody was eager to show everybody else how cool and worldly he was . . . If I jumped in on Vanessa's behalf, they would accuse me of falling in love . . . Everybody would be talking at the basketball court about how I'd caved in and got soft for a bitch. There was no way I was going to put that pressure on myself . . . After a few miserable minutes, I got up and signaled for the next man to take his turn."

Toward the end of the book, the middle-aged McCall recounts a conversation he had in the early 1990s with his teenage son about girls, sex, and consent. He could see that his son was heavily influenced by the macho pulls of his peer culture, and he wrestled with the question of how he could tell him not to do the things he had done. "I told him about the things we did to girls while growing up," he wrote, "and explained to him how much I regretted it now."

I have never been a party to an overt act of violence against a woman, either alone or in a group of men. But I have played various bystander roles in sexist male culture. In fact, much of what I know about male-peer cultures—good and bad—I have learned from personal experience. I grew up in a predominantly white, blue-collar and middle-class suburban community in the late 1970s with a firmly entrenched male jockocracy in which I played a central role. Football ruled in my hometown, then as now, and I was an accomplished high school football player and three-sport varsity athlete. In college and over the past couple of decades I have put in many thousands of hours as a participant-observer doing informal research on intra-male interaction on basketball courts, in locker rooms, in bars of (nearly) every stripe, and in countless workplaces and social organizations. Thus my own intimate knowledge of the power of peer cultures in masculine socialization informs my work as an educator. In 1993, I conceived and cocreated the Mentors in Violence Prevention (MVP) program at Northeastern University's Center for the Study of Sport in Society. The initial purpose of the program was to encourage high-status high school and college male student athletes to speak out on issues like rape, battering, teen-relationship violence, and sexual harassment. The idea was for their example to make it more socially acceptable for less popular men to speak out. The eventual goal was to foster a climate in male-peer culture whereby some men's abusive behavior toward women would be seen by other men as socially unacceptable. While the main focus was on gender violence, MVP also addressed gay-bashing and the harassment of lesbians with the same goal: to create a climate among men where such abusive behavior was seen as intolerable. The MVP model has been well-received in the male athletic subculture and the military because, while the stated goal is to reduce gender violence, the all-male, or nearly all-male, MVP sessions also give men an opportunity to talk about some of the dynamics of their interpersonal and group interaction in a safe space. These are subjects that most men in hypermasculine, hypercompetitive environments would otherwise never dare discuss. In MVP sessions, many men share personal anecdotes about women close to them who have been assaulted. Some talk about their experiences dealing with men they know who have abused women. But a significant portion of the discussion focuses on the roles and responsibilities of men as they are positioned in groups. One of the questions that arises frequently involves the nature of men's responsibilities to their friends, teammates, classmates, and coworkers. Why do some men interrupt other men's sexist behaviors, while others join in or maintain a detached stance?

POLICING MECHANISMS IN MALE-PEER CULTURE
One of the key reasons that few men have been a part of the movements to end domestic and sexual violence is rooted in the concrete dynamics of male-peer culture. Men are silent about these issues because other men keep them silent. They do not want other men to challenge their sexism, so they send off a clear message to "stay out of my business." There are also a number of internal "policing mechanisms" in male culture that are enacted by men, whether or not their conscious intent is to silence each other. The two most important of these policing mechanisms are: (1) Challenges to the manhood of men who speak out about sexism; and (2) Hostile questioning of their heterosexuality. When I ask men to recount terms they have heard—or used themselves—to describe men who vocally support gender justice or challenge other men's sexism, they typically rattle off a number of insults: *wimp, wuss, pussy-whipped, mama's boy, soft, liberal.* The implication is clear: A man who speaks out on these subjects is not a real man. He is weak. He is feminine. It also implies that since he's like a woman he is therefore "less than" a man. (Which is also an insult to women.) In addition to these characteristics, the group nearly always comments about this man's sexual orientation. He's "probably gay." "A fag." "A homosexual." Occasionally they will say he's "an ally," or a "strong man," but these are the exceptions. For substantial numbers of men, men who challenge other men's sexism are not "real men," and they are consequently quite possibly gay. Neither of these assumptions stands up to logical scrutiny. But this hardly matters, because relatively few men ever discuss these tenets of

traditional masculine doctrine in rational terms. I will try to do that here.

Real men don't speak out about sexism

There is a widespread if unexamined assumption in the dominant male culture that men who publicly take the "women's side" in the "battle between the sexes" must not be particularly strong men. But upon close inspection this assumption falls on its face. Consider this: If you are a guy, being "one of the guys" is easy. It does not take anything special. You simply go along to get along. You try your best to fit in with the group. You learn early in life to make it your business to understand the dominant gender ideology of the group, and you conform to it. This process starts in kindergarten and elementary school, when you first learn what William Pollack termed the "boy code." As you progress through adolescence and young adulthood, you continue to pick up cues about what your fellow men expect. If men around you objectify women, tell sexist jokes, frequent strip clubs, and talk about women as if they are on the earth to serve men in the kitchen and the bedroom, if you agree you might join in, and if you disagree you might keep your views to yourself. Either way, it takes nothing special to be "one of the guys." On the other hand, if you are uncomfortable with the sexist attitudes or behaviors of your fellow boys or men, you have to be fairly secure and self-confident to express your opinion. It can be very difficult to challenge other men's sexism, especially in group situations in school, on teams, in fraternities, or in male-dominated workplaces. You have to be willing to risk awkward interactions and even social ostracism.

One thirty-something man I know was faced with a typical dilemma at a bachelor party for one of his friends. The party was held at someone's apartment. There were about twenty men there, all middle-class professionals of one type or another. At some point in the night, a couple of the men arranged to have a stripper come to the apartment. As stripping culture has gone increasingly mainstream, it has become routine practice for men to hire strippers to entertain at private bachelor parties. In large portions of the country this is practically a pre-wedding ritual. Nonetheless, some men are uncomfortable with stripping due to their traditionalist sexual morality or conservative religious beliefs. Other men know that their wives or girlfriends disapprove of the practice and don't want to risk their anger. There are also men who do not frequent strip clubs or welcome strippers at bachelor parties because they find the practice itself to be sexist and degrading—for the men as much as for the woman who is taking her clothes off.

That was the particular nature of this man's dilemma at his friend's party. Unlike some self-described "sex-positive" advocates—both men and women—who see strip culture as innocuous and even sexually liberating for women, he was under no illusions about the deep sexism at work. He is far from a prude, but he knew that many of his fellow party goers had condescending and even contemptuous feelings toward a woman who would show up at a party to strip naked in front of them, and give blow-jobs to guys in the back room. They might enjoy the show and get off on the oral sex, but they had no respect for her. In a *perfect* world, perhaps men would regard a stripper or a prostitute as a woman with a good body who had chosen a simple way to make some quick money. But in *this* world, a lot of guys believe that strippers and prostitutes are "skanky hoes who don't respect themselves, so why should we respect them?"

Some of the men were drunk. *Would the woman be safe?* this man wondered. Private party strippers are often accompanied by male "bodyguards," who are more than likely to be their pimps, but in this case her companion was another woman. They were Latinas; neither of them appeared to speak English. The situation was potentially dangerous. My friend wasn't sure what to do. Should he approach the best man and the other organizers and object to the plan? Should he make it clear to his friends why he did not approve and then leave as a form of protest? How could he balance his desire to be with the guys to celebrate his friend's upcoming wedding with his concern for the women and his own need to dissociate himself from this type of sexist ritual? In the end, he left the party shortly after the stripper arrived; but he did not make any sort of public scene. He just slipped out the door in a kind of silent protest. When he told me this story he was apologetic, as if he had somehow failed to live up to his image of himself as a man who had the courage of his convictions.

Let's return to the popular assumption that men who are uncomfortable with sexism are less than fully masculine. This assumption is in conflict with the long-standing belief in patriarchal culture that it is more "manly" to take a stand for what is right than to blindly follow the majority. Is my friend a wimp because he refused to take part in a sexist event? Because in a sense he refused to be a follower? It is sadly ironic that men who decline to participate in sexist practices—or who muster the courage to confront other men—are called wimps, when they actually have to be stronger than the men who belittle them.

He must be gay

Men who challenge other men's sexism are sure to face questions about their heterosexuality. I hear those questions all the time. Just recently I was told by a man that when he informed a colleague that he was planning to attend one of my trainings, the first thing she said was "Is he gay?" After a speech I gave about men's violence against women at a college in the Midwest, a man raised his hand and said sheepishly, "Please don't take this the wrong way, but I notice you speak with a slight lisp. Do you think people might get the impression that you're gay?" The question caught me a little off guard. Was he trying to mask his own curiosity by referencing other people's impressions? Rather than come right out and say I was heterosexual, I decided to evade the question and at the same time question his premise. As I had been thinking about how to respond, I had noticed that the man's legs were crossed knee to knee. "I noticed that you cross your legs like a woman," I said with no hint (I think) of the sarcasm I was feeling. "Do you think people might get the impression that you are gay?" He did not respond.

An incident one night in 1990 provided me with an entirely new perspective on the stereotype that anti-sexist men must be gay. It was during a protest that I helped organize about an appearance by the misogynist comedian Andrew "Dice" Clay at the Centrum in Worcester, Massachusetts. Dice Clay at the time was a phenomenally successful comic at the height of his popularity. Verbally abusive talk radio "shock jocks" have proliferated since the early 1990s, along with misogynistic rappers like Eminem and Snoop Dogg, so Dice Clay's brand of attack humor has lost some of its shock value. But at the time he made quite a splash with his comic persona as a tough, blue-collar white guy from Brooklyn, who wears a black leather jacket, smokes cigarettes, and verbally attacks women in the angriest and crudest sexual language imaginable. His comedy CDs are still available in most record stores and online, and to this day he regularly performs in Las Vegas casinos. For people who are unfamiliar with his work, Dice Clay draws laughs from his largely (but not exclusively) male audience not so much because of the depth of his comedic insights, but because he dares to express some of men's basest misogynistic impulses. His routines are filled with references to "sluts" and "dish-rag whores" who he regularly "bangs" and tells to "shut the fuck up." In one of his signature comedic bits he takes classic nursery rhymes and changes the words:

Hickory dickory dock
Your wife was sucking my cock
The clock struck two
I dropped my goo
I kicked the bitch down the fucking block.

The purpose of the peaceful protest was not to deny Dice Clay his First Amendment right to commit offensive speech; it was to call attention to the connection between attitudes shaped in popular culture and the ongoing crisis of domestic and sexual violence. Men are not born genetically programmed to assault women; most abusive behavior is learned. If it is learned, it is also taught, and one key area where abusive masculinity is taught is the popular culture. As activists, we wanted to turn the media spotlight away from the entertainment focus ("Shock comedian pushes the envelope") and expose the political nature of an Andrew "Dice" Clay show. What was political about this comedy show? Consider this: At the time, battered women's programs in Massachusetts had to turn away thousands of women and children each year due to a shortage of shelter space. And yet here was a comedian who was set to make hundreds of thousands of dollars for an act where he verbally assaulted and sexually degraded women in front of thousands of cheering men at the sold-out Centrum two nights in a row. At the very least the protest would call attention to the skewed value system in our "free" society.

As we carried our homemade picket signs outside the arena, some of the young men on their way into the show shouted and taunted us. Some were clearly drunk. "Fucking fags!" "Fucking homos!" are among the more articulate epithets I can recall. After I heard that screamed for the umpteenth time, I finally realized its significance. Those guys were saying, in essence, that because we care about women, we must want to have sex with men. At one point I was holding a sign that read, "Love women, don't hate them." It was a rather prosaic slogan. A man walking into the concert saw my sign and stopped about ten steps away. He made a contemptuous face at me and shouted, "I hate women, you faggot!" It was an unintentionally revealing pronouncement. What does it mean that large numbers of people—men and women—question a man's heterosexuality if he is overly concerned about men's violence against women? Most importantly, what does it say about their expectations of heterosexual men? If a man has to be gay to care about women, then *heterosexual* men must not care about women. At the very least, this sends a powerful message to homophobic heterosexual men that they better not publicly admit their concern. Homophobia thus plays a powerful role in keeping heterosexual men from challenging male power and privilege. This will continue as long as homosexuality is stigmatized, and as long as being gay puts men at risk of violence from other men. Many insecure men will predictably conclude that it is better to suffer other men's sexist treatment of women in silence than to run the risk of having someone think they might be gay.

CHAPTER EIGHT

Race and Culture

———— ❖ ❖ ❖ ————————————

"...Racism turns our attention away from real exploitation and danger...by creating myths about family violence and sexual assault. We are taught that men of color and men from other cultures are dangerous. We have stereotypes about rapists being dark (i.e., black) strangers in alleys, about Asian men being devious and dishonest, about Latinos being physically and sexually dangerous. Racism has produced myths about every group of non-white, non-mainstream men being dangerous to white women and children."
—Paul Kivel, *Uprooting Racism*

"The sexist, misogynist, patriarchal ways of thinking and behaving that are glorified in gangsta rap are a reflection of the prevailing values in our society."
—bell hooks

On October 3, 1995, I boarded a plane at the St. Louis airport just a few minutes before the jury was set to deliver its verdict in the O. J. Simpson double murder trial. Like millions of Americans, in their homes, workplaces, and in public spaces, I had been glued to CNN waiting to hear how the latest "trial of the century" would end. A few minutes after takeoff, the pilot came on the PA system. "I bet you're curious about the verdict in the O. J. Simpson trial," he said with a hint of a smirk. "Let me do this. If the verdict is guilty, I'll bank the plane to the left. If he was acquitted, I'll bank it to the right." Intrigued by this creative gesture, we waited for a few tense moments or until all doubt was removed as the TWA jet leaned gently to the right. As the plane tipped, the passengers let out a collective gasp, which quickly turned into expressions of disbelief and anger. Needless to say, most people on board were white.

From the first moments of the infamous white Bronco chase more than a year before, the O. J. Simpson case forced questions of race to the forefront of our national dialogue about gender violence. It was not the first criminal case to do this, but because the alleged murderer was an African American man who had already achieved the status of a cultural icon, and because it took place on the cusp of a dramatic proliferation of 24/7 cable television coverage, it was by far the most culturally consequential.

I have no desire to revisit the specific questions raised by the case about racism within the LAPD, whether Simpson's "dream team" of lawyers simply overpowered the prosecutors, or whether a predominantly black jury chose to deliver a not-guilty verdict to send a statement above and beyond Simpson's guilt or innocence. But I do want to discuss what I learned from the case about the volatile intersection between race and gender, and the manner in which that relationship shapes the national conversation about gender violence.

When I first started giving public lectures about men's violence against women in the late 1980s, I rarely said anything about race beyond the obligatory statement that crimes like rape and domestic violence cut across all the social categories of race, ethnicity, and socioeconomic status. I paid close attention to ongoing intellectual debates about race and gender, and I was certainly familiar with the work of black feminists like Alice Walker, Michelle Wallace, Audre Lord, and bell hooks. I knew the subject was crucially important, but also complex and potentially incendiary, and at the time I doubted my ability to say anything particularly insightful about it. Moreover, because I had already taken on the delicate task of challenging my own and other men's sexism, I worried that in trying to navigate the subjects of sexism and racism simultaneously, I might stumble and inadvertently make an offensive statement. Why take the chance of mishandling a sensitive subject like race and risk diverting my focus away from gender violence? Occasionally this presented a problem, such as when a man— usually but not always African American—forced the issue by yelling out, "Tyson was railroaded!" when I dared broach the subject of male athletes who assault women. Still, I maintained this cautious approach for a few years, until one day, after one of my talks at a large East Coast university, a black female professor approached me and took me aside.

"I noticed that you didn't talk about racial matters in your presentation," she said. "What you are doing is very important, but I think it would be more effective if you said something about race and racial difference so at the very least, people of color—and white people—could trust that you know there are important racialized dimensions to this issue, even if you are not going to focus on them."

She was right, of course. I immediately began to question my cautious strategy. How could I presume to do justice to the huge and multifaceted problem of men's violence against women without acknowledging—at a minimum—some of the ways that race, ethnicity, and culture are involved? I knew, for example, that many African American women in abusive relationships are reluctant to call 911 because they know that black men—especially poor black men—are more likely than whites to receive harsh and often unfair treatment from police and the courts, not to mention the fact that a criminal record would further endanger their already bleak chances for gainful employment. I knew that in certain immigrant communities there is still intense pressure on women to stay in abusive marriages and work things out. Thus how could I talk about efforts to hold batterers criminally accountable for their behavior and not talk about the dramatic difference in perspective between people in a typical white middle-class suburb, who generally trust the criminal justice system, and people in ethnically diverse, poor, and working-class city neighborhoods, who generally do not? It was clear that as a white man I had to address more thoughtfully the unique racial and cultural experiences of women and men of color.

It took me longer to realize that in other ways I *had* been talking about race and culture all along. Every time I said "our culture" teaches boys that being a man means being in control—both of ourselves and others, including women—I was talking about the dominant *white* culture. Because whiteness is the "norm" against which other races/ethnicities are measured, many white people do not even see themselves as having a racial identity, or belonging to a racial/ethnic group with its own set of characteristics. That is one of the most subtle ways that social privilege functions: by remaining invisible. Whenever there is a well-publicized domestic violence incident involving a man of color, it is fair to predict that many whites will casually observe that it is "something about *their* culture" that causes men of color to abuse "their" women. Fernando Mederos, a leader in the batterer intervention movement who has long advocated for culturally competent services and approaches to men who batter, says there is a universal tendency to think that "Our batterers are deviant, theirs are in their cultural mainstream." For example, when was the last time you heard someone say, "It's a white thing" about a white man who was arrested for beating his wife?

During the thousands of hours of TV commentary and debate about Scott Peterson's murder of his pregnant wife, Laci, in 2004, did anyone ever suggest that one of the root causes of the crime might be racial, because *white* men in our society are socialized to view women as disposable objects? On the endless cable news shows and talk radio programs that made fat profits off the case, was there any discussion about the pervasive misogyny of a culture—*our* culture—that produces the likes of Scott Peterson? I must have heard Peterson referred to dozens of times as a cad and a pathological liar. But you would have been hard-pressed to hear Peterson described as a product of a deeply sexist white culture in mainstream media. When white men assault women, it is far less threatening to attribute their behavior to moral failings, or *individual* demons like bad childhood experiences or alcoholism. As a result, white men's violence tends to be examined on a case-by-case basis. Or as the anti-racist educator Tim Wise writes, "When Charles Manson, John Wayne Gacy, Ted Bundy, and Jeffrey Dahmer go out and do their thing, no one thinks to ask what it is about white folks that makes them cut babies out of their mothers' wombs, torture young men and bury them under the house, kill two dozen or more women for the hell of it, or consume human flesh…You say 90 percent of modern serial killers have been white? Well, isn't that puzzling. Next question." By contrast, when African American or Latino men assault women, many white people feel free to make sweeping judgments about their entire racial or ethnic group. The sinister influences of "race" and "culture" are only invoked when the perps are men of color.

The long-standing racist stereotype of black and Latino men as thuggish brutes and sexual predators does incalculable damage to people of color. The image of the dark-skinned man as a threat to white women—and a threat to social order more generally—has been used for centuries by whites to justify all manner of racist social controls. One of the fundamental beliefs under-pinning white European colonialism since the fifteenth century was the racist idea that indigenous peoples throughout Africa, Asia, and North, Central, and South America were "savages" whose violent impulses had to be contained and controlled. Two relatively recent manifestations of those beliefs were the white vigilante practice of lynching African American men in the late nineteenth and early twentieth centuries, and the dramatic overrep-resentation of black and Latino men in prison today. Since the 1960s, conserva-tive white politicians have exploited white fears—of black men especially—with "tough on crime" rhetoric and mandatory sentencing laws, resulting in the incarceration of hundreds of thousands of African American men (most of whom are convicted of non-violent drug offenses).

But the caricature of men of color as violent beasts does more than sim-ply justify racist social or economic policies. Shifting responsibility for vio-lence against women onto the racialized other also keeps the critical spotlight off of white men. Even though FBI statistics clearly indicate that most men who assault women attack those within their own racial or ethnic group, a culturally prevalent message to white women says otherwise. White girls learn from an early age that it is not their own white boyfriends and husbands who present the greatest risk to their safety. The real danger lurks with dark-skinned predators. In spite of decades of multicultural education and consciousness-raising, many white women continue to take this message to heart. Whenever I ask a roomful of (mostly white) college-age women what steps they routinely take to protect themselves against sexual assault, one of their first answers is always "stay away from 'certain' neighborhoods." In his book *Uprooting Racism*, Paul Kivel calls this the "geography of fear," where whites are taught to dread the "inner city," a code word for where African Americans and/or Latinos live. In the hundreds of times I have done this exercise, relatively few women have said they are careful around the white men they hang around with or date—even though statistically those men are much more likely to physically or sexually abuse them. Thus racism plays another of its many functions in our society. When white women focus their self-defense strategies against "external enemies," they are less likely to see—much less do something about—threats from white men that are much closer to home.

The racist but enduring image of black males as violent animals also provides the promise of a built-in alibi for white criminals. A recurring script line on HBO's *The Sopranos* plays on this theme, as white Italian gangsters regularly break the law or double-cross each other, secure in the knowledge that if they are caught, they can always "blame it on the black guy." In one memorable scene, the show's central character, Tony Soprano, the patriarch of a New Jersey mafia family, tearily confesses to his female therapist that he failed to show up and assist his cousin during a planned robbery many years before because he had suffered a panic attack after an argument with his mother. The robbery was botched and the cousin was sentenced to a long prison term. Until that session with his therapist, the violent alpha male, Tony, had never shared the truth with anyone, instead maintaining the socially acceptable cover story that he had been jumped by "a couple of [blacks]."

In 2004, tens of millions of Americans followed the Scott Peterson case, which audiences soaked up as a true crime reality show—replete with betrayed mistresses, clandestinely taped conversations, and tearful courtroom testimonies. The narrative heart of the story was that a white man murdered his pregnant wife and then for weeks successfully deceived his family and friends about what happened. But fifteen years before anyone had heard of Laci and Scott Peterson, another high-profile white domestic homicide riveted the nation. The 1989 murder in Boston of Carol DiMaiti Stuart by her husband

Charles Stuart sent shock waves through white middle-class America. Like the Peterson case, the Stuart case featured a seemingly upstanding white man who had murdered his popular, attractive, pregnant white wife, exposing the hypocrisy of the white middle-class conceit that this kind of thing couldn't happen to "people like us." The two infamous cases had many characteristics in common, but as cultural spectacles there was one big difference. In the Peterson case, both the victim and defendant were white, hence there was no overt or hushed discussion of "race" as a contributing factor. But in the Charles Stuart murder race played a major role. In fact, the alibi that Charles Stuart offered for the murder of his wife provides a textbook illustration of how the demonization of black men can divert attention away from white men's responsibility for violence against women.

The basic facts of the Stuart murder are as follows: On October 23, 1989, Charles Stuart, a thirty-year-old white fur-store manager, fatally shot his pregnant thirty-year-old wife Carol DiMaiti Stuart, a lawyer, in the head as they sat in his car near the Boston hospital where they had just attended a childbirthing class. He then turned the gun on himself, causing a serious wound to his stomach. What came next set the stage for a full-blown racial upheaval. With his car phone Stuart called 911 to report that a black man in a sweat suit had shot him and his wife in a robbery attempt. He was in excruciating pain and his wife was dying next to him in the front seat. By coincidence, the national TV show *911* had a crew in town, and they were able to rush to the scene and provide rare footage of the wounded, bleeding man being loaded into an ambulance. Stuart's chilling call to the dispatcher was also played endlessly on national TV and radio, generating enormous sympathy for him, along with outrage at this brutal and senseless tragedy that had befallen the "perfect couple." Their tragic mistake, it appeared, was venturing into a largely black section of the Mission Hill neighborhood.

While Charles Stuart lay recovering in his hospital bed and expressions of sympathy for the supposedly grieving husband/father poured in, local and national media coverage emphasized the "racially motivated" slaying. Meanwhile, in response to Stuart's description of the black suspect, and under the pressure of national media attention, Boston police began to aggressively stop and search black men on the streets and in housing projects, with little or no probable cause. In a city with an ugly history of white racism and often tense relations between the police and communities of color, the police tactics sparked widespread anger and outrage, and resulted in a series of emotionally charged public meetings and high-profile and angry press conferences by black leaders. A couple of weeks after the shooting, Boston police arrested a black man from Mission Hill with a long criminal record on an unrelated charge. But word spread quickly that he would soon be charged with the murder of Carol DiMaiti Stuart. On January 4, the next bombshell dropped. Charles Stuart jumped off the Tobin Bridge to his death in the Mystic River, an apparent suicide. It was widely believed that he killed himself after learning that his younger brother planned to go to the authorities and confess that he had been an unwitting accessory to the murder of his brother's pregnant wife. The city and much of New England was in shock at the brazenness of Charles Stuart's betrayal—both of his wife and of the many people in the region (not all of them white) who had grieved with him and offered their support and prayers in neighborly solidarity.

Almost immediately there ensued a long round of recriminations and introspection, as white-dominated institutions from law enforcement to city government to the media were accused—and defended themselves against—charges of institutional bias and racism. The questions lingered: why were so many people so quick to believe Charles Stuart's story of a black murderer? No doubt his (presumably) self-inflicted wound enhanced his credibility. Still, when a woman is murdered, her husband is usually the first person to come under suspicion. That assumption seems to have been suspended in this case. If Charles Stuart had killed his wife and concocted a different alibi, would he have been so readily embraced by the white community?

Carol DiMaiti Stuart was probably the most prominent domestic violence murder victim in the U.S. in 1989. But in part as a result of the skill displayed by Charles Stuart in staging an alibi for himself that capitalized on the dominant white culture's willingness to believe the worst about black men, very little commentary in the case related to domestic violence or its causes. In fact, the cover story in *Time* magazine that ran on January 22, 1990, with a picture of Charles Stuart at the crime scene, was titled "A Murder in Boston: How a bizarre case inflamed racial tensions and raised troubling questions about politicians, the police, and the press." The headline writers did not even bother to mention domestic violence. The troubling questions the case raised about (white) men's violence against women were relegated to the status of an afterthought.

As we will see, the racial subtext—however important in and of itself—often serves this diversionary function.

ATHLETES, RACE, AND GENDER VIOLENCE

When people talk about the bad behavior of male athletes—including their mistreatment of women—they might actually be talking in a coded way about the bad behavior of black men. There is certainly a lot of evidence for this. The list of names that typically rolls off white people's tongues is revealing:

O. J. Simpson, Mike Tyson, Kobe Bryant. I suspect that most whites would not consciously want to single out black male athletes as violent misogynists. But running down a list of perps that consists exclusively of black male athletes does reinforce the racist idea that the problem is less about the privileged position of men in a sexist athletic world and more about the racial identity of those men.

It is true that a number of high-profile black male athletes over the past ten or fifteen years have been charged with or convicted of serious crimes of domestic or sexual violence. There is no excuse for their behavior or justification for their crimes. But it is also true that countless white athletes and coaches, including a number of high-profile professional athletes and coaches, have been charged with or convicted of similar crimes. (A Google search with the words "coaches" and "sexual abuse" yields close to two hundred fifty thousand references.) Consider a few of the more prominent cases. Mark Chmura, a married, thirty-two-year-old former all-pro tight end for the Green Bay Packers, was tried in 2001 for sexually assaulting a seventeen-year-old girl who was in a group of teens he had been drinking and hot-tubbing with at a house party after their high school prom. He was acquitted. Bobby Cox, the iconic manager of the Atlanta Braves and one of the winningest coaches in baseball history, was jailed briefly in 1995 on charges of simple battery for assaulting his wife. Patrick Roy, a Canadian who is one of the all-time great professional hockey goalies, was arrested in 2000 and charged with domestic violence after a heated argument with his wife. The charges were eventually dropped. All of these white men are high-profile figures in the professional athletic world, and they have all been linked to questionable incidents involving alleged violence against women. But how often do their names roll off the tongues of people decrying the abysmal gender-violence record of today's athletes?

It is true that mega-stars like Simpson, Tyson, and Bryant are such household names that their transgressions are bound to attract more attention. But that still does not adequately explain why media coverage seems to increase when black males are the alleged perpetrators, and why parents and others rarely use white examples when they rightly decry the negative role-modeling of successful male athletes who mistreat women. I would suggest that in this regard—as in many others—sports are no different than the rest of society. When an athlete of color commits a rape or another assault against a woman, especially if his body is inscribed with ghetto signifiers such as gold teeth and tattoos, the average suburban white fan can dismiss him as belonging to an alien culture with questionable values. He might play for our team, but he is not really *one of us*. This distancing is particularly easy when a black male athlete is accused of assaulting a white woman. In reality the vast majority of white women who are raped are raped by white men, but a heavily hyped black male threat to white womanhood has deep cultural roots in white imagination in the U.S. Thus when a black athlete is charged with a sex crime—especially against a white woman—it is easy to turn him into the dark-skinned "Other," as *Time* magazine attempted to do symbolically by darkening O. J. Simpson's face on its cover after he was arrested in 1994 for the murders of his wife and her friend. When a white athlete is similarly charged, it is much more difficult because he is one of "our guys." His transgression is felt closer to home by white fans, who then have more invested in minimizing the seriousness of the allegations, or denying them outright. One possible psychological explanation is that these tactics help shield the fans from any possible feelings of guilt by association.

A fascinating and disturbing corollary to this over the past couple of years can be found in the reactions of Los Angeles Laker fans to Kobe Bryant, an African American man, after he was charged with raping a white woman in Eagle, Colorado, in July 2003. During the course of the prosecution—before criminal charges were dropped—Bryant received numerous standing ovations at the Staples Center in Los Angeles. These could only be interpreted as explicit shows of support from the crowd, which was overwhelmingly white. But why were the Laker fans so supportive? Several people I talked with in Los Angeles during this time dismissed the idea of attaching any higher meaning to the phenomenon. It was pure Laker partisanship, they said. They believed Bryant because they wanted to believe him. He was too valuable to the team to risk losing to a long prison sentence. But there were other dynamics at play. For example, is it possible that fans who stood and cheered were unconsciously— or consciously—proclaiming that they were not racist because—unlike so many white people throughout our nation's history—they were willing to give a black rape defendant the benefit of the doubt, even when the alleged victim was white? Is it also possible that white men who asserted Bryant's innocence—when they had no possible way of knowing whether he was guilty or not—in a sense privileged their identification with Bryant as a fellow *man* rather than with the alleged white victim as a fellow *white person*? If so, this would be good news for the future of race relations, as it indicates a willingness on the part of significant numbers of white men to reject the racist role of "defender of white womanhood." (What it might indicate about the willingness of men to unite in cross-racial solidarity against women is significantly less inspiring.) It is also possible that at the time he was charged, many white fans saw Kobe Bryant as a basketball superstar who had transcended any sort of threatening black identification. His most notable physical signature was a smile—not a scowl. He had no criminal record, had never been busted for guns or drugs. He had grown up not in the 'hood, but in Italy. He even spoke Italian. At the time he was charged with rape, he did not have any tattoos. Was it possible that his status as a "good black"—unlike black bad boys such as Allen Iverson or Latrell Sprewell—conferred upon him a kind of honorary white citizenship, where white fans were defensive about him in a way they would be if a white superstar for whom they had long cheered ran the risk of being labeled a sex offender?

I am well aware that some whites have little patience for nuanced discussions about race and racism in any circumstance, much less on a topic as loaded as the perpetration of gender violence. They see it as nothing more than excuse-making, as a way that white "liberals" tend to minimize the crimes of men of color in order to assuage their own guilt. Thus many people—including many anti-racist whites—are hesitant to raise the issue of race unless there is absolutely no way around it. A popular way to sidestep the issue is to claim that the conversation about violence by athletes—and our society's toleration of it—has more to do with celebrity and money than it does with race. In the sports culture, race (along with homosexuality) is an especially sensitive subject; more than one sports commentator has referred to it as "the great unmentionable." What this usually refers to is the hesitancy of people—whites and people of color—to talk *publicly* about race, especially when there has been an allegation of violence involving an African American or Latino athlete. (In private, almost everyone talks about race.) But few people even recognize—much less discuss—a racial angle when an incident involves white athletes as perpetrators.

Men's ice hockey, for example, is a sport where the vast majority of players and fans are white. Over the past decade, a number of professional hockey players have been charged with crimes of violence against women. They include premier NHL players such as Philadelphia Flyers goalie Sean Burke and Los Angeles Kings forward Ziggy Palffy. There have been several cases of white college hockey players who were accused of gang rape. But as Dr. Richard Lapchick, a pioneer in the area of combining sport and civil rights issues, recounts in the *Sports Business Journal*, after an incident of domestic violence involving a football or basketball player, reporters inevitably ask him, "What makes football or basketball players more inclined to abuse women?" He asserts that he has never been asked that sweeping question about hockey or baseball players. There is also the matter of fights during games. In the NFL and NBA, sports leagues with a high percentage of African

American players, fighting on the field is not a frequent occurrence, and usually results in fines and suspensions. But in hockey, where most players are white, fighting between players is not only tolerated, it is actively encouraged. Many fans expect to see "red ice," and they call for it from the stands. Only when a player steps over the line and maims another, as the Vancouver Canucks' Todd Bertuzzi did to the Colorado Avalanche's Steve Moore in March 2004, when he struck him on the head from behind and smashed his face into the ice, do sportswriters and fans talk self-righteously about "senseless" violence and "going too far."

There is plenty of discussion of these issues by sportswriters and commentators, and fans in general. Parents who have sons playing youth hockey often worry about the example being set by players at the highest levels. But race is rarely part of the conversation. When was the last time you heard someone say with contempt that violence in hockey is a reflection of the lack of moral values in the white communities where the players come from? Yet when several black NBA players during a game in Detroit in November of 2004 went into the stands and assaulted fans, league officials wondered aloud about the damage done to the "image of the league." This was widely recognized as a coded way of saying they were concerned that many whites believed the league had been taken over by a bunch of violent black thugs with poor morals, who were setting a bad example for the youth of America. It is hard to avoid the conclusion that the key difference between the two phenomena is that black men are typically held more accountable for their violence than are white men.

GANGSTA RAP AND WHITE MASCULINITY

One day in 2000, I was perusing the merchandise in a hip T-shirt store on Cape Cod, with a largely but not exclusively white clientele, when I started listening to the lyrics of a song I heard booming over the sound system. I literally stopped in my tracks. "Bitches ain't nothing but hoes and tricks." I listened intently for a couple of minutes. I knew that a lot of contemporary rap albums that are produced and distributed by the major record labels contain songs with lyrics that are blatantly cruel and woman-hating, but for some reason when I heard this song its cruelty and callousness hit me especially hard. I was struck by an image of how I would have felt as a Jew if I were in a public place in Munich or Berlin in 1935 and heard a song whose lyrics were as vicious toward Jews as these were toward women. I knew how I would feel: I would be afraid for my life. I looked around at the women and girls in the store. Were they listening? Were they aware of the hostility to their sex—to them—that was blaring out of the stereo speakers? I knew from previous conversations with women that many of them have learned to tune these sounds out, to go into a sort of trance where they are aware of the sexism that surrounds them, but refuse to let it invade their psyche or their spirit. It is a survival strategy in a culture that is overrun with audio and visual displays of women's sexual degradation. I looked at some of the young girls. Had they already learned to avert their ears? I thought about girls I had met who actually defended misogynistic male artists, and downplayed the sexism. Then I looked at the men. How many of them were listening to the lyrics? Were they singing along? I could not tell. I decided to approach the white clerk at the checkout counter and ask him what was playing. "It's 'The Chronic 2001,' Dr. Dre," he answered. I brusquely thanked him for the information and walked away. In retrospect, I wish I had at least asked him to put on something less offensive to women—and men. But I was in no mood for a confrontation. As I left the store, I made a promise to myself that I would find a way, together with a growing movement of people of color and anti-racist whites, to publicly challenge the white-owned record companies, television networks, movie studios, music magazines, and newspapers who profited from this sexist and racist exploitation. I would also find a way to challenge artists—regardless of their race—whose music incited men's violence against women.

Up until that time, I had been hesitant to publicly say anything critical about misogyny in rap music. My reticence was validated each time I heard a middle-aged white person lament the sinister influences of popular culture on children, and then, practically in the same breath, say, "like that rap music the kids listen to." Along with references to professional athletes behaving badly, negative comments about rap music often have a thinly disguised racial subtext. As an anti-racist white person, I did not want to participate in this, so I usually chose to say nothing. If put on the spot, I would acknowledge misogyny in rap, but also point out that there was a lot of misogyny in "white" rock music, and thus it was unfair to single out rap. Not to mention the fact that white men own and run most major record companies, including many that produce, distribute, and make enormous profits from rap music. But in the 1990s, as hip-hop took over the music world and entered the mainstream of entertainment culture, it became more difficult for me to evade questions about the unabashed sexism in many rap lyrics, especially in the hugely popular genre that came to be known as "gangsta rap."

One of my younger African American male colleagues often urged me to critique in my writing and public speaking the retrograde gender and sexual politics of many black rappers. He threw my own argument back at me: since the ongoing American pandemic of men's violence against women is fueled by cultural definitions of manhood that teach boys to deny women's full humanity and instead seek to dominate and control them, pop cultural messages that promulgate that ideology must be challenged—by whites as well as by people of color. His view was that I should speak out regardless of the sensitivity of the racial politics. My colleague is a college-educated anti-rape educator from a working-class family, and a devoted member of the hip-hop generation who had become increasingly despondent about the ascendancy of glorified brutality and black-on-black violence in gangsta rap. Like many other progressives and feminists, he had long been inspired by rappers who used their lyrical and musical skills to articulate rage about police brutality, racial profiling, and the daily indignities visited on poor black and brown people. But songs about smacking bitches and pimpin' hoes? That reeked of misplaced anger and hypermasculine posturing—not to mention the fact that black women already suffer disproportionate rates of domestic and sexual violence. It was also based on a racist caricature of black culture that was being packaged and sold by major corporations for consumption by white suburban consumers. As many black feminists have pointed out, gangsta rap not only demeans black women; it also reinforces the most malignant stereotypes of black men as brutal beasts. In addition, while there was never any doubt that he loved rap music and had an encyclopedic knowledge of its history, my colleague—along with many other blacks who have remained silent to avoid being labeled as "Toms" or "haters"—had become increasingly distressed by the anti-gay animus and vicious attitudes toward women that had made it into the rap mainstream. Prominent black feminist writers and activists, such as bell hooks, had been talking about this for years. Their work had created the space and language to hold black male rap artists accountable for the degrading treatment of women in their music, without blaming them for the pervasive misogyny in the larger culture. But not enough men—either men of color *or* white men—had yet joined that conversation in a meaningful public way.

My own hesitation to jump headlong into the roiling debate about gangsta rap—as it moved from the cultural margins in the early 1990s to become a mass culture art form by the end of the decade—was typical of many white men I knew. How could middle-class white men who grew up in the vanilla suburbs unselfconsciously critique a genre of music that took root in the blighted black neighborhoods of the Bronx and Compton? Especially a genre of music that had been celebrated since its birth for giving voice to marginalized and stigmatized black youth. How could educated, middle-class white guys like me call out misogynistic black male rappers without calling attention to our own privileged social position? We would be accused of "misunderstanding" the music and its context, not appreciating the complexity of the narrative or musical structures, or even of attempting to censor authentic voices from the "underclass." We might also face accusations of hypocrisy in terms of our own musical tastes. In my case, I grew up in the pre-hip-hop generation listening to soul and R&B; but as an adolescent I was also heavily into classic white rock bands like Led Zeppelin, the Rolling Stones, and Aerosmith, all of whom did their share of hypermasculine posturing, and none of whom were known for treating women with great respect. There was also a practical concern. As an educator, how could I have any credibility with young black males—and other young men of color— about subjects like "manhood" and violence against women if they thought I was dissing their beloved music? All of this contributed to a deafening silence about rap from me and many other white men in the fields of rape and domestic violence prevention.

During the 1990s, a number of anti-racist legal theorists and sociologists, building on decades of work by civil rights activists, black and brown scholars and other progressive thinkers, began to gain traction with the idea that "whiteness" is a socially constructed category of power and privilege and not a genetic designation. This insight formed the basis of the fast-growing field of critical white studies. As the scholar Ruth Frankenberg put it in her 1993 book *White Women, Race Matters*, "White people have too often viewed themselves as nonracial or racially neutral, so it is crucial to look at the 'racialness' of white experience." Here I discovered the seeds of a new way to think and talk about gangsta rap. In virtually every public discussion about violence against women in rap—from trainings for battered women's advocates to graduate school seminars—someone mentions that its primary consumers are white suburban males. But few people go one step further and ask why. Why do so many young *white* guys get a charge out of lyrics where male narrators boast about slapping bitches around and smokin' hoes? It is important to look at the misogyny of black male rappers and explore what their lyrics say about them, as well as about the fault lines in black culture, especially in relations between the sexes. But we should not ignore what misogynistic rap's popularity among young white males says about *white* masculinity, and relations between the sexes in white culture. The misogynistic fantasies of black male rappers have clearly struck a chord in white male America. These artists and their record companies figured out years ago that there was a big *white* market for lyrics about men treating women like dirt. If a majority of (white) boys and men were turned off by the contemptuous attitudes toward women expressed in rap and other forms of music, market forces in music production and distribution would long ago have caused the sexism to fade.

So we need to turn our attention to the demand side of the marketing equation. What is going on in contemporary white gender and sexual politics that prepares so many white suburban males to accept such crude expressions of anger and contempt for women? Many women in twenty-first-century rap narratives are derided as two-dimensional objects whose only purpose in life is to be penetrated like blow-up dolls by contemptuous men. What do these angry characterizations tell us about the white boys and men who buy the albums, download the songs, and memorize and sing along to them? It is possible that millions of young white men do not even question the misogyny in rap because they grew up with it and thus it seems normal and unremarkable to them. After all, rap had already become the status quo in music culture before many of them were even born. It is also possible that many of them do not feel any particular anger toward women, but nonetheless take on the misogynistic front in response to pressure on them to act "hard" as a means of gaining respect and establishing their "manhood." Notably, this phenomenon long predates hip-hop culture.

Music journalists and scholars of American culture have addressed the general question about white fascination with, and co-optation of, hip-hop culture. Many contemporary writers have attempted to update Norman Mailer's controversial and widely discussed 1957 essay "The White Negro," where he argues that in a conformist white society, the image of the "Negro" is subversive and countercultural, and hence enormously appealing. But the typical focus of these writers is on the process whereby black ghetto style has been commodified to meet white suburban consumers' need to act cool by parroting the speech and styles of the "niggaz" in the 'hood. In a 1996 essay, Robin D. G. Kelley argues that for many white, middle-class male teenagers, gangsta rap provides an "imaginary alternative to suburban boredom," and the ghetto is a place of "adventure, unbridled violence, and erotic fantasy which these young men consume vicariously and voyeuristically." But however insightful, these sorts of essays rarely discuss the reasons why brutally sexist gender politics appeal to white boys and men. More than thirty years after the modern women's movement transformed the social landscape, increasing opportunities for millions of girls and women *and* catalyzing momentous changes in men's lives, why *do* so many white suburban males relate to the retrograde sexism in much of contemporary rap? Why do so many of them gleefully sing along to lyrics about worthless "bitches" whose sole purpose in life is to manipulate unsuspecting men? Why can they identify with male narrators who seem to derive perverse pleasure from having sex with women and then tossing them aside like pieces of meat? They do seem to be caught in a trap. In order to maintain the hard poses that earn the respect of other gangstas, men have to affect a cool distance and never acknowledge vulnerable emotions like caring, affection, and tenderness. They can certainly never acknowledge their longing for sexual intimacy with women. That is sissy stuff. As the wildly popular rapper 50 Cent raps in his hit song "In Da Club," "I'm into having sex/I ain't into makin' love."

But I suspect that one reason why some men's anger toward women is expressed as sexual degradation is that they feel women possess a fundamental power over men—the power to reject them sexually. Women have long possessed this power, but the explosion in porn culture over the past generation has caused a fundamental change. In today's ubiquitous porn culture, heterosexual boys/men have unprecedented access to girls'/women's bodies. But those bodies are often on a video or computer screen, and those boys/men have to pay for them. Young guys want real girls/women to desire them sexually, and they also long for emotional and physical intimacy.

Because of widespread homophobia, they can rarely get this type of intimacy from other boys/men, and so many of them—young and old—seek to achieve it through sex with women. They also seek from girls a means to validate their heterosexual manhood. When boys/men cannot achieve this intimacy and validation, their unrequited desire can often turn into hostility. (I want you/I hate you for not wanting me.) Putting women down sexually with a catchy back beat is yet another way to hurt them as payback for this and other perceived slights.

It is convenient for white conservatives and others to blame our cultural decline on the sinister influence of black artists (Janet Jackson!). But as bell hooks argued in a 1994 essay entitled "Misogyny, Gangsta Rap, and The Piano," young black male rappers alone should not be forced to take the heat for encouraging the hatred of and violence against women that is a central feature of our male-dominated society. Responsibility for these problems needs to be much more widely shared by men—including powerful white men. In fact, it is quite plausible that the widespread acceptance of misogyny in rap is yet another measure of the virulence of the ongoing societal backlash against feminism, particularly against women's organized efforts to achieve equality with men in the economic, social, and political spheres.

BEYOND BLACK AND WHITE

It should be clear that discussions about men's violence against women in contemporary U.S. society must take into account the complexities of race, ethnicity, and socioeconomic class. This recognition of diversity is particularly important in the design of prevention efforts, as they need to be tailored—whenever possible—to meet the needs of specific communities. Furthermore, it is critical to recognize the racialized dimensions of gender-violence issues in white communities, because without this recognition it is much easier for white people—especially white men in power—to deny these are problems in their communities. But it is also important to acknowledge that the United States is an amazingly heterogeneous society and that racial and ethnic differences far transcend the black-white color line.

We know that men who harass, abuse, and assault women and children frequently have rigid and traditional beliefs about appropriate roles for men and women. This is as true for white men as for any other men. Still, there is a great deal of cultural variation in the expectations of men's and women's behaviors—and in the preferred strategy for responding to abuse. Thus, it is not useful to create "one-size-fits-all" prevention strategies, because what works in one community might not necessarily be appropriate for another. For example, as Fernando Mederos explains, in mainstream European American culture there is a "covert or surreptitious system of male supremacy" that underlies batterers' behavior, whereas in Latino communities the male supremacy might be more overt. This does not mean that Latinos are more violent, only that European Americans might be more invested in concealing their controlling and violent behaviors. Or you might say the violence takes different forms. Unless policy makers, service providers, and educators understand these sorts of dynamics, they will not be in a position to design effective prevention strategies.

It is also not accurate or fair to assume that every subcultural group in our diverse society places the same value on such things as family preservation, or women's sexual freedom. For example, in some Asian American communities, both men and women place a high value on preserving marriages—in some cases even when the husband is abusive. This is also true in parts of the white majority culture. Women who are in abusive marriages in these circumstances want the violence to stop, but they often do not have much support from family or friends for leaving the relationship. Abusive men know this, and can use it as a tool to manipulate and control their wives.

I was introduced to an entirely new (to me) set of cultural issues in 2004 when I went to Hawaii to do a gender violence prevention training in conjunction with Girlfest Hawaii, a racially and ethnically diverse arts/film/cultural happening whose goal is to end violence against women and girls through education and entertainment. Hawaii is a complex society where the indigenous cultures have seen their customs eroded and their land expropriated by the awesome colonial power of the United States, which retains an enormous military presence there, and where patterns of immigration from Japan, China, Korea, the Philippines, and the Pacific Islands have created a unique cultural mix. In preparation for my training, I had several conversations with women organizers in Hawaii as I tried to understand some of the issues I would confront when I got there. I asked about some of the important issues I should be aware of. The women made it clear to me that as a "Haole" man from the mainland who was going to be talking about the relationship between cultural definitions of "manhood" and the pandemic of men's violence against women, it would be important for me to have at least some brief background on Hawaiian culture and politics, as well as the sensitivities involved in having a white man come over and "teach" the locals a new way "to be a man."

For example, if I was going to critique the hypermasculine posturing and violence of not only white men, but indigenous men and other men of color, would I also acknowledge that their masculine identities were formed in part in self-defense, as a response to colonial exploitation and the decimation of native Hawaiian culture? Would I accept some responsibility as a representative of the dominant white culture, and not simply point to problems in how men from other cultures treat their women? The Girlfest organizers never once tried to make excuses for abusive men of color; they were clear that colonized men benefited from sexism even as they suffered from racism. Nor did they ask me to mute my anti-violence message. They did give me a lot to think about, including questions about my own cultural biases and filters. Men who do gender-violence prevention in the twenty-first century—especially white men—have an obligation to approach issues of race, ethnicity, and social change from a more nuanced and culturally sophisticated vantage point than our predecessors. This is sometimes uncomfortable, but it is all part of the social change process. And like previous generations of anti-racist, anti-sexist white men, people of color and feminists are often not only our allies in this work, but also our mentors and guides.

CHAPTER NINE

It Takes a Village to Rape a Woman

"[Ours] is a culture in which sexualized violence, sexual violence, and violence-by-sex are so common that they should be considered normal. Not normal in the sense of healthy or preferred, but an expression of the sexual norms of the culture, not violations of those norms. Rape is illegal, but the sexual ethic that underlies rape is woven into the fabric of the culture."
—Robert Jensen

Feminists developed the concept of a "rape culture" decades ago to describe how men who rape are not simply a handful of "sick" or deviant individuals. They are instead the products of a culture that glorifies and sexualizes male power and dominance, and at the same time glorifies and sexualizes female subservience and submission. Rape must be understood not as an aberration in such a cultural environment but as simply the extreme end on a continuum of behaviors. The controversial aspect of this seemingly commonsense argument is that it implicates tens of millions of men who are not rapists. Most men would rather not think about how they participate in a culture that actively promotes—or at the very least tolerates—sexual violence. Many find offensive the mere suggestion of any sense of shared responsibility.

As a result, the mythic image of the rapist as a masked man who hides in the bushes and waits to leap out and attack women continues to resonate powerfully, because while this image strikes fear in the hearts of millions of women and girls every day, it is also oddly reassuring—for both women *and* men. For women, it means that if they are smart and take the necessary precautions, they will drastically reduce their chances of being assaulted. For men, the image of the crazed rapist diverts the critical spotlight away from them. If the male population is divided into two distinct categories—"good guys" and "rapists"—then men who do not rape can easily distance themselves from the problem. But the reality of sexual violence is much more complex than the mythology. Stranger rapes occur with alarming frequency, and can terrorize an entire populace—especially women. But they constitute only about 20 percent of cases. Most sexual violence happens between people who know each other. On college campuses 90 percent of rape victims know their assailants. The perpetrators can be family members or friends of their victims. They are often "nice guys" whom no one would suspect.

Even more troubling is the fact that rape is an act of sexual aggression that can sometimes bear a remarkable similarity to what may be considered "normal" sexual behavior for men—either in heterosexual or homosexual relations. One study showed that one in twelve men admitted to committing acts that met the legal definition of rape. One study by the American Academy of Pediatrics found that 43 percent of college-aged men conceded to using coercive behavior to have sex (including ignoring a woman's protest, using physical aggression, and forcing intercourse). Thus for men—especially heterosexual men—to acknowledge the depths of the problem would require an unprecedented level of introspection. In a sense they would have to question the entire process by which they had been socialized as men.

Not all rapes are the same. As Katharine Baker explains in a *Harvard Law Review* article about motivational evidence in rape law, rapes are not alike in the eyes of the men who commit them, and they are not alike in the eyes of the jurors and the public who judge them. "All rapes are, in part, about sex and masculinity and domination," she writes. "But some…are predominantly about sex, some…are predominantly about masculinity, and some…are predominantly about domination." Like domestic violence, there is no one-size-fits-all description of this crime. There are many different kinds of force, manipulation, coercion, and degrees of consent. Thus it is important to make distinctions between types of rape and rapists in order to successfully prosecute and prevent the crime. The college senior who gets a naïve first-year student drunk and then pushes past her "no's" to insert his penis in her might not fit the same criminal profile as a man who slips through the window into women's bedrooms and rapes them at knifepoint in their own beds—but they are both rapists.

For the purposes of this discussion, I am going to focus on the majority of men who rape—not on the relatively small number of sociopathic or sadistic rapists. We *do* know something about most men who rape. For example, numerous studies have found that while they tend to be more emotionally constricted than nonagressive men, and are often angry and hostile to women, most of them are psychologically "normal." The psychologist David Lisak points out that the old stereotype of the rapist was derived in part from extensive studies with incarcerated rapists, many of whom committed acts of grievous violence against their victims, who were often strangers. But according to Lisak, research over the past twenty years clearly demonstrates that the vast majority of rapes are perpetrated by what he calls "undetected rapists," and they usually know their victims. Undetected rapists are men who typically behave in stereotypically masculine ways, see sex as conquest, and are hypersensitive to any perceived slight against their manhood. But they are not crazy, and they are not sociopaths. "There is simply no evidence, save the rape itself," Katharine Baker writes in the *Harvard Law Review*, "suggesting that all or even most rapists are objectively depraved." Chillingly, she goes on to say that given the social norms that encourage it, there *is* evidence that rape is "culturally dictated, not culturally deviant."

The purpose of this chapter is to explore the role of media and entertainment culture in the transmission of what we might term "rapist values." If large numbers of men who rape women are "normal" guys who perceive their behavior to be acceptable, it makes sense to examine the source of the social norms that feed those perceptions. Obviously social norms are rooted in a complex web of institutional forces. But one of the central insights of the relatively young discipline of cultural studies is that questions of identity ("Who am I?") and ideology ("How does the world work and how do I fit into it?") are intimately connected to the stories that circulate in a culture and give answers to these deeply human concerns. The cultural theorist Stuart Hall explains that we know ourselves when we see ourselves represented. Identity is in a sense a kind of recognition—we recognize ourselves biographically in the stories we tell about ourselves. In the late twentieth and early twenty-first centuries, the mass media is the most significant institution of representation, and the most powerful teacher and transmitter of cultural values. Thus, if we are interested in the question not only of how thousands of average guys become rapists, but how *millions* of men (and women) develop rape-supportive attitudes, it is important to examine the media culture within which young people understand and construct their identities.

In discussions about the normalization of sexual violence, there are two critical aspects of media culture representation. The first is the image of modern Western femininity and how it has been connected with sexuality in contradictory and dangerous ways. Feminist scholars have shown how girls' and women's bodies have become a kind of "war zone" on which are played out all kinds of conflicts of identity. Our culture relentlessly assaults girls and women with the idea that femininity and sexuality are intertwined: that their bodies and their sexual behavior are the only things that are truly valued and desired by heterosexual men. Young girls especially can internalize this story and become obsessed with their appearance and (hetero)sexuality. Millions of them over the past few generations have responded to pressures to become sexual at younger and younger ages. Because they are socially validated largely through boys' responses to their bodies, girls may find it logical to link "feminine" identity with men's use of their bodies. A 2004 article in the *New York Times Magazine* reported on a new phenomenon in the sexual culture of American teenagers called "friends with benefits." It refers to teenagers "hooking up" and having sex with no expectation of a romantic relationship. However, this is hardly an indication of a growing spirit of sexual freedom for both girls and boys. Many of these "hook ups" feature girls performing oral sex on boys, with no hint that the boys would reciprocate. One school counselor I spoke with in an affluent suburb of New York City told me that several girls were dumbfounded when she asked them if the boys performed oral sex on the girls. The possibility had not even occurred to them. And the double standard is still firmly in place, with girls running the risk of being derided as "sluts" if they misstep or hook-up with the wrong boy, while boys enjoy the status they derive from being a "player." It is a disturbingly short step from this sort of non-egalitarian sexual relationship to outright sexual coercion and rape. As one young woman wrote to a colleague of mine:

"I have been raped twice and have had several other sexual assaults. I was not even fully aware that I had been raped either time until much later. It was so ingrained in my mind, personality, behavior, or whatever that this was how things are in the world. I believed that men had a right to my body and I was supposed to let them."

While the forced choice between "virgin" and "whore" has been around for a long time, in the modern period a new twist has been added: girls now have to be *both* virgin and whore. Along with the cultural imperative that "sexuality is everything" is the equally powerful message that "good girls don't." In popular culture over the past decade, this contradiction was best embodied in the figure of the pop star Britney Spears—highly sexualized in everything from appearance to vocals but nonetheless "saving herself 'til marriage." Girls learn early in life that others—especially boys—expect them to be sexy. But not too sexy. In one study published in the journal *Adolescence* in 1995, male and female adolescents who viewed a vignette of unwanted sexual intercourse accompanied by a photograph of the victim dressed in provocative clothing were more likely to indicate that the victim was responsible for the assailant's behavior, more likely to view the male's behavior as justified, and less likely to judge the act as rape. Young women caught in this Catch-22—where social validation comes from sexuality, but the more sexual you act the more you may be despised and blamed if you are victimized—are constantly negotiating an impossible balance, constantly concerned that admiration may change to contempt. If many girls are confused about appropriate ways to behave sexually, it is in part because the culture itself tells a contradictory story about female sexuality. But this contradictory story is not just about female sexuality—it is also about the power of boys and men to shape how women see themselves.

It is crucial, then, to consider a second part of the pop-culture storyline: the way masculinity is constantly equated with power and entitlement, including power over women and entitlement to their bodies. Individuals need to be held accountable for their actions, but violent individuals must be understood as products of a much larger cultural system. By offering up a steady stream of images of sexually aggressive men, and connecting dominant notions of masculinity with the control of women, the mainstream media and entertainment culture—which includes the enormous pornography industry—play a critical role in constructing violent male sexuality as a cultural norm. And here is the paradox: this very "normality" makes it harder to see just how pervasive the problem is. If heterosexual men are routinely turned on by representations of women in which sexiness is indistinguishable from mistreatment, the equation becomes unremarkable—if not part of sexuality itself. Consider the way Marilyn Monroe's vulnerability has been sexualized to this day, more than four decades after her sad life—which was marked by sexual abuse and emotional trauma—ended in self-destruction at age thirty-six. Sexualizing violence against women has the effect of blinding people to its seriousness, because the focus shifts from personal pain and trauma to the pleasures of erotic portrayals.

Over the past several decades, a developing body of research in the social sciences has demonstrated that repeated exposure to depictions of sexualized violence can have the effect of desensitizing viewers—especially males—to the humanity of female victims. This desensitization begins early in life, and today, due to the proliferation of pornographic images on the Internet, cable TV, and increasingly in mainstream film and television, millions of boys and men are exposed to an unprecedented level of sexualized brutality against women. Repeated images and references to women as "bitches" and "hoes" in rap and rock music and accompanying videos, as "cum-guzzling sluts" on countless web porn sites, as objects of sexual bullying on the *Howard Stern Show*, or as scantily clad objects of contempt on pro wrestling telecasts make men's sexual domination of women seem normal, routine, expected, even humorous. In this light, the routine news accounts of gang rapes and countless other sexual abuses should be seen as part of a normative cultural pattern. Sexual violence, in short, is part of a broader cultural pattern in which masculinity comes to be linked with power and control over women.

In the rest of this chapter I am going to look at rape culture through the lens of four distinct phenomena in mainstream media and entertainment: the rape trial of Kobe Bryant; the career of the white rapper Eminem; the popularity of professional wrestling; and the daily familiarity and influence of certain talk radio hosts. While none of these media phenomena directly *cause* men to rape women, each in their own way contribute to a cultural climate that is conducive to the development of "rapist values" in boys and men.

LAKERS FANS SEND A MESSAGE

There is nothing like the rape trial of a famous athlete to remind us of how far we have yet to come in our understanding of sexual violence. The anti-rape movement has accomplished many things over the past three decades in the areas of legal reform, professional training for police, prosecutors, and judges, and public awareness. Arguably the movement's greatest contribution has been to victim services. In most parts of this country, rape victims today can count on a level of compassionate, professional support that is historically unprecedented—and which still does not exist in many other countries. In spite of these positive changes, however, the explosion of victim-blaming unleashed in the aftermath of the sexual-assault charge against Kobe Bryant came as an unexpected wake-up call to many in the anti-rape movement who had been working for years to establish the seemingly straightforward idea that in rape cases the alleged perpetrator is the one on trial—not the victim. Almost from the moment that Bryant's alleged victim—a nineteen-year-old college student—reported that he had raped her in his hotel room at a mountain resort in Eagle, Colorado, people on sports talk programs and around office water coolers began to impugn her morality and question her mental stability, character, and sexual practices. Instead of focusing attention on the behavior, character, and motive of the basketball superstar who was alleged to have raped her, people asked questions like: *Why did she go up to his room? Didn't she know what to expect?*

Public opinion did not just question the victim; it also actively supported the alleged perpetrator. Consider this sequence of events. When Kobe Bryant appeared on a basketball court in Colorado on January 7, 2004, for a game against the Denver Nuggets, the media focus before and after the event was on the fans' response. How loud would the boos be? Would they distract the Laker star to the point of disrupting his game? Was it possible for the authorities to ensure his safety? The Denver fans did not disappoint. Many at the Pepsi Center booed loudly, not only when he was introduced, but every time he touched the ball. It is not surprising that an athlete in the midst of a criminal trial would receive a chilly reception on the road. Especially when he was alleged to have raped a woman in the local area. But the more revealing aspect of the fan response to the Bryant case occurred at the Staples Center in Los Angeles a couple of weeks before and repeated itself several times in the subsequent months. On December 19, 2003, the Laker superstar arrived late for a home game, coincidentally also against Denver. He was late because earlier in the day he had to appear at a court hearing in Colorado; he flew back on a private jet in time to enter the game early in the second quarter. When Bryant emerged from the locker room and made his way over to the Lakers bench, thousands of cheering people sprang to their feet. A second standing ovation ensued when, a few moments later, Bryant first checked into the game. Yes, the Los Angeles Lakers fans gave an enthusiastic standing ovation to an alleged felony rapist. In a legal sense, Kobe Bryant was entitled to the presumption of innocence, and he was surely entitled to defend himself against the charges in a court of law. It is also quite possible that Lakers fans who cheered for Bryant had no conscious intention of making a profound statement about rape—one way or the other. It was not until months later that he issued a dramatic public apology to his alleged victim, in what amounted to a quasi-confession. The cheering merely communicated their loyalty to a flawed but essentially good man (and a great basketball player) as he faced the toughest test of his young life. But regardless of individual fans' intent, there are many possible ways to interpret the meaning of these communal outpourings of affection toward Bryant. It is important to note that there was not simply polite applause when he was introduced, or a spontaneous eruption of joy when he hit a winning jumper at the buzzer; *he got a standing ovation when he came into the arena.*

Three decades after the birth of the anti-rape movement, what are we to make of this? Is it possible to discern any larger meaning from this highly public display of support for the most famous rape defendant of our time? Was it merely indicative of sports fans' tendency to support home team players, no matter what they might have done? Was this unfortunate episode yet further evidence that entertainment values trump all others? It is tempting to chalk the whole thing up to the perversions of our celebrity-obsessed culture. But Lakers fans who stood and cheered inevitably conveyed something beyond support for the beleaguered Bryant. Let's consider the specific messages they sent to (1) girls and women, including those who have been or will become victims of sexual violence, and (2) boys and men, including those who have been or will become sexual violence perpetrators.

The primary message to girls and women is simple enough: if you have been raped, do not tell anyone. Look at the price you will pay—especially if the perpetrator is popular. People will not believe you. They will actually blame *you* for damaging his reputation. Feminist legal reforms notwithstanding, the cultural deck is still stacked against you. Unless the profile of the alleged perpetrator conforms to the stereotype of the predatory monster—which is almost always a poor man of color or a mentally disturbed white guy—public opinion usually sides with the man. Your sexual history will be put on public display in an effort to smear your reputation. Your motives will be questioned. The bottom line: reporting a sexual assault is not worth it. Live with it. Be smarter next time.

The fans' cheers for Bryant also broadcast the powerful message to millions of boys and men that large numbers of people in our society remain eager to excuse "bad boy" behavior. Obviously Kobe Bryant is a larger-than-life figure who lives in a rarified world of privilege and fame. Nonetheless the statement about which party most people will support when there is a rape allegation registered loud and clear. Unless the alleged perpetrator looks like Freddy Kreuger and the victim is a nun, it is the man who can expect the strongest support. This is not by itself going to cause men to rape women. But men who followed the Kobe Bryant case—including men who have raped and men who have thought about it—could clearly see that once Bryant's defense attorneys turned the spotlight onto the alleged victim, many people were eager to make excuses for the defendant. The not-so-subtle message: if it boils down to a he said/she said battle (which men who are charged with rape often claim it is), we are on your side.

Many fans who jumped up and clapped were undoubtedly convinced that Bryant was innocent of the rape charge against him. In other words, they cheered to show solidarity with their falsely accused hero. But if a significant percentage of Lakers fans in the stands believed Bryant had been unfairly accused, this means they believed the young woman from Eagle was either purposely lying or was so mentally unstable as to lack any credibility. It is important to explore the implications of this point of view. According to the FBI, fewer than one in five rapes are ever reported to law enforcement. One reason for this extremely low percentage is that victims typically fear they will not be believed. Why risk compounding the hurt of the original assault by exposing yourself to angry questions about your motives, embarrassing speculations about your sexual history, and the possible loss of friends who may or may not be supportive? In the extraordinary circumstances of the Bryant case, the woman also had to contend with the fact that her alleged rapist received standing ovations—as she received death threats.

When Bryant's alleged victim—with her mother and father at her side—went down to a police station the morning after the alleged incident and filed a claim that the basketball superstar had forcibly raped her, it is hard to imagine that she could have anticipated the ferocity of the backlash that awaited her. Whether people believed her or not, any reasonable person has to acknowledge that reporting this rape was an incredibly bold act by this young woman. But once she reported the incident, matters were no longer solely in her hands. The decision to prosecute was made by the district attorney. Like any prosecutor, he had to know it is very difficult to win a conviction in a rape case, but he had access to all of the available evidence, and obviously he had confidence in her version of the story. It should also be noted that experienced rape crisis counselors and advocates in Colorado who worked closely with the then nineteen-year-old fully supported her. Did all this mean that Bryant was guilty? No. His guilt or innocence was for a jury to decide, after they had heard all the arguments on both sides and consid-ered all the evidence. But in the meantime, thousands of Lakers fans took it upon themselves to vocally support Kobe and thus, by implication, impugn the integrity of his alleged victim. I wonder how many of the fans that cheered for Kobe Bryant have daughters or sisters. Would they have cheered for him if it was their loved one who said she had been raped by him? And if their loved ones are ever raped (by someone else), what is the chance they will feel safe telling a family member or friend who gave Kobe Bryant a standing "o" as he awaited trial? The even-handed approach would have been to withhold judgment—and applause—until all the facts were in.

At the same time, in order for Lakers fans to cheer for him with a clear conscience, they must have believed his claim that the sex was consensual. On what basis should they have believed him? Because he's got a nice smile? Because they have watched him perform magic on a basketball court, and heard his articulate answers in post-game interviews? Because he had a female attorney? Because the alleged victim went up to his hotel room will-ingly? If a significant number of the cheerers believed that Bryant was prob-ably guilty of rape and yet still found it within themselves to applaud him, then our culture is in even deeper trouble than many people think. A benign way to understand the Staples Center standing ovations is that a majority of fans were not consciously trying to send a message—but they were. They might not have been *trying* to silence rape victims by cheering for an alleged rapist—but that was almost assuredly the effect. They might not have *intended* to assert that they believed the pursuit of another title on the court takes precedence over the pursuit of justice—but that's the message they sent.

EMINEM'S POPULARITY IS A MAJOR SETBACK FOR GIRLS AND WOMEN

A couple of years ago I gave a speech about men's violence against women in a packed high school gymnasium in a town in the Midwest. The twelve hundred restless students in the stands were overwhelmingly white. Toward the end of my speech I decided to take a risk and criticize the superstar white rapper Eminem for the blatant woman-hating in his lyrics. I knew I would risk losing the support of some kids. After all, it was the height of his popularity, and it was safe to assume that many of them were fans of the white boy from the "wrong side of the tracks" in Detroit who had made it big in a hip-hop world previously dominated by African American artists. But I reasoned that as a man giving a speech about men's mistreatment of women, if I could not publicly challenge Eminem's misogyny, who could? There were audible moans and groans and whispered comments in response to my statements, but I still received a nice ovation when I finished. As the students filed out I was approached by at least twenty kids, most of whom were positive and supportive. But one small girl stood out. She waited for several minutes off to the side, an indication that she wanted to talk with me in private. She was shaking when she finally approached me. She introduced herself and told me that she was a junior. Then she told me she had been in an abusive relationship. She thanked me for coming, and she assured me that she had gotten out of the relationship and was getting help. Then she started to cry, and asked for a hug. I fought back a tear as she walked away. Twenty minutes later I was in the faculty lounge upstairs when a teacher walked in. She thanked me and then said that in anticipation of my visit, she had instructed her students to read a critical article I had written about Eminem. She was curious to hear how one particular student reacted to my speech. This student—a huge Eminem fan—had read my article and was furious with me, and had told the class that she was going to call me out for dissing her hero when I came to the school. I asked the teacher for the girl's name. It was the girl who had thanked and hugged me.

I realize that social and political critiques of the work of artists are fraught with peril. Artistic tastes vary widely, and so do people's opinions about the social and political responsibilities of art and artists. For example, many

Americans believe that artists have an obligation only to be true to their artistic vision—not to be concerned with the social consequences of their art. According to this perspective, the expression of unpopular or disturbing ideas through art might make people uncomfortable, but that is not necessarily a bad thing. The purpose of art is not to make people feel good, but to give voice to the widest possible range of human experience and emotion. As the recording artist and feminist Tori Amos explains, "If you're singing songs that are about cutting women up, usually these guys (like Eminem) are tapping into an unconscious male rage that is real, that is existing—they're just able to harness it. So to shut them up isn't the answer . . . they're showing you what's happening in the psyche of a lot of people." I would never say that it is necessary to "shut up" Eminem, but I do believe that it is imperative to explore the implications of his popularity. In fact, I do not think it is possible to talk about rape culture in this era and not talk about the man who has been called the "hip-hop Elvis."

If you followed the entertainment media over the past few years, you would get the impression that Eminem has moved beyond controversy and is now entrenched as a larger-than-life cultural force. He certainly experienced a more rapid and broad-based ascent into the mainstream than any black rappers ever have. But he has not been embraced by everyone. At the same time the white music/entertainment establishment was enthusiastically promoting Eminem as one of the most important artists of his generation, many people in the movements against domestic and sexual violence were appalled and profoundly disheartened. For decades, women and men in the field had maintained that rape and domestic violence thrive in a cultural environment where men's violence is not only tolerated but often encouraged. And then along came a charismatic white artist in a black musical genre whose lyrics consistently ridiculed and degraded women, and took images of homicidal misogyny to a new low: "Put anthrax on your Tampax and slap you til you can't stand." But instead of inspiring an anti-sexism backlash, Eminem's music was heralded by many as a brilliant, boundary-crossing contribution to lyrical performance and comic art. Instead of being condemned for stoking the fire of men's fury against women, the songwriter was lionized as an artistic voice for the ages— while his critics were dismissed as cultural rednecks and yahoos, or worse, opponents of artistic expression and free speech.

For people who are not familiar with Eminem's recordings, a sober reading of his lyrics—unadorned by the catchy tunes and infectious beats—can be an emotionally devastating experience. One college professor I know told me that one of her students in a humanities class read aloud the lyrics to several Eminem songs as part of a class presentation. As she read the words, a number of female students began to cry; several got up and left the room. A number of the men in class looked uncomfortable and chagrined. In any assessment of art, it is important to remember that context matters. Critics who defend or excuse Eminem's misogyny often claim that his detractors do not understand his artistic intent when he gives voice to some of the most graphic homicidal rage against women ever captured on record. For example, in one of his most famous songs, "Kim," Eminem presents a chillingly realistic narrative about a verbal confrontation and throat-slitting murder of his then-wife, who is named Kim in real life:

Don't you get it bitch, no one can hear you?
Now shut the fuck up and get what's coming to you
You were supposed to love me
(Kim choking)
NOW BLEED! BITCH BLEED!
BLEED! BITCH BLEED! BLEED!

It is possible that in this song and many others, Eminem uses his lyrical skills to transport the listener inside the mind of a murderer in a way that enlightens us about misogyny even as it entertains. It is possible, as Eminem's defenders assert, that his music contains multiple layers of meaning and that to take it literally is to miss its rich complexity. It is also possible that the very appeal of Eminem's music depends on widespread acceptance of violence against women as a cultural norm.

Whether you love him or loathe him, Eminem is unquestionably an impressive cultural player. He is a multitalented artist: a wildly inventive rap lyricist, a charismatic performer, and an effective actor (essentially playing a glorified version of himself in the 2002 Hollywood biopic *8 Mile.*). What *is* in question is the nature of Eminem's art and image, and its significance. Obviously his unprecedented mainstream success has much to do with his whiteness, and critiques of Eminem have typically centered on the racial politics of his initial rise to notoriety and then to the heights of pop-cultural fame. But there is another way to understand Eminem's popularity, which is that he has achieved success not *in spite* of his virulent misogyny and homophobic utterances—as many critics allege—but in part *because* of them. Richard Goldstein argued in a brilliant piece in 2002 in the *Village Voice* that many of Eminem's male (and some female) fans take "guilty pleasure" in identifying with the aggressor—especially when the victims are women and gays. As Goldstein explains:

"At its hard core, Eminem's poetics is pornography, and it's accorded the same privileges. Just as we've declared the XXX zone exempt from social thinking, we refuse to subject sexist rap to moral scrutiny. We crave a space free from the demands of equity, especially when it comes to women, whose rise has inspired much more ambivalence than most men are willing to admit. This is especially true in the middle class, where feminism has made its greatest impact. No wonder Eminem is so hot to suburban kids . . . He's as nasty as they wanna be."

Several years ago, Eminem was the target of protest from gay and lesbian activists who objected to his lyrical endorsement of violence against them. Other gays have embraced him in spite of this (most notably, and controversially, Elton John). But Eminem's homophobia is not simply a matter of specific lyrics. Rather, it is central to his constructed crazy/tough white guy image. For all of his vaunted "honesty" and presumed vulnerability, the misanthropically cartoonish "Slim Shady" persona that Marshall Mathers—aka Eminem—hides behind requires (at least publicly) a purging of anything that can be associated with femininity. Hence, you hear from Eminem—and his mentor, Dr. Dre—a steady stream of "bitch-slapping" misogyny peppered with anti-gay invective, all in the service of establishing their "hardness." "Now I don't wanna hit no woman but this chick's got it coming/Someone better get this bitch before she gets kicked in the stomach." The irony, of course, is that this hypermasculine posturing—so contemptuous and dismissive of women—produces its own homoerotic tensions, which then requires Eminem (and other rappers) to verbally demonstrate their heterosexuality by attacking gays. It is an embarrassingly predictable process. The popular hip-hop writer Touré provided further insight in this area in a widely circulated *Washington Post* article in 2004 about the sad state of women in hip-hop: "The love in hip-hop is over men, over love, crew love, brotherly love," he said. "It's very sort of ancient Greek. It really doesn't allow for a lot of room for women. Hip-hop at its essence is boys, not men, but boys talking about what they do for and with boys."

Much of the mainstream cultural commentary about Eminem comes, understandably, from music critics and cultural commentators who write in major newspapers, magazines, and websites. Many of these people were initially critical of the misogyny and homophobia in Eminem's work. It was not uncommon to read strong criticism of this in their reviews of his early albums. But as he grew in popularity, criticism of the gender and sexual politics of his music became more muted. Richard Goldstein pointed out the evolution of *New York Times* critic/columnist Frank Rich's thoughts on Eminem in a November 2002 piece in the *Village Voice*. In 2000, Goldstein observed, Rich described Eminem as "a charismatic white rapper [who] trades in violence, crude sex, and invective roughing up heterosexual women, lesbians, and gay men." In 2001, Goldstein wrote, "Rich pondered whether 'racial crossover in the cultural market makes up for a multitude of misogynistic and homophobic sins.'" By 2002, Goldstein reported, "Rich ended up slamming 'moral scolds' for dissing Em, while confessing, 'I've been fascinated with him ever since I first heard his songs at the inception of his notoriety.'"

There is no doubt that as opinion-makers in the music world increasingly praised Eminem's talent, they made more excuses for his anti-woman lyrics. That is one definition of a rape culture: a society where sophisticated people routinely overlook or rationalize rape-supportive attitudes. In the case of Eminem, it is not just that his misogyny has been tolerated. He has been celebrated and honored in a way few artists ever have. He has won several Grammy awards. He even won an Oscar for best song in 2002, for his anthem, "Lose Yourself," from the *8 Mile* movie soundtrack. Can a society that heaps untold riches and praise on a man whose lyrics routinely brutalize women claim that it is serious about eradicating sexual and domestic violence? Consider this analogy. Could a society that claims to care about racism embrace and honor a white artist who glorified racism? Is it even remotely possible that a white artist who regularly rapped and joked about abusing and killing "niggers," "spics," and "kikes," would win critical acclaim—regardless of how artistically inventive he/she was?

The full stamp of cultural approval of Eminem came when the movie *8 Mile* was released in 2002. The Hollywood mythmakers Brian Grazer, Scott Silver, and Curtis Hanson (*8 Mile*'s producer, screenwriter, and director, respectively) blatantly distorted the rapper's story in pursuit of box office glory. They left out the sexism and the homophobia. People who went to see *8 Mile* who had not heard or read the rapper's lyrics came out of the movie with a newfound appreciation for the talented white kid from a trailer park who had the courage to make something of his life. They were spared any exposure to the downside of Eminem's rise to fame, especially his—and his record company's—decision to attack women and girls in his lyrics with a vengeance that was truly breathtaking.

The cultural "meanings" of Eminem are sure to be the subject of debate for years to come. But so far, the national conversation about Eminem has taken place on the terms of fawning critics, flaks for the record and film industries, and lay prophets of the cultural Zeitgeist, all of whom have been incessantly hyping the bleach-blond rapper for the past several years. Give them credit. They have succeeded wildly—Eminem is now a full-blown cultural phenomenon and global merchandising cash cow. But it is time to expand the terms of debate. It is time to offer some counterbalance to the mythologizing distortions from the PR department of Eminem, Inc. In particular, it is time to consider with eyes wide open some of the potentially horrific effects of this art in a world already filled with misogynistic and violent men.

Eminem's lyrics help desensitize boys and men to the pain and suffering of girls and women

Eminem's fans argue that his raps about mistreating, raping, torturing, and murdering women are not meant to be taken literally. I used to hear this regularly from young men and women when I asked them if they had any problems with the way the artist treated women in his lyrics. "Just because we listen to the music doesn't mean we're gonna go out and harass, rape, and murder women," they said. "We know it's just a song." Thoughtful critics of Eminem do not make the argument that the danger of his lyrics lies in the possibility that some unstable young man will go out and imitate in real life what the artist is rapping about. While possible, this is highly unlikely. (Although rare, it does happen. In December 2005, a twenty-one-year-old Eminem impersonator in London was sentenced to life in prison for beating a twenty-six-year-old woman to death and stuffing her body in a suitcase in a case that was widely reported as "life imitating art.") Rather, one of the most damaging aspects of Eminem's violent misogyny and homophobia is how normal and matter-of-fact this violence comes to seem. Rapping and joking about sex crimes have the effect of desensitizing people to the real pain and trauma suffered by victims and their loved ones. The process of desensitization to violence through repeated exposure in the media has been studied for decades. Among the effects: young men who have watched/listened to excessive amounts of fictionalized portrayals of men's violence against women in mainstream media and pornography have been shown to be more callous toward victims, less likely to believe their accounts of victimization, more willing to believe they were "asking for it," and less likely to intervene in instances of "real-life" violence.

Let us not forget that the culture in which Eminem has become a huge star is in the midst of an ongoing *crisis* of men's violence against women. In the U.S., rates of rape, sexual assault, battering, teen-relationship violence, and stalking have been shockingly high for decades, far exceeding rates in comparable Western societies. Sadly, millions of American girls and women have been assaulted by American boys and men. Thousands of gays each year are bashed and harassed by young men. For these victims, this is not an academic debate about the differences between literalist and satirical art. It hits closer to home.

Girls are encouraged to be attracted to boys and men who don't respect women

What began as a tentative dance with the media has become a passionate embrace. After initially airing "misgivings" about featuring the woman-hating rapper, magazines with predominantly young female readership, like *CosmoGirl* and *Teen People*, now regularly feature "Em" on their covers, posed as a sex symbol, as an object of heterosexual female desire. This is not simply the latest example of the star-making machinery of mass media constructing the "bad boy" as desirable to women. It sends a powerful message to girls: He does not really hate and disrespect you. In fact, he loves you. He is just misunderstood. It is the hip-hop version of *Beauty and the Beast*. You know, underneath that gruff exterior, between the lines of those nasty lyrics, lies a tender heart that has been hurt, a good man who just needs more love and understanding.

This is a myth that battered women have been fed for centuries; that his violence is *her* responsibility, that if only she loved him more, his abuse would stop. This is one of the most damaging myths about batterers, and one of the most alarming features of Eminem's popularity with girls. Remember, Eminem is the same "lovable" rapper who wrote a chillingly realistic song ("Kim") about murdering his then-wife (whose real name is Kim), and putting her body in the trunk of his car, interspersed with loving references to their daughter Hallie (their real-life daughter is named Hallie). This is the same "cute" guy who angrily raps about catching diseases from "hoes": "All these bitches on my dick/That's how dudes be getting sick/That's how dicks be getting drips/Falling victims to this shit/From these bitches on our dicks" ("Drips"). This is the same "sexy" artist who raps: "Spit game, to these hoes, like a soap opera episode/and punch a bitch in the nose, 'til her whole face explodes/There's three things I hate: girls, women, and bitches/I'm that vicious to walk up, and drop-kick midgets." This is the same "adorable" man who constantly unleashes torrents of verbal aggression against women, even though he is so sensitive to the potential wounding power of words that he famously refuses to use the "n-word." Why is it not okay for a white rapper to diss "niggers," but it is okay for a man to express contempt for "bitches" and "hoes?"

His credulous female fans counter: He does not really hate women. How could he? He loves his daughter! For battered women's advocates, this is one of the most frustrating aspects of Eminem's popularity. "He loves his daughter" is one of the most predictable excuses that batterers give in pleading for another chance. The fact is, most batterers are not one-dimensional ogres. Abusive men often love the very women they are abusing. And let us not forget that when Eminem verbally abuses his daughter's mother, by extension he abuses his daughter.

We can gain important insight into one key aspect of the Eminem persona by studying both the behavior of men who batter, and people's responses to them. The man who is being lionized as one of this era's emblematic artists shares many character traits with men who batter. One glaring similarity is the folklore that Mathers has actively constructed about his famously difficult childhood. Narcissistic batterers frequently paint themselves as the true victims. It is *them* we are supposed to feel sorry for—not their victims (or the victims/targets of their lyrical aggression). It is well-known that many of Eminem's fans, male and female, reference his abusive family life to explain and rationalize his rage. But it is not as well-known that batterer-intervention counselors hear this excuse every single day from men who are in court-mandated programs for beating their girlfriends and wives. "I had a tough childhood. I have a right to be angry," or "She was the real aggressor. She pushed my buttons and I just reacted." The counselors' typical answer is, "It is not right or okay that you were abused as a child. You deserve our empathy and support. But you have no right to pass on your pain to other people."

Eminem's popularity with girls sends a dangerous message to boys and men

Boys and young men have long expressed frustration with the fact that girls and young women often *say* they are attracted to nice guys, but end up with the disdainful tough guys who treat them like dirt. When I suggest in my college lectures that men need to find the courage to resist putting on the "tough guise" in order to prove their manhood, I frequently hear from sincere young men who approach me seeking advice. "Women want me to be their friend," they say. "But they want to go out with the alpha males. If I don't act hard I go to bed alone." What can I tell them? What are they supposed to conclude when 53 percent of the *8 Mile* audience on opening weekend was female?

What are men to make of *New York Times* columnist Maureen Dowd when she writes, uncritically, that a "gaggle" of her female baby-boomer friends are "surreptitiously smitten" with a certain thirty-year-old rapper whose lyrics literally drip with contempt for women? What are boys to think of an online poll in *CosmoGirl* magazine in 2001 that found him to be the "sexiest musician"? That girls want to be treated with dignity and respect? Or that the quickest route to popularity with them is to be verbally and emotionally cruel, that "bad boy" posturing is a winning strategy to impress naïve (and self-loathing) girls? Surely most of Eminem's female fans would not want to be sending that message to their male peers—but they are.

People who have listened carefully to Eminem's actual lyrics—not just the hit songs or the sanitized movie soundtrack—know that many self-respecting girls who are conscious about the depths of our culture's sexism are repulsed by Eminem's misogyny and depressed by his popularity. Sadly, many of these girls have been silent, fearing they will be branded as "uncool" because they "don't get" the artist who is supposedly the voice of their generation.

There are women who like Eminem because (they say) he is complex and not easily knowable; they would argue that it is dismissive to characterize his art as sexist. But the burden is on them to demonstrate how—in a culture where so many men sexually harass, rape, and batter women—it is possible to reconcile a concern for women's physical, sexual, and emotional well-being with admiration for a male artist whose lyrics consistently portray women in a contemptuous and sexually degrading manner. Girls and women, even those who have been co-opted into Eminem worship, want to be treated with respect. They certainly do not want to be physically or sexually assaulted by men. They do not want to be sexually degraded by dismissive and arrogant men. But they cannot have it both ways. They cannot proclaim their attraction to a man who has gotten rich verbally trashing and metaphorically raping women, and yet reasonably expect that young men will treat them with dignity.

The racial storyline around Eminem perpetuates racist myths

Eminem is popular with white audiences in large measure because the African American gangsta rap icon Dr. Dre and other hard-core black rappers with "street credibility" have conferred on him a certain legitimacy. Dre is Eminem's mentor and producer, signaling to black audiences as well that unlike previous white rappers such as Vanilla Ice, this white boy is for real. What is missing from this story is that Dr. Dre himself is one of the most misogynistic and homophobic figures in the history of rap music. He has produced and performed some of this era's most degrading songs about women. "Bitches ain't shit but hoes and tricks/How could you trust a hoe/Cuz a hoe's a trick/We don't love them tricks/Cuz a trick's a bitch" ("Bitches Ain't Shit"). In other words, Eminem and Dre are modeling a perverse sort of interracial solidarity that comes at the expense of women. It is an old story: sexism provides men with a way to unite across race and class lines. African American people who are happy to see Eminem earning rap greater legitimacy in white America might want to consider that this era's white artist most identified as a bridge to black culture has built that bridge on the denigration and undermining of black women—and all women.

Eminem's success has unleashed a torrent of mother-blaming

One element of Eminem's story of which all his fans are aware is that he and his mother do not get along. He claims that she was an unstable drug abuser who abused him emotionally. She sued him for defamation. Many people psychoanalyze him from a distance and argue that his problems with women stem from his stormy relationship with his mother. This may or may not be true, but it is an excuse that abusive men often make for their behavior. As

Lundy Bancroft observes in his book, *Why Does He Do That? Inside the Minds of Angry and Controlling Men*, battered women themselves sometimes like this explanation, since it makes sense out of the man's behavior and gives the woman someone safe to be angry at—since getting angry at him always seems to blow up in her face. It is hard to say what percentage of Eminem fans relate to his often articulated rage at his mother, but consider this anecdotal evidence: I attended an Eminem concert in southern California during the Anger Management Tour in 2002. At one point, Eminem ripped off a string of angry expletives about his mother (something like "F-you, bitch!") after which a sizeable cross-section of the eighteen-thousand-person crowd joined in a violent chant repeating the verbal aggression against Ms. Mathers (and no doubt other mothers by extension). Why is this aspect of the Eminem phenomenon such a cause for concern? No one begrudges Eminem, or anyone else, the right to have issues—including in some cases being very angry with their mothers. However, it is not a great stretch to see that Eminem's anger can easily be generalized to all women and used as yet another rationale for some men's deeply held misogyny.

Considering Eminem's roots on the economic margins of "white trash" Detroit, class is also a critical factor here. Poor women—especially poor women of color—are easy scapegoats for many societal problems. Eminem's fans presumably know little about the context within which Debbie Mathers (who is white) tried to raise her children. Might we have some compassion for her as we are asked to for him? Why was she constantly struggling financially? How did educational inequities and lack of employment opportunities affect *her* life, her family experiences, her education level, her dreams, her ability to be a good parent? As a woman, how did sexism shape her choices? She became pregnant with Marshall (Eminem) when she was *fifteen*. What was her personal history, including her history with men? Was she ever abused? We know a lot of women with substance abuse problems develop them as a form of self-medication against the effects of trauma. What is the connection between Ms. Mathers's alleged (by her son) substance abuse and any history of victimization she might have? Further, if Eminem's father deserted him and the family when Marshall was young, why is so much of Eminem's verbal aggression aimed at his mother and at women? If you buy the argument that Eminem's misogyny comes from his issues with his mother, then considering his father's behavior, why doesn't he have a huge problem with men? Hint: the answer has to do with sexism. It is easy to blame struggling single mothers for their shortcomings; right-wing politicians have been doing this for decades. A more thoughtful approach would seek to understand their situations, and while such an understanding would provide no excuse for abuse or neglect (if that is what Eminem actually experienced), it would give it much-needed context.

Eminem verbally bullies women and gays and then claims, "I was just kidding around"

Many of Eminem's fans claim that his Slim Shady persona and nasty anti-woman lyrics are just an act. But his misogyny comes out in interviews as well. In a *Rolling Stone* magazine interview in 1999, Eminem tried to explain his writing process:

"My thoughts are so fucking evil when I'm writing shit, if I'm mad at my girl, I'm gonna sit down and write the most misogynistic fucking rhyme in the world. It's not how I feel in general, it's how I feel at that moment. Like, say today, earlier, I might think something like 'coming through the airport sluggish, walking on crutches, hit a pregnant bitch in the stomach with luggage.'"

Elizabeth Keathley points out in a fascinating music journal essay entitled, "A Context for Eminem's Murder Ballads," that many journalists buy the argument that misogyny is a creative response warranted by certain circumstances in an intimate relationship, rather than a world view that informs a person's choices. This rationalization allows them to "overlook" Eminem's misogyny and accept at face value his claim that's he's only kidding. Eminem's defenders—including a number of prominent music critics—like to argue that his ironic wit and dark sense of humor are lost on many of his detractors. This is what his predominantly young fans are constantly being told: that some people don't like the likeable Em because they don't get him, the personae he has created, his transgressive humor. In comparison, his fans are said to be much more hip, since they are in on the joke. As a non-fan, I would offer this response: "We get it, all right. We understand that lyrics are usually not meant to be taken literally. And we have a good sense of humor. We just don't think it is funny for men to joke aggressively about murdering and raping women, and assaulting gays and lesbians. Just like we don't think it is funny for white people to make racist jokes at the expense of people of color. This sort of 'hate humor' is not just harmless fun—no matter how clever the lyrics or spellbinding the backbeats. Music lyrics and other art forms can either illuminate social problems, or they can cynically exploit them. Eminem is arguably a major force in the latter category. Sorry if we don't find that funny."

Eminem's rebel image obscures the fact that men's violence against women is not rebellious.

Eminem has been skillfully marketed as a "rebel" to whom many young people—especially white boys—can relate. But what exactly is he rebelling against? Powerful women who oppress weak and vulnerable men? Omnipotent gays and lesbians who make life a living hell for straight people? Eminem's misogyny and homophobia, far from being "rebellious," are actually extremely traditional and conservative. They are also clearly profitable, both for Eminem and Interscope records, for Nike, with whom Eminem has had a lucrative promotional contract, and with all of the other media that profit from his "controversial" act. As a straight white man in hip-hop culture, Marshall Mathers would actually be much more of a rebel if he rapped about supporting women's equality and embracing gay and lesbian civil rights. Instead, he is only a rebel in a very narrow sense of that word. Since he offends a lot of parents, kids can "rebel" against their parents' wishes by listening to him, buying his CDs, etc. The irony is that by buying into Eminem's clever "bad boy" act, one could argue that they are just being obedient, predictable consumers. It is rebellion as a purchasable commodity. But if you focus on the contents of his lyrics, the "rebellion" is empty. If you are a "rebel," it matters who you are and what you are rebelling against. The KKK are rebels, too. They boast about it all the time. They fly the Confederate (rebel) flag. But most cultural commentators would never dream of speaking positively about the KKK as models of adolescent rebellion for American youth because the *content* of what they advocate is so repugnant. Likewise Eminem would be dropped from MTV playlists and lose his record contract immediately if he turned his lyrical aggression away from women and gays and started trashing people of color, Jews, Catholics, etc. In that sense, Eminem's continued success makes a statement about how this culture regards women and gays. Sadly, it is a statement that many progressive, feminist, egalitarian, and nonviolent people in this era of white male backlash find quite deflating.

WRESTLING WITH MANHOOD

Professional wrestling has escaped serious cultural analysis largely because of its spectacular surface appeal and the common assertion that "it's only entertainment." But its immense popularity and cultural presence, its consistently high ratings, and its aggressive promotion across a range of media channels raise some basic questions: Why is pro wrestling so popular? What does its popularity tell us about gender relations in this era? Given that the audience for World Wrestling Entertainment (WWE) is comprised overwhelmingly of boys and young men, what are the stories it tells them—especially about what it means to be a man or a woman? How does pro wrestling contribute to rape culture?

In the past, discussions about wrestling's effects on "real world" violence have typically centered on the behavioral effects of exposure to it. Does it cause imitative violence? But that question misses the point. The issue is not, "Are children imitating the violence they see?" but "Are boys learning that taunting, ridiculing, and bullying define masculinity?" People who do not watch wrestling are often surprised to learn that real (or simulated) violence actually comprises a small percentage of the length of a pro wrestling telecast. Most of the time is devoted to setting up the narratives, and to verbal confrontation and bullying. In wrestling video games, each combatant not only has signature moves, but also verbal taunts that can be directed against either an opponent or the crowd. The object of the game is to see who can be the most effective bully. There are also numerous storylines that depict men harassing and humiliating women, and imposing their will on women's bodies—often in sexually graphic ways. There are numerous instances of men forcing kisses on women, pouring beer down their throats, and commanding them to perform simulated sex acts. In one scene involving two popular characters, the woman is obviously passed out and lying on the ground. The man gets on top of her to simulate rape as the announcers shriek with delight about how much she enjoys it. "She's liking it," one of them exclaims. "She's euphoric."

We know from decades of research that depictions of violence in the entertainment media create a cultural climate in which such behavior is accepted as a normal, even appropriate, response to various situations. As the pioneering media researcher George Gerbner explains, the problem of violence in media is not so much its graphic depiction but the stories it tells about who has power and who does not, who has the right to use it, and who is an appropriate victim. In that sense professional wrestling tells a powerful story about how "real men" prevail—through intimidation, humiliation, and control, all accomplished by verbal, physical, and sexual aggression. Manhood is equated explicitly with the ability to settle scores, defend one's honor, and win respect and compliance through physical force. Already, this definition of manhood is at the root of much interpersonal violence in our society—including men's violence against women. While it might not be possible to demonstrate a direct relationship between pro wrestling and domestic violence, it is clear that the wrestling subculture contributes to a larger cultural environment that teaches boys and men that manhood is about achieving power and control over women. And when you combine this lesson about manhood with storylines that depict women as two-dimensional objects whose main entertainment function is to take off their clothes, you have a potent recipe for the normalization of rape.

The role of women in the WWE has changed over the past decade. Back in the 1980s, in the days of Hulk Hogan and the Macho Man, women were essentially restricted to a couple of ornamental figures whose main function was to look good and titillate the audience. Today, they play a much more prominent role, either as wrestlers or as bimbo/prostitute sidekicks. In both cases they are highly sexualized and wear little clothing, and function effectively as strippers for the largely male audience. As the WWE's Torrie Wilson explains, "To put it bluntly, [my character] has gotten a little sleazier, the clothes have gotten a little skimpier. I learned through trial and error that I got more popular as the hemlines got shorter." But women in the WWE are not just objects for young men to stare at. As female characters have become more common, they have increasingly been drawn into the narratives. The sight of women being pushed, punched, and brutally slammed by men has become normalized through sheer repetition. There are countless scenes of men knocking women to the mat, punching them in the face, breaking chairs over their back, or mock-raping them. Wrestling might not directly cause men to be abusive to women, but there can be little doubt that it contributes to an atmosphere in which men's violence against women is not taken seriously.

What is perhaps most disturbing about the role of women in the WWE is the deliberate sexualization of men's violence against them. Examples: A scantily clad woman—not a wrestler—is slapped by a male wrestler on her bare buttocks and then pushed out of the ring and onto the ground. A large male wrestler picks up a woman half his size, drapes her semi-nude body across his knees, licks his hand, and spanks her on the butt as the crowd cheers wildly. And in one of the most disturbing sequences of sexual bullying ever shown on television, Trish Stratus, a WWE icon and "one of the most sultry divas ever in sports entertainment," according to her official website, is confronted by WWE CEO Vince McMahon, playing himself. Backstage, he accuses her of some transgression, and then demands that she publicly say she is sorry. Once out in the ring, she does, but he presses on. "If you're really sorry," he says, "if you're really, really sorry, take off your shirt!" She cowers and then complies as the audience roars its approval. He continues to verbally coerce her in this fashion until she is stripped down to her panties, barely covering her surgically enhanced breasts, at which point McMahon shouts at her to get on her knees and bark like a dog. She complies. The entire time, boys in the live arena audience and watching at home on television are treated to a kind of forced strip show, where their sexual arousal is linked to the sexually degrading treatment of an attractive but subservient woman at the hands of a powerful (white) man. On the WWE, men's abusive treatment of their fictional girlfriends and wives is also commonly depicted within a storyline that presents the violence as deserved—a pattern that mirrors similar justifications in the "real world." In one sequence where the wrestler Triple H confronts his "wife" for supposedly lying to him and angrily throws her down on the mat, the announcers literally say she deserves the beating he then inflicts on her. Similarly, wrestling plotlines regularly involve the sexual humiliation of women in the workplace, and treat the entire notion of sexual harassment as a joke. Until the character was discontinued a couple of years ago, in one of the most overtly racist and sexist characterizations on contemporary television, the Godfather, an over-the-top stereotype of a hustling pimp (and one of the few important black figures in the WWE) led out his "hoe train" of scantily-clad women to the leering and jeering crowds. Also, as female sexuality is increasingly prominent in the scripts, the line between the bimbo/prostitute sidekick and the female wrestlers has eroded. During one pay-per-view event, Miss Kitty, a one-time WWE women's champion and a former hyper-sexualized sidekick, removed her top. Big contests for female wrestlers often involve "bra and panties" matches, mud or chocolate baths, Jell-O matches, or the "evening dress" contest (where you lose by having your dress ripped from your body). The most popular female wrestler ever, Chyna (whose real name is Joanie Laurer), built her reputation on her powerful physique. But after numerous cosmetic surgical procedures on her face and body, she posed nude in *Playboy* in 2000 in what became one of the largest-selling issues in that magazine's history.

People who love pro wrestling defend all of this by claiming that it is fantasy and harmless entertainment—and if you don't like it, don't watch. But what does it mean when stadiums around the country are filled with young men cheering and laughing at the staged humiliation and abuse of women? What does it mean that millions of boys and men are entertained by scenes of bullying and ritualized sexual degradation? How realistic is it that boys who are immersed in pro wrestling's cartoonish world of brutish male thugs and compliant female sex objects can switch all of that off and relate to their female (and male) peers in a spirit of equality and mutual respect? It is clear that the WWE sets up girls and women to be little more than compliant victims. But it also sets up boys and men either to be abusers and rapists—or to think like them.

BULLIES WITH A MICROPHONE: HOWARD STERN, TOM LEYKIS, AND RUSH LIMBAUGH

Howard Stern

I understand why Howard Stern is such a popular radio talk show host, especially with his core demographic of eighteen- to forty-nine-year-old white men. He is an undeniably talented radio personality with a fertile creative mind and a great voice. He is a gifted conversationalist. And he is more willing than perhaps anyone in the history of mainstream media to puncture the pretensions of pompous celebrity culture. He talks about sex all the time. He surrounds himself with beautiful young women who are eager to take their clothes off for him and his cohorts. He can also be charming, likable, decent, and funny. One of his winning personality characteristics is his self-deprecation, combined with refreshing bluntness. He constantly refers to his own geeky looks, and does not hesitate to say that he has a small penis. He scores points for his honesty, especially because there is not nearly enough public honesty in modern public discourse—especially from men.

And he is also a first-rate bully. His relentless verbal aggression does far more than just expose the numerous hypocrisies of the rich and famous. Stern seeks out and destroys a variety of human targets, but his special-ty—and a good part of the reason for his popularity with men—is his sexual bullying of women. He constantly belittles, ridicules, and provokes women—often young, surgically enhanced, and desperate to please men—to degrade themselves sexually for their moment of fame. He regularly makes jokes about people's pain. One of the most well-known aspects of his popu-larity—at least according to many of his fans—is his eagerness to say things other men might think but would never dare say out loud. Many of these involve deeply misogynistic feelings. One infamous example is what he said on air shortly after the Columbine massacre in 1999. Talking about the mur-derers Eric Harris and Dylan Klebold, he expressed his disapproval that they did not rape some girls before they killed them. "There were some really good-looking girls running out with their hands over their heads. Did those kids try to have sex with any of the good-looking girls? They didn't even do that? At least if you're gonna kill yourself and kill all the kids, why wouldn't you have some sex? If I was going to kill some people, I'd take them out with sex."

But if Stern is such an abusive person, why is he so popular? We know from research on schoolyard bullies over the past twenty years that they are often popular, talented kids. This does not excuse their abusive behavior; it merely complicates the traditional image of the bully as an unattractive, unloved brute. Just as many people like Eminem, not in spite of his bullying personality but in part because of it, Stern draws legions of male fans that are attracted to his aggressive style and his callous disregard for people's feelings.

Sometimes when I tune in to Stern's radio program, my mind flashes to a moment in the late 1970s when I was a junior in high school and witnessed an incident that is etched in my memory. It was in the school cafeteria. A group of senior boys had secured a table next to the end of the food line. As girls took their trays and headed out to find a table, the boys held up placards numbered one through ten. They hooted and laughed as they rated the girls on their bodies and looks. I did not speak to any of the girls, but I imagine many of them must have felt humiliated and angry at being judged this way. My guess is that some of the boys who participated did not even pause to think how the girls might feel. At the time of this incident I was hardly a feminist thinker; I was a product of the same social environment that produced those boys. But while this event had an impact on me, and I still remember it vividly several decades later, girls and women have to live with boys' and men's often cruel judgments about how attractive they are *every single day*.

Despite the women's movement and the enormous changes in women's lives over the past several decades—especially middle-class women's lives—this sort of abusive ritual is still enacted by boys in middle schools and high schools across the country. Only now, the boys are more likely to get in trouble for it, due in large measure to the passage of sexual-harassment laws that deem such behavior as constituting a "hostile environment" that denies girls equal educational access. But while the laws have changed, other parts of the culture are actually worse than before. In fact, due to the power and reach of mass media, millions of boys and men are in a sense brought into that cafeteria to witness such spectacles on a regular basis.

For example, one of the regular bits on the *Howard Stern Show* features women in skimpy outfits who line up in front of a panel of male judges and prepare to disrobe. They are often strippers, prostitutes, and porn stars, or young women in their late teens or early twenties who aspire to those professions. Either individually or sometimes in a group, the women strip off their clothes as the men comment on their weight, face, and breast size and shape. It is as if the women are African slaves on the auction block, and the men are plantation owners who have to decide which one has the right body for the work they will be forced to do. The judges are typically average-looking Stern sidekicks, but sometimes include oddball characters like an openly drunk and physically disabled alcoholic in his late thirties who angrily calls the women "bitches," or developmentally disabled adult men who are there presumably to be laughed at when they say unpredictable things.

Fans of Stern would no doubt maintain that unlike the cafeteria incident, no one forces the women on his show to subject themselves to this humiliation. They are typically young women who are eager for the exposure on national radio and TV (the cable television channel E! carries Stern's radio program daily). But regardless of the motivation of the women, one has to wonder about the effect on boys and men of watching repeated displays of men making critical and sometimes cruel comments about women's bodies—and everybody laughing it off. Men who make openly sexual comments to women who walk by on the streets—and in other public spaces like sports arenas, bars, and clubs—often insist that "women like that sort of attention." Is it possible that some men believe this because in the pornographic era, they are constantly presented with images of women who willingly participate in their own subordination?

In addition, one effect of Stern's ubiquitous media presence is that he has become an iconic figure in certain parts of male culture. In a sense he is the focal point and preeminent role model for millions of boys and men who listen to his show and are drawn into the electronic community it creates. Like other radio programs such as the *Don Imus Show*, and television programs like Fox Sports's the *Best Damn Sports Show Period*, Stern's program includes several men (and one woman) who are nearly always with him in studio, "shooting the shit," and helping to give the listener the impression that he (or she) is part of an extended "in" group of friends. As such, the norms that are established in that studio have wide influence in male culture. How wide? In 2004 Stern signed a five-year contract for $500 million with the satellite radio service Sirius, where Stern's misogyny and pornographic imagination will not be bound by the strictures of FCC regulation.

Tom Leykis

If "incitement to rape" is ever made into a crime, the Los Angeles-based talk radio host Tom Leykis would make a great candidate for the first man to be prosecuted. The Tom Leykis program makes the *Howard Stern Show* sound like a feminist seminar. Leykis, who is number one in his time slot with males in LA, routinely calls women "bitches," "whores," and "sluts." The overweight "shock jock" routinely makes demeaning statements like "Fat chicks serve a purpose—poor guys need love," and instructs young men to stay away from women over thirty because they are dried up, needy, and desperate for attention. He has told countless women callers over the age of thirty that they have passed their "expiration date." As a man approaching fifty who has been married and divorced four times, he brags about dating very young women, using them, and dumping them the minute they place any sort of demand on him. He got a burst of national attention during the Kobe Bryant rape trial, when he was the first prominent media person to unapologetically mention on air the name of Bryant's alleged victim—whom he angrily denounced as a "lying slut." (Most media outlets withhold the names of alleged sexual-assault victims out of respect for their privacy and concern that unwanted publicity could further traumatize them.) And he got tons of free media coverage in Canada in 2003 when he offered to donate $50,000 to charity if a woman newscaster in Vancouver agreed to bare her breasts and let him autograph them (she declined).

Leykis's misogyny is so extreme and over the top that an unsuspecting listener who comes across his program on their radio dial might believe that he is a satirist who parodies the worst aspects of traditional masculinity. But he always stays in character, and his listeners generally accept his pronouncements as authentic. One promotion for his show referred to the sexual-harassment allegations against the TV game show host Bob Barker. "He's seventy years old and sexually harassing twenty-year-olds," he said. "He's my hero!" It is important to remember that this sort of talk is not on some restricted access porn channel. The *Tom Leykis Show* is distributed by Westwood One radio network and is syndicated in sixty markets that include San Francisco, Dallas, Seattle, and Detroit. And as Ann Simonton, the founder of Media Watch, points out, it is often broadcast in afternoon time slots when children are listening.

One of the most popular features on his show is a recurring segment entitled "Leykis 101," where "Professor Leykis" dispenses advice to young men about their relationships with women. It is really a how-to for young, horny men about how they can get laid, because in the "relationships" that Leykis promotes, women are basically there to service a man's sexual needs and little else. He tells men never to spend more than forty dollars on a date, to dump a "chick" if she hasn't "put out" by the third date, and to resist any sort of emotional attachment, which can only end badly. It gets worse. On the air he has repeatedly called women "sperm depositories" and "human urinals." In Leykis's universe, women are "scheming bitches" who only want a man's money and maybe a father for their children, and men are perpetual adolescents who only want sex without commitment, and maybe someone to cook dinner for them. He says all of this with calm certitude, as if he is merely stating the truth. When women call to challenge him, he typically tries to discredit them by stating outright that they must be unattractive or "over thirty." If they persist in their position that his show promotes harmful and demeaning stereotypes of women, he simply tells them that he speaks for men and his show's popularity speaks for itself. On the rare occasion when a male caller takes issue with him, he attempts to discredit him with the charge that he has been "pussified," or allowed a woman too much influence on his life.

One of the most disturbing aspects of his show is the steady stream of female callers who not only excuse his woman-hating rants but actually affirm them. On one show in 2005, a number of women called to say they like it when guys "throw them up against walls," tell them to shut up, and don't ask what they want sexually but just do what the men want. It is sad to think that young male listeners might actually take all of this to heart and treat women sexually with contempt because "that's what girls want."

On one representative show in 2005, Leykis asked his callers for stories about "dialing while drunk." One young man recounted a story about a time when he was drunk and called his ex-girlfriend. It is possible that she already had a restraining order against him, because according to the guy, his ex recorded the conversation, and he was subsequently convicted of threatening her, for which he spent a year in jail. The spirit of his call was to warn that guys have to be careful when they are drunk and pick up a phone, because they can get themselves in serious trouble. Leykis did not chastise the man for his threatening behavior. He betrayed no hint of empathy for women who are on the receiving end of harassing phone calls from men, no acknowledgment that men stalking women is a big problem in the U.S., or that alcohol is correlated with all sorts of violent behaviors.

But this is positively benign compared to what he did on a show in 2000. In what has to be counted as one of the lowest moments in the history of talk radio, Leykis devoted an extended segment to a discussion of how men could use women's sexual abuse histories as a manipulative trick to get them into bed. The segment started with Leykis reading letters from male listeners who say women who have been sexually molested "put out" more. He used that as a stepping-off point to talk about the ethics of men doing whatever it takes to get laid. At one point, he had a female caller on the line who tried to argue that using a woman's weakness in order to get laid is like playing on a child's innocence in order to molest them. Leykis disagreed, arguing that:

"All men do it . . . we find different weaknesses. Sometimes, we find out you have a weakness to, uh, have a couple of drinks and then you get, uh, kind of loose. Sometimes, we find out that you like to smoke pot and we get you stoned. Sometimes, we find out that you have a weakness for money so we take you out and we spend a lot of money on you and then, uh, you'll bend over for us . . . We find out all kinds of weaknesses you have and that's how we get in."

The female caller asked if he thought this was a little cruel. He denied it. "I mean, men want to get laid," he said. "We're not here to . . . to . . . to get to know you." If a man finds out a woman has been molested, Leykis continued, "You're more likely to put out. You're more likely to be good in bed. That's what guys are saying." When the woman continued to insist that it is cruel to exploit a woman's problems in this way, Leykis did not budge from his position. "It seems horrible but I don't think it's as horrible as it seems."

Before he became an unapologetic sexist and sexual bully on the airwaves, Tom Leykis used to host a political talk show from a liberal perspective. But in the mid 1990s when his career fortunes were sagging, he made the decision to copy the lucrative formula pioneered by Howard Stern, which combined sexually explicit talk with ugly and aggressive advocacy from the so-called "men's perspective." Like the *Howard Stern Show*, the *Tom Leykis Show* derives much of its influence from the claims of its host and fans that it speaks for all men. That leaves men who love and respect women and believe in equality between the sexes with a clear choice. Unless these men make their voices heard in public and private, the Sterns and Leykises of the world will continue to speak for men, and thus do a major disservice to countless women who have learned not to expect more from the other sex. They will also continue to do a disservice to countless men who, I am convinced, want intimacy and connection—along with sexual pleasure—from women as well as other men; but they will never find it by following the advice of cynical manipulators like Stern and Leykis.

Rush Limbaugh

I would suspect that most of Rush Limbaugh's fans would not be pleased to see his name on a list of radio personalities who contribute to rape culture—especially when the list includes the likes of Howard Stern and Tom Leykis. Limbaugh is certainly not as crude and openly misogynistic as those two. But he merits inclusion on a list of talk-radio personalities who support a rape culture on the sole basis of his relentless attacks on feminists. People can legitimately differ with positions feminists take on various issues. In fact, there is often healthy debate and disagreement *between* feminists. But Limbaugh does not simply express disagreement with feminists; he routinely ridicules and personally insults them. That is, he routinely demeans the very people who created and sustain the anti-rape movement. Let's be clear. There would be no rape crisis centers—or battered women's programs—without them. Millions of women and children would not be protected by the laws feminists helped write and enact over the past generation. Rape within marriage would still be legal. Without feminists there would be virtually no anti-rape education in the schools. So when Limbaugh stigmatizes feminists by calling them names like "feminazi," he is attacking those women who have been most successful in the fight against rape. This indirectly helps foster a rape culture to the extent that it weakens its most effective opponents.

But in addition to his attacks on the leaders of the anti-rape movement, Limbaugh's comments about the Abu Ghraib prison torture scandal that broke in 2004 were textbook examples of "rape-supportive" attitudes. When news reports confirmed that United States Army personnel had abused Iraqi prisoners with torture techniques that included sexual humiliation, threats of rape, forcing male detainees to masturbate while being photographed and videotaped, forcing naked male detainees to wear women's underwear, and arranging naked male detainees in a pile and then jumping on them,

Limbaugh used his highly influential radio forum to minimize the abuse and undermine the legitimacy of Americans who were outraged that such abuses took place in their name. In fact, Limbaugh made a series of statements that "downplayed, dismissed, and even endorsed" Iraqi prisoner abuse, according to the liberal watchdog website Media Matters for America. For example, Limbaugh said that Pfc. Lynndie England and other accused soldiers were engaging in acts that he compared to hazing and fraternity pranks, "Sort of that kind of fun." He compared the chilling pictures of naked Iraqi men stacked on top of each other to "good old American pornography," and claimed that the soldiers had just been "blowing off steam." Furthermore, he asserted that the reaction to the "stupid torture" is an example of the "feminization of this country."

The Abu Ghraib torture scandal did incalculable damage to perceptions of the United States around the world, and it badly undermined American claims to moral authority in the volatile Middle East. For a time, it looked like there might be pressure to hold senior officials accountable for this scandal, and not just the ordinary soldiers who claimed to be following orders. Limbaugh's comments at the time were widely seen as an attempt to deflect criticism away from higher ups in the chain of command, up to and including the White House. But in playing this transparently partisan role, the nation's number one talk radio personality did what powerful men have done for eons: he sided with the perpetrators of sexual violence over its victims. The rape culture will persist as long as influential people—for whatever reason—make excuses for sex crimes instead of firmly and unwaveringly declaring that sexual abuse will never be condoned, tolerated, or excused.

CHAPTER TEN

Guilty Pleasures: Pornography, Prostitution, and Stripping

"Pornography hates men. It tells them that they are cruel, pathetic creatures who can sustain erections but not relationships. Porn is based on the premise that men will buy into this image rather than see it for what it is—a cold, calculated strategy to manipulate them into buying billions of dollars of woman and man-hating propaganda."
—Gail Dines

"Who are the 'johns,' those people who buy women and girls in prostitution? Johns are average citizens rather than sadistic psychopaths. They are from all walks of life—doctors, judges, famous actors, and CEOs, as well as construction workers, social workers, and traveling salesmen. Rich and poor, young and old, the men . . . are from every race/ethnicity in the world. Most are married . . . One woman reported that as she was about to perform fellatio on a man in his Volvo, she heard a cry from behind her, turned around, and saw a year-old baby, strapped into a car seat."
—Melissa Farley, Prostitution Research and Education,
  San Francisco, California

It has long been understood that what people do for entertainment—and sexual pleasure—can be shockingly revealing. But until recently, most discussions about pornography, prostitution, and stripping have focused on the women and girls in those industries—who they are, how they got into that life, and what happens to them once they do. These are important areas of discussion, and over the past couple of decades activists and researchers have learned a great deal about the reality of women's and girls' lives in the commercial "sex industry"—largely as a result of the courageous testimonies of women who have survived it. But if we hope to *prevent* sexual violence and other forms of sexual exploitation, we must begin to ask another set of questions: How does heterosexual men's use of pornography as a masturbatory aid help to shape not only their view of women and girls, but their own manhood and sexuality? What is the influence on boys' sexuality of early and repeated exposure to the pornography industry's particular representation of "normal" sex? Is it possible to discuss sexual violence in our society and not talk about the influence in male culture of the $10 billion pornography industry? What is the relationship between the sexual abuse of children and the proliferation of media products that deliberately sexualize young girls— and in some cases boys? How do men treat prostitutes, and what impact does this have on the way they treat their wives, girlfriends, female coworkers, and fellow students? As strip culture seeps ever more visibly into the mainstream, what effect does this have on men's and boys' attitudes toward women? What can be done about what seems to be a steady movement away from the idea of sex as mutually respectful? Short of creating our own version of a Taliban-like theocracy, is it possible to reverse the seemingly inexorable societal trend toward the pornographic fantasy of men using women like blow-up dolls?

These are uncomfortable questions, and what makes them even more difficult is that not everyone wants to know the answers. Men have an obvious incentive to change the subject. But it is also true that many women are not eager to find out about what goes on in certain parts of male culture that historically have been off-limits to them, especially when it gets personal and involves men close to them. And who can blame them? The "truth" about some men's callousness, cruelty, and need for sexual dominance that is revealed in pornography, prostitution, and strip culture is a lot to stomach. Some women carry the added burden of having done things sexually with men to accommodate a man's pornographic fantasy, which in another context they might feel compromised their integrity. It also must be painful for women to admit to themselves that their fathers, brothers, sons, and lovers are often the very same men who rent videos with titles like *A Cum-Guzzling Slut Named Kimberley*, pay twenty-year-old strippers for lap dances at "gentlemen's clubs" on the way home from work, get blow jobs from prostitutes at friends' bachelor parties, and in some cases travel abroad to have cheap sex with twelve-year-old girls.

REVOLUTIONARY HONESTY

The writer John Stoltenberg once said that pornography tells lies about women, but it tells the truth about men. I think Stoltenberg is only partially right. Unless it can be proven that male infants are born hard-wired for sexism, the only truth about men that pornography reveals is that they are products of their environment. Thus if we want to reduce the level of sexual violence perpetrated by boys and men, we need to critically examine the environment in which we socialize boys and establish norms in male culture. This will not be easy, especially since so many men have conscious or unconscious feelings of guilt about how they have objectified women, or perpetuated their oppression through their treatment of them as purchasable commodities. But in order for men to transform their feelings of guilt into something more constructive, they need to do something about the underlying problem. They need to move beyond defensiveness and ask themselves how they can help to change the sexual rituals and norms in male culture that are harmful to women and children. A good place to start this process would be to commit—in private and public—what Stoltenberg calls acts of "revolutionary honesty" about their lives, loves, and guilty pleasures.

In this spirit of revolutionary honesty, I want to come clean about some of my own guilty pleasures. At the very least, I want to make sure that I am not self-righteous or moralizing in this discussion. I do not characterize myself as a "good guy" while other guys who use porn or pay prostitutes are "bad guys," or irredeemably sexist. I have never had nonconsensual sex or sex with a prostitute, but I am far from prudish. In my teens and twenties, before I was politically conscious about the sexist exploitation at the heart of the "sex industry," I went to strip clubs and used pornography. But I never saw myself as oppressing women. I denied any connection between my private pleasure and the perpetuation of rape culture. At first I did not know, and then I did not want to know, how badly some men (and women) treat the women and girls in those industries. It was only as I came to hear and read about their life experiences—and reflect on the feminist idea that the high incidence of rape and sexual harassment in the U.S. is linked to the pervasive sexual objectification of women in our society—that I consciously refused to support or condone the commercial sex industry. Still, the effects of my earlier conditioning have stayed with me to this day. For example, I am sometimes aroused by images that I know are sexist and degrading to women. I appreciate the complexity of the human erotic imagination, but I wonder how much my fantasy life—and the fantasy life of tens of millions of my fellow men—has been shaped by the increasingly angry and misogynistic porn that has flooded the culture and our psyches in recent decades. I would never hold other men to a standard which I do not hold for myself. Any man who wants to fight gender violence—and all forms of sexism— needs to be careful not to condemn in others what he refuses to acknowledge about himself. The solution I have found is simply to be honest about my own self-doubts and contradictions. In my work with men, I have found that most of them respect and appreciate this, even if they do not agree with all of my interpretations or conclusions.

ANTI-SEXIST MEN AND THE PORN WARS

Pornography is usually thought of as a women's issue. But as the sociologist Gail Dines bluntly states, "Men make, distribute, and get rich on porn. They jerk off to it. Tell me why it's a women's issue." Although men are overwhelmingly the producers and consumers of porn, they are nonetheless dramatically underrepresented among the people who take the time to reflect on and discuss its societal function. In fact, millions of men use pornography, but I suspect very few have ever had a serious conversation about it. (Pornography marketed to gay men is a huge industry itself, and many feminist critics—gay and straight—have called attention to the ways in which much of gay porn eroticizes power and control and sexual violence. For the purpose of this discussion, I am focusing on by far the largest segment of the pornography market: heterosexual men and boys.) I know that countless men with whom I have worked over the past twenty years report they had never even heard—much less discussed—thoughtful critiques of the role of porn in men's lives, and the possible negative affect it has had on their sexuality and ability to connect with real women. Some men avoid this sort of introspection because it is still awkward to talk honestly about sex in this culture, and they are embarrassed. Other men like to shift the conversation about pornography into political arguments about free speech and censorship and away from questions about how boys and men use it, what types of porn they find pleasurable and why, and what affect heavy porn use might have on their feelings about women's bodies and sexuality. I am certain that part of their motivation for these evasions is personal: if they engaged in serious discussions about pornography, men might have to ask themselves troubling questions about what effect pornography has on how they view *themselves*, their bodies, and their desires for intimate connections with women.

The debate in this country about hot-button issues like pornography and the sexualization of children in advertising has become so polarized that to the casual observer, there are only two positions: either you are for porn or against it, with no thought given to the complexity of the subject. In real life, people tend to have much more nuanced views of these matters. People in the movements to end sexual and domestic violence are often falsely accused of prudery by the self-described "sex positive" advocates and of being "in bed with the Christian right" if they dare to critique the behavior of "consenting adults." In fact, over the past couple of decades, pornography has even been a divisive issue among people who call themselves feminists. There are two major camps. Anti-porn feminists take the position that pornography sexualizes women's subordination, and is a critical factor in maintaining gender inequality. It might not directly cause men's violence against women, but it portrays men's domination and control of women as sexy. In practice, the porn industry is also a heartless corporate enterprise which can be quite brutal and exploitative of the largely working-class women (and men)—many of them in their late teens and early twenties—whose bodies provide the main attraction, but whose careers in the unforgiving adult film business—Jenna Jameson notwithstanding—are nasty, brutish, and short.

Pro-porn feminists, by contrast, argue that unbridled sexual expression— even if much of it is sexist and produced by and for men—is in women's self-interest because one of the cornerstones of women's oppression is the suppression of their sexuality. True emancipation requires the celebration of women's right to do whatever they want with their bodies—which includes their right to appear in pornography, strip, and sell sex.

Notably, these arguments about pornography have largely taken place between women.

Until recently, men who have a public voice about pornography tended to fall into one of two categories: conservative Christians or pro-porn enthusiasts. In the former category are men like the Reverend Jerry Falwell and Dr. James Dobson, who publicly chastise the purveyors of "obscenity" and "filth," and who also oppose women's reproductive freedom, readily available contraception for young people, and school-based sex education. In the latter category are libertarians like Howard Stern who talk endlessly about how much they love porn, along with men in the porn industry itself who write and speak about its positive effects and savagely attack its right-wing and feminist critics.

But as a growing number of men enter the sexual violence prevention field, a new men's conversation about pornography is beginning to take shape. These men frequently bring an "insider" perspective on the role of pornography in the lives of boys and men. They do not have to debate in the abstract about whether they think the pornography industry is harmful to women. For many of them, the answer flows out of their lived experience and observations of the men around them. There are no formal studies on this topic, but my sense is that a sizable majority of men who have worked in college and community-based anti-rape organizations over the past fifteen or twenty years share the anti-porn feminist view that pornography contributes to the problem of sexual violence, and at the very least desensitizes men to women's sexual subordination. There is by no means unanimity of opinion among these men about what can be done to counteract the popu-larity and influence of the porn industry in boys' and men's lives. And there are ongoing debates on college campuses and email Listservs about whether all pornography is objectification, and hence bad, or whether the real prob-lem is the misogynistic vision of women's sexuality and men's power that the multi-billion dollar porn industry has sold to the public as normal and even liberating. (Note: There are competing definitions of pornography. But to simplify matters, consider the definition Gail Dines uses in her work. Pornography, she says, consists of those materials that are produced by the multi-billion dollar pornography industry. "The industry knows exactly what it is producing," she says.)

It is also important to note that the vast majority of men in the rape pre-vention world who are critical of the pornography industry do not object because they think public displays of sex are obscene, but because of the harm inflicted on women and children by sexist displays of women's and men's sexuality. In fact, I would bet that most of these men would celebrate uninhibited expressions of women's sexuality. Their opposition to pornogra-phy stems from their belief that most of the magazines and videos produced by the pornography industry actually *limit* women's sexual freedom, while setting women up to be sexually victimized by men. The problem is not only that a high percentage of women in porn are sexual abuse survivors, some of whom were coerced into the business when they were troubled or naïve teenagers by predatory pimps and other abusive older men. It is not only the reduction of women to what University of Texas journalism professor Robert Jensen, writing in the *Sexual-Assault Report*, painfully describes as "three holes and two hands." It is the way the pornography industry helps to define heterosexual *men's* sexuality. Every time a video portrays a scene where a woman asks to be penetrated by a succession of men who ejaculate all over her face as they contemptuously call her a "cum-guzzling whore," it also por-trays men getting pleasure from the sight of that "cum-guzzling whore" get-ting what she wants, and deserves. It normalizes the men's pleasure-taking as it sexualizes the woman's degradation. The idea that consumers of porn can masturbate and have orgasms to that kind of treatment of women and not have it affect their attitudes toward the women and girls in their lives is more a fantasy than anything the most creative porn writers can conjure up.

Mainstream pornography has changed a lot in the past couple of decades. People of a certain age who still associate heterosexual porn with "girlie magazines" and air-brushed photos of big-breasted women shot in soft light on luxurious beds with big pillows would be shocked by the brutality, outright contempt for women, and racism that is common in today's product. One need not search out the extremist fringe of porn culture to find this. A simple Google search will suffice to see some of the "adult" titles readily available: *A Cum-Sucking Whore Named Francesca, Rectal Reamers, Brianna Banks aka Filthy Whore #1, Love Hurts,* and *Ride 'em and Wreck 'em.* There are thousands of porn videos that sexualize some of the most racist caricatures of women and men of color, with titles like *Big Black Beast, Slaves on Loan, Asian Fuck Sluts,* and *Three Black Dicks and a Spanish Chick.* The Web is full of porn sites that advertise not just "sex," but the sexual degradation of women. One such site is called *Violated Teens: Cum in and use them,* which boasts of "Teens forced to fuck, exploited for hard cash: we do what we want to them and they have to love it." Consider one of the most popular porn sites on the Internet, called BangBus. Since its debut in 2001, this site has pioneered what has been called "reality porn," a new genre of "humilitainment" that features what Shauna Swartz in *Bitch* magazine calls "some of the most violent and degrading porno scenes to hit the mainstream." BangBus consists of a couple of average guys who drive around southern Florida in a van, "in search of every girl's inner slut." What they are looking for—the viewer is led to believe—are young women who will agree to go for a ride with them on the promise that they will be paid a few hundred dollars to do something sexual on camera. The videotape documents the initial pick-up on the side of the road, followed by a brief conversation inside the moving van, where the men convince the seemingly naïve woman to take off her clothes. As the handheld camera rolls, the woman has vaginal or anal sex with one of the guys, or she performs oral sex on him. He then withdraws and ejaculates on her face, as the narrator with the camera shrieks in delight. Then after the sex act, the men figure out some way to get the woman out of the van, in one instance to let her pee, in another so she can wash off in a lake. Once she is outside, they hit the gas and race away without paying her. The men laugh and congratulate each other on another successful "drop off," as the young woman's face registers disbelief and then shame as she realizes she has been duped and literally kicked to the curb. The success of this site—which in recent years has drawn huge crowds at the porn industry's major convention in Las Vegas—has predictably spawned a series of imitators, including a site called Trunked, which boasts, "It's simple. Throw the bitch in the trunk. If she doesn't like it, she can get out. Oh yeah. We're goin' 55 mph."

The word "pornography" translates from Greek to mean "writing about prostitutes," and there is no doubt that just as women's bodies are the center of attention in heterosexual pornography, most of the people who have written about pornography as a cultural phenomenon have written about how it affects women's lives. This is understandable and appropriate, because it is primarily the bodies of women and girls that pornography producers use and abuse for profit. But if our goal is to dramatically reduce the incidence of sexual violence, we must turn our attention to the demand side of the pornography question and begin to look critically at the role of pornography in the lives of boys and men.

In the previous chapter, I discussed the concept of rape culture, which starts with the premise that sexual violence is common in our society not because there are so many sick men, but because we socialize *normal* boys to be sexually dominant and *normal* girls to be sexually subordinate. The pornography industry is clearly a key area in the culture where "normal" boys learn to objectify and dehumanize girls and women. For example, Diane Rosenfeld, who teaches gender violence at Harvard Law School, says that her students worry about whether the male judge who watched a porn movie last night is taking her seriously at all.

But sexual objectification notwithstanding, Robert Jensen has written that people are mistaken in assuming that pornography is such a difficult and divisive issue because it is about sex. On the contrary, Jensen maintains that our culture struggles unsuccessfully with pornography because it is really about men's cruelty to women, and the pleasure men sometimes take in that cruelty. Like many women in the anti-rape movement who have studied pornography, Jensen has spent thousands of hours coding and analyzing the content of mainstream porn videos and magazines. His research focuses on men's use of pornography, and how that might shape their attitudes toward women or their own sexuality. In his prolific popular writings on the subject, he cites numerous examples as evidence, realizing that people who are not familiar with contemporary heterosexual porn—especially women—can be skeptical about feminist claims that porn is less about naked bodies and "sex," and more about the eroticization of men's dominance and control of women. The following extended quotation is from an article by Jensen that was published in 2004 in the *Sexual-Assault Report*.

> One of the ten scenes in the film *Gag Factor #10*, a 2002 release from J. M. Productions, begins with a woman and man having a picnic in a park. He jokes about wanting to use the romantic moment to make love to her mouth, and

then stands and thrusts into her mouth while she sits on the blanket. Two other men who walk by join in. Saying things such as "Pump that face, pump that fucking face," "All the way down, choke, choke," and "That's real face fucking," they hold her head and push harder. One man grabs her hair and pulls her head into his penis in what his friend calls "the jackhammer." At this point she is grimacing and seems in pain. She then lies on the ground, and the men approach her from behind. "Eat that whole fucking dick. . . . You little whore, you like getting hurt," one says, as her face is covered with saliva. "Do you like getting your face fucked?" one asks. She can't answer. "Open your mouth if you like it," he says, and she opens her mouth. After they all ejaculate into her mouth, the semen flows out onto her body. After the final ejaculation, she reaches quickly for the wine glass, takes a large drink, and looks up at her boyfriend and says, "God, I love you baby." Her smile fades to a pained look of shame and despair.

Jensen recounts several similar scenes from a variety of bestselling porn videos, and then concludes that because the vast majority of people who rent or buy these sorts of videos are men, "we have to ask why some men find the infliction of pain on women during sexual activity either (1) Not an obstacle to their ability to achieve sexual pleasure, or (2) A factor that can enhance their sexual pleasure." The *optimistic* way to read the contemporary market demand for cruelty in pornography is that men and boys have been so desensitized to women's suffering that they are not bothered by the cruelty. This is a frightening development by itself, with serious implications for the present and future of relations between the sexes. If present trends continue, heterosexual sex—at least that which is represented as such in the commercial sex industry—would seem to be growing increasingly impersonal, and men's pleasure increasingly linked to displays of masculine power and dominance. In other words, transforming the rape culture could become even more of a difficult challenge than it is at present.

The more pessimistic assessment is that some men's sexual pleasure is actually enhanced by the mistreatment and degradation of women. Sadly, there is a wealth of documentary evidence which suggests that the producers of porn are quite conscious in their attempt to provide men with an outlet for their anger and feelings of sexual aggression. Consider the words of Max Hardcore, a popular porn director and actor whose name calls up over one million hits on Google. In an interview with *Hustler* magazine that is recounted by Robert Jensen and Gail Dines in their book *Pornography: The Production and Consumption of Inequality*, Hardcore said, "There's nothing I love more than when a girl insists to me that she won't take a cock in her ass, because—oh yes she will!" He described his trademark as being able to "stretch a girl's asshole apart wide enough to stick a flashlight in it," and went on to say that he doesn't hate all women, just "stuck-up bitches." The porn performer Amanda McGuire told this story about him in *Icon* magazine: "He has made girls cry and lots of girls puke—that's not unusual. I was there once when he throat-fucked a girl so hard she puked and started bawling." Hardcore, whose work has been referred to by porn reviewers as "pseudo-pedophilia" because of how he dresses up his "actresses" to look like young girls, explained the challenges he faces making his films. "It's pretty easy to get a slut to spread solo for the camera," he said. "And quite a different matter to get her to take it up the ass and puke up piss."

In spite of these sorts of statements by men in the industry, its defenders—including women such as the "thinking man's porn star" Nina Hartley—downplay or even deny that porn culture is saturated with misogyny and sexism. They point to the small percentage of porn written and produced by women, or they emphasize the growing popularity of "couples porn," which is typically less misogynistic and abusive than the majority of products that are aimed at the predominantly male market. However, veteran porn director and actor Bill Margold comes right out and admits what he and so many other pornographers are trying to do:

> I'd like to really show what I believe the men want to see: violence against women. I firmly believe that we serve a purpose by showing that. The most violent we can get is the cum shot in the face. Men get off behind that, because they can get even with the women they can't have. We try to inundate the world with orgasms in the face.

Examples like this of the sort of open misogyny and woman-hatred that comes out of the mainstream pornography industry still have the potential to shock young women, because due to the segmentation of the porn market, many of them have never been exposed to it. Dines says that her women students who think they know what's out there in porn are often devastated to learn what their boyfriends consider "normal." This is because the guys are more likely to use the "gonzo" porn referenced above to masturbate by themselves—with effects on their sexuality that we have not yet even begun to understand.

BOYS AND PORN

Three young white men were convicted in March 2005 of sexually assaulting an intoxicated sixteen-year-old girl in the summer of 2002 in Orange County, California. The central piece of evidence in the trial that gained national notoriety was a videotape of the crime made by the defendants. The then-sixteen- and seventeen-year-old men had made a twenty-one-minute video of them shoving a Snapple bottle, lit cigarette, apple juice can, and pool cue into the vagina and anus of the unconscious victim. One of the young men, whose father was then the assistant sheriff of Orange County, had proudly shown the video to some acquaintances, some of whom thought the girl was a corpse and called the police. Many media discussions of the crime and trial took their cues from the defense lawyers' offensive strategy, and focused on the actions of the victim. According to R. Scott Moxley in the *OC Weekly*, the lawyers for the young men called the girl—named Jane Doe for the court proceeding—a "slut" and a "whore," who loved giving "blow jobs" and enjoyed "doggy-style" sex. They claimed that she dreamed of becoming a porn star and had staged the entire episode in order to get them to gangbang her on film. With so much attention fixated on Jane Doe's morals and motives, there was little room to discuss the heart of the case: the morals, motives, and mindsets of the young men. What were they thinking as they molested her? How could they be cruel enough to rape and degrade this girl, and brazen enough to videotape the entire thing and then brag about it? What did those actions say, not about the character of the girl, but about their characters, and the values of the white-affluent culture that produced them? What did this case reveal about young men's attitudes toward women's sexuality? What did it say about sexual norms in male culture, and the role of pornography in establishing or maintaining those norms? Is it so hard to believe that "normal" boys could videotape a grotesque gang rape when porn sites that brag about "invading privacy to the limit" and feature "Gym Cam, Locker Room Cam, Up-Skirt Cam, Toilet Cam, and the Infamous Gyno Cam" are just a mouse click away and part of millions of boys' sexual socialization?

The Orange County gang-rape case was far from an aberration. Over the past decade there have been numerous criminal cases, some of which made the national news but most of which did not, that involved boys and young men who videotaped sexual activity with girls and then shared it with their friends. In a number of these cases, the young men involved were normal, primarily law-abiding kids who did not see anything wrong with what they had done—until they were held accountable. For example, an eighteen-year-old soccer star and high school honor student in Ohio was charged in 2001 with posting nude pictures of a girl in an Internet chat room. He posted the pictures the same night that a seventeen-year-old girl had changed her clothes at his home. He called the incident a practical joke, but was charged with unlawful use of a minor in nudity-oriented material or performance, which is a second-degree felony. Interestingly, in 1999 the U.S. Justice Department formed a partnership with the Information Technology Association of America to educate people about computer responsibility in the Internet age. One goal of the program was to help children and young adults develop an "awareness of potential negative consequences resulting from the misuse of the medium." This seems like a smart initiative, because everyone knows teenagers—like adults—have a tendency to sometimes act without thinking. But any serious attempt to help boys think through their decisions about how to treat girls has to examine those places in male culture where sexist and abusive behavior is presented as normal and masculine and even expected—and where there are no real consequences for hurting people, including through Internet pornography. Even hit Hollywood films present this attitude, such as *American Pie*, where the main character arranges to videotape himself having sex with a Czech exchange student and broadcast it by web cam to his friends watching in another room. When *American Pie* was released in 1999, critics hailed it as good clean fun. Practically no one mentioned that one of the main plot points turned on the lead character's stumbling attempts to commit an unforgivably cruel and sexist act—the type of act that ruins lives when it happens in the real world.

Girls and women suffer the most harm from a culture awash in misogynist pornography, but boys and men are hurt, too. It is important to discuss this hurt both for pragmatic reasons, and out of genuine concern for these boys and men. In order to stem the tide of cruelty, callousness, and brutality toward girls and women that is now mainstream fare from the porn industry, men and boys in sufficient numbers will need to make the decision to stop paying for porn magazines, videos, and Internet porn sites. Some men will be motivated to give up their porn habits as they develop a greater sensitivity to the damage that eroticized cruelty does to girls and women—inside and outside the porn industry. But altruistic concern for harm done to women cannot motivate anywhere near as many men and boys as enlightened self-interest. In other words, if they can be shown that porn hinders rather than facilitates a healthy sex life for *men*, there is at least a chance that enough men will reject it to truly make a difference. But unless heterosexual men perceive that they have a personal stake in a sexual culture that is not dominated by the cartoonish version of sexual fulfillment created by middle-aged businessmen in windowless studios in the San Fernando Valley outside Los Angeles, it is hard to see how the current trend toward greater acceptance of sexualized brutality will be reversed in coming generations.

It is clear that the men who own and run the pornography industry will do anything to girls and women in pursuit of massive profits. But it is also true that they do not have much regard for boys and young men. If they cared about boys and their longings for intimacy, love, and sexual connection with girls, then why would they relentlessly sell them an endless supply of videos, magazines, and websites that heap scorn on girls and women, and reduce them to a set of orifices to use up and discard? As Dines and Jensen write in an article titled "Pornography Is a Left Issue," "Take away every video in which a woman is called a bitch, a cunt, a slut, or a whore, and the shelves would be nearly bare." In the cold and exploitative world created by hardcore pornographers, who are heterosexual boys supposed to have relationships with? With the cum-guzzling sluts who are forced to drink gallons of cum? The big-titted bitches who they can fuck in every hole? The dirty little sluts who want to get their pussies drilled by various farm animals? It is no coincidence that the porn industry does not want boys to establish real intimate connections with girls, because then who would purchase their product?

It is not fair to blame boys (or girls) for being seduced by the porn world's promise of sexual excitement and pleasure. Technological progress—especially home video and the Internet—have made it possible for them to access the most graphic sexual images with the touch of a button. For many boys going through puberty and adolescence, the temptations of porn are irresistible. After all, it promises a kind of sexual gratification with no strings attached—and no chance of rejection. In pornography, even unattractive and unpopular boys can have sex with beautiful girls. Pornography is also so mainstream now that many kids are unfazed by it. In the digital age, it is all around them: online, on cable, video, chat rooms. Porn is now available on cell phones. It is also a common plotline on TV shows such as *Friends* or *The OC*; and many MTV and BET videos look like porn videos. In fact, several rap stars now produce their own porn videos. With porn images all around them, many young Americans simply see it as an unremarkable feature of the cultural landscape.

But this has come at a cost. Because there is so little sexual content in media that is not pornographic, and because there is so little quality sex education in schools, pornography fills a void for millions of sexually inexperienced kids. What they see in pornography helps to establish a template for "normal" sexual behavior that they then feel pressure to emulate. They might not initially be drawn to pornography because of all the misogyny and brutality, but that is what they are getting from the stories being depicted in most mainstream porn today. I heard a story from a rape prevention educator about a question one of his colleagues received from a ten-year-old boy during a presentation. The boy had walked into a room where his older brother was on an Internet porn site, and saw on the screen a man shoving a pool cue into a girl's vagina. The young boy wanted to know: do girls like that sort of thing? A colleague of mine recounted this story: At the college where she teaches, a male and female student, both virgins, had sex for the first time. When the man was about to reach orgasm, he withdrew and ejaculated on his partner's face. They both thought this was the way normal people are supposed to have intercourse. Neither of them was aware that this practice derived not from "real life" but from pornography, where it had developed as an aggressive act by men to express contempt for the women they had just conquered.

"PIMPS AND HOES"

In *Beyond Beats and Rhymes*, Byron Hurt's documentary film about hyper-masculinity and misogyny in hip-hop culture, he interviews young men outside a rap music event who matter-of-factly identify many of the women across the street as "hoes." He then walks over and asks the women what they think of being labeled this way. They reject the label and assert their right to wear short shorts and bikini tops in the hot Florida sun. The viewer is left with the sad impression that these women are either oblivious to how some men view them, or they are so beaten down that they expect it and are unfazed. The term "ho" has become such a routine part of everyday conversation that it has lost much of its initial sting. In this context, it is worth remembering that "ho" is shorthand for "whore," which itself is a colloquial expression for a prostituted woman (or man). So when men (or women) call women "hoes," they are comparing them to prostitutes. To what effect? As a growing body of research shows, some men treat prostitutes with shocking brutality. According to one study, about 80 percent of women in prostitution have been the victim of a rape. As Susan Kay Hunter and K. C. Reed said in a 1990 speech at a conference sponsored by the now-defunct National Coalition Against Sexual Assault, "It's hard to talk about this because . . . the experience of prostitution is just like rape. Prostitutes are raped, on the average, eight to ten times per year. They are the most raped class of women in the history of our planet." Contrary to the *Pretty Woman* stereotype, most prostituted women are young, poor, and desperate. A large majority are incest survivors. Many of them are women of color. The average age that "women" in the United States are drawn into prostitution is *thirteen* or *fourteen*. So the term "ho" is not just a thoughtless epithet. When men (or women) call a woman a "ho," they not only demean and degrade her. In a sense they send the message to people who know her that she deserves to be treated like a prostitute. In this way it sets her up—like a prostitute—to become a rape victim.

If casual use of the word "ho" sets women up to be rape victims, then it follows that casual use of the word "pimp" sets men up to be rapists. In fact, in the moral universe created by the phrase "pimps and hoes," the true "nature" of women is that they should be sexually subservient, and the true "nature" of men is that they should dominate and control women. In a world that operates according to the cold and unforgiving values of the market-place, the only distinction between men is whether they own women or rent them. As the white rap/rocker Kid Rock raps in "Pimp of the Nation": "There's only two types of men/Pimps and Johns." There is no doubt about which one is the true "man's man."

Over the past few years, the word "pimp" has become a non-controversial word in popular discourse. From Nelly's Pimp Juice beverage to the MTV show *Pimp My Ride*, from guys displaying "Pimpin' Ain't Easy" bumper stickers on their cars and trucks to men high-fiving each other for that "pimpin' stereo system you got there, man," the word "pimp" has not only become a routine part of the language—it has actually become a compli-mentary term. To what effect? What are the possible consequences of this glamorization of pimps? First, a little reality check. The traditional image of a pimp in this country is an African American street hustler. So casual talk about pimps always has a racial subtext that perpetuates one of the most racist caricatures of black masculinity: They're sex-crazed jive-talkers who treat their women like shit. But regardless of their race, pimps are criminals who make money off the crass exploitation of girls' and women's bodies. (And boys' and men's.) Many of them are rapists and batterers. Regardless of how "cool" the image of the pimp has become in mainstream media culture, in real life pimps are incredibly cruel and callous men. The Council for Prostitution Alternatives estimates that 85 percent of prostitutes are raped by pimps. Some pimps are sociopaths. As Kathleen Barry explains in *The Prostitution of Sexuality* (1995):

> Pimps target girls or women who seem naive, lonely, home-less, and rebellious. At first, the attention and feigned affec-tion from the pimp convinces her to "be his woman." Pimps ultimately keep prostituted women in virtual captivity by

verbal abuse—making a woman feel that she is utterly
worthless: a toilet, a piece of trash; and by physical coercion—beatings and the threat of torture. Eighty to 95 percent of all prostitution is pimp-controlled.

Let's be clear. A culture that celebrates pimps is a culture that teaches men
that masculinity is about power and control. It teaches them that they are
entitled to sell, abuse, and rape women. Of course many men reject that and
refuse to accept the one-dimensional caricature of manhood it implies. Still,
to the extent that "pimps and hoes" becomes increasingly synonymous in
people's psyches with "men and women," the fight against sexual violence
will be like shoveling sand against the tide.

THE DEMAND SIDE OF SEX TRAFFICKING

In 2003, a Los Angeles-based group called Captive Daughters partnered with
the International Human Rights Law Institute of DePaul University College
of Law to organize the first-ever conference on the demand side of prostitution and sex trafficking. The "demand side" is a euphemism for the men who
pay for sex with women and children, either here in the U.S. or around the
world. The rationale for shifting the paradigm this way is obvious. It is
imperative that the victims of prostitution and sex trafficking—who are typically poor girls and women from Asia, eastern Europe, and Central and
South America—get the services they need, including medical care, drug
abuse counseling, job training, and a host of other assistance. But these services are often too little, too late. Many of the girls' and women's lives are
already badly damaged, their family and community relationships severed.
On the other hand, without the demand from johns, traffickers' profits
would shrink, and the international prostitution syndicates would either dis-
solve or move into other areas of criminal activity.

When the focus of attention shifts to the demand side of the equation, a
number of relevant questions emerge: Who are the men who buy sex from
trafficked women and children? What percentage of them are "normal" guys,
and what percentage are sexual predators? In a 2004 *New York Times Magazine*
cover story on sex trafficking, the author, Peter Landesman, said that many
formerly trafficked women he talked to said that the sex in the U.S. is "even
rougher" than what the girls face in Mexico. One woman he spoke with in
Mexico City who had been held captive in New York City said that she
believed younger foreign girls were in demand in the U.S. because of "an
increased appetite for more aggressive, dangerous sex." Who are the men with
this increased appetite, and why do they seek out these types of experiences?

On a practical level, how do they find the prostitutes to service them? In ads for "escort services" and mail-order bride companies? In the classified advertising sections in the back of hip newsweeklies? On the Internet? Does the travel industry collude when agencies organize and promote trips for johns to go to favored destinations for sex tourism, where they have easy access to cheap sex with young girls and boys? To what degree is the U.S. military complicit when it averts its institutional eyes as brothels spring up near bases and U.S. service members continue the long tradition of taking quick trips on weekend leave to solicit prostitutes in Asia? There are a host of public health concerns that revolve around men. When American men travel to Southeast Asia or South America to have sex with children, do they wear condoms? Or do they force the girls and boys to have sex without them, which increases the chance that either party—but especially the prostituted person—might contract HIV or other sexually transmitted infections? Do the men's wives, girlfriends, and boyfriends back in the States know about their unprotected episodes when they return from their travels and have sex with them?

Unless men's demand for sexual services subsides, in a world where there are billions of poor and desperate people, there will always be a steady supply of women and children who are forced, tricked, or blackmailed into prostitution by criminal pimps and organized crime syndicates. The trouble is that until recently, few people even mentioned the demand side, much less sought to analyze it systematically. It was simply expected—and accepted—that millions of men would want to procure prostitutes or pay to have sex with young girls or boys. And to this day, few people seem willing to name and challenge the colonialist exploitation at the heart of the globalized prostitution business. Exhibit A: the increasing number of American and European men who travel to impoverished Third World countries to have sex with dark-skinned young women and girls, and boys. When you add that degree of overt racism to the already rampant sexism of prostitution, the problem can seem overwhelming. I know that for some women, this entire subject is simply too sensitive to raise, especially because some men can be defensive and hostile when women challenge them on the subject of their "private" sexual behaviors.

A woman I know who works as a rape advocate described to me a conversation she had with her neighbor, a man she considered very sensitive to women's issues, about a new book she was reading by Melissa Farley.

She said, "I'm reading this book on prostitution and post-traumatic stress. It describes the experiences of prostitutes around the world and their experiences parallel those of rape and physical battery…"

The neighbor replied, "No, I don't believe that. It's the woman's decision."

"Is it?" she replied. "Do you really think they want to have sex with all those men? In the book it talks about how many are forced into it and then controlled by pimps or boyfriends, husbands."

"They make a lot of money," he said.

"…that the pimps keep."

"I don't know. It's still their choice to do it."

"What other choices do they have?"

"No one puts a gun to their head!"

At that point, according to the woman, her neighbor became defensive to the point of belligerence. He grew angrier as the conversation continued, while she felt a mixture of frustration and sadness. She also felt a chill coming on in their friendship. "He became a stranger to me in that moment," she said.

This conversation is not unusual. The entire subject of men's participation in the purchase, sale, and rental of women's bodies has long been shrouded in denial, euphemisms, and evasions. The anonymity of pimps and johns in discussions about sex trafficking has been maintained in the same way that domestic violence and sexual assault have been defined as women's issues. The language used to discuss it obscures men's role. For example, the *New York Times* lead editorial on New Year's Eve 2005 offered a series of resolutions for bipartisan national action, and it highlighted sex trafficking as one area where Republicans and Democrats could work together. But men were not mentioned in the editorial. There were references to "helping women in the third world" and earnest pronouncements that this kind of "exploitation of women" remain on the international agenda. But one would search in vain for any acknowledgment that the demand for the illegal business of sex trafficking is men's desire to purchase sex with "exotic" women—and young girls—that they can use and abuse with virtual impunity. There was also no mention of pimps or johns. The editorial suggested the focus of the anti-sex trafficking agenda should expand beyond the poor countries where trafficking begins to include the wealthy nations where the sex slaves are imported, such as the Scandinavian countries, Japan, and the U.S. This is a step in the right direction. The next step is to say that the focus needs to be on the criminal *men* in the poor and wealthy countries who coerce and enslave women and children in order to exploit their bodies for financial gain, and the *average guys* whose money fuels the demand.

STRIP CULTURE GOES MAINSTREAM

In the early 1990s, I was a guest on a television talk show where the subject was "feminist strippers." The question: does strip culture empower women or degrade them? Most discussions about strip culture on mainstream TV focus on the titillating and sexy aspects of strippers' lives, or the conflicts that arise in women's relationships when their husbands or boyfriends patronize the clubs. I was there to argue that it is impossible to discuss stripping without taking into account the prevalence of sexual violence in our society. We can speculate about whether or not strip clubs would be popular in a non-sexist, rape-free world, but that is not the world we live in. Predictably, one or two of my fellow guests, as well as several members of the studio audience, countered that the popularity of male strip shows like Chippendale's proves that stripping culture is not sexist. *Women love this stuff. They go crazy at male strip shows.* But even the slightest peek beneath the surface of these comparisons reveals a huge difference between female and male strip culture. That difference provides interesting insight about some of the ways that the sex industry contributes to the sexual violence pandemic.

The male and female strip cultures are not even close in size and scope. Male strip shows make up a tiny fraction of the "exotic" dancing industry. It is a challenge to find any strip clubs that cater exclusively to heterosexual women who want to watch men take their clothes off, although there are "male stripper" nights at strip clubs that offer naked women dancers every other day and night of the week. And male strippers typically do not fully disrobe. As someone said of the bikini, what it reveals is exciting, but what it conceals is vital. Male strippers rarely appear totally naked with their genitals on full display, while in a great many of the twenty-five hundred strip clubs across the United States, women take everything off. Even more revealing is the difference between how female and male strippers pose. Like women in pornography, female strippers pose in vulnerable positions—writhing around poles, back arched, legs spread, bending down with their rear ends up in the air and facing toward the audience. The intent is to invite the male patron to fantasize about penetrating them. Male strippers, on the other hand, do not pose in vulnerable positions. They strut around stage and thrust their bodies forward, posing in ways that reinforce not their vulnerability but their sexual and physical power. Even their choice of costumes is revealing in their celebration of traditional masculine strength: male strippers frequently pose as police officers, cowboys, construction workers. Compare that with female strippers' costumes of choice: garter belts and lace, cheerleader skirts and pom-poms, or the classic French maid's outfit. (One exception: the dominatrix is another popular stripper persona.) In other words, in strip culture as in pornography, men's power and women's vulnerability is presented as sexy. Not coincidentally, that is the same dynamic that underlies and defines rape culture.

In patriarchal culture, women's sexuality and physical appearance is one of their defining features, a sexist presumption that the institution of female stripping confirms and perpetuates. By contrast, heterosexual men's sexual attractiveness is much less based on their looks. So, when women go to "ladies night" at the strip club, or hire a male stripper for a private bachelorette party, part of the pleasure is in the role reversal. They can act like men for a night. In fact, one reason there is so much laughter at such shows is that for men to put themselves on sexual display for women in this way is still relatively uncommon; the humor resides in the subversion of the norm. This has begun to change over the past twenty years, as male "beefcake" and "hunk" calendars have become more of a regular feature in the cultural landscape.

Spokespeople for the strip industry insist that many of today's prominent strip clubs are not the sleazy strip joints of decades past: they are more likely to be housed in attractive steel and glass buildings with nice furniture and clean bathrooms, and the deeper pockets of their owners allows for higher quality advertising than the cheap XXX signs that you still see in windowless strip clubs near highway truck stops or in economically depressed urban or rural areas. But these upgrades do not hide the danger for women that lurks just beneath the surface of the stripping industry. In fact, perhaps the most important difference between the male and female strip cultures is the threat of violence that is absent from the former and ever-present in the latter. Female strippers rely on continuous protection from male bouncers and security officers, who are present in every strip club to shield the dancers from aggressive, disrespectful men—many of them drunk—who do not recognize or accept the "official" boundaries between the dancers and the customers. Unlike male strippers, female strippers have to worry about their safety *after* they leave the club, and not only for the reasons that all women are vulnerable to men's violence. Female strippers, like prostitutes, are more vulnerable to sexual violence outside the club.

Most men who go to strip clubs do not assault women, and they respect the boundaries put forth by the establishment. But some men clearly do not respect the women, and after a few drinks they have no shame or reluctance to express their contempt. One former stripper told me that it was common for men to yell insults to women on stage as they walked by, and many dancers she knew had experienced everything from slaps and pinches to digital penetration. One of the open secrets of the sex industry is that some male customers believe that once they have paid a woman for sex they have the right to treat her any way they want. This includes some men who go to strip clubs and watch women strip, and it certainly includes men who pay women for lap dances, where the line between stripping and outright prostitution is deliberately vague. They might not have touched the woman with their own hands or naked penises, but in their minds they have paid women for sex, and are thus entitled to them.

In some cases, this sense of ownership plays out in disturbing and violent ways. Prostitutes are regularly beaten and raped, both by pimps and by customers. According to the prostitution researcher Melissa Farley, women in prostitution report that half of their customers demand sex without a condom. Many women who strip are also prostitutes, but in the minds of many men, there is not a big difference between the two. The good girl/bad girl dichotomy is alive and well, and when a woman is a bad girl, some men who have been socialized in our deeply misogynistic culture believe she is no longer worthy of their respect. In fact, when a woman so much as takes her clothes off in public, some men think she has given up her right to control when and with whom she wants to have sex. I have talked with several former strippers who say they cannot tell men whom they are interested in romantically that they used to strip, because they fear the men will assume that means they are ready to have sex with them practically on the spot.

It is one thing to argue that a woman has a right to do whatever she wants with her body, which includes taking her clothes off for men so she can put clothes on the backs of her children. But for anyone to say that stripping is an expression of women's sexual freedom or empowerment is laughable, given that most men read it as confirmation of their degraded "whore" status. In fact, this is how some men think about all girls and women who dare to be explicitly sexual—not just strippers. This presents young heterosexual women with a difficult dilemma as they try to negotiate the line between sexual self-expression and physical safety in a world where men's violence is a common occurrence. Lynn Phillips thoughtfully explores some of these challenges for young women in her book *Flirting With Danger: Young Women's Reflections on Sexuality and Domination* (2000). The disconnect between what women intend when they express themselves sexually and how some men interpret that expression also helps explain the ongoing debate about the legacy of the pop star Madonna. Madonna is celebrated by many in the media and academia for being an unapologetically sexual woman and artist who is unafraid to transgress the boundaries of proper femininity. But as noted by the cultural theorist Elayne Rapping, Madonna's critics argue that the many young girls who imitated her dress and style were likely to be met, in the real world, by a male public very much in the dark about the liberatory intent of the pop diva's work. Or as a sixteen-year-old boy in a detention center in the mid-1980s said to me when I asked him what he thought of Madonna, "Boy, I'd like to fuck her."

Women who work as prostitutes and strippers are routinely subject to brutal violence from pimps and johns, and they are a favorite target of serial killers. They live in a dangerous world, where they never know if the next john they meet will kill them, or if the polite schoolteacher who sits in the front row at the strip club will turn into the stalker from hell. This ever-present danger is one of the reasons why so many women in the sex industry develop symptoms of post-traumatic stress disorder. There have been numerous media stories in recent years about a trend in high-end strip clubs toward friendlier environments for women patrons, and some women who describe themselves as feminists claim to be empowered by the experience of watching other women take their clothes off. But no matter how many positive stories the strip industry tries to sell to a public eager to avert its eyes from sexism and exploitation, women strippers remain particularly vulnerable to harassment, abuse, and violence from men—inside and outside the clubs.

A particularly tragic example of this took place in June 1996, in Peabody, Massachusetts, on the north shore of Boston. A tall, blond, twenty-seven-year-old woman, Kristen Crowley, stopped at a Mobil Mini-Mart on her way home from work one night to pick up a can of ravioli and some water and soda. It was around midnight, and two drunk white men, Timothy Dykens, twenty-three, and John Keegan, twenty-five, were in front of the store, talking to the nineteen-year-old clerk, who was having a cigarette. Earlier, the men had been drinking in the Golden Banana, a local strip club where women danced in cages. Keegan reportedly saw Kristen get out of her car and said to Dykens, "Wow, look at that. I want a piece of that." The nineteen-year-old clerk, perhaps in a spirit of male-bonding, shared a piece of titillating information with his temporary acquaintances.

"She's a stripper," he said.

"You know what we've gotta do," said Dykens. According to the clerk he repeated the phrase several times.

Kristen made her purchases and left the store to drive home. The clerk watched as the two men got in their car and followed her back to her condo complex, where they jumped her as she walked across the parking lot with the bag of groceries. They dragged her to a ravine where they tore off her clothes and tried to rape her, and then smashed her skull with a large boulder and left her to die, just a few dozen yards from where her husband of eighteen months sat in their apartment, awaiting her return. Not surprisingly, media accounts of the murder highlighted Kristen Crowley's part-time work as a stripper at men's private birthday and bachelor parties: "Dancer murdered in Peabody." "Jury selection begins in dancer murder." The victim-blaming undertones were subtle but unmistakable. There is a well-established narrative in this culture that sexual women get punished for their freedom and libido. It is a favorite theme in Hollywood films, most famously in Alfred Hitchcock's *Psycho*, where Janet Leigh plays the sacrificial sexy blond whose brutal and eroticized murder scene in the shower has titillated audiences and wowed critics for more than four decades.

What was not explored in great detail in the media coverage of this horrific murder was the connection between the men's patronage of a strip club earlier that night and their crude objectification of this woman. There wasn't even much discussion about whether their discovery that she was a stripper contributed to the crime. There was only one substantial piece in the mainstream Boston media that suggested a relationship between strip culture and men's violence against women. It was a November 1996 article in *Boston Magazine* entitled, "Pretty Girl Dead," by J. M. Lawrence, and I have used it to draw some of the facts of the case for this account. But few people in media seemed eager to examine some of the critical questions raised by this murder: Do men who frequent strip clubs learn to objectify women even more than men who do not? If men are already misogynistic and angry with women, do certain aspects of strip culture—like women in cages—validate their feelings of superiority and feed their contempt? How do men read the act of women taking off their clothes for men in public? What are some of the differences between men in the way they interpret this experience? No doubt some men remain unfazed by all of the sexist trappings of strip culture, and simply like to stare up at the stage and fantasize about having sex with an attractive woman. They see it as just another type of entertainment, some eye-candy in the background while they have a few drinks. But other men have less benign intentions. For them, strip clubs are places where they feel special license to vent their hostility toward sexual women. A former stripper I know tells this story:

> One time I was on stage dancing and this guy walks up to the stage and waves a $100 bill in front of me and gives me a wry grin. I remember being so happy because no one had ever given me a tip that big. When I bent down and opened my garter for him to put the money in, he yanked it back, called me a slut, laughed, and walked away.

Would it have made any difference if someone had confronted Timothy Dykens and John Keegan earlier in the evening when they were making tasteless and vulgar comments to strippers at the Golden Banana? Probably not. How about earlier in their lives? Would Kristen Crowley still be alive today if someone a little older and wiser had provided better guidance for them years before, when they were young and impressionable, and still learning how a decent man is supposed to treat women?

J. M. Lawrence reported in the *Boston Magazine* piece that the name of the Mobil Mini-Mart clerk was impounded by request of the district attorney's office after he was threatened by a man claiming to be a member of Hell's Angels. She also quoted one of Kristen's friends, who said she did not blame the nineteen-year-old clerk for the murder, although his comment ("She is a stripper") might have triggered the entire episode. "He was just a kid," the friend said. "It was just guy talk to him." It is probably safe to assume that he wishes he had not been "one of the guys" that night. The other guys in the case surely have their own regrets. Dykens is serving a sentence of life in prison without the possibility of parole. Deegan was convicted of murder in 1998 but will eventually be eligible for parole, after his lawyer convinced the jury that his client was too drunk to lift the boulder that killed Kristen Crowley.

HUNTING FOR BAMBI

At first it seemed like either a crude satire or an elaborate hoax. Or maybe it was true. In July 2003, a Las Vegas television station broke the news about a new business, called Hunting for Bambi, where men in camouflage outfits hunted naked women and shot them with paintball guns. The idea of men paying thousands of dollars to shoot women dressed in nothing but tennis shoes and hiding behind bushes in the Nevada desert was at first too outrageous for many people to believe. The news sped rapidly across the Internet, and then made a rotation on the 24/7 cable news channels. The story made great TV: it combined a titillating Las Vegas mix of sex and violence, and it came complete with home-made video footage of naked women scampering around outdoors.

The concept of this new business was so over the top that the rational response, at first glance, was to think the entrepreneurs responsible were simply looking to profit from the shock value of their demented idea. This is a tried and true marketing strategy. Outrageousness sometimes does move product. Hence the dilemma faced by women's groups and others: how to fight back? If they responded with outrage, it would fuel the controversy that brings free media, and even more people would be exposed to the offensive product. On the other hand, if they ignored it, they would run the risk of sending the message that men pretending to kill women for sport was not only socially acceptable but might even be profitable. Cultural critics also faced a dilemma in seeking to understand this phenomenon. Should they treat Hunting for Bambi as a cultural aberration—in which case the media storm that surrounded it could be viewed as the response of a healthy society to a violation of its central norms? Or should they treat this new "pastime" as a chilling but nonetheless understandable development in a culture where the objectification of women is common and men's violence against women is in the news on a daily basis? There is no doubt that it was more comforting to think of Hunting for Bambi as an aberration, because the focus then would not have been on "normal" men, but on the amoral businessmen who created it and the pathetic wackos who supposedly paid big bucks to play the game.

Soon after the initial burst of publicity, the urban legends website *Snopes* declared that Hunting for Bambi was a hoax. Eventually the promoter, Michael Burdick, acknowledged there were no actual hunts—they were staged for TV news as a way to sell Hunting for Bambi videos. Many media commentators breathed a sigh of relief, grateful to hear that our culture had not yet sunk quite that far. But why did so many people easily believe there were men who were willing to pay thousands of dollars to play out murderous fantasies about stalking and shooting women like scared animals? For that matter, why are there men who would buy a video that depicts this? And as the sociologist John Glass pointed out, why should the actual hunt be considered degrading to women, but a video of it should not? As of this writing, the video is still available for purchase on Amazon.com, where one reviewer called it "Lewd, crude, and funny . . . watch this video at a bachelor party or at a hunting camp and roll on the floor laughing."

The Hunting for Bambi controversy did not appear out of nowhere. It emerged in the context of a broader entertainment culture where the degradation of women has been normalized, and male sexual aggression celebrated. Is the idea underlying Hunting for Bambi so unbelievable? Not when you consider that in the U.S. in the early twenty-first century over ten thousand new porn videos are produced each year, with titles like *The Stalker, Flesh Hunter,* and *Anal Intruder*; or that *Grand Theft Auto: Vice City*, a video game that gives players the opportunity to simulate sex with a prostitute *and then beat her to death* is one of the all-time leaders in video game sales. Men's violence against women—or the minimizing and excusing of it—was a pervasive presence in our entertainment culture long before Hunting for Bambi came on the scene. Still, there is something revealing about this ugly episode. While media stories about this new form of "adult" entertainment focused mostly on the degradation of women, the fact that so many people believed the Hunting for Bambi hoax says more about how we feel about *men* than it speaks to how we view women. During his deception, Michael Burdick— who named his company Real Men Outdoor Productions—told the Las Vegas TV station KLAS that the majority of men who paid the $5,000 to $10,000 to play the game were the submissive, quiet types. "For the individual who's used to saying, 'I can't go out with the boys tonight,' or the wimp

206 ❖ The Macho Paradox

of America," he said, "it's a chance for him to come out and vent his aggression and really take charge and have some fun." No such authentic individual was ever identified. But it is a fair bet that Burdick markets the video of the staged hunt to men who fit that description. It is an open secret that tens of thousands of average Joes with similar motivations come to Las Vegas ("What happens here, stays here") each year to explore those sorts of sexual power fantasies with prostitutes in hotel rooms, or in the legal brothels nearby. What Burdick was banking on is what feminists regard as a truism: you can look like a nice guy in public and still do—and fantasize about doing—abusive and degrading things to women and girls in private.

CHAPTER ELEVEN

MVP: Athletes and Marines

"There's nothing better than excelling at a game you love. There's nothing worse than thinking your accomplishments as a player outweigh your responsibilities as a person."
—Doug Flutie

"If a marine is a great warrior on the battlefield and he comes home and beats his wife, he is not a good marine."
—Lt. General George Christmas, United States Marine Corps (Ret.)

It was while in graduate school in the early 1990s that I developed the beginnings of MVP, a program to work with high school and college male student athletes on the issues of rape, battering, sexual harassment, and all forms of men's violence against women. I was not interested in working with "jocks" simply because of their particular problems. There is no question that men's violence against women is a serious problem in the male sports culture—at all levels. Anyone who has paid the slightest attention to the sports pages over the past couple of decades knows how sadly common it is to read about alleged assaults by male athletes. There is a widespread public perception that male college student athletes are disproportionately responsible for acts of sexual aggression against women, although to date no full-scale national studies have conclusively proven this point. But my interest in the male sports culture had less to do with athlete perpetration and more to do with the leadership platform afforded male athletes. The rationale was simple. Male athletes, as exemplars of traditional masculine success, already have status with their fellow men. If they could be persuaded to speak out about sexual and domestic violence, they could have influence not only in the athletic subculture, but in the larger male culture that continues to look to athletics for definitions of what it means to be a "real man." In particular, leadership from men in athletics could make it safer for other men to "come out" against sexism. Eventually, this would result in a growing intolerance in male culture for some men's sexist violence.

Striking examples of this strategy can be found in politics. Political scientists and historians frequently observe that President Richard Nixon, a renowned anti-communist, was the first U.S. president to open relations to communist China. Because of his anti-communist credentials, no one could credibly accuse Nixon of being a weak-kneed liberal who was ready to sell out American interests to the Chinese. And surely it is more than historical coincidence that Lyndon Johnson, a white southerner from Texas who talked like a good ol' boy, was able to champion civil rights and was critical to the enactment of historic federal civil rights legislation.

Another interesting illustration of this leadership concept comes from the world of beer marketing. Consider this mini-history of Miller Lite beer: In 1972, Miller Brewing Company bought the rights to Meister Brau Light, a "diet" beer the small Chicago brewery had been attempting to market to women. Miller's market research had determined that men wanted a beer that would not fill them up, but they did not want to drink a "feminine" beer. So Miller had a problem, because in 1972 men made up approximately 85 percent of the beer market in the U.S. Miller's strategy was to run an advertising campaign that showed famous football players drinking Miller Lite beer. The most popular featured Dick Butkus, an iconic white linebacker for the Chicago Bears, and Bubba Smith, an iconic African American defensive lineman for the Baltimore Colts. They placed Butkus and Smith in a bar room scene surrounded by their friends, with a Miller Lite beer in their hands. The unspoken message of the campaign was: Dick Butkus and Bubba Smith can drink Lite beer and no one is going to accuse them of being wimps. You can, too. As a result, the Miller Lite campaign became one of the most successful advertising campaigns in TV history. It won Clio awards for advertising excellence in 1977 and 1978, and throughout the 1980s and 1990s Miller Lite was the official beer of the National Football League.

How did a beer travel the distance in just a few short years from being considered a "wimpy diet beer" to becoming the official beer of the NFL? First, a smart marketing person identified the problem. Millions of men are hypersensitive about appearing unmanly, so the challenge is to make it manly to buy the product. The best way is to create an association between the Lite beer and recognizably masculine figures. In other words, if Dick Butkus and Bubba Smith take a "risk" and publicly identify themselves with Lite beer, it is easier for men with less status in the masculine hierarchy to do likewise. The same principle applied in recent years when Mike Ditka, the tough-as-nails football coach, appeared on television commercials and exhorted men to take the "Levitra challenge" and use a male sexual-enhancement drug, or when Rafael Palmiero, the home-run-hitting major league baseball star, made a similar pitch for Viagra.

Why not utilize this approach to get more men to speak out about gender violence? As we have seen, a set of unexamined beliefs in male-peer culture has historically kept men silent. It is wimpy to confront other men's sexism. It is wimpy to question men's enjoyment of women as sex objects. Men who treat women with dignity and respect cannot be real men. What could be more effective to counteract the silencing power of these beliefs than to enlist the support of recognizably masculine men? And where better to find them than the sports culture?

In 1992 I approached Dr. Richard Lapchick, the civil rights activist and director of Northeastern University's Center for the Study of Sport in Society, and proposed the idea of a program to train high school and college male student athletes to be leaders in gender-violence prevention. With initial funding from the U.S. Department of Education, I, Lapchick, and the center's associate director, Art Taylor, started the Mentors in Violence Prevention (MVP) program in 1993. The program was designed to train student athletes and other student leaders to use their status to speak out against rape, battering, sexual harassment, gay-bashing, and all forms of sexist abuse and violence. A female component was added in the second year with the complementary principle of training female student athletes and others to be leaders on these issues. Today, when MVP is implemented in the sports culture and other educational settings it is a mixed-gender initiative, although a key feature of the model is small-group, single-sex discussions of the issues.

MVP is the most widely utilized gender violence prevention model in college athletics—for both men and women. Numerous Division I athletic programs such as Kentucky, Wisconsin, Notre Dame, and the University of Florida regularly participate in MVP trainings conducted by members of the MVP staff, who are all former college and professional athletes. In 2005, the Southeastern Conference (SEC) became the first major college athletic conference to fund MVP training for schools conference-wide. The National Collegiate Athletic Association uses MVP materials in their Life Skills program.

Since 1998, the 2002, 2004, and 2005 Super Bowl champion New England Patriots football club have held MVP trainings each year with the players in rookie camp, along with the coaching staff and front office personnel. The 2004 World Series champion Boston Red Sox implemented the program for the first time in spring training of 2005, along with other sports organizations such as the New York Jets and Major League Lacrosse.

MVP has also been implemented in the United States military. In fact, the MVP program is the first system-wide gender-violence prevention program in the history of the U.S. Marine Corps. MVP trainers have been working all over the world with marines since 1997. MVP trainings and workshops have also been held with officers and enlisted personnel from the army, navy, and air force, as well as personnel from the service academies.

BEYOND SPORTS CULTURE

Although MVP began in the sports culture and is increasingly utilized there, the MVP model is equally effective with the general population of college and high school students, and in other institutional settings. When a high school implements MVP, for example, student athletes and coaches are typically part of the program, but so are band members, kids in the drama club, and student government leaders—as well as skater kids, smoker kids, and kids who have nothing to do with traditional student leadership groups. On college campuses, athletic programs can implement MVP, but so can the housing department, Greek affairs, health education, and new student orientation.

The MVP model is one of the first educational initiatives to utilize the concept of "bystanders" in an approach to gender-violence and bullying prevention. It focuses on men not as perpetrators or potential perpetrators, but as empowered bystanders who can confront abusive peers—and support abused ones. It focuses on women not as victims or potential targets of harassment, rape, and abuse, but as empowered bystanders who can also take leadership roles. In this model, a "bystander" is defined as a family member, friend, classmate, teammate, coworker—anyone who is imbedded in a family, social, or professional relationship with someone who might be abusive, or experiencing abuse.

The heart of the MVP model is interactive discussion, with both single-sex and mixed-gender applications. One of its goals is better inter-gender dialogue about issues like sexual violence, relationship abuse, and sexual harassment. But single-sex sessions provide young men and women with a comfortable space within which to explore some of the more charged aspects of these difficult subjects. In all-male sessions, men will sometimes say things they simply would not say with women present (and vice versa).

As noted by one of the pioneers of sexual assault prevention education with men, the psychologist Alan Berkowitz, all-male workshops on rape and other forms of gender violence allow men "to speak openly without fear of judgment or criticism by women." This is by no means intended to disparage coeducational learning, or the contributions women make to men's education on this or any other issue. But I and many of my colleagues have co-facilitated countless single-sex discussions where men have said things we know they would not have said if women were present.

Sometimes I wish my female friends and colleagues could eavesdrop on these conversations, because they would be fascinated by the dialogue and impressed by the insightful—and sometimes courageous—comments men make. For example, one night in the mid-1990s Byron Hurt and I were conducting a workshop with an entire Division I college football team in the South. The group of a hundred was too big for an intimate conversation, and a lot of guys were joking and making snide remarks. Then a young man in the back rose and addressed his teammates. "You guys laughing and talking better listen to what these guys are saying. My mom went through something like this, and it wasn't pretty," he said. "This shit is serious." The mood in the room instantly changed, and the rest of the session was animated but respectful.

Other times I am thankful there are no women in the room, because some men's misogynistic attitudes and victim-blaming propensities can come pouring out in an all-male setting. In those settings, for example, I have heard more than a few high school boys and college men claim that it is okay to make aggressive sexual comments about girls' bodies to girls in school hallways, in malls, or out on the streets. "Girls like that," some of them will say. "Especially if they dress sexy." When someone points out that regardless of how they dress, girls do not appreciate this sort of male commentary, some guys are dismissive. "What's the big deal anyway? They should get over it." If a young man had the chutzpah to say that in a mixed-gender setting (in my experience, most do not), one of his female peers would more than likely confront him—sometimes angrily. I have seen this happen: A guy makes a victim-blaming comment like "She should have known what to expect," about a woman who was raped at a party. "I can't believe how ignorant some guys are!" one of his female classmates exclaims. "Do guys actually believe that girls like to be treated as if they're in a porn video? You guys are so immature." Her female friends nod or shout out their agreement. Meanwhile, the guy who made the controversial comment desperately tries to defend himself. His friends jump in to support him. The conversation then quickly turns into a "battle between the sexes" with everyone feeling pressured to take the side of their sex. The whole scene sends a strong message to other guys who either agree with the original speaker, have a more complex view of the issue at hand, or completely disagree with him. The message is to stay silent, because they could easily be accused by the girls of being insensitive or sexist, or attacked by the boys for not maintaining male solidarity. The result is that the dialogue is less productive than it could be if people were comfortable being honest.

Chances are a conversation about the same subject in an all-male setting would play out differently. MVP sessions are typically led by people who are slightly older than the target group. They are not authority figures laying down the law, but more like older brothers and sisters there to provide guidance on difficult issues. In many settings, high school juniors and seniors work with incoming ninth graders, or with middle school students. In college, upperclassmen (and upperclasswomen) work with first-year students, etc. A male MVP trainer might respond to the victim-blaming comment by saying, "Are you sure you want to say that? Doesn't a girl have the right to say no to sex whenever she wants? Wouldn't you want that right for yourself?" This gives the guy a chance to hear another young man's perspective, and while it might challenge his beliefs, it does so in a way that allows him to reconsider, rather than retreat into defensiveness and hostility.

Many all-male (or all-female) MVP sessions begin with an interactive exercise. The exercise is designed to highlight the role of the bystander by asking people to visualize a powerful and clear-cut bystander scenario. MVP trainers explain to participants that they will be asked to visualize a woman (or man) close to them who is being assaulted—physically or sexually—by a man. In most cases, this exercise takes place in single-sex groups, although it has been used in mixed-gender settings (it was originally designed for men only). In either case, MVP trainers are instructed to tell people not to participate if they feel uncomfortable in any way. As the exercise begins, participants are asked to close their eyes (unless they choose not to) and think about a woman (or man) close to them—such as a mother, sister, wife, girlfriend. Then they are asked to imagine that she/he is being assaulted by a man. After they let that sit for a moment, the MVP trainers ask the group to imagine there is another man in the room who is in a position to stop the assault, but he does not. He either stands there and watches, or gets up and leaves. Once people think about this for a few moments, they are asked to open their eyes. As you might expect, men often react strongly to this exercise. They are upset about the assault, and angry at the bystander who failed to act. They often say the bystander is "just as guilty" as the perpetrator. One marine said, "He gets the second bullet."

Then the MVP trainers ask the following questions: how did you feel when you imagined a woman (or man) close to you being assaulted, and how did you feel about the bystander? In answer to the first question, it sometimes takes a while for men to say they felt any emotions aside from the socially approved "masculine" ones of anger and rage. There is no doubt that many men experience a range of feelings, such as powerlessness and sadness. One goal of this exercise is to validate publicly in a roomful of men that it is okay and common for men to have such feelings. But the chief goal of the exercise, and the reason it was created, is to get people to contemplate the role and responsibility of the bystander. The imagined scenario is deliberately clear-cut, and people usually express anger at the bystander for failing to intervene. Anger at the perp, sadness, and helplessness about the victim are also common reactions. Many people—men and women—say they choose not to visualize the scenario because it is too painful or difficult to experience.

But here is the catch. When MVP sessions get into discussions about different real-life bystander scenarios, people often give all sorts of nuanced reasons why they or other bystanders do not or would not get involved. Real life quite often turns out to be a lot more complex than that exercise. By referring back to the clarity of people's perceptions and expectations of the imagined bystander, this comparison makes a powerful point about those nuances and complexities and how they can obscure the central moral question: what can a responsible person do when faced with the opportunity to prevent an act of violence?

MVP uses real-life situations that speak to the experiences of young men and women in college, high school, and other areas of social life. The chief curricular innovation of MVP is a training tool called the Playbook, which consists of a series of realistic scenarios depicting abusive male (and sometimes female) behavior. The scenarios have names that are taken from sports. The Playbook—with separate versions for men and women—transports participants into scenarios as witnesses to actual or potential abuse, and then challenges them to consider a number of concrete options for intervention before, during, or after an incident. Consider the following scenario from the MVP Playbook for high school males, which goes by the name "Slapshot":

> You're in the hallway between classes. You see a couple you
> know arguing, then you see the guy push his girlfriend into
> her locker. The guy isn't a close friend of yours, and neither
> is the young woman, but you do hang around with the same
> group of people. Nobody else is doing anything.

Many people mistakenly believe that they have only two options in instances of actual or potential violence: intervene physically and possibly expose themselves to personal harm, or do nothing. As a result, in MVP sessions when we initially introduce the idea that bystanders have a responsibility to act, people often voice fears about their safety, and say that they would not want to get involved because the price of intervention is too high. However, physical force and passive acceptance are only two of countless possible options. There are numerous ways that bystanders can prevent, interrupt, or intervene in abusive behaviors, and the majority carry little or no risk of physical confrontation. Since this variety of possible interventions is not always self-evident, part of the process of working with men as bystanders is to introduce them to as many nonviolent, non-threatening options as possible. But first, the MVP model helps men to develop a train of thought about the costs and benefits of intervention:

> This is an ugly situation . . . This guy is being real rough with this girl . . . I wonder what's going on? Should I say something? But if nobody else is stepping in, why should I? If I say something, he might come after me. Am I ready to get into a fight, if it comes to that? What if he's got a weapon? Besides, if he treats her like that and she stays with him, who am I to get involved? Is it any of my business? But if I don't do something, I'm saying it's okay for a guy to abuse a young woman. What should I do in this situation?

Although they focus on specific cases of abuse, MVP scenarios are designed to stimulate wide-ranging discussions about the dynamics of male-peer culture, masculinity, sex, violence, abuses of power, and conformist behavior. In all-male sessions, boys and men discuss such questions as: Why do men hit women? Why do men sexually assault women? How do cultural definitions of manhood contribute to sexual and domestic violence and other sexist behaviors? Why do some men make it clear that they won't accept that sort of behavior from their peers, while others remain silent? How is the silence of peers understood by abusers? What message is conveyed to victims when the abuser's friends don't confront him? Why do some heterosexually identified men harass and beat up gay men? Does the accompanying silence on the part of some of their heterosexual peers legitimize the abuse? Why or why not?

After they read the "train of thought," the facilitators spark discussion with a series of questions designed to explore the role of the bystander:

- Why would a guy who is a bystander in this scenario not say something?
- What are the risks of saying or doing something to interrupt or confront the abusive behavior?
- What is the message to the victim when no one speaks up or acts on her behalf?
- What is the message to the perpetrator when no one confronts him or expresses disapproval of his abusive behavior?
- What, if anything, is the responsibility of the bystander to the victim?
- What, if anything, is the responsibility of the bystander to the perpetrator or potential perpetrator? (Note: in the scenario the bystander is usually positioned as a friend, teammate, or coworker of the boy or man who is being abusive.)

The answers typically reveal a great deal about the dynamics of male-peer cultures and the pressures on young men to conform. For example, many guys admit that they would not be happy to see a guy treat his girlfriend this way, but they would not say anything. The guy who is abusing his girlfriend might be older than him, or bigger. He might be more popular. People might think he is not "cool" if he tries to get involved. It is much easier to intervene in theory than it is when the pressure is on, your palms are sweaty and your heart is pounding.

Once the participants have had time to discuss these questions, the conversation shifts to the options:

1. Nothing. It's none of my business.
2. Attempt to distract the couple somehow, maybe by talking loudly, in order to defuse the situation.
3. Shout out something so that everyone in the hallway hears, like, "Hey, what are you doing? Leave her alone!" and stick around to make sure the situation has "cooled" down.
4. Talk to the girl at some point and let her know I saw what was going on and am willing to help her.
5. Don't do anything immediately. But as soon as possible, that day or later, I should make a point of talking to the guy and suggesting he get some counseling to deal with his abusive behavior.
6. Talk to a group of his friends, and/or talk to a group of her friends. Tell them what I saw and urge the group to make a decision about how to proceed.
7. Talk to my parents, a guidance counselor, the school social worker, a teacher, or the school nurse, and ask their advice on what to do.
8. Personal option.

When he was a member of the original MVP program in the 1990s, the

documentary filmmaker Byron Hurt used to recount an incident he witnessed in college. He was in the cafeteria at lunchtime with a group of men
and women friends who were seated around a large table. Another male student whom they all knew came into the room, walked over to one of the
women and leaned over to tell her something. She kissed him on the cheek.
It all seemed innocent enough, until he abruptly reacted to the kiss with
anger. He grabbed her by the shirt, lifted her out of her seat, and pushed her
up against a concrete post next to the table. She started to cry. Everyone saw
what happened, but no one said anything. Not even "hey, what do you think
you're doing?" No one asked her if she was all right. Hurt sat there in shocked
silence. At the time, he was the quarterback of his college Division I AA football team. He was well-known and well-respected. He was built more like a
linebacker than a quarterback. Why didn't he speak up? "The dude was kind
of cool," he said. "I was scared and paralyzed by the thought of what might
happen if I said something." If the quarterback of the football team is intimidated into silence, imagine the pressure on average guys.

The overall goal of the MVP model is to stimulate dialogue and critical
thinking about the ethical choices bystanders face when they witness abusive
behaviors, and to help people think through the costs and benefits of action
or inaction. It is also to reposition the bystander—the one who speaks out
and confronts his abusive peer—as strong and courageous, not "weak,"
"uncool," or a "narc." It is not appropriate to tell people how they should act
in every situation; there are too many unknown variables to be prescriptive.
It is likewise not realistic to expect a group of guys to agree about the best
course of action to consider in any given scenario, especially since there are
no "right" or "wrong" answers. The idea is to provide people with a greater
menu of options in the hope that if at some point they are in a position to
act, they will have more good options to choose from. The only option discouraged in MVP is to "do nothing."

The following scenario from the college men's playbook, called "Illegal
Motion," describes a disturbingly common event:

> At a party, you see a friend trying to get an obviously drunk
> woman to leave with him. She's not just buzzed; she's stum-
> bling over her own feet. You know the woman, and she
> seems reluctant.

This scenario always sparks lively dialogue, in part because it involves two
of the central preoccupations of contemporary college social life: getting
drunk and having sex. The MVP trainers ask the men if they would intervene

in this situation, and if not, why not. Most college and high school men say they would not. It's not their business, they say. It happens all the time. How do you know it is going to end badly? Many of them have been in these situations—and not only as bystanders. The train of thought gives them more to think about:

> Men and women who are drinking hook up all the time . . . Then again, she looks really drunk. Maybe she's not in a position to make a good decision . . . I know a lot of "date rape" involves alcohol. Could this be one of those situations? . . . But what if I'm overreacting? Won't my friend be mad at me? Will he even listen to me? . . . But if I don't do something, I might be letting her down. What should I do?

After they read the "train of thought," the facilitators spark discussion with a series of questions:

- What, if anything, is the responsibility of the bystander to the drunk woman?
- Does it matter how well you know her, or if you know her at all? How would you feel if a woman you loved found herself in this situation, and no one intervened on her behalf?
- Does it matter how she ended up drunk? Is that relevant? What if you have seen her drunk before? Does that matter? What if someone slipped a roofie in her drink? Is it possible to tell?
- What, if anything, is the responsibility of the bystander to the guy who is trying to "hit it" with her? Does it matter how well you know him? What if he is your teammate or fraternity brother? Do you have a special responsibility to stop him from doing something that could get *him* in trouble?
- How many people here know the state law on the matter of sexual consent involving alcohol? Under the law in every state a person is considered unable to give consent if they are inebriated, which means that if a man sexually penetrates a drunk woman (or man) he can be prosecuted for rape.

I ask the men whom they feel they have a responsibility toward: the woman who is drunk, the man, or both. Their answers are sometimes encouraging, like when they say they care about both of them: her because she is vulnerable, and him because he might get in trouble. But on several occasions I have heard college-aged men state matter-of-factly that if the woman got herself in that predicament and she's eighteen or older, they are not responsible to her because "she knew what she was doing." Those coldly presented sentiments confirm what some feminists have maintained for decades: that in our sexist and increasingly pornographic culture, boys and men are socialized to objectify and dehumanize women—especially young sexually active women.

This is disturbing, but not as revealing as some of the responses by men who say they *would* do something. Some guys say they would "get their friend out of there," because he might do something stupid, or face a false accusation of rape the next day. In other words, help *him* before he puts himself in a compromising situation, be his friend by looking out for *his* interests—not the woman's—in a potential rape scenario. Just as often, guys assert that they would urge the drunk woman's friends to look out for *her* interests by getting her out of there. Many men want to avoid the possibility of a direct confrontation with their friend even when they know he might be trying to take sexual advantage of a drunk and vulnerable young woman. Perhaps they are anxious about the possibility of violence. They might realistically be concerned that the guy could get belligerent and take a swing at them. But their reticence is also undoubtedly rooted in social anxiety, their fear based on an unconscious awareness that if they come to the defense of a vulnerable woman they might be seen as soft or sensitive, and hence lose standing among their peers.

The "Illegal Motion" scenario also provides the context for a discussion about false accusations of rape. Many men in college—athletes, fraternity members, and others—believe they or their friends are at significant risk of being falsely accused of rape by a woman. This phenomenon is what Alan Berkowitz refers to as men's "false fear of false accusation." I do not immediately tell the men how I feel about this fear, but I do share with them the FBI statistic about the number of rapes that are *not* reported: between 80 and 90 percent. In other words, the vast majority of women (and men) who are raped never report it to the officials. I ask them why they think this is. With help they usually come up with many of the key reasons: the rape itself was traumatic, and they don't want to put themselves through the trauma of the legal process; doing a "rape kit" to collect evidence is painful, invasive, and can be highly embarrassing, as medical professionals need to extract pubic hairs and swabs from a woman's genitals or anus; the woman's sexual behavior and character are often attacked by people who take the side of the alleged rapist; perhaps the woman knows the man who raped her and is furious with him, but even so does not want to see him to go to prison. Once the men have gone through this list, I pose the question: if these disincentives are powerful enough to keep the vast majority of actual rape victims from reporting the crime, how realistic is it to believe that large numbers of women are falsely doing so? Why would they want to invite the heartache and social stigma? I always make sure to acknowledge that false reports of rape do occur—in anywhere from 2 to 8 percent of cases, depending on how one defines "false" and whose research they rely on. (See endnotes for further discussion.) There is no doubt that being falsely accused of rape is a horrendous and potentially traumatizing experience. It is also important to recognize that men of color have a slightly more justified fear of false accusation, even though it is, as Berkowitz says, primarily a "false fear."

The conversation in an MVP session—whether it is with a group of high school students or in a roomful of marines—really picks up when someone confesses that he would not say anything if he saw one of his boys in a situation like the "Illegal Motion" scenario because "I wouldn't want to be a blocker." A "cock-blocker," or "CB," is a widely used term in the hip-hop generation, but most people over thirty have never heard it, unless they work closely with kids or have kids of their own who speak openly with them. A "CB" refers to a man who gets in the way of another man's "game," or attempt to hook up with a woman. Needless to say it is not a term of endearment. If a guy develops a reputation as a cock-blocker, he risks a possible loss of status in the male hierarchy, which amazingly for many men is too high a price to pay for preventing a possible rape.

Once there is some discussion about these questions, the facilitators move to the options:

1. Do nothing. It's really none of my business.
2. Try to get my friend to leave her alone. Tell him he has to be real careful dealing sexually with a drunk woman.
3. Find some of her friends and try to convince them to get her home safely.
4. Approach the woman and ask her how she feels, and if she wants help getting home.
5. Try to find the person whose apartment or house it is, or someone who seems responsible, and ask them to assist me in defusing this situation.
6. Get a group of my friends together, male and female, and confront my friend, firmly telling him to stop pursuing this drunk woman.
7. Personal option.

Not all of the MVP scenarios involve incidents of physical or sexual abuse. For example, one scenario in the high school boys' playbook is called "Offsides":

You're riding in the back seat of your friend's car late one afternoon with two other male friends. Someone spots a young woman jogging a few hundred yards ahead and the driver starts to slow down. Your friend in the passenger's side of the front seat starts to roll down his window to yell something at her.

This scenario provides an opportunity for young men to imagine how young women's experience of the public world differs from their own. How is it possible for one person (or three) to regard this as harmless fun and another to experience it as harassing and threatening behavior? Although they live together and go to school together, boys' and girls' lives are very different, especially because one sex learns early in life to fear the other. As amazing as this sounds to many of my women friends, young men in MVP sessions—high school and college students—often report that they had never even thought about girls' feelings in situations like this. (White people in anti-racist workshops often report similar feelings when they are asked to put themselves in the shoes of people of color.) When this scenario is discussed in mixed-gender settings, some young men begin to realize for the first time how easily they can scare girls and women and limit their ability to move freely in the world. After all, how do the girls know that guys in the car are not rapists who are going to lie in wait around the corner? Numerous men I have talked to over the years describe one of their first "aha" moments about male privilege as the time they realized women feared them as they walked or drove by on the streets—even when the men themselves felt non-threatening.

Of course not all young men are quite as empathetic. Some express impatience with the entire premise of this scenario. I have heard more than a few men say they know girls who look for that sort of attention from men, so what's the big deal? They react defensively to the suggestion that behavior which they consider normal "guy behavior" is being defined as problematic. Young men also frequently maintain that it is totally unrealistic to expect one of them to say something to his friends in this scenario—even if he knows that what they are about to do is wrong.

The train of thought provides further material for discussion:

What's my friend going to say? Will it be something sexual, or is he just going to yell out something stupid? Does it matter?…How will this girl feel to hear a group of guys in a car shouting at her? Will she be scared? We're just a harmless group of guys, but how could she know that?…I know girls who jog. I wonder if they ever get harassed by guys in cars…Can I say something to stop my friends from saying

something? Won't they get ticked off at me? What should I
do in this situation?

After someone reads aloud the "train of thought," the MVP trainers ask
questions like:

- Does anyone have a sister or girlfriend who jogs? Have you ever talked
to her about how she feels when guys in cars yell things at her? What did
she say?
- When guys shout at girls out of a car window, what are they trying to
accomplish? Who are they trying to impress? The girl? Their friends?
- Does a young man have a responsibility to support or defend a girl he
does not know and might never meet?

The scenario ends with a discussion of the options:

1. Don't say anything. It's just harmless fun and speaking up would do
more harm than good.
2. Try to change the subject in order to distract my friends and get their
attention off of the female jogger.
3. Tell the driver to speed up and say, "Come on, guys, let's leave her alone."
4. Don't say anything right then, but later, tell my friends that I don't
think we should be harassing girls like that.
5. Talk to a female friend of mine who runs and find out how she feels
when guys drive by and say things.
6. Personal option.

One of the enduring lessons of MVP is that when you approach men
with the intent of enlisting them as allies in the fight against gender violence—rather than as potential perpetrators—many of them rise to the challenge. Men who have participated in MVP sessions often say the experience
was nothing like what they expected. Whether from personal history or
paranoia, a lot of men expect to be lectured at in a gender-violence prevention workshop. Many of them are impressed when they find out instead that
it's not a lecture but a dialogue, and that rather than being blamed for men's
violence against women they are being challenged to do something about it.
Jeff O'Brien, who has directed MVP since 1999, tells this story about a session with a professional football team:

> The guys were predictably reluctant as we began our first of
> three trainings with the group. We had good discussions on
> the first day, and when we began day two, a big linebacker just
> bluntly stated "You guys are some cool motherfuckers…when
> you first showed up I thought this was going to be bullshit,

but y'all are keepin' it real." That's a compliment in "guy-speak," and the best way he could express his appreciation for the value of the discussions we were having and still be a "man."

On another occasion, when O'Brien and some colleagues finished a training with an elite college football team, they were given the "double-clap," a gesture reserved for their inner-team activities, and a sign of solidarity and respect. This is notable because MVP trainers do not pander to pampered male athletes—they confront sexist beliefs and victim-blaming statements when they arise and challenge the men to resist peer pressure and become leaders—*off* the field. One indication that the MVP approach resonates with a lot of men is that many of them stay after sessions to talk with the trainers. O'Brien, a former All-American college football player who has conducted hundreds of MVP trainings across the U.S. with high school, college, and professional athletes, explains it this way: "We do gender-violence prevention, but for us this means having honest conversations with guys about how we've all been socialized as men. I believe that most men are longing for male relationships that have some depth and genuineness. Outside of a ninety-minute training, we are complete strangers, yet guys ask us for advice on all sorts of life issues."

MVP IN THE MARINE CORPS

There is no doubt that a violence *prevention* program with marines sounds like an oxymoron at first glance. After all, marines have a well-deserved reputation for being hypermasculine warriors, not advocates for non-violence and gender equity. When people hear that I run a version of the Mentors in Violence Prevention program for the United States Marine Corps, they ask: aren't marines trained to commit—rather than prevent—acts of violence? I certainly understand people's skepticism, in part because I was once a skeptic myself. But today, after many years and dozens of trainings on Marine Corps bases around the world, I have a much different perspective on the Corps, especially the individuals that it comprises.

This shift in perspective came about when I first met and started working with the Marines in 1997. I quickly came to see that beneath the façade created by their hard bodies and crisp uniforms, marines were complicated people just like everybody else. In fact, one thing I make sure to tell civilian MVP trainers before they work with marines for the first time is that they should not be fooled by the combat fatigues and short haircuts. Marines—and other military members—have professional commitments that differentiate them from civilians—especially in a time of war. But male marines have more in common with civilian men than either group might think. After all, before they are marines they are fathers, brothers, sons, and lovers of women and girls. As such, gender-violence issues are as personal for them as they are for any civilian. In addition, most Marines are only in the service for four years, after which they return to their families and communities, largely in small towns in rural America and poor and working-class sections of big cities. What they learn in the Marine Corps thus affects not only them but all of the people they come in contact with throughout their lives.

In my experience—and contrary to the expectations of many of my civilian colleagues—working with Marines on domestic violence and sexual assault prevention is no more difficult than working with other groups of men. In fact, there are some characteristics of the Marine Corps that make our trainings with them run *more* smoothly than in other places. This is because MVP adopts a positive approach to working with Marines that is similar to the approach used by the Duluth Domestic Abuse Intervention Project in their groundbreaking work with the Corps during the 1990s. In a fascinating article entitled "Strange Bedfellows: Feminist Advocates and U.S. Marines Working to End Violence," Valli Kanuha, Patricia Erwin, and Ellen Pence explain that D.A.I.P. tried to use key aspects of Marine Corps ideology to argue that domestic violence was not only illegal but "un-Marine-like." In their words, "Instead of resisting the hyper-patriotic and paternalistic aspects of [Marine Corps core values], we embraced them as tools to build buy-in." The D.A.I.P.'s attempt to institute a comprehensive coordinated community response to domestic violence in the Marine Corps ultimately failed when marine leaders in the late 1990s discontinued the ambitious program, but not before this group of self-described "feminist outsiders" had successfully made allies of countless marines who agreed there was a need to bolster a warrior identity that did not include abusing women and children.

The language of leadership that is so important to the success of the MVP approach resonates especially strongly in the Marine Corps. When MVP trainers say that our culture desperately needs more male leadership in the gender-violence area, many Marines hear and respond to this as a positive challenge; and they are used to challenges. It is deeply imbedded in the ethic of the Marine Corps that Marines are not average or ordinary people. They proudly stand apart from the rest of society, and do things that others are not able or willing to do: they endure spartan living conditions, they work long hours for low wages, and they take significant risks with their lives in the service of helping others. There is much to discuss and criticize about the tasks to which marines are assigned by their political leaders. And there are many aspects of Marine Corps culture that offend progressive sensibilities—especially issues of gender and sexual equality. Not surprisingly, the Marine Corps has the lowest percentage of women in the U.S. military, approximately 6 percent. But in spite of all this, individual Marines are characteristically highly motivated, they have the courage of their convictions, and they are ready to sacrifice for the common good. Their credo is Honor, Courage, Commitment. This is perfectly consistent with the MVP philosophy of empowering men—and women—to speak up when they see a person mistreat another—even if doing so entails some personal risk.

The MVP model is basically the same in the Marine Corps as it is any place else. The language in the playbooks is slightly different; instead of "teammate," the Marine Corps playbooks say "squad member." But the key concepts are the same, especially the idea that silence in the face of abusive behavior is consent to that behavior. Consider the following scenario from the Marine Corps playbook, called "Barracks Heroes":

> In the barracks or gym one afternoon, some of your squad members are making sexist and degrading comments and jokes about a female Marine who is a friend of yours. They say she's a "bitch in heat" who can't lay off anyone, and several state they'd like to $#@% her.

Some guys—inside and outside the Marine Corps—think this is taking things too far. They might say, "Rape and abuse is wrong, but this is getting so I can't even tell jokes or look at women without people jumping down my throat." But this scenario raises some important questions about the relationship between attitudes and behaviors. For example, is it ever just "harmless fun" when a group of guys tell each other sexist jokes with no women around? Once in the late 1990s when a colleague and I were doing this scenario at an MVP-MC training in Quantico, Virginia, the Marines in the room could not see why this would be a problem. There was laughter and commotion in the room and we seemed to be losing control of the session. "Okay," I said. "Let me ask you this. Would it be okay if a group of white Marines was making racist comments and telling racist jokes about black or Latino Marines, even if there were no black or Latino Marines present? Would that be okay behavior in the United States Marine Corps?" One Marine, a charismatic African American gunnery sergeant, turned to his fellow Marines and said sincerely, "That's it. It's a slam dunk. There's no way I'm gonna argue with that," as the mood in the room noticeably shifted.

For more than five years, MVP-MC has been part of the curriculum at the Staff Non-Commissioned Officer (NCO) academies throughout the Marine

Corps. The academies employ Marine Corps instructors who provide courses to Marines as they are promoted through the ranks of enlisted leadership, from corporal to sergeant major. This is one way to institutionalize gender-violence prevention as a leadership issue. The message to Marines is that they need to be educated about what they can do, not because they are "good guys" who care, but because they are leaders and it is their responsibility. MVP-MC is far from a comprehensive program, and there is much more that the Marine Corps and all the other services can do to prevent gender violence. Large-scale reforms in this area are in the works throughout the Department of Defense, largely in response to congressional pressure following numerous domestic-violence and sexual-assault scandals in the military over the past decade. Whether or not these reforms will successfully reduce men's violence against women in the U.S. military is far from certain. But in an authoritarian institution like the military, responsibility for what the troops do resides at the top. Command sets the tone. So while programs like MVP-MC and others that target junior level leaders and young service members are important, ultimately the buck stops with senior leadership. If the male leadership in the Department of Defense—starting with the president of the United States—began to treat gender violence prevention not as a distraction or a public relations challenge but as an absolute institutional priority, the rates of domestic violence, sexual assault, and sexual harassment perpetrated by members of the armed forces would begin to decline precipitously.

CHAPTER TWELVE

Teach Our Children Well

"There's a lot of ugly things in this world, son. I wish I could keep 'em all away from you. That's never possible."
—Atticus Finch, *To Kill a Mockingbird*, by Harper Lee

"The belief that violence is manly is not carried on any chromosome, not soldered into the wiring of the right or left hemisphere, not juiced by testosterone. Boys learn it."
—Michael Kimmel

A public service announcement produced by the Family Violence Prevention Fund highlights the need for adult male leadership in the lives of boys. It features three vignettes where young boys approach older men. In the first, a boy walks up to a letter carrier on the sidewalk. "Excuse me," he says to the man. "I've been getting mixed messages about women and violence. I need a little clarification." In the second, a boy is riding on a train, seated next to his uncle. "Uncle Bill," he asks, "how am I supposed to grow up to respect women when I have such lousy role models?" In the third, a boy approaches a man on a basketball court and says, "Can you help me reshape my attitudes toward women?" As the piece ends, a male narrator intones in an authoritative voice, "Boys are never going to approach you. You need to teach them that violence against women is wrong."

The Fund's Coaching Boys Into Men campaign is a highly visible example of a positive development in the field of gender violence prevention: an increased focus on boys and young men. The idea behind this approach is simple. Since domestic and sexual violence are largely learned behaviors, it is important to reach boys *before* they learn to abuse girls. And since these types of violence are so closely linked to men's beliefs about what it means to be a man, it is also important to provide boys with alternative ideas about manhood to counterbalance all of the hypermasculine posturing and misogyny they encounter in their peer culture and the media.

There is general agreement among researchers in the domestic and sexual violence fields that boys' and men's violence against girls and women is not the expression of innate, biological impulses, but is the result of some combination of personal experience and social conditioning. Theories differ on the exact nature of this social conditioning, but by far the most influential one of why gender violence is so common in our society begins with the premise that men's violence against women is the result of the power imbalance between men and women, which carries with it a set of cultural messages to boys and men, including the idea that "real" men are *supposed* to control and dominate women. The ultimate solution to the problem of men's violence against women, therefore, is equality between the sexes. The closer we get to a society where there is economic, social, and political equality between the sexes, the less need there will be for one sex to learn how to dominate the other. But despite the historical gains of the multicultural women's movement, a truly egalitarian society is still a long way off. Thus we are faced with a daunting challenge: how to keep victims safe and hold offenders accountable, even as we work toward a society where boys and men do not learn the sexist attitudes and beliefs that lead some of them to emotionally, physically, or sexually abuse girls and women.

Where do boys learn to abuse girls? Many people assume they learn it at home, in a self-perpetuating cycle of violence which is passed down from one generation to the next. But numerous studies of men who batter show something different. Boys who witness wife abuse are much more likely to abuse their wives than are boys who grew up in non-violent homes. But the vast majority of boys who witness do not become abusive. In addition, the strong majority of men who are abusive toward women did *not* grow up with fathers who were batterers. It is useful to think about the intergenerational transmission of violence in terms of the intergenerational transmission of alcoholism. Children of alcoholics are at greater risk of developing their own drinking problems. Research shows that when one parent is an alcoholic, the children have a greater statistical chance of becoming alcoholic; when both parents are alcoholic, their chances are even higher. But the majority of children of alcoholics do not become alcoholics—and *the majority of alcoholics did not grow up in alcoholic families.*

So if most men who physically or sexually abuse women are not simply perpetuating a sad family tradition, where did they learn to be abusive? Unless you believe that each abusive man is unique, and that his attitudes and behaviors bear no relation to those of millions of his fellow abusers, the answer is not reassuring. They learn to be abusive in the same way they learn to be men. In other words, they do not just learn to be violent; they learn that violence is manly. One of the most important theoretical contributions of the battered-women's movement is the insight that men's abusive behavior in relationships is best understood as a manifestation of a masculinist ideology of power and control. The crime of domestic violence is not simply caused by men's poor anger management skills. Instead, it is the product of a *belief system*—itself deeply rooted in male dominance—whose central tenet is that men *should* be in control in a relationship, their needs should come first, and if force is necessary to gain the woman's compliance, then that is just an unpleasant fact of life. Similarly, one of the most important theoretical insights of the rape crisis movement is that rape is not about a man's inability to control his sexual desire; it is more about his need to conquer and possess another person.

Where do so many men develop this burning need for dominance? Take a look around. Everywhere you turn, you see manhood equated with power and control—of other men as well as women. Some boys get this message at home, from influential adult male role models. But there are many other sources: their neighborhood, their peers, and the media. They learn it on Saturday morning cartoons and trips to the toy store, where "action heroes" with rippled muscles convey the powerful lesson that might makes right; on the playground, where recent research shows that bullies are not social misfits but often the most popular kids; in the sports culture, where dominating one's opponent is seen as the height of athletic achievement; in NASCAR racing, whose most popular icon was nicknamed "The Intimidator"; in hip-hop, where rich and famous rappers denigrate women and gays; in professional wrestling, where ritualized bullying, humiliation, and sexual harassment is normal behavior, and caricatured portrayals of brutish manhood are celebrated; in video games, where mastery of the joystick and the ability to "kill" at will—and sometimes beat up prostitutes—is equated to manly competence; and in the larger adult world, where they see abuses of power by men in business and government.

At the same time that impressionable boys absorb these lessons about how to earn respect in the world of men, they get the complementary message that what is considered "feminine" has less value than what is considered "masculine." It is a short step from there to the belief that women are supposed to be subordinate to men—and sexually available to them. Despite important gains in gender equity sparked by the modern multicultural women's movement—or perhaps because of them—our culture is saturated with stark visual evidence of women's continued subservience to men, especially in the sexual realm. The stylistic conventions of pornography have become decidedly mainstream. From advertising billboards to magazine covers, scantily-clad female bodies are ubiquitously on display as objects for men to use and discard. Pornography itself—the vast majority of which eroticizes male dominance and control—is a $10 billion-a-year industry. Major recording artists glamorize pimps, and radio shock jocks openly humiliate women—with little or no public outcry. In the context of this cultural environment, can we credibly profess to be surprised when boys and men verbally, physically, and sexually harass and abuse girls and women?

The values and beliefs of men who become batterers and rapists in their twenties and thirties typically begin to take shape when they are much younger. That is why there is a growing clamor for prevention strategies that target kids in middle school. Early adolescence is a time of rapid growth and development, and it is a time when both girls and boys learn powerful lessons about femininity and masculinity. If young boys at that critical juncture are provided with guidance from men—and women—who can impress upon them that strong, confident men respect women as their equals and do not feel the need to put them down or control them in order to feel good about themselves, they are much more likely to successfully resist sexist pressures in the dominant male culture. But if this is true, what did abusive men learn about what it means to be a man when they were younger? Studies of men who batter show that while there is variation between types of abusive behavior, and not all batterers have the same psychological makeup, they tend to believe in men's superiority and "natural" right to control women. Similarly, on the Rape Myth Acceptance Scale, an instrument used to measure the belief systems that underlie rapist behavior, men who rape tend to score high on belief in "traditional" and rigidly defined gender roles, acceptance of violence as part of relationships, and the idea that relationships are basically exploitive. There can be warning signs early in a boy's life that should alert adults to serious problems. For example, boys who abuse animals have a high risk of becoming domestic-violence perpetrators when they grow up. However, just because the crimes of batterers and rapists often have earlier roots in their socialization does not mean that their later behavior was predictable.

When I was in my twenties, I worked as a counselor in the Boston area in a detention center for adolescent males. The boys, aged ten to seventeen, had committed crimes ranging from petty theft to rape. Many of them came from troubled, poor families (although not always); many had already been abused and neglected by parents and other caregivers; many had alcohol and drug problems. To someone reading about their crimes in the newspaper, or encountering them on the streets, a lot of these boys could appear intimidating and incorrigible. But youth counselors like me who worked with them saw a more complex reality. Mostly we saw vulnerable, needy boys. As survivors of physical and sexual abuse, many of them had built walls around themselves long before they were taken into custody. They were clearly at risk for committing more crimes and hardening into adult criminals. Still, with a little bit of love and a lot of guidance from firm but caring adults—both sorely lacking in most of these kids' lives so far—many of them stood a good chance of turning their lives around. In fact, to this day some of the best counselors in the juvenile justice system were in that system when they were kids.

Countless studies show that boys who are exposed to violence in their families are at greater risk for violence themselves. But "greater risk" does not imply inevitability. There are so many "resiliency factors" that can mitigate their damaging experiences, so many possible interventions along the way, that it is unfair to write them off as hopeless. In fact, most experts believe that if they receive quality professional attention, even boys who have been physically traumatized or sexually abused are not destined to repeat the familiar pattern.

This raises the question: is it ever too late to intervene? It is clearly important to reach boys when they are very young with messages challenging sexism and separating manhood from violence, provided it is done sensitively in an age-appropriate manner. But a person's gender ideology is not fixed. We do not simply have to accept that the ideas about manhood which boys learn early in life can never be challenged or changed. This point was reinforced for me at—of all places—a Marine Corps base in the desert at Twenty-Nine Palms, California. I had just started working with the Marines, and I was giving a talk to about one hundred uniformed, non-commissioned officers. I began to explain the MVP approach, discussing the need to teach young men not to be passive bystanders in the face of their friends' abusive behaviors toward women. I had been talking for a few minutes when a thirty-something male Marine raised his hand and with a dismissive tone said, "If you think this is going to work here, you're mistaken. These young guys come to us at seventeen, eighteen, nineteen. Their attitudes about women, relationships, and those kinds of things were formed years before. It's a done deal. You're not going to change them." Since the program I co-founded, MVP, begins with the premise that gender violence is learned behavior and thus can be unlearned, this man was essentially challenging the very heart of the program.

I knew I had to respond forcefully; as a civilian who had just started working with the military, my credibility was on the line. But I never got the chance. Instead, another Marine turned toward him and asked, incredulously, "What do you think boot camp is for? If you think a man can't change once he's reached eighteen, what are you doing in the Marine Corps? We resocialize guys all the time. We take 'em from all sorts of backgrounds—healthy and unhealthy—and make Marines out of 'em."

It is no secret that an important part of what the military seeks to accomplish when it resocializes young men—and women—is to prepare them to kill other human beings. This is clearly the opposite of violence *prevention*. But implicit in military training is the idea that it is never too late to introduce someone to a new social norm, or expect them to conform to it. There are many graduates of court-ordered domestic violence programs who speak in public about their experiences and teach other men to rethink old abusive definitions of manhood. I know men who were physically or sexually abusive to women who nonetheless became powerful advocates for anti-sexism and non-violence. I have watched colleagues of all ages go through profound personal transformations when they started to engage in discussions with other men and women about the subject of sexism and men's violence against women. On the outside, many of these men have traditional masculine resumes. They are former college or professional athletes, or they have had military experience. Some are police officers. Some were drawn to the subject matter by chance, others by the professional or personal interests of a woman close to them. But as they began to read and think critically about masculinity, violence, sexism, and homophobia, and listen to other men who were grappling with many of the same questions about male identity, it dawned on them that they had never been fully comfortable in a social system that trains men to devalue and dominate women. It would be an overstatement to argue that most of these men would willingly relinquish all the perks of male privilege. But when they realized that a lot of other men shared their discomfort with certain forms of sexism and male dominance, they were eager to hear ideas about how they could help other men, and boys, along a similar questioning path.

Boys Learn What We Teach Them

In an earlier chapter, I argued that use of the passive voice in discussions about gender violence ("How many women are raped?") shines the critical spotlight on the victims instead of the perpetrators—and the society that produces them. This is useful if the goal is only to take care of victims. But if the goal is to stop the abuse from happening in the first place, critical attention needs to be turned onto the people most responsible for it. In a similar fashion, to say that boys *learn* to mistreat girls either at home or out in the world shifts attention away from the role adult men play in *teaching* boys to mistreat girls. This is subtle but significant, because when you shift the topic of conversation back to how men *teach* boys to be violent it puts the onus for change back on adults. It frames the question as one about the responsibilities adults have to children. For example: When daddy goes out to Hooters with friends after a softball game, *what message does he send to his twelve-year-old son* about how men view women? When a male coach tries to motivate his underperforming male players by comparing them to a "bunch of ladies," *what information does he communicate to them about women's worth?* When there is a public march against violence against women and only a handful of men show up, *what message do all of the absent men send* to the boys (and girls) who might be there with their mothers?

In the rest of this chapter, I am going to explore briefly three areas where adult men (and in some cases women) teach—or fail to teach—boys and young men how to treat girls. First I want to discuss some of the issues for fathers—and mothers—of sons. Then I will talk about the role of adult male leadership in the schools. This includes the leadership role of men in the highly influential culture of school athletics. And finally, I will make the case for a dramatic expansion of media literacy education—in schools and elsewhere—in order to provide young people with tools to counteract the one-dimensional, sexist, and distorted images of manhood that pervade contemporary media and entertainment.

PARENTS

In the early years of the twenty-first century, parents of girls and boys have ample reason to be worried about their kids. Many of them recall their own childhoods as relatively carefree in comparison to what kids face today, and this is especially true when it comes to sex and violence. The sexual abuse of children is not a new phenomenon, but there is vastly greater public awareness of it than there was a generation ago. What is new is the degree to which children's sexualized bodies are on display in the media. Moreover, since the advent of the Internet, sexual predators have had unprecedented access to their young victims. Although most children who are sexually or physically abused know their abusers, in our highly mobile and increasingly impersonal society, children are also more vulnerable to random acts of violence. It seems every time you turn on the news you hear about another young girl or boy abducted by a man on the street or in a mall parking lot. And for parents of daughters, recent research on the prevalence of violence in girls' relational lives is profoundly unsettling. A 2001 survey in Massachusetts done by the Harvard School of Public Health found that *one in five* teenage girls had been physically and/or sexually abused in a relationship. Extrapolated nationally, that would amount to *millions* of girls. Millions more experience subtle and blatant forms of sexism and objectification on a daily basis. When I address groups of adult male professionals, I often ask them to raise their hands if they have daughters. The goal is to remind them that gender violence prevention is not only their professional responsibility—it is in their personal self-interest. This is also true for parents of sons. Boys are clearly vulnerable to sexual abuse, often by men who earn their trust and then betray it. The signature example of this in our time has been the Catholic priest pedophilia scandal. But the challenge for parents of sons has an added dimension. Their responsibility is not just to shield their sons from harm; it is to raise sons who will not mistreat girls and women—or remain silent when their peers do.

This is a challenging task for parents of sons, especially parents who want their sons to grow up as members of a new generation of anti-sexist men. The work of these parents is crucial to the success of gender violence prevention efforts, as energy in the field shifts away from the risk-reduction model for girls, and toward a true prevention approach that addresses head-on men's and boys' attitudes and behaviors. Some parental challenges cut across sex differences, while others are specific to fathers or mothers.

Fathers

Clearly one of the most important roles a father—or a father figure—can play in his son's life is to teach by example. If men are always respectful toward women and never verbally or physically abuse them, their sons in all likelihood will learn to be similarly respectful. Nonetheless every man who has a son should be constantly aware that how he treats women is not just between him and the women—there is a little set of eyes that is always watching him and picking up cues about how a man is supposed to act. If a man says demeaning and dismissive things about women, his son hears it. If he laughs at sexist jokes and makes objectifying comments about women's bodies as he watches TV, his son hears it. For years anti-racism educators have maintained that it is the responsibility of white parents to teach their children not to be racist. It is time more men became aware that they have a similar responsibility to teach their children not to be sexist.

Fathers also need to teach boys that it is not acceptable to be silent when their friends harass or abuse girls. Among the many ways they can do this: by not remaining silent when their own friends say or do something sexist; by speaking out in their workplace; by encouraging dialogue about gender violence as a men's issue at their church, synagogue, or mosque; or by using their platform as a coach of a youth soccer, Pop Warner football, or Little League baseball team to speak to the kids about sexual harassment and teen-relationship abuse.

Take the case of a twelve-year-old boy who wants his parents to buy him the wildly popular video game *Grand Theft Auto*. Perhaps his mother does not want him to have it in the house, because it is extremely violent and misogynistic, and she worries that playing such games will desensitize him to violence and the mistreatment of women. If the father reluctantly tells his son that he has to live without *GTA* in the house because "you know how your mother feels" about it, he sends a powerful message to the boy that the problem is not the sexist video game, or the fact that millions of boys—and grown men—find it pleasurable to play a game where they pretend to beat up a prostitute they just had sex with. No, the problem is his *mom's* discomfort about all of this. Consider the impression he would make on his son if the father said this instead: "I don't want *GTA* in my house because it is disrespectful to women. It teaches boys to think violence against women is just a big joke. Think about your mother, your sisters. You wouldn't think it was harmless fun if someone hurt them, would you? You can play whatever video games you choose when you go out the door, but *as a man* I will not spend my money on this and I don't want it in my house. You might not like it now, but I hope some day you'll understand why I feel this way."

Men who grew up in abusive homes have a special set of concerns when they become fathers of sons. They may be intent on breaking the cycle of violence in their own family. Many of these men make a commitment to themselves, their wives, or their co-parents that they will not put their sons (and daughters) through what they experienced. Victor Rivers, the actor and spokesperson for the National Network to End Domestic Violence, is one of many courageous men I know who have done this successfully. In their own way all of these men are true anti-violence activists. Terry Real, whose 1997 book *I Don't Want to Talk About It* was a groundbreaking study of men's emotional lives, calls them heroes. But for some men, the effects of trauma they suffered as children can resurface later and wreak havoc in their adult lives. Unless they have done a lot of personal work—often including psychotherapy—some men can be at risk for repeating old patterns. It has become a cliché to say, "I always said I would never be like my father, but just the other day I was under a lot of stress and I heard myself say something nasty to my wife in front of the kids just like he used to, and it scared me." For men with these kinds of concerns, one of the best things they can do for their sons—and all of their loved ones—is to give *themselves* permission to seek both personal and professional help and support.

Mothers

Women I know who teach college courses on gender report that some of their best male students are those who were raised by strong, assertive women, and maintained close relationships with them throughout adolescence. These young men are less defensive and more open to learning about sexism and women's lives in part because they have already learned a lot from their mothers. In a sense they have already seen the world through a woman's eyes. In a related phenomenon, I have found that in gender-violence workshops with college men, some of the most powerful moments come when young men disclose that their mothers have been assaulted. They know too well that the problem is real, but it has not yet occurred to many of them that there is a way for them to channel their sadness and anger into constructive efforts to prevent future violence—and spare other children the pain of having to go through it themselves.

Whenever mothers bring their teen or pre-teen sons to one of my talks, I assume there is a back story. Are they single mothers who are eager for their sons to hear a man publicly denounce men's violence against women? I know that is sometimes the case because the women often introduce themselves, or contact me later. The words of an anti-sexist man—even someone they do not know—can be an invaluable asset to a formerly battered woman who is trying to raise a son after she has left the boy's father. One tactic many abusive men use to justify or excuse their behavior is to claim that they act the way they do because "that's just how men are." When men who do not agree say so publicly and without equivocation, it can leave a strong impression with boys, allowing them to see the fallacy in their father's claims. This does not necessarily demonize the man, who is still the boy's father, with whom the boy may want to maintain a relationship. But it helps the son to see his father's rationalizations for what they are, and it might give him hope that he can become a man who does not repeat the same mistakes.

Part of the reason why many women work to end men's violence against women is out of love for their sons. They want to help build a society, and a world, where boys will not be forced to dominate others—and deny their own humanity—in order to "make it" as men. They want to build a world where their sons will not be brutalized and bullied in school or sexually abused by predatory men (or women). At the same time, because they work with the female victims and survivors of men's violence, these women see on a daily basis the damage that some men inflict on women and children. It would be understandable if these women became thoroughly disillusioned with men. But part of what keeps them going, they often say, are their loving relationships with men—their sons, husbands, boyfriends, brothers, and friends.

For mothers who are survivors of physical and sexual abuse by men—and there are millions of them—raising a boy can sometimes be an emotional minefield. Consider the experience of a woman I know, a college professor on the East Coast. One afternoon she overheard her fourteen-year-old son and his friend talking in the next room. The friend called a girl he knew, and at some point said to her, "If you don't tell me what school you're going to next year, I'll track you down and rape you." The woman asked her son's friend if she truly heard him correctly, and he said he was only kidding around. She told him she took violence against women very seriously, and that he would not be welcome in their home if she ever heard words like that again. Her son later told her he was worried that his friend wouldn't want to come over any more. To complicate matters further, when the woman's husband came home and she told him what had happened, he pointed out that she could have used the incident as a "teachable moment" with both of the boys. The woman, who is a rape survivor, was upset that her husband did not immediately understand her reaction. As she explained it, when she heard the boy's violent threat—even if it was meant in jest—at that moment she was not in educator mode. Her feelings took precedence over the boys' need to be educated.

Many women who became feminists in the 1960s and 1970s had sons, who are now in their twenties, thirties, and forties. These men grew up—one hopes—with an elevated consciousness about sexism and the oppression of women. They may or may not have chosen to get involved in social justice advocacy. But one reason for hope in the gender violence prevention field over the next couple of decades is that the sons of women who were at the forefront of a social revolution a generation ago are now by age, experience, and accomplishment moving into position to be part of a transformative generation of progressive men.

MALE LEADERSHIP IN SCHOOLS: THE SOUNDS OF SILENCE

Why is gender violence prevention education not an absolute priority in the schools? When you consider that some studies show as many as a third of high school- and college-age youth experience violence in an intimate or dating relationship, why isn't teen-relationship abuse talked about in every high school in America? Why, when more than half of all rape victims are assaulted by the age of eighteen, and 29 percent are assaulted *by the age of eleven*, is there such a meager amount of anti-rape programming in high schools and middle schools—if not elementary schools? Sexual harassment is even more a part of students' daily lives. One national study found 83 percent of girls in school have experienced some form of it. Nan Stein, one of the nation's leading experts on school-based sexual harassment, writes in her book, *Classrooms and Courtrooms: Facing Sexual Harassment in K-12 Schools*, that this harassment has become "ordinary, expected, and public," and that "normalized and public performances of harassment, assault, and battery in schools may have consequences" for students' relationships later in life. In all of its various forms, violence clearly hurts students' academic performance, can lead to depression and other emotional and physical illnesses, and can contribute to substance abuse and delinquency. Schools often cannot adequately address every important issue, and it is not fair to blame educators for their failure to solve deep and pervasive social problems. But schools play a critical role in the socialization of children and adolescents. What students learn and experience there can affect them for the rest of their lives.

Most gender-violence prevention education has historically—and understandably—been initiated and implemented by women. Women have been the foremost pioneers, reformers, and guiding forces in this work. Their achievements are especially impressive when you consider that they have undertaken to educate not only girls but boys, too, as well as their male colleagues and friends. But since most formal positions of leadership in education, including a majority of principals and an overwhelming percentage of superintendents and athletic directors, are occupied by men, this is another area where men's leadership has been sorely lacking. There are numerous possible explanations for this, but consistent with the theme of this book, I want to explore some of the gender politics of male educators. By "gender politics" I mean such factors as a man's beliefs about proper gender roles for men and women, his level of self-awareness, his relationships with other men as well as women, where he stands in his peer culture, his body image, and his overall concept of what it means to be a man. How do these factors influence the exercise of a man's educational role, especially his potential for activism in gender violence prevention? How do men's gender politics contribute either to problems, or to potential solutions?

In many schools prevention programs are initiated by one impassioned person, usually a woman, who devotes personal time above and beyond her professional obligations. Some of the most effective efforts I have observed were initiated by women (and rarely, men) who held no formal positions of institutional power. However, administrators bear a disproportionate share of responsibility for what goes on (or does not go on) in their schools. It should not fall solely on the shoulders of health educators or public safety personnel to make sure the school is doing all it can to prevent trauma and harassment in students' lives. It is true that educational leaders face numerous, and sometimes overwhelming, pressures. This is particularly true in resource-poor areas, where educators confront numerous and seemingly intractable social problems daily. The challenges—and the opportunities—for educators in those systems have been powerfully addressed by numerous academic as well as popular writers. In recent years, school administrators have faced the added burden of conforming to the mandates of the No Child Left Behind Act of 2001, which makes it difficult for schools to devote time to subjects that are not measured by state administered tests. But gender violence is one of our most urgent and far-reaching social problems, and it affects impoverished city schools as well as wealthy suburban school districts.

Some male principals, superintendents, athletic directors, college presidents, and deans have devoted significant resources, including personal time, to gender violence prevention work. Unfortunately, however, many male administrators, even those who support gender equity efforts and are generally responsive to feminist concerns, do not often recognize the extent of their potential for anti-sexist leadership. Instead, they see it as their responsibility to delegate administrative authority in this area to a woman. Their explicit or implied rationale is that it is more appropriate for women to be handling "gender-related" issues.

The leadership of women, of course, has made possible the very discussion of how men should be involved. But pandemic rates of men's and boys' violence have persisted despite these feminist efforts. And while we cannot ascribe this persistence to any single factor, one factor is surely the absence, society-wide, of effective anti-sexist male leadership, including active male involvement in primary prevention education efforts aimed at boys. Administrators have to cater to the concerns of various constituencies, including school boards, faculty, students, parents, and community groups. It would be unfair to minimize the political sensitivity of their position. But anti-sexist leadership, in professional as well as personal spheres of life, requires men to make decisions and take actions that might be personally uncomfortable, unpopular, or controversial. Exercising this leadership can sometimes feel very lonely. Men who have the courage to stake out a position as bold anti-sexist leaders may sometimes feel as if they have little support, especially among their male colleagues. One of the consequences of breaking the historical conspiracy of men's silence about sexism is a certain degree of isolation. You risk being seen as having "broken ranks" with your fellow men, many of whom do not appreciate being held accountable to other men about the way they treat women—either in the school setting or in their private lives.

As a result, too often men in positions of influence, instead of speaking out about the sexist attitudes and behaviors of boys and men, leave it to women—mothers, teachers, female colleagues, or coworkers—to raise concerns or try to hold abusive males accountable. For many male leaders this is an unconscious process; they have never been forced to think through their responsibilities as anti-sexist *men* in these situations. But counting on women is also a way of avoiding some of the difficult burdens of leadership. It is important to note that this phenomenon is not specific to education. Relatively few men in the corporate world, the professions, or in white- or blue-collar workplaces have distinguished themselves as powerful anti-sexist leaders. Most men are not abusive, but they have not spoken out about the sexism and abusive behavior of their peers and other males in their circles of influence.

Another reason for male administrators' relative inaction might be that it rarely occurs to them that they have an extra responsibility *as men* to do something proactive about boys' abusive behaviors. They might see themselves as administrators, with a set of professional responsibilities, and not *male* administrators with special obligations. For some of these men, the first big step toward action is to think about how they can use the influence, mentoring role, visibility, and resources of their professional positions to better serve the needs of their students, families, friends, and community. How can these men be most helpful? First and foremost, by doing whatever is in their power to support victims and hold offenders accountable. But male educators who wish to help stop gender violence *before it happens* can also be leaders in developing gender violence prevention programs in their schools. On a personal level, they can provide an invaluable service if they choose to engage boys and other men in critical dialogue—in assemblies, classes, on the playing fields, in trainings for faculty and staff, and in private conversations—about what it means to be a man, especially as this relates to attitudes and behaviors toward women. In facilitating this dialogue, they need to take risks and talk about their own thoughts and feelings about manhood—the downsides as well as the privileges they enjoy. They must also provide ample opportunities for young men, in safe and respectful educational spaces, to talk about their life experiences as *boys* and *young men*, not simply as "kids," or "teens," or "youth." All of this is not easy, because both the educators and the students live in a culture that often misinterprets male introspection and vulnerability as weakness. Part of their challenge is to model anti-sexist masculinity as a stark contrast to the omnipresent cultural images on television, in movies, comedy, sports, and music that equate strength in men with power, dominance, and abuse toward women. One way of doing this is to co-teach classes and co-facilitate workshops with women. When men and women work together they can model the very sort of inter-gender partnership and respect that stands in diametric opposition to sexism and abuse.

Walking the talk

Male educators who get involved in school-based anti-sexist efforts need to know that their personal behavior is likely to be more thoroughly scrutinized. A male principal, teacher, or coach who takes a public anti-sexist stance, which inevitably means talking about male responsibility and accountability, invites attention to his own "walking the talk." Before he can teach a class, initiate programming for students or faculty, or otherwise provide anti-sexist leadership, he must assess whether or not his private life, personal history, or daily conduct in interactions with women in any way contradicts his public role. If it does, he invites the charge of hypocrisy, both from others and, if he is honest, from himself. Men in any visible line of work or profession who take a public anti-sexist stance must be aware of this dynamic.

In part because they are still a small minority of men, the personal motives of avowedly anti-sexist or pro-feminist men are constantly under suspicion. Of course, because of this, it is even more critical for those seeking to increase the number of anti-sexist men, inside and outside of schools, to be very cautious about embracing men who might have personal transgressions to hide. This does not mean that all men who want to be effective anti-sexist educators must have a perfect record. Young people can learn a lot from a man who openly takes responsibility for abusive behavior in his past, especially if he has done the personal work required to understand how and why he chose to act the way he did toward women (or gays, people of color, etc.). On the other hand, if he is not fully honest, he risks providing motivation for women or girls—from his past or present—to reveal the truth. This sort of unmasking not only causes pain and embarrassment to the parties involved, it also impacts the level of trust afforded all men who speak out against sexism, and deepens the skepticism of those who wonder why a man would really care about these issues in the first place. Admittedly, this degree of mistrust is not unfounded. There have been more than a few cases across the country in the past few years where seemingly supportive male educators, clergymen, coaches, politicians, and business leaders have sexually assaulted and/or harassed either young girls and boys, or their own female peers.

Fortunately, most potentially active anti-sexist male educators are not paralyzed by fears of being found out. Most men have never assaulted a woman. Rather, their reticence to get involved has more to do with a self-critical appraisal. Some men have confessed to me that they feel reluctant to "tell other men how to behave" on account of their having had "politically incorrect" experiences, such as use of blatantly misogynistic pornography. There is clearly a need for much more honest dialogue among men, and between women and men, about the sometimes hard-to-define distinctions between sexual attraction, objectification, and abuse. It is also important that men are honest with themselves and confront their own sexist attitudes and behaviors. In the meantime, however, scandalous rates of rape, battering, and sexual harassment continue, and few men speak out. For this reason, it is important to mention that for men to be effective anti-sexist leaders, they must dispense with self-righteousness—and the idea that they must be free of any ideological inconsistencies or inevitable human contradictions.

In addition to being able to "walk the talk," male educators need to have an adequate personal-comfort level in talking to other males about these issues. Considering the intensely competitive male hierarchies in which most men are socialized, this is easier said than done. There are many personal reasons why men might be uncomfortable talking about issues that may hit close to home. What if a man grew up in a home where his father abused his mother, and he has never talked about it outside of his family? What if he has an abusive relative or friend, and has never confronted him? What if a woman close to him is a rape survivor? What if a male educator is a survivor of childhood sexual abuse or some other sort of violent mistreatment? How do these life experiences affect a man's willingness to talk to young people about these issues? Some men are silenced by their continuing shame at having been bullied, as kids or even as adults. One embarrassing secret of many male high school teachers is that they are intimidated by outwardly tough male students. The popular discourse about teachers being intimidated by students typically conjures up the setting of a decaying urban high school with a teacher scared of his or her young black or Latino students who might have access to knives or guns. So societal fear of boys of color—not just "boys"—shapes people's perceptions. But this phenomenon is present in upper-middle-class white towns as well.

As Bernard Lefkowitz reports in *Our Guys*, his book about the 1989 gang rape of a mentally retarded girl by a group of popular white high school male athletes in Glen Ridge, New Jersey, the inside clique of abusive "real jocks" in the school intimidated everyone around them:

> The peacock image they projected was not something they
> had picked up overnight in high school. They had spent

years perfecting it. For these young men, the essence of jockdom was a practiced show of contempt for kids and teachers alike. They tried to humiliate any wimpy guy who got in their way, but they reserved their best shots for girls who ignored them or dared to stand up to them.

Lefkowitz reports one incident where a girl tells of being grabbed by the arms and legs by two of the boys, who began dragging her through the hallway of the school.

They are carrying me off the ground, and they're trying to pull off my pants. I'm screaming my head off, and this teacher sticks her head out the door and she doesn't say anything because none of the teachers wanted to deal with them. So nobody did anything until they finally let me go.

In this case the intimidated and irresponsible teacher was a woman, but Lefkowitz makes it clear that these aggressive young men silenced male teachers, administrators, and coaches as well. This type of abuse by young males is hardly unique to suburban New Jersey; it occurs across the country. In the face of this sort of bullying, is it surprising that many male educators hesitate before jumping into overt anti-sexist advocacy? A related question concerns men's body politics. For example, how does the anti-sexist teaching strategy of a man who is short and slight of build differ from one who is tall and muscular? How does a male physical-education teacher and coach, wearing a warm-up suit, differ in the way he talks about issues and is responded to by students from a math teacher who is less athletic but perhaps more bookish and cerebral? Each can be effective, but perhaps for different reasons. If men in every ethnic and racial group are, in the words of the anthropologist Alan Klein, "in a dialogue with muscles," how does that dialogue influence pedagogical choices in gender violence prevention education efforts?

Consider the following scenario. A male English teacher is leading a discussion of a book or short story with an explicit gender theme. In the course of conversation, a charismatic and aggressive male student says something sexist or victim-blaming (e.g., a woman who was raped was asking for it). The teacher does not respond directly, challenging the sexism of the statement, but instead moves on to another point. Some of the female students quietly fume; the teacher gradually develops a reputation for being insensitive to girls. I have heard variations of this very situation from many female educators, as well as from students about their high school teachers or college professors. The women often assume that male teachers are silent in these circumstances not because they are insecure or unprepared to respond, but because they agree with the sexist statements. This might be true, but there is another, perhaps more subtle, explanation for the teacher's silence. He might appear to be a mature, confident adult man, but in truth he is frightened by the sexist student and his male peers, and he also worries about what other male faculty will think of him. This intimidation, from students or colleagues, rarely takes the form of a physical threat. Rather, it has to do with the teacher's confidence and security *as a man* and whether or not he can withstand potentially overt or covert ridicule. For male teachers in their twenties and thirties, memories of sexist and homophobic male high school and college peer cultures might still be fresh. They might have experienced these peer cultures as oppressive, but never had the strength or standing to speak out. If they have not yet addressed the issue of their silence and insecurity in the male group dynamic, they will be much less likely to respond to other men's sexism, inside or outside of a classroom. Male teachers who do not meet the stereotypical standards of a "man's man" might also be compromised in their ability to confront belligerently sexist male students. They might even, in some circumstances, feel physically threatened or bullied. Closeted gay teachers might not want to risk being outed by the inevitable gossip that follows anti-sexist men. ("He must be gay, a 'real man' wouldn't be talking about 'masculinity.'") Many homophobic heterosexual men also chafe at this sort of gossip. Some men are so policed by their own internalized homophobia that just the possibility that others will think they are gay is enough to keep them silent, even if they are uneasy in the face of other men's sexism. There might also be relevant racial and cultural factors. African American men who teach in majority white suburban schools, for example, have to be prepared to deal not only with the sexism of their students, but potentially with their racist beliefs about black male sexuality. Asian American male teachers who dare to challenge young men's macho posturing may have to be self-confident enough to overcome their stereotypical image, in the words of the Japanese American actor Mark Hayashi, as "the eunuchs of America." On the other hand, white male teachers who have a large percentage of students of color might be hesitant to confront sexism out of fear of being accused of ignorance or insensitivity. It is very difficult for any educator, male or female, to maintain a strong anti-sexist position in a discussion when you are being forcefully told, "you don't know what it's like in my culture."

In any cultural setting, teachers who are privately anti-sexist might not want to risk losing whatever credibility or popularity they have acquired in the school's dominant male culture, whether it be jock-centric or not, by calling some boys out on their sexism, or calling girls out on their complaisance. In some cases, the motivation might be related to concerns about career advancement. There is little reason to suspect that men who challenge the male power structure are likely to be speedily promoted as a reward for principled dissent or ideological independence.

It is one thing for educational-policy makers to agree, in principle, that more male participation is needed in school-based gender violence prevention education; but who would decide which men? What if the majority of current male faculty, for many of the reasons outlined above, resists taking on these issues? Can a small minority of concerned men in a school system make a sufficient impact to affect the school climate? If so, who trains them? Out of whose budget? The most common model of gender violence prevention programming in schools consists of a mix of various components, including classroom presentations, forums for teens, theater troupes, peer leadership programs, and support groups for at-risk students. While there is no comprehensive data documenting the sex of faculty involved in this work, there are, to be sure, male educators who have been teaching and mentoring students, attending trainings and conferences on gender equity and violence issues, and providing other sorts of anti-sexist male leadership. But we are a long way from this sort of participation being the norm.

In the meantime, schools that want a knowledgeable, confident, anti-sexist male presence realistically will have to bring in educators from the community. Currently, only a few communities in the U.S. have anti-sexist men's groups that provide this service. Battered women's and rape crisis programs often have youth outreach programs, but many more men are needed to co-facilitate classes with the women who typically present the material. Unfortunately, chronically underfunded women's programs rarely can provide compensation for these positions, unless they are fortunate enough to obtain funding through sources such as the Violence Against Women Office at the Department of Justice. There are also significant drawbacks to the model of male community educators coming into the schools. Time limitations are always a factor. Even if they can gain the respect and attention of the students, community educators are only briefly in the school. And if they can manage to be effective despite the constraints, sometimes the very teachers and coaches who brought them in can undermine their influence. At one urban high school where two of my colleagues were conducting a series of all-male workshops, a student told them that his football coach had called him a "fucking pussy" for not diving to block a punt. At another session in the same school, a physical education teacher in his late twenties was handing out passes to students about to participate in an MVP workshop. He said to one boy, "You're not only a member, you're the president of the fag club." This was in front of my colleagues, who were there to talk and facilitate dialogue about men's sexist and abusive behaviors. Amazingly, this same man told my colleagues later that day, "I'm so on top of these issues, I could have done this training myself." While this is highly debatable, what is not in question is whether enough male educators have accepted the responsibility of full participation in gender violence prevention efforts. Clearly they have not.

Can women teach boys?

Many women who provide sexual assault and teen dating violence education in schools wrestle constantly with the question of whether their approach is effective with boys. They often report that in mixed-gender settings, where most of this education takes place, they know they are reaching the girls, but they are not sure about the boys. Many women have shared horror stories with me about boys ignoring them, joking at inappropriate moments, or openly defying them. This prompts the question: is it possible for women to educate boys about gender violence, especially when this education involves the examination of sensitive and loaded questions about masculinity, femininity, power, and control? Clearly some boys and young men are capable of learning new insights about manhood from women. In fact, I have no doubt that the majority of men in the gender-violence prevention field have been profoundly influenced by women writers and educators. Many have female mentors who played an indispensable role in their evolution into anti-sexist men.

Just the same, many boys and young men are too immature and insecure to truly listen to a woman they perceive to be challenging their manhood—especially in a school setting in front of their male—and female—peers. By mid-adolescence, some boys have already learned to devalue what women say. Boys might be uncomfortable with the very idea that a woman has something to teach them about how a "real man" is supposed to behave, a discomfort that parallels a process that is going on at home with their own mothers. Early-to-mid adolescence can be a time of great tension in mother-son relationships, because of cultural pressure on sons to push their mothers away, and pressure on mothers to disengage emotionally from their sons if they want them to be successful in the world of men. (Where presumably there are no "mama's boys.") Feminist theorists have maintained that this pressure is not a law of nature, but is rather a cultural belief that needs to be examined and transcended.

Regardless of the reasons, more than a few boys are not open to learning about relationship abuse and sexual violence from women educators. For these boys, it can help to have a man introduce the subject, especially a man they cannot write off as hopelessly out of touch with the realities of boy's lives and the pressures on them to conform to masculine norms. Of course it can be very effective for women and men to co-teach, allowing them to model inter-gender collaboration. When no male educators are available, women who want to defuse criticism that they are "male-bashers" can use video clips of men talking about these issues—including public service announcements which feature anti-rape and anti-domestic violence testimonials from high-profile men, such as professional athletes. They might also get quotes from anti-sexist men, or articles by them, and have the class read and discuss them. The idea is to bring men's voices (if not their actual persons) into the classroom to support the woman, and disarm the boys (and possibly girls) who might attempt to discredit the information the woman is presenting by impugning her motives. Another strategy for women who do gender violence prevention education with boys—in single-sex or mixed-gender settings—is to identify a handful of potential male allies in the class and approach them, say, one week *before* the class period when they are scheduled to raise testy issues. The women can tell the young men that they have noticed their maturity and thoughtfulness, and ask them to speak up in class and support them—if they agree with what the teacher is saying—when a controversial discussion is on the table.

The Role of the School Athletic Subculture

Sports culture is often accurately viewed as one of the key sources of sexist and homophobic male attitudes and behaviors. As the sport sociologist Don Sabo points out, sports, especially contact sports, train boys and men to assume macho characteristics like cut-throat competitiveness, domination of others, tendency toward violence, emotional stoicism, and arrogance toward women. Men and boys in the male-dominated school sports culture often have a disproportionate impact on what sorts of masculine styles and sexualities in that school are accepted or marginalized, celebrated or bullied. But while many critiques of the relationship between sports culture and gender violence understandably stress its complicity in covering up, if not actively promoting, men's violence against women, the male sports culture can also be a source of creative anti-sexist strategies. As noted above, the dearth of male participation in gender violence prevention efforts over the past generation is partly a failure of male leadership. Due to the popularity, power, and privileged status of boys' sports (particularly team sports) within many suburban, rural, and urban schools, the athletic subculture—in the persons of athletic directors, coaches, and student athletes—is in a position to provide some of that missing leadership. If one reason so few male educators have participated in this work is that it has been stigmatized as "unmasculine," what better strategy than to enlist some of the most traditionally "masculine" men in the work?

Of course, this approach is not without its contradictions. One could argue that by utilizing the potential for leadership in the male sports culture, we reinforce its legitimacy, instead of diminishing its power. But if high status male student athletes (e.g., varsity members, team captains, seniors, all-stars) were offered special anti-sexist training that focused on their role as leaders and did not target them as potential perpetrators, their leadership could help make this work more acceptable for males with less social standing. This is just as true for athletic administrators and coaches, who belong to their own peer cultures in the school and community. One promising initiative in this area is the Family Violence Prevention Fund's campaign called Coaching Boys Into Men which recognizes the unique leadership platform of coaches, and highlights the positive role they can play in gender-violence prevention. For example, if coaches attend gender violence prevention trainings, cosponsor events with school-based health educators or community-based women's programs, and otherwise endorse anti-sexist efforts, it is possible that their non-athletic peers on the faculty or in the administration would be more likely to get involved. Politically, the interdepartmental and community contacts fostered by these sorts of coalitions could also help indirectly to reduce the resistance of influential male athletic directors, coaches, teachers, and others to school-based gender-equity and anti-homophobia efforts.

My colleagues and I have given speeches and presented workshops in numerous schools where the athletic department has been a cosponsoring partner. In most cases, a woman administrator or teacher initiated the effort, and solicited support from the athletic department in part by emphasizing our sports backgrounds and credentials. The success of these partnerships is hardly assured. Many male athletic administrators, coaches, and student athletes resist efforts to get involved with these types of educational interventions, in some cases due to simple defensiveness. Some are angry about the widespread public perception that male athletes, at the high school, college, and professional level, are out of control generally, and are disproportionately involved in crimes against women. Advocates for African American male athletes are concerned that in the national media, black males are the implied focus of this discussion, thus allowing white male athletes and non-athletes to evade critical scrutiny. In some cases, it is necessary to defer talk about positive leadership and instead spell out how it is in the self-interest of athletic departments to get involved (e.g., to prevent student athletes from getting themselves, their coaches, and the school in trouble).

There are many other strategies that school systems, through athletic departments, can implement to help mandate and institutionalize male participation in gender violence prevention efforts. One is to provide regular training for coaches and student athletes. But it would represent great progress in the educational system if school boards, superintendents, and principals were to write job descriptions for prospective athletic directors that explicitly mention gender-based violence prevention programming as part of the job. Hiring preference would go to candidates, male and female, who had previous experience in this area or who had done related college or graduate work. Likewise, if athletic directors communicated, in their job postings for coaches' positions, that undergraduate and graduate course work and other demonstrated knowledge of and interest in gender issues would help (male and female) candidates distinguish themselves, this would prompt many otherwise indifferent undergraduate or graduate students (who have an interest in the coaching profession) to take these kinds of courses. While there is no national uniformity in this sort of coursework, and no guarantee that education will result in an increase in commitment to non-violence and gender equity, one effect on men of taking gender studies courses is an increased awareness of the pervasiveness of sexism and all forms of men's violence against women. Studying gender is also likely to lead to a better understanding, by men who are training to be leaders in athletic departments, of the potential abuses of masculine power and privilege. This insight, and the self-knowledge it often catalyzes, is one of the reasons why this education is still politically controversial.

Lessons about Accountability

In a just world, adults and adolescents should be held accountable for their behavior, especially when it harms others. But sadly, in recent years accountability—for adults or young people—has not been greatly in evidence in male sports culture. That is why an event that occurred at a school in Baltimore in 2001 was so notable. A sixteen-year-old junior varsity lacrosse player at St. Paul's, a prestigious, predominantly white, independent school whose lacrosse team was ranked number one in the nation, videotaped himself having sex with a girl from another private school. He then showed the tape, made without the girl's knowledge, to a small group of teammates, and a few nights later a varsity player showed it to two dozen team members. When the girl found out and her parents alerted the authorities, the reckoning was swift and sure. The school's headmaster expelled the male student and suspended several others. Then, at a school with a long and proud lacrosse tradition, he sent an unmistakable message to the rest of the team. *He canceled the varsity season.*

The girl suffered a traumatic event whose effects she might feel for a long time. She immediately withdrew from school. For the young men on the lacrosse team, some of whom have by now graduated from college, this regrettable episode provided one of those life lessons that coaches like to talk about as one of the benefits of team sports. The lesson is about silence and complicity. There were many disturbing aspects of this case, but the one that probably caused the most second-guessing is the fact that numerous guys had prior knowledge of their teammate's plans, but none said or did anything to prevent or interrupt them. Not even seniors or the team captains. Why not? One possible explanation is that few of the boys on the team grasped the extent of the harm they were doing. They had grown up immersed in a popular and pornographic culture where the sexual degradation of women is so common as to seem unremarkable. In that sense it should not surprise us that they did not stop to think about how humiliated the girl would feel.

There is another explanation. In organized team sports, leadership on and off the field is constantly invoked as a highly prized ideal. Yet when it comes to men speaking out about other men's sexism or violence toward women, few high school boys, or adult men, have been willing to provide that leadership. This is not an insignificant failure. Several recent surveys have shown that 25 to 40 percent of teens know someone in their school who has been in an abusive relationship. Most gender violence is perpetrated by men who are not athletes. But when male athletes in high school, college, or the pros are caught treating women in stereotypically sexist, physically abusive, or sexually assaultive ways, because of their status and prominence in male culture they reinforce the idea that being disrespectful to women is part of the very definition of being a man. On the other hand, when individual male athletes or entire men's sports organizations take an active public stance against gender violence, they set a powerful example for other men and boys. When respected athletes support the cause, more than any specific piece of wisdom they might impart, they send the message to other men that it is okay for them to speak out, too. If we want to reduce gender violence, we need to discourage men from being passive bystanders in the faces of their peers' abusive behavior. Fortunately, it appears that a growing number of high school and college student athletes are getting involved in programs aimed at reducing teen-relationship abuse, rape, and sexual assault. But positive peer influence is not enough. Potential perpetrators need to know that there will be consequences for abusive behavior. Responsible leaders in the sports culture, including athletic directors, coaches, and general managers, increasingly need to display the kind of courage that the headmaster at St. Paul's did when he refused to excuse the thoughtless cruelty of the lacrosse team. If we want our boys to become healthy men who treat women—and each other—with respect and dignity, we need to put an end to the rationalization that "boys will be boys" and demand a higher standard, because someday "they will be men."

MEDIA LITERACY

In my educational video, *Tough Guise: Violence, Media, and the Crisis in Masculinity*, I argue that media do not directly cause violence, but that violent masculinity is a cultural norm. In other words, when boys and men act out violently, we should not profess to be shocked; the culture teaches boys every day that part of being a man means being violent, or using the threat of force to establish or maintain power and control. Therefore, since media is the great pedagogical—or teaching—force of our time, it is critical to examine the stories we tell in media that link violence and masculinity.

Tough Guise is part of the growing media literacy movement. One of the chief goals of this movement is to assist people in developing analytic tools to understand how media works on their individual psyches as well as in their communities. Once people understand better the way media representations help to shape people's identities and thus to affect their behavior, the negative images will have less of a pernicious effect. In order to help people analyze or deconstruct media messages, educators need to bring the images themselves into the classroom. In our media-saturated culture there is an endless supply of material for critical assessment. For example, teachers can ask students to analyze front pages of newspapers, ads from magazines, song lyrics, and scenes from television programs they have taped or movies they have watched. The students need to consider many aspects of media culture: Who produces most of the images and stories in mainstream media? Whose interests do the producers of media images represent? Do they present a realistic or distorted portrait of people or events? What stories about manhood and womanhood do media convey? Sex and violence might attract audiences, but what kinds of sex? Whose violence? When do media representations merely reflect existing relations of power, and when do they subvert them? In the growing number of schools that have the technological capability, classes can view websites together and critically assess the benefits—and the drawbacks—of the revolutionary changes in the flow of information that have been catalyzed by the growth of the Internet and the World Wide Web.

Media literacy is already a crucial aspect of some rape and domestic violence prevention education, and in the coming years it will only become more important. If we are going to achieve dramatic reductions in incidents of domestic and sexual violence, we must face squarely the roots of this violence in the system of gender inequality—otherwise known as "patriarchy." A crucial component of the patriarchal system is the gender ideology that is transmitted to young people through media, and plays such a powerful role in their understanding of what it means to be a man, or a woman. How much can things change if successive generations of men are taught that part of being a man means dominating and controlling women? And how can we change that sexist and oppressive definition of masculinity unless we address the 24/7 media culture that reinforces it?

It is clear to me that many high school and college students are eager to understand not only how media contributes to our society's violence pandemic but how they can be part of the effort to counteract it. Many sexual-assault and teen-relationship-abuse educators use *Tough Guise* in their trainings. They use it to provide insight and spark dialogue among young women and men about the relationship between cultural definitions of manhood and the way some men treat women. Many of these programs use other educational videos, such as Jean Kilbourne's *Killing Us Softly 3*, to study images of women in advertising and to examine questions about cultural definitions of womanhood and how they influence girls and women. One of the first educational videos to look explicitly at the relationship between media images and sexual violence is Sut Jhally's *Dreamworlds*, which is about the sexual objectification of women on MTV. Jhally, a professor of communication at the University of Massachusetts-Amherst, initially produced *Dreamworlds* with a tiny budget to educate his students. But the response was so overwhelming that he decided to create the Media Education Foundation, a Northampton, Massachusetts-based non-profit organization that produces dozens of educational videos—many on gender and media-related themes—that are used in college and high school classes across this country, and other parts of the world.

CHAPTER THIRTEEN

More Than a Few Good Men

"As long as we take the view that these are problems for women alone to solve, we cannot expect to reverse the high incidence of rape and child abuse ... and domestic violence. We do know that many men do not abuse women and children; and that they strive always to live with respect and dignity. But until today the collective voice of these men has never been heard, because the issue has not been regarded as one for the whole nation. From today those who inflict violence on others will know they are being isolated and cannot count on other men to protect them. From now on all men will hear the call to assume their responsibility for solving this problem."
—President Nelson Mandela, 1997, National Men's March,
   Pretoria, South Africa

Since the very beginning of the women-led movements against domestic and sexual violence in the 1970s, there have been men who personally, professionally, and politically supported the work of those women. In addition, over the past several decades there have been repeated attempts by men to create organizations and targeted initiatives to address men's roles in ending men's violence against women. Some of the early efforts were undertaken by groups of concerned men who responded to the challenge from women's organizations to educate, politicize, and organize other men. Some of these men chose to volunteer in supportive roles with local rape crisis centers or battered women's programs. Others contributed to the development of the fledgling batterer intervention movement in the late 1970s and 1980s. Some of the better known programs for batterers were Emerge in

Cambridge, Massachusetts; RAVEN (Rape and Violence End Now) in St. Louis, Missouri; and Men Stopping Violence in Atlanta, Georgia. Still other men created political and activist educational organizations, like the National Organization for Men Against Sexism (NOMAS), which has held "Men and Masculinity" conferences annually since 1975; the Oakland Men's Project in the San Francisco Bay Area; Men Stopping Rape in Madison, Wisconsin; DC Men Against Rape; and Real Men, an anti-sexist men's organization I co-founded in Boston in 1988.

The rapidly growing field of "men's work" also produced community centers that combine batterer-intervention and counseling services for men with educational outreach and social activism. One of the groundbreaking programs in this field is the Men's Resource Center of Western Massachusetts, founded in Amherst in 1982. In the 1990s anti-sexist men's initiatives in the U.S. and around the world increased dramatically. One of the most visible has been the White Ribbon Campaign, an activist educational campaign founded by a group of men in Canada in 1991. They started the WRC in response to a horrific incident on December 6, 1989, at the University of Montreal, where an armed twenty-five-year-old man walked into a classroom, separated the women from the men and proceeded to shoot the women. Before he finished his rampage, he had murdered fourteen women in cold blood—and shaken up an entire country. The significance of the white ribbon—which has been adopted on hundreds of college campuses and communities in the U.S. as well as a number of other countries—is that men wear it to make a visible and public pledge "never to commit, condone, nor remain silent about violence against women."

Despite these notable efforts over the past thirty years, the movement of men committed to ending men's violence against women has only recently picked up significant momentum. There are more men doing this work in the United States and around the world than ever before. Halfway through the first decade of the twenty-first century there is reason for optimism, especially about the emergence of a new generation of anti-sexist men. But there are nowhere near enough men yet involved to make a serious dent in this enormous problem. Several key challenges lie ahead:

• How to increase dramatically the number of men who make these issues a priority in their personal and professional lives
• How to expand the existing infrastructure of men's anti-rape and domestic violence prevention groups, and other campus and community-based initiatives
• How to institutionalize gender violence prevention education at every level of the educational system

- How to build multiracial and multiethnic coalitions that unite men across differences around their shared concerns about sexist violence and the sexual exploitation of children
- How to insure that federal, state, and local funding for efforts to reduce gender violence are maintained and expanded in the coming years
- And finally, how to make it socially acceptable—even cool—for men to become vocal and public allies of women in the struggle against all forms of men's violence against women and children

A "BIG TENT" APPROACH

As I have made clear in this book, there is much that we can do to prevent men's violence against women—if we find the collective will in male culture to make it a priority. I am convinced that millions of men in our society are deeply concerned about the abuse, harassment, and violence we see—and fear—in the lives of our daughters, mothers, sisters, and lovers. In fact, a recent poll conducted for Lifetime Television found that 57 percent of men aged sixteen to twenty-four believe gender violence is an "extremely serious" problem. A 2000 poll conducted by the Family Violence Prevention Fund found that one-quarter of men would do more about the issue if they were asked. And some compelling social norms research on college campuses suggests that one of the most significant factors in a man's decision to intervene in an incident is his perception of how other men would act in a similar situation. Clearly, a lot of men are uncomfortable with other men's abusive behaviors, but they have not figured out what to do about it—or have not yet mustered the courage to act on their own. So there is great potential to increase dramatically the number of men who commit personal time, money, and institutional clout to the effort to reduce men's violence against women. But in order to achieve this we need to think outside the box about how to reach into the mainstream of male culture and social power.

One promising approach employs elements of what might be called "big tent" movement building. The big tent concept comes from politics, where it has been used most famously to describe efforts to unite various constituencies and single-issue special-interest groups under the Republican Party label. A number of questions arise when this concept is applied to gender violence prevention: How do we attract individuals and organizations not known for their advocacy of the issues of men's violence? What are some of the necessary compromises required in order to broaden the coalition of participating individuals and groups? What are some of the costs and benefits of engaging new partners, who might not have the depth of experience or the ideological affinities of the majority of women and men currently in the movement?

Growing pains always accompany growth. A bigger movement will inevitably create new conflicts. One way to think about the question of broadening the base of the movement is to consider the concept embodied in the geometric model of the Venn diagram. The Venn diagram captures the idea that coalition building involves identifying shared objectives between groups with different interests, not creating a perfect union between fully compatible partners. The diagram consists of two overlapping circles. In this case we might say that one circle represents the needs and interests of the battered women's and rape crisis movements. The other circle represents any men's organization that has not historically been part of these movements. Clearly, there are large areas where the circles do not overlap. But the big tent approach does not dwell on the areas of disconnection. It focuses on the center area, where there are points of agreement and shared objectives. If individuals and groups of men and women can agree that reducing men's violence against women is an urgent objective, then perhaps they can agree for the moment to table their other differences.

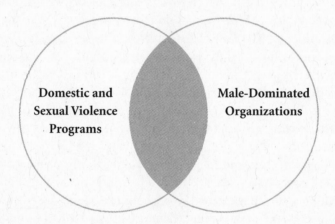

Domestic and Sexual Violence Programs

Male-Dominated Organizations

CHALLENGES

There are obvious downsides to incautiously expanding the big tent. Take, for example, the costs and benefits of working with men in the sports culture. Many women in domestic and sexual violence advocacy have long seen the benefit to partnering with athletic teams or utilizing high-profile male athletes in public service campaigns. But some of these same women worry about the potential risks inherent in such collaboration. They fear that a male athlete who speaks out publicly against men's violence could undermine the integrity of the movement if his private behavior does not match his public rhetoric. Happily, in recent years this fear has begun to dissipate as more male athletes speak out, in part because with increased men's participation there is less pressure on any one man to be the "perfect" poster child for anti-violence efforts. We can also never lose sight of the fact that professional sports teams are not social justice organizations. They are businesses that sometimes have huge investments in players. Say a team takes a public stand against men's violence, and then at some point one of its star players is arrested for domestic violence or sexual assault. Is the team likely to respond based on what they think is best for the community, or for their own bottom line?

The participation of faith-based organizations in the big tent presents significant opportunities, but comes with its own unique set of challenges. As the Rev. Dr. Marie Fortune, a pioneer in the movements against domestic and sexual violence and founder of the FaithTrust Institute in Seattle, Washington, points out, "Millions of men participate in faith-based communities whose leaders, often male, typically enjoy significant moral authority and shape in important ways the values and behaviors of men in their congregations." There are male clergy in every denomination who are strong allies of women in the domestic and sexual violence prevention movements. But many clergy and religious leaders have received no training on the issue of men's violence against women. To this day many male clergy are reluctant to take strong public stands on issues of sexual and domestic violence. What further complicates matters is that many religious traditions have "reflected and reinforced," in the words of Rev. Fortune, "patriarchal values that have been at the core of violence against women." But perhaps even more troubling are the clergy sex abuse scandals that have become routine in recent years. It is plain to see that even men with impeccable religious credentials can be private hypocrites.

The participation of faith-based organizations in gender violence prevention also raises the question of how much ideological incompatibility is tolerable in the quest for big tent inclusiveness. Can feminist religious and secular leaders work in coalition with religious leaders who have resisted the advancement of women in the family and the pulpit? Can progressive religious and secular leaders who support full sexual equality work side by side with religious leaders who oppose gay civil rights?

Similar questions arise about an organization like the Boy Scouts. Scouting plays an important role in the lives of millions of boys and adolescent males. Many local Boy Scout chapters have participated in events of domestic violence and sexual assault awareness month. But if the Scouts went a step further and made participation in gender violence prevention a major nationwide organizational goal, they could have a tremendous impact, especially since the Scouts have a presence in many communities where there is currently little male participation in domestic and sexual violence programs. But many progressive organizations refuse to work with the Boy Scouts because their official policy discriminates against openly gay scouts and scoutmasters. Does their anti-gay stance make the Boy Scouts an unacceptable coalition partner in the struggle against teen-relationship abuse and sexual assault?

Until now most men in the movement to end men's violence against women have been pro-feminist and politically liberal or progressive. But this does not preclude them from framing one aspect of the gender-violence issue in language about crime and punishment that resonates with conservatives. In fact, many politically conservative men have played an important role in this fight—particularly men in law enforcement, the military, and government. After all, domestic and sexual violence are more than social problems; they are crimes. Nonetheless, millions of abusive men continue to receive suspended sentences, probation, and other light penalties, which signals that their crimes are not taken seriously. In order to be effective, decisive action is required by police, prosecutors, and judges. The goal of punishment is to send the message to would-be perps that the price for transgression is steep. Conservative as well as progressive men who take the idea of personal responsibility seriously should support policies that hold law-breakers accountable, and advocacy that strengthens the community's desire to do so. But a criminal justice approach is also fraught with potential problems. For one thing, there are not enough jail cells to house all the men who could be prosecuted for domestic and sexual violence. As I have discussed, class bias and racism are factors in any discussion about the criminal justice system. Efforts to attract conservative men's support by emphasizing a law enforcement approach might exact too high a cost—and jeopardize the increased participation of people of color who are concerned about both gender violence *and* the over-representation of men in color in the "prison industrial complex." In addition, since most gender violence—including the vast majority of rape—is currently not reported, it is questionable how effective a criminal justice approach can be.

MEN AND WOMEN

The special challenge of gender violence prevention politics is that women's trust of men is not a given. Some women are understandably wary of men's motivations and skeptical about their commitment to gender justice. As increasing numbers of men get involved, they worry that men might try to "take over" the movement, or take it in a direction that suits men's needs rather than women's. Women are always eager to see whether men "walk their talk." For example, an administrator in a domestic-violence agency recently told me about a talented young man who had applied for a youth outreach position. He seemed to know the issues really well, she explained, and he grasped some of the subtle racial and ethnic issues involved in this work. He also had an engaging personal style. But he had not yet mastered the "micro-politics" of how to interact with women in positions of leadership. He often cut off women co-presenters, or talked over them in an effort to prove his knowledge. Was it worth the risk of hiring him?

For their part, some men are well-meaning but oblivious to the sensitivities required for effective inter-gender collaboration on an issue where women have historically been the leaders. For example, I have heard stories too many times about earnest young men on college campuses who were inspired to start anti-rape groups, but neglected first to check in with women who were already engaged in rape prevention work, like the director of the campus women's center. These sorts of political missteps can cause unnecessary tension and discord at the earliest stages and can undermine successful coalition-building.

Even so, there are numerous examples across the country of men and women working together to create and sustain sexual and domestic violence prevention initiatives. In fact, many successful college men's anti-violence programs have actually been started by women. Among the more well-known are Men Against Violence at Louisiana State University, begun by Dr. Luoluo Hong, and the Fraternity Anti-Violence Education Project at West Chester University in Pennsylvania, led by Dr. Deborah Mahlstedt.

WHAT CAN MEN DO?

At a small state college in the Northeast, a controversy erupted in early 2005 when the editors of the student newspaper distributed a sex survey across campus that included a question about which professor on campus they would most like to "get it on with." The person chosen was the coordinator of the women's studies program, who responded with a lengthy letter to the editor in which she wrote that it was "offensive and hurtful" to be disrespected by students in this way, and as a professional it undermined her ability to do her job. In her letter she posed a number of questions for an alternative survey, including one to men which asked, "What are you willing to do to help reduce rape and sexual assault among college students?" In response, a male columnist for the student newspaper wrote dismissively: "I will not rape anyone. Is there anything more I should add to this?" The student's response might have been glib and a bit obnoxious, but he spoke for a lot of men. Many of them have never even considered the wide range of choices men have to reduce rape and sexual assault, and every other type of gender violence. What follows is a brief discussion about how men can be effective anti-sexist agents, both as individuals and in their various public and private leadership roles within institutions.

Have the courage to look inward

One of the most important steps any man can take if he wants to be an ally to women in the struggle against gender violence is to be honest with himself. A key requirement for men to become effective anti-sexist agents is their willingness to examine their own attitudes and behaviors about women, sex, and manhood. This is similar to the sort of introspection required of anti-racist whites. It is not an easy process, especially when men start to see that they have inadvertently perpetuated sexism and violence through their personal actions, or their participation in sexist practices in male culture. Because defensiveness is the enemy of introspection, it is vital that men develop ways to transcend their initial defensive reactions about men's mistreatment of women and move toward a place where they are grounded enough to do something about it.

Support survivors

In a social climate where women who report sexual and domestic violence are often disbelieved and called "accusers," it is crucial that men personally and publicly support survivors—girls and boys, women and men. This can mean the offer of a supportive ear in a conversation, or a shoulder for a friend to cry on. It can also mean challenging others—men and women—who seek to discredit victims' accounts of their victimization. For example, when a girl or woman reports a sexual assault and her alleged attacker is a popular guy with a network of supporters, people often rally around him—even when they have nothing more than his word to go on that she is lying. Sadly, some of them try to smear her character and reputation. It is not fair to assume the man's guilt; he is entitled to a presumption of innocence until proven guilty. But alleged victims are entitled to a presumption as well—the presumption that they are telling the truth about what was done to them. They also have the right to be treated with respect, and to expect the people around them to defend their integrity if it is ever questioned.

Seek help

Men who are emotionally, physically, or sexually abusive to women and girls need to seek help now. But first they have to acknowledge to themselves that they have a problem. I once gave a speech about men's violence against women at a big state university in the West. After the event was over, a blond-haired college student in jeans and a T-shirt approached me in the main lobby of the student center. His voice quivered as he said, "I just realized that I have done bad things to women." He did not elaborate, nor did I ask him to. But I could tell he had a troubled conscience by the look in his eyes, and because he waited nearly half an hour to talk to me. The question of what to do about men who have been abusive will take on ever greater urgency as more men become involved in the movement against gender violence. Many men who were formerly abusive to women have become effective profession-als in batterer intervention programs. They share their personal stories and serve as models for how men can grow and change. This is crucial because millions of men have committed mild or severe acts of cruelty toward women and children, and whether they were charged with and convicted of a crime or not, we have to figure out ways to integrate most of them back into our families and communities. Of course, sometimes this is easier said than done. For example, in recent years families in communities across the U.S. have faced the challenge of living in neighborhoods alongside convicted child molesters. This raises another set of questions: When do the rights of children and their parents to be free from the threat of sexual abuse and violence out-weigh the rights of men (or women) who have served their sentences and are seeking to rebuild their lives? If a man has committed acts of sexual or domestic violence, should those acts define him for the rest of his life?

Refuse to condone sexist and abusive behavior by friends, peers, and coworkers

As I have argued in this book, if we want to dramatically increase the num-ber of men who make men's violence against women a priority, it is not use-ful to engage them as perpetrators or potential perpetrators. Instead, it makes sense to enlist them as empowered bystanders who can do something to confront abusive peers, or who can help to create a climate in male peer culture that discourages some men's sexist attitudes and behaviors. This is often easier said than done, because it can be quite awkward for men to con-front each other about how they talk about and treat women. Consider an experience I had when I was in my early thirties at a wedding of an old friend of mine. A few minutes after I was introduced to the best man at a cocktail reception the day before the wedding, he confidently told me and a group of other guys a tasteless joke about battered women. I was not sure how to react. If I said something, I feared that it could create a chill between us, and this was the first day of a long weekend. But if I did not say something, I feared my silence might imply approval of the joke. I felt similar to how I would have felt if a white friend had told a racist joke. There was an added concern: How could I—or anyone else—know the full context of his joke-telling? The guy may have been personally harmless, but at the very least his gender politics were suspect, and at the worst he also may have been a closeted batterer who was subtly seeking public approval for his private behavior. I managed to mutter a feeble objection, something like, "Surely you have other topics to joke about." But I never told the guy how I really felt.

Sometimes men who take a strong stand against gender violence can face serious interpersonal consequences for their efforts. Mike LaRiviere, a police officer who is deeply committed to domestic and sexual violence prevention, trains police across the country in domestic violence policies and procedures. He recounts an incident many years ago when he was relatively new to his small-city New England police force. He and his more senior partner answered a domestic violence call, and when they arrived at the apartment it was obvious that the man had assaulted the woman. Mike thought it was clear they should make an arrest, both for the victim's safety and to hold the man accountable for what he had done. But the senior partner had another idea. He just wanted to tell the guy to cool down. Mike and he had a hushed but heated conversation in another room about what to do. They finally arrested the man, but for the next five or six months, Mike's partner barely spoke with him. The atmosphere in the squad car was tense and chilly, which in police work can be dangerous as well as unpleasant, because you can never be certain that someone who seethes with resentment will always have your back.

In spite of how difficult it can be for men to challenge each other about sexism, it does happen. In fact, it might happen more often than many people realize. In any case, it is important for men to hear each other's stories about this type of intervention, so they can see that other men feel as they do and so they can get potentially useful ideas. I heard one such story about a bachelor party road trip that Al Emerick, a leader of Men Against Violence Against Women in Jacksonville, Florida, took a couple of years ago with some friends. They were a group of well-off white guys in their thirties who had been playing poker together for nine years. There were four married men in the car along with the groom, and the discussion came up about strip clubs. The best man was ready to drop a pile of one-dollar bills on some "fine ladies' asses." Al said he would not be joining them, and the guys immediately got on him. "Whattya gay?" "What's the big deal, the wife's not here." "Cut loose." Because the guys had known Al for quite some time, they knew he was no prude, nor were his objections based on his religious beliefs. But they did know he had been working with a men's group that was affiliated with the local domestic violence shelter. He told them he did not want to take part because he had a problem with the objectification of women—even when it is voluntary. As he tells it, this group of friends spent two hours in an "intense but wonderful" conversation about sexism, domestic violence, male privilege, power, and control. In the course of the conversation Al fielded a range of predictable challenges like: "I'm not an abuser because I look at chicks." He countered with questions like, "What about men in the audience who might be abusers or rapists? By us being there and supporting the action, aren't we reinforcing their behaviors?" In the end, they never went to the strip clubs. Since that event, they have had further conversations about these issues, and according to Al, one of the guys has even offered to help produce a public service announcement for the anti-sexist men's group.

Make connections between men's violence against women and other issues

Gender violence contributes to a wide range of social problems that include youth violence, homelessness, divorce, alcoholism, and the transmission of HIV/AIDS. Men who care about these problems need to educate themselves about the relationship between gender violence and these issues, and then integrate this understanding in their work and daily life.

Perhaps nowhere are the effects of gender violence more pronounced than with HIV/AIDS, the global pandemic that has already killed twenty million people and infected forty-five million. Across the world, there is an inextricable linkage between men's violence against women and transmission of the virus. Forms of gender violence that are fueling transmission include sexual coercion and rape, men's refusal to wear condoms, and married or monogamous men's solicitation of prostitutes followed by unprotected sex with their wives or partners. Gender violence also takes the form of civil and customary laws that perpetuate male privilege and prerogative and deny women's human rights. This might include civil and customary laws that do not recognize marital rape or the dangers of early marriage, as well as systematic prohibitions against females inheriting wealth and property—a reality that ultimately forces millions of widows and daughters to lives of abject poverty and economic dependence on men. But according to M.I.T. research fellow and United Nations consultant Miriam Zoll, while heterosexual transmission may be the primary route of HIV/AIDS infection today, few HIV-prevention programs actually address the underlying gender, power, and sexual dynamics between men and women that contribute to infection, including violence. In a 2004 report entitled "Closing the HIV/AIDS Prevention Gender Gap?" Zoll surveyed men's and women's attitudes about gender and sexuality on several continents. She found that men and women's cultural definitions and perceptions of masculinity and femininity often reinforced men's power over women in ways that make sexually transmitted infections more likely. In the report, Zoll featured the work of men and women who are implementing promising gender-based prevention strategies. For example, Dean Peacock is a white South African who lived for many years in the U.S., where he worked in San Francisco as a facilitator in a batterer intervention program. Peacock returned to South Africa a couple of years ago to lead HIV prevention work with men in a program called Men As Partners, sponsored by Engender Health and Planned Parenthood of South Africa. As Zoll reports, from his unique vantage point Peacock observed with groups of men in prevention trainings in South Africa many of the same ideas about masculinity that he encountered with batterers in the U.S.: "A real man doesn't negotiate with a woman." "A real man doesn't use condoms." "A real man doesn't worry about his health status." "A real man doesn't get tested." "A real man has sex with multiple partners." Even so, Peacock says that men in South Africa with whom he has worked are very open to gender equitable work. "The paradox of the HIV/AIDS epidemic is that it has opened the door to gender equality. We say to these men, 'If you work with us, your life will become richer.' We appeal to them as moral agents. We ask them, 'What is your responsibility to take this to the community, to challenge other men's behaviors, to confront men who are violent, to confront other men who are placing their partners at risk?'"

Contribute financial resources

Men with significant financial resources need to think creatively about what they can do to help support the growing number of domestic and sexual-assault prevention initiatives that target boys and men. This is the cutting edge of prevention work, and the field is new enough that a small number of wealthy men could make an enormous impact. Ted Waitt, founder of the Gateway Computer Company, has been one of the early leaders in this area. Philanthropic individuals and organizations can and should continue to fund services for women and girls who are victims and survivors of men's violence, especially when state and federal funds are being cut; funds that target work with men and boys should never compete with funds for direct services for women and girls. But they should not have to, because the pool of available resources should increase as more influential men get involved and bring new ideas and energy to the task of preventing men's violence against women.

Be creative and entrepreneurial

A number of enterprising men have used their imagination and creativity to raise other men's awareness of sexism, and to challenge the sexist attitudes and behaviors of men around them. Any list of these individuals is necessarily subjective and abbreviated, but I would nonetheless like to spotlight a handful of exemplary anti-sexist activist men. Chris Kilmartin, a professor of psychology at Mary Washington University, performs a one-man show around the country where he uses his skills as a stand-up comedian to satirize traditional masculinity. His first solo theatre performance was called *Crimes against Nature*, and his most recent show is entitled *Guy Fi: The Fictions That Rule Men's Lives*. Through these dramatic presentations and scholarship, Kilmartin has helped to expand the focus of sexual assault prevention to include discussions about the pressures on young men to conform to gender norms that limit their humanity as well as set them up to hurt women.

Another man who has made a unique contribution to this work is Hank Shaw, who in 2000 produced a glossy brochure about men and gender violence that is called, "It's Time for Guys to Put an End to This." Shaw, whose day job is in marketing and corporate communications, wanted to reach average guys with a piece written in "guy language" for men who would likely never read a book about gender violence. The brochure, tens of thousands of which have been distributed across the U.S., Canada, and elsewhere, is cleverly written and beautifully illustrated, and contains such features as the "Mancipation Proclamation": "Henceforth guys are no longer under any gender-oriented, testosterone-derived, penis-related or penis-associated obligation to hurt, harass, or otherwise mess up (or mess with) the lives of female employees, coworkers, students, family members, friends, neighbors, or other female personages who may or may not be personally known to the party of the first part. When all people of the male persuasion get this message, it will spare everyone a whole lot of grief. Plus it will save the country about a gazillion dollars per year."

Another man who has become influential in the gender violence prevention field is Don McPherson, the former professional football player and star quarterback for Syracuse University in the late 1980s. One of the first highly successful black quarterbacks, McPherson runs the Sports Leadership Institute at Adelphi University in New York, and travels widely and gives speeches about violence toward women and what it means to be a man to a variety of high school, college, and professional audiences. What makes McPherson an effective gender violence prevention educator is that while he has the credentials as "The Man" due to his success in sports, he openly admits that he was never comfortable in the role that so many men fantasize about: "I had to carry myself in a different way," he told Oprah Winfrey, "sometimes not showing emotion, not showing weakness or any kind of vulnerability. It meant being in control all of the time. Most people expected me to be shallow . . . I struggled with who I really was on the inside versus my need to be a part of the guys who were cool." In his popular lecture, entitled, "You Throw Like a Girl," McPherson makes the connection between what the culture expects of "real men," and men's widespread mistreatment of women.

New technologies are changing the nature of social activism, and this is as true for anti-sexist men's work as it is for any social movement. In particular, the Internet and the Web have become indispensable tools in anti-sexist men's organizing. The ability to instantaneously transmit information and facilitate connection between people across the country and the world continues to amaze some of us who have vivid memories from the 1980s and 1990s of standing on street corners handing out leaflets. One man who has made a significant contribution to harnessing the power of the Internet is Marc Dubin, founder and executive director of CAVNET, Communities Against Violence Network, at www.cavnet.org. CAVNET is a diverse network of professionals and advocates who work on issues related to violence against women and children, human rights, genocide, and crime victims with disabilities. People in the network regularly share a wealth of information and resources—including points of contact for anti-sexist men's organizations nationally and internationally. Dubin, who works tirelessly—and virtually without pay—to maintain and expand CAVNET's database and connect people to each other, is a former federal prosecutor with extensive experience prosecuting domestic violence, sexual assault, rape, child abuse, and hate crimes. He formerly served as special counsel to the Violence Against Women Office at the United States Department of Justice and is an expert in the federal civil rights of people with disabilities.

Start anti-sexist men's groups

The power of individuals to catalyze change increases exponentially when they work together to create new institutions and organizations. A growing number of organizations have made significant contributions in recent years to gender violence prevention efforts with men and boys. Some of these groups have paid staff and operate along the lines of traditional non-profit educational organizations; others are more grass roots and volunteer-oriented. It is not possible to provide anything close to a comprehensive list of these various initiatives, but consider a handful of examples from around the country: The

Washington, D.C.-based group Men Can Stop Rape regularly conducts anti-rape trainings with high school, college, and community organizations. Their "strength campaign" posters and other materials have been widely circulated. The Institute on Domestic Violence in the African American Community, headed by Dr. Oliver Williams, regularly brings together scholars and activists to discuss issues of particular interest to men (and women) of color, such as the potential role of the hip-hop generation in preventing men's violence against women. The anti-rape men's group One in Four has chapters on dozens of college campuses. In 1999, a group of men in the famous fishing town of Gloucester, Massachusetts—carpenters and clergy, bartenders and bankers—started Gloucester Men Against Domestic Abuse. They march annually in the town's popular Fourth of July parade and sponsor a billboard that says "Strong Men Don't Bully," a public testimonial of sorts that features the names of five hundred Gloucester men. The Men's Leadership Forum in San Diego, California, is a high-profile annual conference held on Valentine's Day. Since 2001, MLF has brought together a diverse group of men and boys (and women) from across the city to learn how men in business, labor unions, the sports culture, education, the faith community, and the human services can contribute to ending men's violence against women. Some men are politicized about sexism out of concern for their daughters, or as a result of things that have happened to them. One of the most effective organizations that addresses these concerns is Dads and Daughters, a Duluth, Minnesota-based advocacy group led by Joe Kelly. Part of the mission of DADS is to mobilize concerned fathers to challenge companies whose marketing is sexist and exploitative—especially when it involves the sexualization of young girls or adolescents, or treats men's violence against women as a joke.

In addition to some of these now well-established organizations, anti-sexist men on college campuses and in local communities have worked—often in collaboration with women's centers or domestic and sexual violence programs—to educate men and boys about the role men can play in confronting and interrupting other men's abusive behaviors. One venue for this collaboration has been the proliferating number of V-Day events held on college campuses. While V-Day is woman-centered, male students have played all sorts of supportive roles, such as organizing outreach efforts to men and coproducing and promoting performances of the Eve Ensler play The Vagina Monologues.

Some anti-sexist men's efforts have been ad hoc and customized to fit the needs and experiences of various communities. For example, in 2003 a group of Asian American men in Seattle organized to support the local chapter of the National Asian Pacific American Women's Forum in their opposition to a restaurant that was promoting "naked sushi" nights, where patrons took sushi off the bodies of semi-nude models wrapped in cellophane. And in the summer of 2004, a group of men (and women) in the "punk, indie, alternative" music scene organized a Different Kind of Dude Fest in Washington, D.C. Along the lines of the Riot Girrls and Girlfest, Hawaii, they sought to use art as an organizing tool. Their goal was to call attention to the ways in which progressive political punk culture, while promising liberation from other forms of social conformity and oppression, nonetheless helped to perpetuate sexism and patriarchal domination. The organizers of the music festival also explicitly affirmed the need for men to be allies of feminists in the fight for gender justice and social equality.

Champion institutional reform

Men who hold positions of power in government, non-profit organizations, business, and labor unions can do much to prevent men's violence against women if they take two critical steps: 1.) Recognize domestic and sexual violence prevention as a leadership issue for men, and 2.) Start to think creatively about how they can push their institutions to address it. The problem is that many men in positions of institutional authority do not yet see gender violence prevention in this way. That is why I strongly suggest that public or private institutions who want to begin serious primary prevention initiatives first arrange trainings for men in positions of senior leadership—and the more senior, the better. If done well, gender violence prevention training for men can be transformative. Men often come out of such trainings with an entirely new sensibility about their professional and personal responsibilities to women and children, as well as to other men. This is important because in the long term, dramatic reductions in the incidence of men's violence against women in the U.S. and around the world will only come about when people with power—which often means *men* in power—make gender violence issues a priority. Among other things, this means that male leaders must set and maintain a tone—in educational institutions, corporations, the military—where sexist and abusive behavior is considered unacceptable and unwelcome, not only because women don't like it but because other men will not stand for it. This sounds good, but people often ask me how to get powerful men to take these issues seriously. For example, how do you convince male legislators, educational administrators, business leaders, or military commanders to attend gender violence prevention training? There are a variety of strategies, but the bottom line is that they do not necessarily have to be motivated—at least initially—by altruism or concerns about social justice. They need instead to be persuaded that prevention is a widely shared institutional goal, and that it is their responsibility to be as knowledgeable and proactive about these issues as possible.

Think and act locally and globally

The focus of this book has been mostly on the U.S., but obviously men's violence against women is an issue everywhere in the world. Since 9/11, many Americans have learned what many people around the world have long known—in the modern era, what happens in foreign cultures thousands of miles away can affect people right here at home, sometimes in ways that are impossible to predict. That is the irrevocable reality of the global environment in which we now live. As I have maintained throughout, gender violence is best seen not as aberrational behavior perpetrated by a few bad men but as an expression of much more deeply seated structures of male dominance and gender inequality. This is much easier to see when you are looking at someone else's culture. For example, in radical fundamentalist Islamic countries, women have few rights, and in many instances men's violence against them is legal and even expected—especially when they defy male authority. In other words, men's violence against women functions in some cultures to maintain a highly authoritarian, even fascistic male power structure. In that sense, gender violence is clearly a political crime with potentially far-reaching consequences. As a result, the way that men in distant lands treat women—individually and as a group—cannot be dismissed as a private family or cultural matter. It has too much bearing on political developments that could affect all of us—like the possibility of nuclear war, or the constant threat of terrorist attacks.

At the same time, it is tempting for some Americans to hear and read about the way men mistreat women in foreign cultures and attribute that mistreatment to cultural deficiencies and even barbarism. But it is important to remember that by world standards, the incidence of men's violence against women here in the U.S. is embarrassingly high. No doubt many American men would be offended to hear people in other countries speculating about the shortcomings of American men—and the inferiority of the culture that produced them.

Fortunately, the growing movement of men who are speaking out about men's violence against women is international in scope. There are anti-sexist men's initiatives in scores of countries across the world. In addition, one of the most promising developments in the history of international human rights law is the growing international movement to identify men's violence against women as a human rights issue. A pivotal moment in that movement came in 2001, when the United Nations war crimes tribunal named rape and sexual slavery as war crimes. And today, a number of international organizations—most prominently Amnesty

International—have begun to focus on gender violence and link the physical and sexual exploitation of women to a host of other social and political problems. One of the major challenges for American anti-sexist men in the coming years will be to make connections between men's violence against women in the U.S. with violence around the world, and to support efforts everywhere to reduce men's violence and advance gender equality— not only because it is the right thing to do, but also because it is arguably in our national interest.

What's in it for men?

Men who occupy positions of influence in boys' lives—fathers, grandfathers, older brothers, teachers, coaches, religious leaders—need to teach them that men of integrity value women and do not tolerate other men's sexism or abusive behavior. Obviously they have to lead by example. But that is not enough. In a cultural climate where the objectification of women and girls has accelerated, and boys are exposed to ever more graphic displays of brutality toward women disguised as "entertainment," men need to preemptively provide clear guidelines for boys' behavior. This does not always have to be defined in negative terms, e.g., "Don't hit women." It can be framed as a positive challenge to young men, especially if they aspire to something more special than being "one of the guys" at all costs.

In fact, when I give talks about men's violence against women to groups of parents, I am often asked by parents of sons if there is something positive we can offer young men as a substitute for what we are taking away from them. "We constantly say to our kids, 'Don't do this, don't do that, I wish you wouldn't listen to this music.' We tell them they shouldn't treat girls a certain way, they shouldn't act tough. We spend a lot of time telling our sons what they shouldn't be. It's so negative. Why shouldn't they just tune us out? What's in it for them?"

My answer is really quite simple, and it is as true for the fathers as it is for the sons. When we ask men to reject sexism and the abuse of women, we are not taking something away from them. In fact, we are giving them something very valuable—a vision of manhood that does not depend on putting down others in order to lift itself up. When a man stands up for social justice, nonviolence, and basic human rights—for women as much as for men—he is acting in the best traditions of our civilization. That makes him not only a better man, but a better human being.

ACKNOWLEDGMENTS

This book is the product of intense labor over the past year or two, but in truth I have been working on it much longer. I am therefore deeply grateful not only to those who generously helped me navigate the painstaking writing process, but also to those who have inspired me personally and professionally over the years, whether through friendship or by sheer example. Writing is a lonely endeavor, but in meaningful ways it is still very much a collaborative process, and this book is testimony to that fact.

I want to thank my family for giving me decades of support and patience, especially my mother, Frieda Miller, my sisters Janet Miller and Julie Katz, and my cousin Rivka Polatnick. I grew up surrounded by exceptional women, and I feel their influence daily.

My teacher Ann Ferguson, professor of philosophy and women's studies at the University of Massachusetts-Amherst, provided an early and enduring example of how to combine a passion for knowledge with unflinching political commitment. If she was skeptical about a young man fresh out of a small-town football jockocracy who was inspired by philosophy and women's studies, she never let on.

Some of my closest friends have been a great source of love, camaraderie, and late-night brainstorming over the years. In particular, I want to thank two soulmates: Miriam Zoll, my feminist fellow traveler since college, and Jeremy Earp, my confidant and intellectual partner with whom I have been connected for nearly thirty years. I also want to thank Gail Dines and David Levy, who have long been a source of personal and political solidarity, and

Dode Levenson, who has stood by my side from the time I was a struggling activist with big dreams and bad apartments.

The process of bringing this book to print started with my search for a literary agent, no easy task with a subject as difficult as this one. I am grateful that James Levine was up to the challenge. I thank Rosalind Wiseman not only for recommending Jim, but also for her friendship and support over the years. I also want to thank my publisher, Sourcebooks, for believing in this project from the beginning, and for never doubting that a book by a man about men's violence against women was worth getting out to as wide an audience as possible. In particular I want to thank my editor, Sarah Tucker, for her brilliant editing work, her patience, and her calm reassurance in the face of my many harried phone calls from airports and taxis. Thanks also to Michelle Schoob, a talented editor at Sourcebooks whose resourcefulness and flexibility made the late-stage editing process much less painful than I had anticipated.

I want to thank my mother-in-law Jan Bue for her love and encouragement, and for being so generous in providing the best conceivable child care at crucial times during the writing process.

I am also indebted to several people who read and commented on portions of the manuscript or contributed useful anecdotes: Daryl Fort, Gail Dines, Diane Rosenfeld, Caroline Heldman, Alan Berkowitz, Rhonda Hammer, Doug Kellner, Lori Strauss, Angie Aaron, Heather Sturm, Marie Brodie, Kristen Houser, Molly Dragiewicz, Laura Vargas, and Zeus Leonardo. Thanks to Giannina Cabral for research assistance. Of course none of them bears any responsibility for any errors or omissions that may have made their way into the final product.

Throughout all phases of the writing process, I had the additional privilege of being able to draw inspiration from the work and friendship of innumerable activists and educators. I wish I could acknowledge them all, but my all-star team begins with Judy Stafford, Cindy Waitt, Alan Heisterkamp, Nancy Beardall, Annette Lynch, Denise Thomson, Dean Peacock, James Lang, Barbara Kasper, Hank Shaw, Patti Giggans, Abby Sims, Mary Atwater, Bob Haynor, Lori Strauss, Carolyn Ramsay, Mark Dubin, Verna Taber, Steve Allen, Ann O'Dell, Gerry Sea, Victor Rivers, Nina Cummings, Al Emerick, Sally Laskey, Marissa Mezzanotte-Zadrozny, Linda Blanshay, Beverly LeMay, Rashmi Luthra, Bob Paret, Kathy Xian, Grace Caligtan, Sally Spencer-Thomas, Joe Kelly, Hollie Ainbinder, Leah Wyman, Steve Sherblom, Amy Levine, Rob Okun, Jerri Lynn Fields, Claire Kaplan, Peter Jaffe, Shelia Hargesheimer, Evelyn Brom, Linda Tangemann, Jeff Share, and Jill Montoya. I have also benefited immensely from work I have done with Mary Dixon, Toby Graff and Meredith Wagner at Lifetime Television, and Maria Kalligeros at PT and Co.

Since first hearing him lecture on masculinity when I was an undergraduate, Don Sabo has remained a steady source of wisdom and guidance. The same is true of Lundy Bancroft, Terry Real, Alan Berkowitz, Nan Stein, Jean Kilbourne, Michael Kimmel, John Stoltenberg, Leah Aldridge, Debby Tucker, Sarah Buel, Mike Messner, Mariah Burton Nelson, Paul Kivel, Sandy Caron, Harry Brod, Sandy Holstein, Michael Kaufman, Rus Ervin Funk, Ann Simonton, David Lisak, Tim Beneke, Marie Fortune, Susan Bailey, Ron Slaby, Connie Sponsler-Garcia, Tom Gardner, Warren Blumenfeld, Jamie Kalven, Sherryl Kleinman, Helan Page, Myriam Miedzian, John Badalament, Craig Norberg-Bohm, Barbara Ellis, Delilah Rumburg, Agnes Maldonado, Michael Flood, Steve Bergman, Nina Huntemann, and bell hooks.

I want to thank my lecture agent, Kevin MacRae, at Lordly and Dame, for his belief in my vision and for our many years of productive collaboration. I also want to thank the lecture agents Kevin and Jayne Moore, who helped me get started in the college lecture world.

I will always be grateful to Rich Lapchick and Art Taylor for working with me to create MVP at Northeastern University's Center for the Study of Sport in Society in 1993. MVP has been a magnet for many talented people. I especially want to thank Jeff O'Brien for his inspired leadership and friendship, and Don McPherson for his willingness to provide even more leadership off the field than on it. I also have MVP to thank for my long-time collaboration and friendship with the filmmaker Byron Hurt, from whom I have learned a great deal and about whom I brag at every opportunity. Thanks also to Michelle King, Dave Kay, Miles McLean, Craig Alimo, and Tom Penichter for their early and important contributions to the development of MVP.

My deepest appreciation also goes out to Randy Eltringham and Claire Lebling for their roles in initiating my work with the Marine Corps. And I want to thank all of those Marines, too numerous to name, who have supported my prevention program in the Corps. Thanks, too, to Marney Thomas, Brian Leidy, Mary Page, and Ellen Pence for working so productively with my colleagues and me in our years with the Marines, and to all the civilian and military members of the Defense Task Force on Domestic Violence in the Military, for all their insights, friendship, and camaraderie.

I have had the additional benefit of working over the years with the gifted staff of the Media Education Foundation (MEF), in particular the producers Ronit Ridberg, Susan Ericsson, Loretta Alper, Sanjay Talreja, Jeremy Smith, and Jeremy Earp. I especially want to thank MEF's founder and tireless executive director, my friend Sut Jhally, who believed in me enough to make a longtime vision of mine a reality with the film *Tough Guise*, and has since then enabled me to reach ever-wider audiences with the films *Wrestling with Manhood* and *Spin the Bottle*. One of the most encouraging developments in gender violence prevention in recent years has been the emergence of a new generation of anti-sexist men, both college students and young professionals. In the latter category I want especially to thank Chad Sniffen, Brad Perry, Kaili McCray, Ross Wantland, Brian Pahl, Keith Edwards, Kevin Ladaris, Matt Ezzell, and Ben Atherton-Zeman for specific contributions to my work and thinking, and also for the intangible inspiration their dedication has given me.

I want to state clearly that my work and that of many other men would not be possible were it not for the pioneering work of countless feminists past and present, women of color as well as white women, some of them famous but many more who never sought nor received public acclaim for their world-changing activism. Sadly, the woman who perhaps did more than any other individual in history to enlighten both women *and* men about men's violence against women died while I was writing this book. I never had the opportunity to thank Andrea Dworkin in person, so I do so here in recognition of her extraordinary grace and courage in the face of ruthless caricatures and dismissals of her work.

Finally, I am grateful to the two people closest to me. My work can be quite dispiriting at times, but when I experience my son Judah's enthusiasm and joy for life my hope is renewed. And then there is Shelley Eriksen. More than any other single person, Shelley made this book possible. She was the foundation of my intellectual and emotional support system throughout its writing. She nobly endured the burdens it placed on her, and made sure I had the time, space, and encouragement I needed to get it done. Her wise counsel, judicious editing, and love improved not only this book, but also the quality of my life while writing it. From the bottom of my heart, Shelley, I thank you.

iii *"After hundreds of years of anti-racist struggle"*: from bell hooks, "Men: Comrades in Struggle," in Men's Lives, p. 535.

CHAPTER 1: VIOLENCE AGAINST WOMEN IS A MEN'S ISSUE

10 *"In the end…we cannot change society unless we put more men at the table"*: See Soler, 2000.

11 *The better angels of their nature:* Abraham Lincoln. First Inaugural Address, March 4, 1861.

11 *Violence Against Women Act (VAWA):* Here is a brief history of VAWA provided by the Family Violence Prevention Fund: "VAWA is the first comprehensive federal legislation responding to violence against women. It was introduced in 1990. While the U.S. Senate held several hearings and reported bills out of committee, not until the 103rd Congress was there finally traction on the issue in both the Senate and the U.S. House of Representatives. With the help of outspoken advocates across the country…the Violence Against Women Act (VAWA) was finally signed into law in August of 1994 as a part of the Violent Crime Control and Law Enforcement Act of 1994….VAWA created new penalties for gender-related violence and new grant programs encouraging states to address domestic violence and sexual assault including law enforcement and prosecution grants (STOP grants); grants to encourage arrest; rural domestic violence and child abuse enforcement grants; the National Domestic Violence Hotline; and grants to battered women's shelters." The Fund's website says that "no one felt this completely addressed the needs of victims of domestic violence, (but) almost all involved believed this was a vital first step in our nation's efforts to treat domestic violence as a serious problem.

"Because the authorization for the original VAWA provisions expired in 2000, the Congress took up the reauthorization of this landmark legislation in 1999 and completed its efforts in the fall of 2000 with the passage of the Violence Against Women Act of 2000. The House version of the bill, known as H.R. 1248, passed on September 26 by a vote of 415–3, and the Senate version, known as S. 2787 passed on October 11 by a vote of 95–0. During the course of final negotiations, VAWA 2000 was merged with the Victims of Trafficking and Violence Protection Act of 2000 and several smaller bills, and President Clinton signed the legislation into law on October 28, 2000." VAWA was reauthorized by Congress in 2005. Advocates lobbied for and secured funding for several new initiatives, including prevention and education with boys and young men.

In spite of the wide bipartisan support VAWA enjoys in Congress, many right-wing groups oppose the legislation, which they call "anti-family." They have sought its demise since it was initially passed in 1994.

11 *Social norms theory:* For more information about social norms theory, see "The Social Norms Approach: Theory, Research, and Annotated Bibliography," 2004, at www.alanberkowitz.com.

11 *Significant numbers of men are uncomfortable:* See Fabiano, et al., 2003.

12 *A major national poll released in 2003 by the New York-based Center for the Advancement of Women:* Fisher, Luchina, "Women's Top Worry Is Domestic Violence," *Women's e-news,* www.womensenews.org, August 8, 2003.

15 *Men are the primary perpetrators:* For a thorough debunking of the distorted use of social science data by the so-called "men's rights" movement, see Kimmel, M. 2002.

CHAPTER 2: FACING FACTS

19 *"If a man is offered a fact"*: Bertrand Russell, *Proposed Roads to Freedom,*1918, Chapter 6.

21 *20 percent of adolescent girls have experienced physical or sexual abuse by a date:* See Silverman et al., 2001.

21 *Nearly one-third of American women report being physically or sexually abused:* The Commonwealth Health Fund, *Health Concerns Across a Woman's Lifespan: 1998 Survey on Women's Health,* 1999.

21 *Nearly 18 percent have been raped:* "Prevalence, Incidence, and Consequences of Violence against Women: Findings from the National Violence Against Women Survey," National Institute of Justice and Centers for Disease Control and Prevention, November 1998.

21 *Studies show that between 15 to 38 percent of women and 5 to 16 percent of men:* See Fergusen, D., et al., 1999.

21 *The average age a child is first abused sexually is ten:* See Finkelhor, D. et al., 1990.

21 *As many as 324,000 women each year:* See Gazmararian, J.A. et al., 2000.

21 *Women are much more likely than men to be killed:* Bureau of Justice Statistics Crime Data Brief, *Intimate Partner Violence,1993–2001,* 2003.

21 *One national survey found that 83 percent of girls reported:* See Stein, N., 1999.

21 *Between one in four and one in five college women:* See Fisher, B.S. et al., 2000.

21 *Ten thousand porn videos are released:* Timothy Egan, "Technology Sent Wall Street into Market for Pornography," *New York Times,* October 23, 2000: A1 and A20.

21 *The average age of entry into prostitution is thirteen or fourteen:* According to the prostitution research website www.prostitutionresearch.com. See Silbert, M.H., 1982, or fourteen years, See Weisberg, D.K. Most of these thirteen- or fourteen-year-old girls were recruited or coerced into prostitution.

21 *Forty percent of girls age fourteen to seventeen:* Children Now/Kaiser Permanente poll, December 1995.

21 *There are twenty-five hundred strip clubs in the U.S.:* See Yancey, K., 2003.

21 *One study found that 70 percent of women with developmental disabilities:* Sobsey, D. and T. Doe. 1991. "Patterns of Sexual Abuse and Assault," *Journal of Sexuality and Disability,* Vol. 9, No. 3, pp. 243–59.

21 *One study showed that 37.5 percent of American Indian and Alaska Native women:* "Extent, Nature and Consequences of Intimate Partner Violence: Findings from the National Violence Against Women Survey." Patricia Tjaden and Nancy Thoennes.

22 *Eight percent of women and 2 percent of men in the U.S. have been stalked:* "The Crime of Stalking: How Big is the Problem?" Patricia Tjaden, National Institute of Justice, November 1997.

22 *In one study, lifetime risk for violent victimization was so high:* Goodman L. A., M. A. Dutton, M. Harris: "Episodically homeless women with serious mental illness: prevalence of physical and sexual abuse." *American Journal of Orthopsychiatry* 65:468–473, 1995

22 *A study of prisons in four Midwestern states:* Struckman-Johnson, Cindy and David Struckman-Johnson, "Sexual Coercion Rates in Seven Midwestern Prisons for Men," 80 *The Prison Journal* 379 (2000), available at www.spr.org/pdf/struckman.pdf.

22 *The estimated annual health-related costs:* National Center for Injury Prevention and Control. "Costs of Intimate Partner Violence against Women in the United States." Atlanta, GA: Centers for Disease Control and Prevention, 2003.

22 *Studies suggest that between 3.3 and 10 million children witness:* Carlson, Bonnie, 22.

22 *Between 50–70 percent of men who abuse:* See Bowker, L. et al., 1990. E. "Children's observations of interpersonal violence" in A.R. Roberts (Ed.) *Battered women and their families,* 1984. pp. 147–167. Straus, M.A. "Children as witnesses to marital violence: A risk factor for lifelong problems among a nationally representative sample of American men and women" *Report of the Twenty-Third Ross Roundtable,*1992.

23 *The violent deaths of poor women of color:* A 2005 article in the *Los Angeles Times* explored a related phenomenon: over the past couple of years "missing women" stories have become a staple of cable news programming, but few of the cases tracked involve women of color. See O'Connor, A., 2005.

24 *One in three women worldwide:* See Heise, L., et al., 1999.

25 *Members of dominant groups have a critical role:* For a documentary history of men in the U.S. who fought for women's rights, see Kimmel, M., et al., 1992.

27 *However, 88 percent of men whose actions:* See Warshaw, R. 1988.

26 *Why Does He Do That?:* Bancroft, L., *Why Does He Do That: Inside the Minds of Angry and Controlling Men,* 2002.

28 *Deeply disturbed individuals inspire morbid fascination:* For a study of the phenomenon of serial murder that locates this gruesome crime in systems of gender and power, and particularly in cultural constructs of masculinity and the deep misogyny in Western cultures, see *The Age of Sex Crime,* Caputi, J., 1987.

28 *Was the killer next door?:* See Chu, J., 2005.

28 *Most perpetrators are, in fact, "our guys":* For an exceptionally well-done journalistic account of one the most notorious gang rapes of the past quarter century, see Lefkowitz, B., 1997.

30 *Some might even revere* Hustler *founder Larry Flynt:* For a discussion of the way the biopic *The People vs. Larry Flynt* helped to construct the misogynous pornographer as a heroic figure, see Ramsay, E. M., 2005.

30 *Chester the Molester:* For more information about Tinsley and a discussion of the role of cartoons in *Hustler,* see Dines, G., et al., 1998. As Dines writes: "Cartoons, because of their claim to humor, allow *Hustler* to depict 'outrageous and provocative' scenarios such as torture, murder, and child molestation, which may, in a less humorous form such as pictorials, deny the magazine access to the mass-distribution channels." p. 55.

CHAPTER 3: TAKING IT PERSONALLY

35 *"My father was a violent man":* This quote from Joe Torre is from the Coaching Boys Into Men playbook, available from the Family Violence Prevention Fund. Go to www.endabuse.org for more information.

39 *This phenomenon was addressed memorably in the hit film* Good Will Hunting: For a fascinating (and much
    deeper) analysis of this scene, see Terrence Real's 2002 book *How Can I Get Through To You?* p. 57-60. In
    his books, Real brilliantly examines the emotional/psychological processes that sometimes underpin men's
    destructive behaviors, including violence. Like the author James Gilligan, Real emphasizes the importance
    of understanding shame as a prime motivating force in the lives of men who choose to act out violently.

41 *Regardless, countless boys and men have suffered:* For a thoughtful and informative guide for men (and women)
    who are "secondary victims" of gender violence, see "Responding to Secondary Victims: Impact of Trauma,
    Factors in Healing," by Brad Perry, Virginians Aligned Against Sexual Assault, *The Advocate,* Winter 2002. Also
    see Alan McEvoy, et al's excellent publications, including the books *If She Is Raped: A Guidebook for Husbands,
    Fathers and Male Friends* and *If He Is Raped: A Guidebook for Parents, Partners, Spouses, and Friends.*

43 *Many of the Democrats on the committee were noticeably silent:* For more background on the politics
    and personalities involved in the Thomas-Hill hearings, see *Strange Justice: The Selling of Clarence
    Thomas,* by Jane Mayer and Jill Abramson, Houghton-Mifflin, 1994.

44 *What sorts of messages would be most likely to attract men:* The Family Violence Prevention Fund
    website (www.endabuse.org) has more information about their campaigns to reach men and boys,
    including *Coaching Boys into Men.*

44 *The boy initiated a "parental divorce":* Webster, K., "Murderer dad agrees to 'divorce' by son,"
    Salon.com, July 26, 2004.

46 *How does the violence done to a mother affect her children:* See Bancroft, L., 2004. For more research
    on the effects of adult domestic violence on children, see Edelson, J., 1999. "Children's Witnessing of
    Adult Domestic Violence," *Journal of Interpersonal Violence,* 14(8), 1999. p. 839–870.

49 *There is no difference between being raped:* Piercy, Marge, "The Rape Poem" *Circles on the Water,* 1982.

50 *The late comedian Sam Kinison:* Sam Kinison, (1953–1992) was the talented son of a preacher who
    became a highly popular comedian in the 1980s. Kinison attracted a large audience with routines
    that were often surprisingly cerebral, but he combined weightier subject matter (such as his critique
    of religion) with a rock and roll-style, hard-partying image, overt and angry misogyny, and signa-
    ture screams. He was killed by a drunk driver at age thirty-nine in 1992.

50 *The manager of the New York Yankees, Joe Torre:* Torre is founder and chairman of the Joe Torre Safe
    At Home Foundation, Grand Central Station, P.O. Box 3133, New York, NY 10163, Phone: (toll-free)
    877–878–4JOE, (main) 212–880–7360. On the web at www.joetorre.org.

52 *His murder saddened and enraged millions of heterosexuals:* See Loffreda, Beth, 2000.

54 *Many women had an unconscious desire to be taken care of:* See Dowling, Colette, 1981.

54 *Black women long for "the stuff of romantic fantasy":* See hooks, bell, *We Real Cool,* 2000, p. 119–120.

54 *Why many women are drawn to socially conservative movements:* Dworkin, Andrea, *Right Wing
    Women,* New York, Perigree Books, 1983.

55 *In the era of girl power and self-defense classes:* There are numerous self-defense initiatives that focus
    on women's ability to protect themselves from sexual assault. For example, see *Defending Ourselves:
    A Guide to Prevention, Self-Defense and Recovery from Rape,* by Rosalind Wiseman, New York: Farrar,
    Straus, and Giroux, 1994; Model Mugging; and the Rape Aggression Defense (RAD) program,
    www.RAD-Systems.com.

57 *Not until 1993 that marital rape was considered a crime:* See Bergen Raquel, *Wife Rape: Understanding
    the Response of Survivors and Service Providers,* Thousand Oaks, CA: Sage Publications, 1996.

CHAPTER 4: LISTENING TO WOMEN

61 *Women comprise less than 20 percent of opinion columnists:* See Dowd, Maureen, "Dish It Out,
    Ladies," *New York Times,* March 13, 2005.

63 *Women whose voices have been stymied:* See Gilligan, Carol, *In a Different Voice: Psychological Theory
    and Women's Development,* Cambridge: Harvard University Press, 1982.

64 *Take Back the Night rallies:* Take Back the Night rallies and marches started in England in the 1970s
    as a protest against the fear that women experienced walking the streets at night. The first TBTN in
    the U.S. was held in San Francisco in 1978.

64 *One of the most powerful public education/political art campaigns:* The Clothesline Project was found-
    ed in 1990 in Cape Cod, Massachusetts. For more information, go to www.clothesline project.org.

66 *Black women have historically been trained:* See Robinson, Lori, *I Will Survive: The African American
    Guide to Healing from Sexual Assault and Abuse,* Emeryville, CA: Seal Press, 2003.

70 *Women—especially young women—frequently hear unsolicited comments:* Maggie Hadleigh-West's
    documentary film *War Zone* powerfully illustrates this phenomenon on the streets of New York.

CHAPTER 5: MALE-BASHING?

74 *Who are feminists?:* A staggering amount of propaganda and disinformation about feminism has been put out by the political and cultural right for decades, leading many women to disidentify with the term. In fact, the saying "I am not a feminist, but…" is routinely uttered by women who agree with most of the major principles of feminism. For a very reader-friendly introduction to feminism, see hooks, bell, *Feminism Is for Everybody,* Boston: South End Press, 2000.

75 *Who were the Nazis:* For a fascinating social psychological analysis of the sexual and family politics of the German National Socialist Party, see *The Mass Psychology of Fascism* by Wilhelm Reich, originally published in 1933, with a paperback edition published by Farrar, Straus, and Giroux, 1980. Another fascinating analysis of far-right-wing misogyny and masculine violence can be found in *Male Fantasies Volume 1: Women, Bodies, Floods, History,* by Klaus Theweleit. University of Minnesota Press, 1987. Theweleit does a literary analysis of the writing of men in the Freikorps, a murderous Aryan men's movement in Germany that was a precursor to the Nazis.

75 *The Way Things Ought To Be:* Rush Limbaugh, Pocket Books, 1993. Although much of Limbaugh's published and broadcast commentary about feminists is embarrassingly superficial and often factually inaccurate, he has been highly effective at smearing the reputation and integrity of feminists, and thus to counteract his polemics it is important to read what he has actually written and said about them whenever possible.

76 *Orwellian quality of the term "male-basher":* See George Orwell's famous 1946 essay "Politics and the English Language."

76 *I Am the Central Park Jogger: A Story of Hope and Possibility:* Trisha Meili, New York: Scribners, 2003.

76 *Amber's Frey's memoir: Witness: For the Prosecution of Scott Peterson,* by Amber Frey, New York: Regan Books, 2005.

76 *They would betray their fellow men in an effort to be "politically correct":* The term "politically incorrect" has been used by the right *and* some liberals to ridicule men, white people, and heterosexuals who struggle to be fair and egalitarian and not exercise illegitimate privilege through language—or any other way. For an illuminating discussion of the linguistic politics of the term "politically correct," see Lakoff, 2000.

78 *In almost every category they are its primary victims:* A prime example of how men and boys are both the victims and perpetrators of most violent crime is prison rape. The subject of prison rape has only recently emerged from the shadows and entered the public discourse, however tentatively. Dostoevsky wrote that the degree of civilization in a society can be judged by entering its prisons. If so, our civilization in many respects is terribly callous and cruel; one measure of this is the routine incidence of sexual violence in prison that is tolerated by the authorities and continues to fly under the radar of public outrage. For some chilling insights into the pervasiveness of prison rape see the website of the organization Stop Prisoner Rape: www.spr.org.

79 *The feminist newsjournal Off Our Backs:* Volume XXXIV, nos. 9, 10, September–October, 2004.

82 Men's Health *magazine ran a feature:* The September 2000 article was entitled "The Best and Worst Campuses for Men." *Men's Health* was widely criticized for this article; not long after it was published the editor in chief was replaced.

85 *Who Stole Feminism?:* Christina Hoff Sommers, New York: Touchstone Books, 1994.

85 *A number of other conservative women, including Ann Coulter and Laura Schlesinger:* It is hard to know whether Coulter truly believes many of the silly things she says and writes. But it is undeniable that she is popular with many conservative men, who enjoy hearing a putatively educated, assertive woman verbally assault feminists, like when she wrote in *Slander: Liberal Lies about the American Right,* that Gloria Steinem is a "deeply ridiculous figure."

86 *Camille Paglia writes that a lot of battered women stay in abusive relationships:* Here is more of what she wrote in an essay entitled "The Rape Debate, Continued," in her 1992 book *Sex, Art, and American Culture:* "Feminists have no idea that some women like to flirt with danger because there is a sizzle in it. You know what gets me sick and tired? The battered-woman motif. It's so misinterpreted, the way we have to constantly look at it in terms of male oppression and tyranny, and female victimization. When, in fact, everyone knows throughout the world that many of these working-class relationships where women get beat up have hot sex. They ask why won't she leave him? Maybe she won't leave him because the sex is very hot. I say we should start looking at the battered-wife motif in terms of sex. If gay men go down to bars and like to get tied up, beaten up, and have their asses whipped, how come we can't allow that a lot of wives like the kind of sex they are getting in these battered-wife relationships? We can't consider that women might have kinky tastes, can we?" p. 65.

86 *The War Against Boys:* See Sommers, 2000.

CHAPTER 6: STUCK IN (GENDER) NEUTRAL

91 *"The young Jonesboro suspect's stated motive: Christian Science Monitor,* April 2, 1998. Dr. Yllo is a sociologist and prominent domestic violence researcher.

93 *In the late 1970s, the pioneering legal theorist Catherine MacKinno:* See MacKinnon, 1979.

93 *Against Our Will:* See Brownmiller, 1975.

93 *The Politics of Rape:* See Russell, 1975.

95 *Reagan's first budget included plans to dramatically cut federal funds:* For background on the rise of Reaganism and the New Right and how the conservative movement regarded the early domestic violence movement, see Pleck, 1987, pp.196–198.

99 *Raising Cain:* See Kindlon, Dan and Thompson, Michael, 1999.

102 *The Puerto Rican Day Central Park rampage:* Portions of this section were previously published in the *Los Angeles Times* on June 25, 2005 in an op-ed article I co-authored with Sut Jhally entitled "Put the Blame Where it Belongs: On Men."

108 *Rape in the Military: Female Troops Deserve Much Better: USA Today,* February 5, 2004.

109 *Take the infamous Janet Jackson-Justin Timberlake performance:* For a detailed discussion of this major pop-culture event, see Wenner, 2004.

110 *The novelist Andrew Vachss makes a related point:* See Vachss, 2005.

CHAPTER 7: BYSTANDERS

113 *John Steinbeck,* Of Mice and Men: Thanks to Michael Kimmel for this quote, from *Manhood in America.*

115 *The movie was loosely based on an infamous real-life incident:* The gang-rape victim in the Big Dan's case was a twenty-one-year-old single mother of two. According to several eyewitnesses, she ran into the middle of the street—naked from the waist down—with a look that one man described as "the most scared he had ever seen a human being ever." Four men—Portuguese immigrants—were convicted of raping her in a highly publicized case that according to some accounts exacerbated tensions in the Portuguese community between recent immigrants and longstanding members of the community. Even more tragically, the victim was ostracized from the community and moved to Florida, where a few years later she was killed in a car accident.

119 *Men care a great deal about what other men think of them:* See Kimmel, 1996, p. 7.

120 *Media Culture:* See Kellner, 1995.

121 *What's Going On:* See McCall,1997.

122 *War, Battering, and Other Sports:* See McBride, 1995.

123 *D.C.-based group Men Can Stop Rape:* MCSR can be contacted through their website at www.mencanstoprape.org.

123 *Male Athletes Against Violence:* For more information about MAAV, go to www.umaine.edu/maav.

123 *Emotional detachment, competitiveness, and sexual objectification of women are often the criteria:* See Bird, Sharon R. "Welcome to the Men's Club: Homosociality and the Maintenance of Hegemonic Masculinity." *Gender & Society, 10(2),* pp. 120–132. April, 1996.

123 *Makes Me Wanna Holler:* See McCall, 1994.

124 *In 1993, I conceived and cocreated the Mentors in Violence Prevention program:* For more information about the MVP program at Northeastern University's Center for the Study of Sport in Society, go to www.sportinsociety.org. For narrative about the origins of the MVP model, go to www.jacksonkatz.com.

126 *What William Pollack termed the "boy code":* See Pollack, 1998.

129 *At the time, battered women's programs in Massachusetts:* The shelter space crisis has eased in recent years, but women and children are still turned away due to lack of available beds.

CHAPTER 8: RACE AND CULTURE

131 *"Racism turns our attention away from real exploitation":* See Kivel, 1996, p. 52.

131 *"The sexist, misogynist, patriarchal ways of thinking":* See hooks, 1994.

140 *Dr. Richard Lapchick, a pioneer in the area:* The article "Race, Athletes, and Crime," special to the *Sports Business Journal,* is available at www.sportinsociety.org.

145 *For many white, middle-class male teenagers:* See Kelley, R. cited in Keathley, E., 2002.

147 *In mainstream European American culture:* The entire article is available from the Melissa Institute. See Mederos.

147 *Girlfest Hawaii, a racially and ethnically diverse arts/film/cultural happening:* For more information about Girlfest, go to www.girlfesthawaii.org.

148 *It would be important for me to have at least some brief background:* An important event that focuses intense attention on Hawaiian race, class, and sexual politics is the 1932 Massie case, which some

people say remains the most notorious criminal incident in modern Hawaii in history. Thalia Massie, the twenty-year-old white wife of a Pearl Harbor Navy officer, falsely accused five working-class and impoverished men of Asian descent with raping her. From the start, based on little or no evidence, the men were described in local newspaper accounts as "thugs" and "degenerates." After a three-week trail, a jury failed to reach a verdict, and a mistrial was declared. Before a decision could be made about retrying the men, one of the defendants was beaten by a carload of sailors, and another was kidnapped and murdered by Massie's husband and mother. The vigilantes—who were represented by the famous attorney Clarence Darrow toward the end of his career—were eventually convicted of manslaughter after a highly publicized trial, but their sentences were commuted to one hour by the territorial governor. For more information about the Massie case, see the *Honolulu Advertiser* article by David Stannard.

CHAPTER 9: IT TAKES A VILLAGE TO RAPE A WOMAN

149 *"A culture in which sexualized violence, sexual violence, and violence by sex are so common":* The full article by Robert Jensen which contains this quote is entitled "Rape Is Normal," on the *Counterpunch* website: www.counterpunch.com/jensen0904.html.

150 *As Katharine Baker explains in a* Harvard Law Review *article:* See Baker, 1997.

151 *But according to Lisak, research over the past twenty years:* See Lisak and Miller, 2002.

151 *In discussions about the normalization of sexual violence:* I am indebted to Sut Jhally for some of the key points in this section, as some of it is drawn from a piece that we coauthored that was originally published in the *University of Massachusetts Magazine* in the winter issue, 2001, entitled "Big Trouble, Little Pond: Reflections on the Meaning of the Campus Pond Rapes," pp. 26–31.

152 *Friends with benefits:* The full title of the *New York Times Magazine* article is "Friends, Friends With Benefits and the Benefits of the Local Mall," by Benoit Denizet-Lewis, May 30, 2004.

152 *In one study published in the journal* Adolescence: See Cassidy L., 1995.

153 *As objects of sexual bullying on the* Howard Stern Show: Stern is typically described in mainstream commentary—as well as in some liberal and progressive publications—as a "shock jock," a "raunchy" radio personality, a "potty-mouthed" provocateur, etc. These descriptions, while not complimentary, obfuscate the deeply misogynous character of his personality and his radio program. Calling him a sexual bully shifts the conversation away from his childish and adolescent fixations on body functions or "sex" and onto his abuses of power.

154 *There is nothing like the rape trial of a famous athlete:* For more discussion of the Kobe Bryant case, see my 2003 article "When You're Asked about the Kobe Bryant Case," at www.jacksonkatz.com/bryant.html.

159 *As the recording artist and feminist Tori Amos explains:* The full text of Amos's remarks about Eminem can be found at www.mtv.com in an article entitled "Eminem's Fictional Dead Wife Spoke to Her." September 28, 2001.

159 *A sober reading of his lyrics:* For people who want to study Eminem's lyrics, there are countless websites that provide all of the lyrics to his songs at no charge. Just type in "Eminem lyrics" to any major search engine.

160 *Critics who defend or excuse Eminem's misogyny often claim:* One talented and prominent music critic who repeatedly lavishes praise on Eminem and—to this reader—seems only slightly bothered by the white rapper's relentlessly misogynous lyrics is Robert Hilburn of the *Los Angeles Times*. For example, in a glowing concert review of a show on the 2002 Anger Management tour in southern California, Hilburn writes that "the ugly portrayal of women in such songs as the macho-minded 'Superman' is disheartening," and in a review of Eminem's 2004 release "Encore," he writes that if Eminem had "restrained himself to fifty minutes (instead of a bloated seventy-seven minute record), he could have left out moments of juvenile silliness and the further put-down of women that undercut some of the poignant reflection of 'Yellow Brick Road' and 'Mockingbird.'" Is it conceivable that a prominent music critic writing in a major metropolitan daily would describe as "disheartening" a white rapper who attacked people of color in his lyrics?

160 *Richard Goldstein argued in a brilliant piece in 2002:* To locate the full text of Goldstein's article, see the bibliography. Here is one crucial paragraph: "There *is* a relationship between Eminem and his time. His bigotry isn't incidental or stupid, as his progressive champions claim. It's central and knowing—and unless it's examined, it will be free to operate. Not that this music makes men rape any more than the Klan-lionizing imagery in *Birth of a Nation* creates racists. The real effect is less personal than systematic. Why is it considered proper to speak out against racism and anti-Semitism but not against sexism and homophobia? To me, this disparity means we haven't reached a true consensus about these last two biases. We aren't ready to let go of male supremacy. We still think something central to the universe will be lost if this arrangement changes."

161 *The love in hip-hop is over men, over love, crew love, brotherly love:* To locate the full text of the article, see Wiltz, 2004.

161 *Richard Goldstein pointed out the evolution:* To locate the full article, see Goldstein, November 2002.

163 *A twenty-one-year-old Eminem impersonator:* Here is a summary of a Reuters news report by Michael Holden on December 5, 2005: A British man, who was so obsessed with rapper Eminem that he dressed like him, had the same tattoos, and used to perform the same dance routines, was jailed for life on Monday for battering a woman to death.

Christopher Duncan, twenty-one, forced his victim to undergo a torrid sexual ordeal before he beat her round the head with a metal baseball bat and, although she was still alive, crammed her into a suitcase where she died up to ninety minutes later.

On the night of he murder, Duncan had met his victim in a London karaoke bar where the manager said he had been "aggressively" performing songs by Eminem, notorious for his violent and misogynistic lyrics.

"You treat women as sexual objects and have a sadistic sexual fantasy life," Judge David Paget said as he ordered that Duncan should serve a minimum term of twenty-five years. "It may well be you pose such a danger to women it will never be safe to release you."

Prosecuting lawyer Jonathan Laidlaw said Duncan's victim, twenty-six-year-old law student Jagdip Najran, a promising singer herself, had fallen for Duncan.

"One of the tragic features of this case is the terrible misjudgment she made of him," Laidlaw told the Old Baily criminal court.

165 *What are men to make of* New York Times *columnist Maureen Dowd:* See Dowd, 2002.

168 *A fascinating music journal essay:* See Keathley, Elizabeth, 2002.

169 *Wrestling With Manhood:* I am indebted to Sut Jhally for many of the ideas in this section. Much of it is drawn from the Media Education Foundation video *Wrestling With Manhood* that he directs and in which I am featured, and from a *Boston Globe* article in February 13, 2000 that I cowrote with him, entitled "Manhood on the Mat: The Problem Is Not That Pro Wrestling Makes Boys Violent. The Real Lesson of the Wildly Popular Pseudo-Sport Is More Insidious."

169 *Professional wrestling has escaped serious cultural analysis:* For a short article about World Wrestling Entertainment that explores some of the political economy of this entertainment phenomenon, see www.jacksonkatz.com/manhood.html.

171 *WWE's Torrie Wilson explains:* From a video clip on *Wrestling With Manhood,* Media Education Foundation, Northampton, Massachusetts, 2002.

173 *One infamous example is what he said on the air:* For a discussion of Stern's comments and media commentary about them, see Jennifer L. Pozner's article "Journalists Trivialize Howard Stern's Advocacy of Rape as 'Insensitivity,'" in the July/August 1999 issue of *Extra!*, the publication of the progressive media watchdog group Fairness and Accuracy in Reporting (FAIR).

177 *One of the lowest moments in the history of talk radio:* The transcript from Leykis's show of 12–27–99 was circulated on the Internet in early 2000.

179 *"Good old American pornography":* Limbaugh claims that he said this somewhat sarcastically in the context of pointing out the hypocrisy of "liberals," whom he accuses of defending pornography in the U.S. while condemning it in the case of Abu Ghraib. Of course, in spite of whatever harms pornography might cause in the lives of women or men, there is no moral equivalence between pornography that presumably documents sex between consenting adults and the way some U.S. servicemembers sexually abused prisoners in their custody.

CHAPTER 10: GUILTY PLEASURES

181 *"Pornography hates men":* From personal conversation with Gail Dines.

181 *"Who are the 'johns,' those people who buy and sell women in prostitution?":* This quote is from the article "The Demand for Prostitution," by Melissa Farley, PhD. It is available on the website of the organization Captive Daughters: dedicated to ending sex trafficking, at www.captivedaughters.org/demanddynamics/demandforprostitution.htm.

184 *"Men make, distribute, and get rich on porn.":* From personal conversation with Gail Dines.

185 *Until recently, men who have a public voice about pornography:* One notable and powerful exception to this is John Stoltenberg's 1989 collection of essays *Refusing to Be a Man: Essays on Sex and Justice.* Another thoughtful contribution to men's writing about pornography—pro and con—is Michael Kimmel's *1990 book Men Confront Pornography*, a groundbreaking and highly readable collection of essays from men about various ways that pornography functions in men's lives.

185 *A new men's conversation about pornography is beginning to take shape:* Feminists who criticize the pornography industry are often characterized by "pro-porn feminists" as "prudes" and "Victorian moralists" who do not like the sexual or erotic choices some women make and hence seek to couch

their discomfort in language about women's exploitation. Anti-porn feminists are also often accused of being anti-male, or of caricaturing heterosexual men's sexuality. As a heterosexual man who takes—in this book and elsewhere—a strong stance against the pornography industry for its misogyny and contribution to rape culture, I want to make it clear that I preemptively reject any attempt to characterize me as prudish or moralizing. Since my years in college when I led student opposition to the New Right and groups such as the Moral Majority, organized banned book displays, distributed contraceptive information to women and men, and participated in a pioneering peer sexuality education program at the University of Massachusetts, I have fought for women's sexual and reproductive freedom and will continue to do so for the rest of my life. Criticism of the pornography industry is NOT criticism of women's fundamental right to sexual expression, nor is it inherently anti-male. In fact, as I have argued in this book, in spite of some people's efforts to produce "nonviolent, non-exploitative, non-sexist" erotic porn, I believe the pornography industry as a whole over the past generation has done incalculable damage to both women's and men's sexuality.

186 *Robert Jensen…painfully describes as "three holes and two hands":* See Jensen, 2004.

190 *There's nothing I love more than when a girl insists to me":* From Dines, Jensen, and Russo, p. 81.

190 *Its defenders—including women such as the "thinking man's porn star" Nina Hartley:* For a fascinating left/feminist response to Nina Hartley's defense of pornography that links opposition to the porn industry's exploitation of women (and men) to other forms of class exploitation, see Stan Goff's piece, entitled "The Porn Debate: Wrapping Profit in the Flag," available at: www.notforsale-book.org/Articles/Goff_Hartley.html

191 *The lawyers for the young men called the girl:* The full text of Moxley's article, entitled "Justice Takes a Pool Cue," from the July 2–8, 2004 edition of the *OC Weekly,* can be found at the paper's web site at www.ocweekly.com.

192 *The Information Technology Association of America to educate people:* For more information about this initiative, see www.cybercrime.gov/cybercit2.htm.

193 *Why would they relentlessly sell them an endless supply of videos:* In "Pornography Is a Left Issue," Dines and Jensen write: "This misogyny is not an idiosyncratic feature of a few fringe films. Based on three studies of the content of mainstream video/DVD pornography over the past decade, we conclude that woman-hating is central to contemporary pornography. Take away every video in which a woman is called a bitch, a cunt, a slut, or a whore, and the shelves would be nearly bare. Take away every DVD in which a woman becomes the target of a man's contempt, and there wouldn't be much left. Mass-marketed pornography doesn't celebrate women and their sexuality, but instead expresses contempt for women and celebrates the charge of expressing that contempt sexually."

194 *Beyond Beats and Rhymes:* Hurt's groundbreaking documentary features surprisingly candid interviews with rappers Fat Joe, Jadakiss, and Busta Rhymes, as well as Sarah Jones, Michael Eric Dyson, and student activists from Spellman College who received national attention for their criticism of the rapper Nelly after his song/video Tip Drill that showed a man running a credit card through a woman's bare buttocks.

195 *Pimps target girls or women who seem naïve, lonely:* See Barry, Kathleen, 1995. *In a 2004 New York Times Magazine cover story on sex trafficking:* For the full article, see Landesman, 2004.

200 *In fact, perhaps the most important difference between the male and female strip cultures:* Women who strip experience a high amount of physical, sexual, and verbal abuse by men. In one study of eighteen women in strip clubs in the Minneapolis/St. Paul area, Kelly Holsopple found that:

    44 % reported that the men threatened to hurt them
    39 % experienced vaginal penetration with fingers
    17 % experienced anal penetration with fingers
    · 11 % experienced attempted penetration with objects
    17 % experienced forced masturbation from customers
    11 % experienced rape

For more details of this study and a highly informative look at strip clubs through the experiences of women who work in them, see Holsopple, 1998.

201 *This presents young heterosexual women with a difficult dilemma:* Ariel Levy covers another aspect of this subject in her provocative polemic *Female Chauvinist Pigs: Women and the Rise of Raunch Culture* (2005). Although she only briefly touches on sexual violence, she chides women who have deceived themselves into thinking that lifting their shirts for *Girls Gone Wild* cameras, going to strip clubs, or surgically altering their bodies in order to look "hot" for men somehow demonstrates true sexual freedom.

201 *Madonna's critics argue that the many young girls who imitated her dress and style:* From a 1995 piece by Rapping entitled "Power Babes and Victim Feminists" in the informative but now-defunct magazine *On the Issues: The Progressive Woman's Quarterly.*

CHAPTER 11: MVP

207 *"There's nothing better than excelling at a game you love":* This quote by college and professional football star Doug Flutie comes from the *Coaching Boys Into Men Playbook,* produced and distributed by the Family Violence Prevention Fund. Go to www.endabuse.org for more information about the Coaching Boys Into Men campaign.

207 *"If a marine is a great warrior on the battlefield":* One of the first things I did when I started working with the Marines in the mid-1990s was to attend a luncheon in the Washington D.C. area in honor of General Christmas's retirement. He said this in his speech.

209 *When Rafael Palmiero, the home-run-hitting major league baseball star:* Palmiero, whose reputation was severely damaged when he tested positive for steroids in 2005, made some revealing comments about being a pitchman for Viagra in a 2002 interview with the *Fort Worth Star-Telegram.* As Richard Sandomir reported in the *New York Times* on August 2, 2005, Palmiero said that being the athletic front man for the little blue pill was "not like doing a Nike commercial or something. I think it takes courage, and I think I've got what it takes to do this."

210 *Although MVP began in the sports culture:* The first community to embrace MVP city-wide is Sioux City, Iowa. With visionary leadership from Judy Stafford and Cindy Waitt, and funding from the Waitt Family Foundation, MVP has been implemented in all of the public high schools in that heartland city. The principal of North High School, Alan Heisterkamp, has provided exemplary leadership in bringing in and sustaining MVP, and in developing structures to evaluate and measure outcomes.

212 *MVP sessions are typically led by people:* MVP has been implemented in dozens of high schools and middle schools in eastern Massachusetts. One of the most successful institutionalizations of MVP has been in the Newton, Massachusetts, public schools. Over the past six years, hundreds of Newton high school students have been trained in MVP and subsequently have given presentations to thousands of middle school students. A Newton public school teacher, Nancy Beardall has been the guiding force and tireless advocate who has nurtured MVP's growth there.

213 *The chief curricular innovation of MVP is a training tool called the Playbook:* MVP playbooks are customized for target populations. For example, there are separate playbooks for high school boys, high school girls, college men, and college women. There are also trainer's guides that accompany each playbook. For information about how to order copies, see www.jacksonkatz.com/playbooks.html.

215 *Personal option:* The scenarios in MVP playbooks include several options for bystander intervention before, during, or after an incident, but the list is by no means comprehensive. A "personal option" is included in each scenario to suggest the idea that individual creativity and resourcefulness are critical aspects of successful bystander intervention.

219 *False report rapes do occur:* The question of how often rape is falsely reported is controversial. Many professionals and researchers in the sexual assault field believe the number to be extremely low. The reason why some studies—such as the Uniform Crime Reports—arrive at a higher number (8 percent) is that in spite of major advances in training in recent years, many law enforcement personnel unilaterally determine rape allegations to be "unfounded" if the alleged victim is drunk or on drugs, presents inconsistencies in her (or his) story, or otherwise does not meet the definition of a sympathetic victim. In some states, as recently as the 1980s rape victims were forced to take lie detector tests, which are not only highly unreliable but also serve to stigmatize victims and discourage them from coming forward.

CHAPTER 12: TEACH OUR CHILDREN WELL

227 *"The belief that violence is manly":* See Kimmel, 2000.

237 *Male Leadership in Schools: the Sounds of Silence:* Portions of this section were first published in a chapter I wrote for the book *Masculinities at School,* ed. Nancy Lesko, published by Sage Publications, Thousand Oaks, CA: 2000.

239 *It would be unfair to minimize the political sensitivity of their position:* A significant obstacle to the implementation of good gender violence prevention in many schools is the impassioned opposition by so-called "social conservatives"—often parents—to any educational initiatives that deal honestly and non-judgmentally with issues of sexual orientation and homophobia. At the very least, comprehensive gender violence prevention education has to include discussions about homophobia, because it plays such a powerful silencing role in male (and female) peer cultures. Also, if it is important in principle that men speak out against the abuse of women, it is equally important that heterosexuals speak out against the abuse of gays, lesbians, and bisexuals, as well as transgendered people.

244 *In the words of the Japanese American actor Mark Hayashi:* For an interesting discussion of some of the gender and sexuality issues facing Japanese American men, see David Mura's 1996 book *Where the Body Meets Memory.*

245 *The most common model of gender violence prevention programming in schools:* See Hanson, 1995.

245 *While there is no comprehensive data documenting the sex:* Nan Stein and Dominic Cappello designed an excellent teacher's guide that incorporates the teaching of gender violence prevention into existing curricula, thus making it easier for classroom teachers to teach this material, rather than relying on outside presenters. Published in 1999 by the Wellesley Centers for Women, it is entitled *Gender Violence/Gender Justice: An Interdisciplinary Teaching Guide for Teachers of English, Literature, Social Studies, Psychology, Health, Peer Counseling, and Family and Consumer Sciences* (grades 7–12). I have several exercises in this guide, including an explanation of the "Sexual assault in the daily routine" exercise that I recount in the Preface to this book. To order GV/GJ, go to www.wcwonline.org/title282.html

249 *Lessons about Accountability:* Portions of this section first appeared in an op-ed I wrote entitled "The Price Women Pay for Boys Being Boys," that was published in the *Seattle Post-Intelligencer* on May 13, 2001.

251 *In my educational video,* Tough Guise: There is a study guide for *Tough Guise* available for free online at www.mediaed.org.

251 *Who produces most of the images and stories:* For a powerful introduction to the topic of media ownership and the implications of increased corporate media consolidation on the ideological content available to the mainstream, see McChesney, 1999.

CHAPTER 13: MORE THAN A FEW GOOD MEN

252 *Emerge:* For more information about this program, which in 1977 became the first batterer intervention program in the country, go to www.emergedv.com.

253 *"As long as we take the view":* For the full text of President Mandela's speech, go to www.anc.org.za/ancdocs/history/mandela/1997/sp971122.html.

254 *RAVEN:* RAVEN was founded in 1978. For more information about RAVEN and its history in the batterer intervention movement, go to www.ravenstl.org.

254 *Men Stopping Violence:* Men Stopping Violence, founded in Atlanta in the early 1980s, describes itself as "a social change organization dedicated to ending men's violence against women. MSV works locally and nationally to dismantle belief systems, social structures, and institutional practices that oppress women and children and dehumanize men themselves. We look to the violence against women's movement to keep the reality of the problem and the vision of the solution before us. We believe that all forms of oppression are interconnected. Social justice work in the areas of race, class, gender, age, and sexual orientation are all critical to ending violence against women." For more information, go to www.menstoppingviolence.org.

254 *National Organization for Men Against Sexism (NOMAS):* For more information about the history of NOMAS and its ongoing activities, go to www.nomas.org.

254 *Oakland Men's Project:* The Oakland Men's Project, founded in 1979, was a pioneering, community-based model for anti-sexist men's advocacy. It was also an early leader in developing educational materials about men's violence against women, masculinity, racism, homophobia, and the connections among and between them. For example, OMP developed the highly effective "Act Like a Man" box exercise, which has been used by progressive educators for decades, and which was incorporated into MVP trainings starting in 1993. For more information about how to use the box exercise, go to http://toolkit.endabuse.org/Resources/ActLikeAMan. Some of the early activist-educators who created OMP and contributed to its work include many well-known figures in anti-sexist men's work such as Paul Kivel, Robert Allen, Allen Creighton, and Victor Lewis.

254 *Men Stopping Rape:* Founded in Madison, Wisconsin, in 1983, Men Stopping Rape is an anti-sexist men's organization devoted to promoting sexual assault education for men. The membership of MSR consists of students on the UW-Madison campus and men working and living in the community. According to its website, MSR covers a wide range of ages, upbringings, orientations, and experiences: "We share a desire to live in a world free of violence against women and against men. Men join MSR for a variety of reasons: many of us have known someone in our lives who has been assaulted; some of us have come to question our own behavior and the role violence has played in our 'initiation' into modern masculine culture, and we desire to learn how to avoid perpetrating assault; all of us benefit from an atmosphere of support and understanding."

Among its many activities, MSR has provided workshops for dormitories, fraternities, academic departments, high schools, group homes, church groups, prisons, and service providers for "at risk" youth. Workshop presenters are volunteers who have completed MSR's thirty-hour workshop training program, gaining facility to discuss such topics as sexuality, masculinity, enculturation, homophobia, racism, violence/abuse, male survivors, and personal safety. They produce and market a brochure entitled "What One Man Can Do to Help Stop Rape," a poster series describing the myths surrounding sexual assault, and a thirty-minute video and study guide which have been distributed to campus and community organizations throughout the U.S., Canada, and Australia. For more information, see www.men-stopping-rape.org.

254 *DC Men Against Rape:* The nationally well-known group Men Can Stop Rape is an outgrowth of D.C. Men Against Rape (formerly Men's Rape Prevention Project) a volunteer profeminist collective founded in 1987 by a handful of men seeking to raise their own and their community's consciousness about men's violence against women. In 1997, MCSR incorporated as a nonprofit organization with the goal of carrying forward and expanding on its original mission to increase men's involvement in efforts to end men's violence. Through awareness-to-action education and community organizing, MCSR promotes gender equity and builds men's capacity to be strong without being violent. MCSR describes itself as "a concerned community of men and women of all ages, from many walks of life, working locally and nationally for peace, equity, and gender justice. We are men and women who find strength in compassion and nonviolence and who strive to support young men who are courageous enough to challenge the 'rape culture' in which we live." Their web site is www.mencanstoprape.org.

254 *Real Men, an anti-sexist men's organization:* Real Men was an all-volunteer activist organization from 1988–1998 whose main purpose was to call public attention to men's role in ending men's violence against women. We produced and distributed literature (e.g., "10 Things Men Can Do to End Gender Violence"); organized fundraisers for battered women's programs; sponsored lectures, speak-outs, and debates; handed out leaflets at Fenway Park and the old Foxboro Stadium that urged fathers, coaches, camp counselors, and youth workers to speak out against men's violence; organized protests against sexist media, including the comedians Andrew Dice Clay and Sam Kinison; and appeared on radio and television talk shows.

254 *Men's Resource Center for Change:* The stated mission of the Men's Resource Center for Change (formerly the Men's Resource Center of Western Massachusetts) is to "Support men, challenge men's violence, and develop men's leadership in ending oppression in ourselves, our families, and our communities. Our programs support men to overcome the damaging effects of rigid and stereotyped masculinity, and simultaneously confront men's patterns of personal and societal violence and abuse toward women, children, and other men." According to the organization's website, the roots of the Men's Resource Center for Change go back over twenty years. In 1981 the National Conference on Men and Masculinity's seventh gathering was held at Tufts University in Medford, Massachusetts. Several men who attended were moved by the ideas they heard about redefining male roles in healthier, non-violent directions. They returned home inspired to create an anti-sexist men's network, and in 1982 these men founded what was originally called the Men's Resource Connection (MRC). A grassroots organization, the MRC was committed to developing a strong local network among men, and between men and women. Soon after they began publishing a men's newsletter which has evolved into *Voice Male*, a magazine with a print run of ten thousand that is distributed throughout parts of New England and New York and mailed to subscribers across North America and overseas. Over the years, the MRC has offered classes, workshops, consultations, and trainings at schools, colleges, and universities, and for agencies and organizations across the Northeast and beyond. Among its other public activities have been a statewide fathers' conference, newspaper signature ad campaigns, the "Challenge and Change" annual awards banquet, and a four-day Men's Walk to End Abuse, which was initiated in October 2003.

In 1988, the MRC incorporated as a non-profit organization and began offering an array of programs, projects, and services, including batterer intervention, male survivor support groups, and youth education. The Men's Resource Connection officially changed its name to the Men's Resource Center of Western Massachusetts in 1993. In October 2003 the MRC officially went international, with a twelve-day training visit to Japan in which staff talked about the MRC's approach to stopping domestic violence. For many years the MRC has hosted numerous visitors from many countries, including Sweden, Norway, South Africa, and the former Soviet Republic of Kyrgyzstan. In May 2005, in recognition of the fact that their work extends well beyond western Massachusetts, the MRC changed its name to the Men's Resource Center for Change. For more information, go to: www.mensresourcecenter.org.

254 *The White Ribbon Campaign:* The Canada-based WRC bills itself as "the largest effort in the world of men working to end men's violence against women." It relies on volunteer support and financial contributions from individuals and organizations. Each year, the WRC urges men and boys to wear a ribbon for one or two weeks, starting on November 25, the International Day for the Eradication

of Violence against Women. (In Canada men wear ribbons until December 6, Canada's National Day of Remembrance and Action on Violence against Women.) The WRC is an educational organization that encourages "reflection and discussion that leads to personal and collective action among men." Throughout the year, the WRC encourages men to do educational work in schools, workplaces, and communities; to support local women's groups; and to raise money for the international educational efforts of the WRC. They also distribute Education and Action kits to schools, speak out on public policy, and maintain a website: www.whiteribbon.ca. Information about the European version of WRC can be found at www.eurowrc.org.

255 A *"Big Tent" approach:* Portions of the section on a "big tent" approach first appeared in an article I wrote for an online discussion series hosted by the Family Violence Prevention Fund. For a full text of my article, go to endabuse.org/bpi/discussion1/Discussion1-long.pdf

255 A *recent poll conducted for Lifetime Television:* In the same poll, 75 percent of women in the same age group believe gender violence is a "serious problem." For more information about this poll, go to www.mcgrc.com/releases/lifetime.

257 *"Millions of men participate in faith-based communities":* These comments by Rev. Fortune are taken from a piece she wrote in 2003 for an online discussion series hosted by the Family Violence Prevention Fund. Go to http://endabuse.org/bpi/discussion1/V.rtf for the full text.

264 *Few HIV-prevention programs actually address the underlying gender:* For the full text of Miriam Zoll's report, from which these quotes are drawn, go to www.zollgroup.com.

265 *Don McPherson:* For more information about Don McPherson or the Sports Leadership Institute which he runs, go to: www.adelphi.edu/communityservices/sli/mcpherson.php.

265 *I would nonetheless like to spotlight a handful of exemplary anti-sexist men:* Ben Atherton-Zeman is another man who uses elements of dramatic performance and comedy to educate college students and others about domestic and sexual violence. In his one-man show, *Voices of Men,* he plays iconic hypermasculine cinematic characters such as Rocky Balboa and James Bond, as well as Austin Powers, in the unlikely role of messengers who deliver anti-violence, profeminist messages to sometimes difficult-to-reach audiences of men and women. See www.voicesofmen.org.

Scott Berkowitz is an important leader in the movement against sexual violence. He is the founder and president of the Rape, Abuse & Incest National Network (RAINN), which bills itself as the nation's largest anti-sexual assault organization, and has been ranked as one of America's 100 Best Charities by *Worth* magazine. Among its programs, RAINN created and operates the National Sexual Assault Hotline at 1-800-656-HOPE. According to the RAINN web site www.rainn.org, this nationwide partnership of more than 1,100 local rape treatment hotlines provides victims of sexual assault with free, confidential services around the clock. The hotline helped 133,000 sexual assault victims in 2004 and has helped more than 900,000 since it began in 1994.

267 *The anti-rape men's group One in Four:* One in Four was founded by Dr. John Foubert, author of "The Men's Program." For more information, go to: www.nomorerape.org.

267 *Some men are politicized:* For more information about Dads and Daughters, go to www.dadsand-daughters.org.

267 *A growing number of organizations have made significant contributions in recent years:* One highly innovative and effective initiative is Boys To Men based in Portland, Maine. The year-round mission of Boys To Men is to help reduce interpersonal violence by offering programs that support the healthy development of adolescent boys, provide assistance and educational resources to boys and those who raise them, and increase community awareness about the specific needs of boys. Since 2000, Boys To Men has held an annual conference that brings middle and high school-aged boys from across the state together with fathers and other adult mentors. The conference features workshops on diverse topics such as guitar-making, cooking, and hip hop music-making, but a key theme of the conference is encouraging nonviolent and pro-social ways of being a man. According to its web site, BTM focuses on boys because (many) boys do not hear anti-violence messages and alternatives ways of being male from the men in their lives—even though studies show that adolescent boys respond to messages they hear from adult males they most respect. See www.boystomen.info.

270 *One of the major challenges for American anti-sexist men: New York Times* columnist Nicholas Kristof deserves special commendation for repeatedly calling attention in his columns to men's rape and sexual exploitation of poor girls and women in Southeast Asia, South Asia, and elsewhere.

BIBLIOGRAPHY

Baker, Katharine K. "Once a Rapist? Motivational Evidence and Relevancy in Rape Law." *Harvard Law Review*, 110 Harv. L.R. 563, January, 1997.

Bancroft, Lundy. *When Dad Hurts Mom: Helping Your Children Heal the Wounds of Witnessing Abuse*. New York: G.P. Putnam and Sons, 2004.

Bancroft, Lundy. *Why Does He Do That: Inside the Minds of Angry and Controlling Men*. New York: G.P. Putnam and Sons, 2002.

Barry, Kathleen. *The Prostitution of Sexuality*. New York: New York University Press, 1995.

Beneke, Timothy. *Men On Rape: What They Have To Say About Sexual Violence*, New York: St. Martin's Press, 1982.

Bergen, Raquel. *Wife Rape: Understanding the Response of Survivors and Service Providers*. Thousand Oaks, CA: Sage Publications, 1996.

Bevacqua, Maria. *Rape on the Public Agenda: Feminism and the Politics of Sexual Assault*. Boston: Northeastern University Press, 2000.

Bowker, Lee H., Michelle Arbitell, and Richard McFerron. "On the Relationship Between Wife Beating and Child Abuse," in Kersti Yllo & Michele Bograd, eds. *Feminist Perspectives on Wife Abuse*. Thousand Oaks, CA: Sage, 1990.

Brownmiller, Susan. *Against Our Will: Men, Women, and Rape*. New York: Simon and Schuster, 1975.

Canada, Geoffrey. *Reaching Up For Manhood: Transforming the Lives of Boys in America*. Boston: Beacon Press, 1998.

Caputi, Jane. *The Age of Sex Crime*. Bowling Green, OH: Bowling Green University Popular Press, 1987.

Cassidy, L. Hurrell RM. "The Influence of Victim's Attire on Adolescents' Judgments of Date Rape." *Adolescence* Vol 30, 1995, 319–323.

Chu, Jeff, "Was the Killer Next Door? Dennis Rader Was a Husband, Father, Church Leader—And Is Now the Man Accused of Terrorizing Wichita." *Time Magazine*, March 14, 2005.

Cohn, Carol. "Wars, Wimps, and Women: Talking Gender and Thinking War," in *Gendering War Talk*, Cooke, Miriam, and Woollacott, Angela, eds. Princeton, NJ: Princeton University Press, 1993.

Coulter, Ann. *Slander: Liberal Lies about the American Right*. New York: Crown, 2002.

DeBecker, Gavin. *The Gift of Fear: Survival Signals That Protect Us from Violence*. Boston: Little Brown: 1997.

Dines, Gail and Robert Jensen. "Pornography Is a Left Issue." ZNET, www.zmag.org.

Dines, Gail, Robert Jensen, and Ann Russo. *Pornography: The Production and Consumption of Inequality*. New York: Routledge, 1998.

Dowd, Maureen. "The Boomers' Crooner." *New York Times*, November 24, 2002.

Dowling, Colette. *The Cinderella Complex: Women's Hidden Fear of Independence*. New York: Summit Books, 1981.

Dworkin, Andrea. *Right-Wing Women*, New York: Perigee Books, 1983.

Edelson, Jeff. "Children's Witnessing of Adult Domestic Violence," *Journal of Interpersonal Violence*, Vol. 14(No. 8), 1999. p. 839–870.

Fabiano, P., W. Perkins, A. Berkowitz, J. Linkenbach, and C. Stark. "Engaging Men As Social Justice Allies in Ending Violence Against Women: Evidence for a Social Norms Approach." *Journal of American College Health*. Vol. 52,(No.3), Nov./Dec.2003.

Faludi, Susan. *Backlash: The Undeclared War Against American Women*, New York: Crown, 1991.

Farley, Melissa. *Prostitution, Trafficking, and Traumatic Stress*. Binghamton, New York: Haworth Press, 2004.

Fergusen, D. and P. Mullen. "Childhood Sexual Abuse: An Evidence-based Perspective." Thousand Oaks, CA: Sage Publications, 1999.

Finkelhor, David., G. Hotaling, I.A. Lewis, and C. Smith. "Sexual Abuse in a National Survey of Adult Men and Women: Prevalence, Characteristics, and Risk Factors." *Child Abuse and Neglect*, Vol. 14, 1990. pp. 19–28.

Fisher, B. S., F. T. Cullen, M. G. Turner. "The Sexual Victimization of College Women." Department of Justice, National Institute of Justice, Washington, D.C., 2000.

Frankenberg, Ruth. *White Women, Race Matters*. Minneapolis: University of Minnesota Press, 1993.

Frey, Amber. *Witness: For the Prosecution of Scott Peterson.* New York: Regan Books, 2005.

Funk, Rus Ervin. *Stopping Rape: A Challenge for Men.* Philadelphia: New Society Publishers, 1993.

Gazmararian, J. A., R. Petersen, A. M. Spitz, M. M. Goodwin, L. E. Saltzman, J. S. Marks. "Violence and reproductive health; current knowledge and future research directions." *Maternal and Child Health Journal,* Vol. 4(No. 2), 2000. pp.79–84.

Gilligan, Carol. *In A Different Voice: Psychological Theory and Women's Development.* Cambridge: Harvard University Press, 1982.

Gilligan, James. *Violence: Our Deadly Epidemic and Its Causes.* New York: Putnam, 1996.

Goldstein, Richard. "The Eminem Shtick: What Makes a Bigot a Genius? Presiding Over Guilty Pleasures." *The Village Voice,* June 12–18, 2002.

Goldstein, Richard. "The Eminem Consensus: Why We Voted for Slim Shady." *The Village Voice,* November 13–19, 2002.

Hammer, Rhonda. *Antifeminism and Family Terrorism: A Critical Feminist Perspective.* Lanham, MD: Rowman and Littlefield, 2002.

Hanson, Katherine. "Gendered Violence: Examining Education's Role." *Working Paper Series #4, Education Development Center,* Center for Equity and Cultural Diversity, Newton, MA, 1995.

Heise, L., M. Ellsberg, and M. Gottemoeller. "Ending Violence against Women" Johns Hopkins University, *Population Reports,* Series L, (11), 1999.

Hilburn, Robert. "Minus the Chain Saw, Eminem Seems a Bit More Mature." *Los Angeles Times,* August 9, 2002.

Hilburn, Robert. "With Encore, Eminem Melts: The Album Shows the Rapper to Have a Tender, Even Apologetic, Side." *Los Angeles Times,* November 8, 2004, p. E1.

Holsopple, K. "Stripclubs According to Strippers: Exposing Workplace Sexual Violence." *Making the Harm Visible: Global Exploitation of Women and Girls. Speaking Out and Providing Services.* Kingston, RI: Coalition Against Trafficking in Women, 1998, pp. 253–276.

hooks, bell. *Feminism Is for Everybody.* Boston: South End Press, 2000.

hooks, bell. *Misogyny, Gangsta Rap, and the Piano. Z Magazine,* February, 1994.

hooks, bell. *We Real Cool: Black Men and Masculinity.* New York: Routledge, 2000.

Jensen, Robert. "Cruel To Be Hard: Men and Pornography." *Sexual Assault Report,* Spring 2004, pp. 54–58.

Kalven, Jamie. *Working with Available Light: A Family's World after Violence.* New York: W.W. Norton and Company, 1999.

Keathley, Elizabeth. "A Context for Eminem's Murder Ballads." *Echo: A Music-Centered Journal,* Vol. 4, (No.2), Fall 2002.

Kelley, Robin D. G. "Kickin' Reality, Kickin' Ballistics: Gangsta Rap and Postindustrial Los Angeles." *Droppin' Science: Critical Essays on Rap Music and Hip-Hop Culture.* W. E. Perkins, ed. Philadelphia: Temple University Press, 1996.

Kilmartin, Christopher. Sexual Assault in Context: Teaching College Men about Gender. Holmes Beach, FL: Learning Publications, 2001.

Kellner, Douglas. *Media Culture: Cultural Studies, Identity, and Politics between the Modern and Post-Modern.* London: Routledge, 1995.

Kimmel, Michael and Michael Messner, eds. *Men's Lives.* Boston: Allyn and Bacon, 2001.

Kimmel, Michael and Tom Mosmiller, eds. *Against the Tide: Pro-Feminist Men in the United States, 1776–1990.* Boston: Beacon Press, 1992.

Kimmel, Michael. "Gender Symmetry in Domestic Violence: A Substantive and Methodological Research Review," *Violence Against Women,* Vol. 8, (No. 11), 2002, 1332–1363.

Kimmel, Michael. *Manhood in America: A Cultural History.* New York: Random House, 2005.

Kimmel, Michael. *Men Confront Pornography.* New York: Crown, 1990.

Kimmel, Michael. "Searching for a New Boyhood: The Testosterone Vs. Feminism Debate." *Voice Male: The Magazine of the Men's Resource Center of Western Massachusetts. Winter, 2000,* pp. 8–10.

Kindlon, Dan and Michael Thompson. *Raising Cain: Protecting the Emotional Life of Boys.* New York: Ballantine Books, 1999.

Kivel, Paul. *Uprooting Racism: How White People Can Work for Racial Justice.* Philadelphia: New Society Publishers, 1996.

Klein, Alan. *Little Big Men: Bodybuilding Subculture and Gender Construction.* Albany: State University of New York Press, 1993.

Lakoff, Robin Tolmach. *The Language War.* Berkeley: University of California Press, 2000.

Landesman, Peter. "The Girls Next Door." *The New York Times Magazine,* January 25, 2004.

Lawrence, J. M. "Pretty Girl Dead." *Boston Magazine,* November, 1996.

Lefkowitz, Bernard. *Our Guys: The Glen Ridge Rape Case and the Life of the Perfect Suburb.* Berkeley: University of California Press, 1997.

Levy, Ariel. *Female Chauvinist Pigs: Women and the Rise of Raunch Culture.* New York: Random House, 2005.

Limbaugh, Rush. *The Way Things Ought to Be,* New York: Pocket Books, 1993.

Lisak, David and Paul Miller. "Repeat Rape and Multiple Offending Among Undetected Rapists." *Violence and Victims,* Vol. 17, (No. 1), 2002.

Loffreda, Beth. *Losing Matt Shepard.* New York: Columbia University Press, 2000.

MacKinnon, Catherine. *Sexual Harassment of Working Women: A Case of Sex Discrimination.* New Haven, CT: Yale University Press, 1979.

Mayer, Jane and Jill Abramson. *Strange Justice: The Selling of Clarence Thomas.* Boston: Houghton-Mifflin, 1994.

McBride, James. *War, Battering, and Other Sports: The Gulf between American Men and Women.* New Jersey: Humanities Press, 1995.

McCall, Nathan. *Makes Me Wanna Holler: A Young Black Man in America.* New York: Random House, 1994.

McCall, Nathan. *What's Going On: Personal Essays.* New York: Random House, 1997.

McChesney, Robert. *Rich Media, Poor Democracy: Communication Politics in Dubious Times.* Champaign-Urbana, IL: University of Illinois Press, 1999.

Mederos, Fernando. "Domestic Violence and Culture: Moving Toward More Sophisticated Encounters." Available at www.melissainstitute.org/handouts.html.

Meili, Trisha. *I Am the Central Park Jogger: A Story of Hope and Possibility.* New York: Scribners, 2003.

Mura, David. *Where the Body Meets Memory: An Odyssey of Race, Sexuality, and Identity.* Garden City, NY: Anchor Books, 1996.

Nelson, Mariah Burton. *The Stronger Women Get, The More Men Love Football: Sexism and the American Culture of Sports.* New York: Harcourt Brace and Company, 1994.

O'Connor, Anne-Marie. "Not Only Natalee Is Missing: Is the Media Inattention to Missing Women Who Aren't White Due to Deliberate Racism or Unconscious Bias?" *Los Angeles Times,* August 5, 2005. p. E1.

Paglia, Camille. *Sex, Art, and American Culture.* New York: Vintage Books, 1992.

Phillips, Lynn. M., *Flirting with Danger: Young Women's Reflections on Sexuality and Domination,* New York: New York University Press, 2000.

Piercy, Marge. "The Rape Poem" *Circles on the Water.* New York: Knopf, 1982.

Pleck, Elizabeth. *Domestic Tyranny: The Making of American Social Policy against Family Violence from Colonial Times to the Present.* Oxford: Oxford University Press, 1987.

Pollack, William. *Real Boys: Rescuing Our Sons from the Myths of Boyhood.* New York: Henry Holt, 1998.

Ramsey, E. M. "Protecting Patriarchy: The Myths of Capitalism and Patriotism in *The People vs. Larry Flynt.*" *Feminist Media Studies,* 5.2, 2005, pp. 197–213.

Rapping, Elayne. "Power Babes and Victim Feminists." *On the Issues: The Progressive Woman's Quarterly,* Summer 1995, p. 11.

Real, Terrence. *I Don't Want to Talk About It: Overcoming the Secret Legacy of Male Depression.* New York: Scribner, 1997.

Reich, Wilhelm, *The Mass Psychology of Fascism.* New York: Farrar, Straus, and Giroux, 1980.

Rivers, Victor Rivas. *A Private Family Matter: A Memoir.* New York: Atria Books, 2005.

Russell, Diana E. H. *The Politics of Rape: The Victim's Perspective.* New York: Stein and Day, 1975.

Robinson, Lori. *I Will Survive: The African American Guide to Healing from Sexual Assault and Abuse.* Emeryville, CA: Seal Press, 2003.

Russell, Bertrand. *Proposed Roads to Freedom.* New York: Globucz Publishing, 1918.

Schwartz, Martin and W. DeKeseredy. *Sexual Assault on the College Campus: The Role of Male Peer Support.* Thousand Oaks, CA: Sage Publications, 1997.

Silbert, M. H. and A. M. Pines. "Victimization of Street Prostitutes." *Victimology: An International Journal,* Vol. 7: 1982, pp. 122–133.

Silverman, J., A. Mucci Raj, J. Hatha. "Dating Violence against Adolescent Girls and Associated Substance Use, Unhealthy Weight Control, Sexual Risk Behavior, Pregnancy, and Suicidality." *The Journal of the American Medical Association,* Vol. 286, No. 5, 2001.

Silverstein, Olga, and Beth Rashbaum. *The Courage to Raise Good Men.* New York: Penguin, 1995.

Snodgrass, Jon, ed. *For Men against Sexism: A Book of Readings.* Albion, CA: Times Change Press, 1977.

Soler, Esta. "News from the Home Front." Newsletter of the Family Violence Prevention Fund, Fall/Winter, 2000, p.2.

Sommers, Christina Hoff. *The War against Boys: How Misguided Feminism Is Harming Our Young Men.* New York: Simon and Schuster, 2000.

Sommers, Christina Hoff. *Who Stole Feminism: How Women Have Betrayed Women.* New York: Touchstone Books, 1994.

Stannard, David. "The Massie Case: Injustice and Courage." *Honolulu Advertiser.com,* October 14, 2001.

Stark, Christine and Rebecca Whisnant. *Not For Sale: Feminists Resisting Prostitution and Pornography.* North Melbourne, Victoria, Australia: Spinifex Press, 2004.

Stein, Nan. *Classrooms and Courtrooms: Facing Sexual Harassment in K-12 Schools.* New York: Teachers College Press, 1999. p.12.

Stoltenberg, John. *Refusing to Be a Man: Essays on Sex and Justice.* Portland, OR: Breitenbush Books, 1989.

Tarnas, Richard. *The Passion of the Western Mind: Understanding the Ideas That Have Shaped Our World View.* New York: Ballantine Books, 1991. p. 468.

Theweleit, Klaus. *Male Fantasies Volume 1: Women, Bodies, Floods, History.* Minneapolis: University of Minnesota Press, 1987.

Thornhill, Randy and Craig T. Palmer. *A Natural History of Rape: Biological Bases of Sexual Coercion.* Cambridge, MA: The M.I.T. Press, 2001.

Vachss, Andrew. "If You Want to Fight against the Abuse of Children, Watch Your Language." *Parade Magazine,* June 5, 2005.

Warshaw, Robin. *I Never Called It Rape.* New York: HarperCollins, 1988.

Weisberg, D. K. *Children of the Night: A Study of Adolescent Prostitution.* MA: Lexington Books, 1985.

Wenner, Lawrence. "Recovering (From) Janet Jackson's Breast: Ethics and the Nexus of Media, Sports, and Management." *Journal of Sport Management,* October 2004.

Wiltz, Teresa. "Hip-Hop Nation: 30 Years of Rap, Ladies Last." *Washington Post,* December 31, 2004, p. C01.

Yancey, Kitty Bean. "Stripping's New Side." *USA Today,* October 28, 2003, p. 2D.

Media Education Foundation (MEF), 273
Media literacy, 251–252
Meili, Trisha, 278, 289
Men. *See* Anti-sexist men
  abuse, help (seeking), 261
  assistance. *See* Women
  bashing, 73, 75
  behavior, 240
  callousness/cruelty
    reduction, 192
    truth, 182
  concern. *See* Boys; Girls; Women
  control, importance, 133
  creativity, 265–266
  defensive hostility, 25–26, 32
  disrespect, 43
    girls, attraction, 163–165
  dominance, need, 229
  education, women (impact), 61
  Eminem
    lyrics, desensitization, 163
    popularity, danger, 165–166
  empathy, 220
  entrepreneurship, 265–266
  honesty, 260
  influence, 122
    rewards, 270
  issues, 12–18
  loyalty. *See* Brothers; Friends
  measuring up, 123
  misogynistic attitudes, 211
  opinions. *See* Sexism
  peer pressure, 118–122
  perpetrators. *See* Violence
    focus, 5–6
  personal responsibility, seriousness, 258
  power, usage, 268
  primary perpetrators, 15–16
  relationship. *See* Women
  self-help, 259–270
  sexism (challenge), gay stereotype, 127–129
  sexual pleasure, assessment, 189–190
  silence, complicity, 25
  stories, 46–49
  suffering, 277
  support. *See* Women
    increase, 47
  testimonies, 48–49
  traditional roles, viewpoint, 147
  truth, selectivity. *See* Real men
  values/beliefs, 230
  violence
    cessation, 50
    connection, 263–264
    impact, nonrealization, 38
    problem, historical dimensions, 21–22
  women
    defense, reasons, 83–84
    fighting, rationale, 84
    loyalty, 84
    trust, question, 258–259
Men Against Violence, 259
Men Against Violence Against Women, 262
Men and Masculinity conferences, 254
Men As Partners, 264
Men Can Stop Rape (MCSR), 123, 267, 284
Men of color

caricature, 134–135
  dismissal. *See* Athletes of color
  status quo, maintenance, 41
Men Stopping Rape (MSR), 254, 284
Men Stopping Violence, 254, 284
Men's Health, 279
  Orwellian inversion, 82
Men's Leadership Forum, 267
Men's Rape Prevention Project, 284
Men's Resource Center for Change, 285
Men's Resource Connection (MRC), 285
Men's rights movement, disinformation, 15
Men's work, field (growth), 254
Mentors in Violence Prevention (MVP), 124, 209
  bystanders, concept (usage), 210
  conversations, shift, 215–216
  development, 207
  impact. *See* Athletes; Marine Corps
  model
    goals, 216–217
    usefulness, 214
  participation/expectation, 221–222
  real-life situations, usage, 213–214
  scenarios, 216–217
    abuse focus, 214–215
  SEC funding, 209–210
  sessions, 125, 283
    conversations, 219
    initiation, 212
  train of thought, impact, 217–218, 220–221
  trainers, response, 212, 213
  trainings, 284
  workshops, athletic department (acting cosponsor), 248–249
Micro-politics, 259
Miller, Paul, 289
Miller Brewing Company, 208
Misogynistic culture, women (socialization), 9–10
Misogyny, 228. *See also* Eminem; Leykis; Rap music; White rock music
Mob psychology, 103
Mock-rape, 171
Moore, Steve, 141
Mosmiller, Tom, 289
Mothers
  blaming, Eminem success (impact), 166–168
  impact. *See* Boys
  role/teaching, 236–237
Movements, experience, 94
Moxley, Martha, 105
Moxley, R.Scott, 191
MRC. *See* Men's Resource Connection
MSR. *See* Men Stopping Rape
Mullen, P., 288
Multicultural movements, political attacks/bureaucratic inertia, 94
Mura, David, 289
MVP. *See* Mentors in Violence Prevention

N

National Asian Pacific American Women's Forum, 267
National Basketball Association (NBA), player assault (league image), 141
National Center on Domestic and

Sexual Violence, 59
National Collegiate Athletic Association, MVP material (usage), 209–210
National Conference on Men and Masculinity, 285
National Domestic Violence Hotline, 275
National Network to End Domestic Violence, 77, 235
National Organization for Men Against Sexism (NOMAS), 254, 284
National Victim Center, 110
National Women's Studies Conference, 111
Nelly, Pimp Juice beverage, 195
News
  gender-violence tragedies, 6
  impact, 20–33
Nixon, Richard, 208
No Child Left Behind Act of 2001, 239
NOMAS. *See* National Organization for Men Against Sexism
Non-egalitarian sexual relationship, 152

O

Oakland Men's Project (OMP), 25, 254, 284
O'Brien, Jeff, 221–222, 273
O'Connor, Anne-Marie, 289
Off Our Backs, 279
Offender accountability, 96
Offsides scenario, 219–220
Okun, Rob, 272
OMP. *See* Oakland Men's Project
One in Four, 267
Orange County, gang rape trial, 191–192
Organized team sports, leadership (prized ideal), 250
Out-of-context media coverage, 23–24

P

Paglia, Camille, 85, 279, 289
Palffy, Ziggy, 140
Palmer, Craig T., 87, 290
Palmiero, Rafael, 283
Parental divorce case, 44
Parents, awareness/worry, 233–237
Passive voices. *See* Voices
  usage, 108–109
Peacock, Dean, 264
Peer cultures
  dynamics, 122
  policing mechanisms. *See* Male-peer culture
Peer culture. *See* Boys; Men
Pence, Ellen, 223, 273
Penelope, Julia, 111
Perkins, W., 288
Perpetrators. *See* Men
  accountability, 118_
  characteristics, 28
  focus, 15–16
Petersen, R., 288
Peterson, Scott, 133–134
  audience involvement, 135
Phillips, Lynn M., 201, 289
Piercy, Marge, 49, 277, 289
Pimps
  impact, 194–196

ABOUT THE AUTHOR

Jackson Katz is internationally recognized for his groundbreaking work in gender violence prevention with men and boys, particularly in the sports culture and the military. He is cofounder of the multiracial, mixed-gender Mentors in Violence Prevention (MVP) program at Northeastern University's Center for the Study of Sport in Society. MVP is widely used in college athletics, and is also used by both the 2005 Super Bowl champion New England Patriots and the 2004 World Series champion Boston Red Sox. Katz also directs the first worldwide gender violence prevention program in the history of the United States Marine Corps. His award-winning educational video *Tough Guise*, his featured appearances in the films *Wrestling with Manhood* and *Spin the Bottle*, and his nationwide lectures have brought his insights into masculinity and gender violence to millions of college and high school students. Since 1990, he has lectured at over nine hundred colleges, prep schools, high schools, middle schools, professional conferences, and military installations in forty-three states. A native of Boston, he lives with his family in the Los Angeles area. For more information see www.jacksonkatz.com.